Suspects in Europe

Procedural Rights at the Investigative
Stage of the Criminal Process in the
European Union

Editors:
Ed Cape
Jacqueline Hodgson
Ties Prakken
Taru Spronken

Suspects in Europe

Procedural Rights at the Investigative Stage of the Criminal Process in the European Union

AGIS 2005

With financial support from the AGIS
Programme European Commission –
Directorate-General Justice, Freedom
and Security

INTERSENTIA

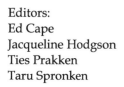

Ius Commune Europaeum

Editors:
Ed Cape
Jacqueline Hodgson
Ties Prakken
Taru Spronken

Suspects in Europe. Procedural Rights at the Investigative Stage of the Criminal Process in the European Union

ISBN 978-90-5095-627-7
D/2007/7849/5
NUR 824

IUS COMMUNE EUROPAEUM

A peer-reviewed book series in which the common foundations of the legal systems of the member states of the European Community are the central focus.

The *Ius Commune Europaeum* series includes horizontal comparative legal studies as well as studies on the effect of treaties within the national legal systems. All the classic fields of law are covered. The books are published in various European languages under the auspices of METRO, the Institute for Transnational Legal Research at the Maastricht University.

Editorial Board: Prof.Dr. J. SMITS (chair), Prof.Dr. M. FAURE and Prof.Dr. E. VOS.

Recently published:

PREFACE

This book is the result of an international research project examining the nature of the legal protections provided to suspects in the investigative stage of criminal proceedings in a range of EU countries – Belgium, England and Wales, Germany, Greece, Italy, the Netherlands and Poland – from both a theoretical and practice-based perspective. Knowledge of procedural rights such as criminal defence provision across Europe is patchy and the accounts that exist often differ widely from practice. The study aims to provide a more contextual understanding of the criminal defence role across different European jurisdictions, considering the legal and procedural rules in place and the implications which the pre-trial stage process has for the trial stage.

The context for this project is the increasingly proactive nature of EU activity in matters of criminal justice, concerning both transborder crime and domestic provisions. In spring 2004 the European Commission proposed that minimum safeguards for criminal investigation be agreed by member states and published a draft framework decision comprising *inter alia* the right to legal assistance. Since then, negotiations have continued with increasing opposition to the proposal emerging from member states. One of the main arguments against a framework decision is that the ECHR already guarantees procedural rights to suspects, and member states are obliged to comply with this. At the time of the completion of this book it is still uncertain whether an agreement on minimum standards in compliance with the ECHR for suspects in criminal proceedings within the EU can be reached.

The contributions in this book demonstrate that procedures vary enormously across EU jurisdictions as does the level of legal protection of suspects in criminal proceedings in practice. It also makes clear how important it is to gain an understanding of the ways in which these systems function, when policies are to be adopted that aim to develop standards and consistency in the protection of rights of individuals in the EU. They also demonstrate that there is still a great deal of research that remains to be done.

This book would not have been possible without the participation of academics and practicing lawyers in the research group, willing to share their experience and expertise in discussions that have encouraged critical reflection. We want to express our thanks to Michele Caianiello, Stef De Decker, Zinovia Dellidou, Jan Fermon, Giulio Illuminati, Piotr Kruszyński, Christos Naintos, Franz Salditt, Frank Verbruggen and Thomas Weigend for their support, inspiration and contributions.

Our warm thanks also go to Dorris de Vocht and Mark Jackson for their editorial support and Yleen Simonis at METRO, the Institute for Transnational Legal Research at the University of Maastricht for editing the text of the book.

Last but not least we are grateful for the financial support provided by the AGIS Programme 2005 of the European Commission – Directorate–General Justice, Freedom And Security, without which this project would not have been possible.

March 2007

Ed Cape
Jacqueline Hodgson
Ties Prakken
Taru Spronken

TABLE OF CONTENTS

BIOGRAPHIES

1.   Michele Caianiello

Michele Caianiello is Assistant Professor in Criminal Procedure at the University of Bologna, Faculty of Law. He also lectures in Criminal Evidence at the L.U.I.S.S. 'Guido Carli;' University of Rome. He graduated in 1994, with a thesis on pre-trial detention. He was awarded his PhD in 2000, with a thesis on International Criminal Tribunals. In 2005, he won a competition as Associate Professor promoted by the University of Lecce. He has studied the decision to charge a suspect with a crime, especially the legally recognised rights of victims and private citizens in this matter. He has also conducted research in the field of evidence law in international criminal justice systems. He is the author of two books (*Poteri dei privati nell'esercizio dell'azione penale*, Giappichelli, 2003; *L'ammissione della prova davanti ai Tribunali penali internazionali per la ex Jugoslavia e il Ruanda e alla Corte penale internazionale*, ConquistE, 2004). He practiced as a lawyer in the field of Criminal Law from 1998 until 2006.

2.   Ed Cape

Ed Cape is Professor of Criminal Law and Practice at the University of the West of England, Bristol, UK, where he is Director of the Centre for Legal Research. As a former criminal defence lawyer in practice in Bristol, he has a special interest in criminal justice, criminal procedure, police powers, the legal profession, legal aid and access to justice. He is the author of a leading practitioner text, *Defending Suspects at Police Stations* (5th edition, 2006), and has contributed to and edited a number of books on aspects of criminal justice. He is the author of many articles in academic and professional journals, including the 50th anniversary article on the criminal defence profession in *Criminal Law Review* (2004). His research includes the contracting of publicly funded criminal defence services, cost drivers in criminal legal aid, victim impact statements, and an evaluation of the pilot Public Defender Service in England and Wales. He has acted as consultant to the Law Society and the Legal Services Commission, and he regularly presents courses on police station practice to the legal profession.

3.   Stef De Decker

Stef De Decker graduated from the Catholic University of Leuven with a Master of Laws (2004) and a Master in Tax Law (2006), where he has been a junior member of academic staff at the Institute of Criminal Law since 2004. He teaches in the areas of Criminal Law, Criminal Procedure and Corporate Criminal Law. His research interests include white collar crime, the procedural treatment of illegally obtained evidence, special investigation methods, and pre-trial detention.

4.   Zinovia Dellidou

Zinovia Dellidou completed her undergraduate legal studies at the University of Warwick in England and the University of Lille II in France, and obtained a Master's degree in European Community Law at the College of Europe in Bruges. She has a PhD in Law from Warwick University where she taught on the undergraduate law programme for two years. Her thesis concerned the role of defence counsel and the right to legal aid and assistance in Europe. She has worked in a law practice in Greece and for the Representation of the European Commission in Athens. She was a research assistant at the College of Europe on the consolidation of European Community Law project. Her research interests include European law, social law, human rights, Justice and Home Affairs and comparative criminal justice.

5.   Jan Fermon

Jan Fermon graduated in law at the Free University of Brussels (VUB) in 1983. He has practiced as a lawyer at the Brussels Bar since 1989 and specialises in international humanitarian law; international, EU and Belgian criminal law; and in immigration law. He is a member of the Progress Lawyers Network – PLN (<www.progresslaw.net>) and is a senior lawyer in their Brussels office. He is also a member of the Bureau of the International Association of Democratic Lawyers (with official consultative status to the United Nations Economic and Social Council ECOSOC). In September 2006 he joined the Faculty of Law of the University of Maastricht and began work on his doctoral thesis on the protection of professional privilege within the EU.

6.   Jacqueline Hodgson

Jacqueline Hodgson is Professor of Law in the School of Law, University of Warwick, UK, teaching Criminal Law and Criminal Justice and Human Rights in Europe. She graduated with an LLB and PhD from the University of Birmingham. She has conducted a range of empirical research projects in the UK and in France. She is the author of *French Criminal Justice* (2005) and co-author (with Belloni) of *Criminal Injustice* (2000) and (with McConville, Bridges and Pavlovic) of *Standing Accused: The Organisation and Practices of Criminal Defence Lawyers in Britain* (1994).

She has published widely in the area of UK, French and comparative criminal justice, notably on the right to silence, the role of the criminal defence lawyer in Britain and in France, comparative criminal justice and procedural models of justice, the investigation and supervision of crime in France and human rights and criminal justice. She has advised the House of Lords Select Committee on the European Union and taught postgraduate comparative criminal procedure as visiting professor at the University of Bordeaux IV from 2004-2006.

7.   Giulio Illuminati

Giulio Illuminati is Professor of Criminal Procedure at the Faculty of Law of the University of Bologna, and Head of the Department of Law. He also lectures in Criminal Procedure at L.U.I.S.S. 'Guido Carli' in Rome. He graduated in Law in 1969 at the University of Bologna where, in 1971, he was granted a research fellowship and went on to work there as an assistant from 1974 to 1980. From 1980 to 1989 he was Professor at the University of Camerino, lecturing in Criminal Procedure and General Theory of the Legal Process. Between 1987 and 1989 he was appointed as a member of the Committee for the Reform of the Italian Criminal Process, established by the Minister of Justice, which drew up the current Code of Criminal Procedure. His main research fields have so far concerned the constitutional rights of the accused, the rights of the arrested person, and more recently, human rights in international criminal law. His main publications include *La presunzione d'innocenza dell'imputato* (1979) and *La disciplina processuale delle intercettazioni* (1982); he also contributed to the textbooks *Casi e questioni di diritto processuale penale* (1995), *Compendio di procedura penale* (3rd edition, 2006), and co-edited the volume *Crimini internazionali tra diritto e giustizia* (2000). He is a member of the Editorial Board of the review *Cassazione penale*.

8.   Piotr Kruszyński

Piotr Kruszyński, is an Attorney as well as Professor and Director of the Institute of Criminal Law in the Law and Administration Department, Warsaw University. He is the author of approximately sixty publications, including two monographs dedicated to the legal status of the defence lawyer in criminal proceedings and is co-author of an academic student text on the scope of criminal law. He has participated in numerous scientific conferences, either in Poland or abroad (Germany, Austria, France, the Netherlands, Italy and the United Kingdom). He has contributed, as an expert, to the work of several parliamentary committees dealing with substantive criminal law and criminal procedure. As a defence lawyer, he has participated in several famous cases; recently (in 2006) he has defended Poland's present Deputy Prime Minister, Prof. Zyta Gilowska, in her vetting trial before the Court of Appeal in Warsaw.

9. Christos Naintos

Christos Naintos studied law and political science at the Aristotle's University of Thessaloniki between 1997-2001 and 2002-2004, and was awarded scholarships during this time. Between 2002 and 2004 he studied a Masters degree in Penal Law and Criminal Procedure at the University of Thrace, in Komotini, where he has studied as a PhD student in Penal Procedure since 2004. He has taught Criminal Procedure at the Komotini Police College, as well as teaching at the university of Thrace. He has published two articles in student magazines concerning the use of weapons by the police and the use of community service as a criminal penalty. He has been working as a lawyer in Thessaloniki since 2003.

10. Ties Prakken

Ties Prakken graduated in law at Amsterdam University. She started her career as a practising lawyer in Amsterdam, before going on to teach criminal law at Utrecht University (1971-1985) and completing her PhD there in 1985 on the subject of legal aid and legal activism. From 1985 to 1998 she left academia in order to return to practice as defence counsel, working on many politically important and controversial cases. In 1998 she became a professor in criminal law at Maastricht University, from where she retired in 2004. Throughout her career she has published across a range of areas in criminal law, in particular the law of criminal procedure. Most recently, she has co-authored (with Taru Spronken) a Manual for Criminal Defence Lawyers (2003) and she continues to research and practice in the area of criminal law.

11. Franz Salditt

Franz Salditt has been a defence lawyer in private practice since 1971, specialising in the defense of tax and other white-collar cases. He was a member of the criminal law committee of the German Lawyers' Association (*Deutscher Anwaltverein*) from 1991 to 2002 and co-founded the European Criminal Bar Association (ECBA) in 1997, serving as its vice chairman from 1997 to 2002. He has published extensively on issues of criminal law and criminal procedure. He holds an honorary professorship at the FernUniversität (University for Distant Learning) at Hagen, Germany.

12. Taru Spronken

Taru Spronken is Professor of Criminal Law and Criminal Procedure at the University of Maastricht and defence lawyer at the *Advocatenpraktijk, Universiteit Maastricht*. She is Chair of the Legal Development Committee of the European Criminal Bar Association, Chair of the Advisory Committee on Criminal Law of the Dutch Bar Association and an honorary judge in the Court of Appeal of Arnhem. As both an academic and a practitioner she specialises in proceedings before the

European Court of Human Rights in Strasbourg. She has written a thesis on the role and professional responsibility of the defence counsel in the Netherlands and has published extensively on the position of the defence in criminal proceedings.

13. Frank Verbruggen

Frank Verbruggen is professor at the Institute of Criminal Law of the Catholic University of Leuven, Belgium. He teaches Criminal Law, the Law of Criminal Sanctions, European Criminal Law and International Criminal Law. He has studied the impact of the fight against organized crime and terrorism on criminal law and procedure. His current research focuses on pan-European principles legitimizing and limiting mutual recognition in criminal matters and on the reform of Belgian sentencing and penitentiary law within a European context. He served as an expert to the Belgian parliament in the debate on the Bill for a new Belgian Code of Criminal Procedure (2006). He also is a lawyer at the Brussels Bar, as of counsel with Liedekerke-Wolters-Waelbroeck-Kirkpatrick.

14. Thomas Weigend

Thomas Weigend is professor of criminal law and criminal procedure at the University of Cologne, Germany. He has studied law at the Universities of Hamburg, Freiburg and Chicago and received the degree of *Dr. jur.* from the University of Freiburg in 1977. In 1985, he obtained the *Habilitation* (license to teach law) from the University of Freiburg. Since 1986, he has been a member of the law faculty of the University of Cologne. He has published several books and more than one hundred articles in German and foreign law reviews, mostly on problems of (comparative) criminal procedure and recently on international criminal law. He has been co-editor of *Zeitschrift für die gesamte Strafrechtwissenschaft* since 1988 and managing editor of that journal from 1982 to 2004. He taught as a visiting professor at the University of Chicago (1976/77), the University of Tokyo (1991 and 1996) and New York University (2001).

Ed Cape
Jacqueline Hodgson
Ties Prakken
Taru Spronken

PROCEDURAL RIGHTS AT THE INVESTIGATIVE STAGE: TOWARDS A REAL COMMITMENT TO MINIMUM STANDARDS

1.   Introduction

Crime and criminal justice policies are increasingly crossing jurisdictional borders. As Karstedt has observed, crime policies are 'travelling,' and they 'increasingly travel within a transnational and global institutional context.'[1] This 'import' and 'export' of crime and criminal justice policies involves interpretation and re-interpretation both of specific policies and of the contexts within which they operate and are (mis)understood – the legal procedural traditions, the roles and functions of legal personnel, the daily routines and practices of criminal justice and the ways in which these are informed and influenced by existing legal cultures. The transfer of crime and criminal justice policies is nowhere more evident than in and between the member states of the European Union (EU). Yet the variety of legal traditions, and the cultural and institutional differences, mean that understanding how criminal processes work, let alone seeking to ensure that they observe minimum standards, is a difficult and complex task.

In this book we examine the investigative stage of the criminal process and, in particular, the legal protection of persons suspected of crime, in a number of EU countries: Belgium, England and Wales, Germany, Greece, Italy, the Netherlands and Poland. For each country, academic and practicing lawyers critically examine the pre-trial stage of the criminal process and its relationship to the trial stage. In doing so, the authors do not simply describe, in formal terms, criminal procedural rules but, drawing on empirical research (where available) and other relevant materials, and on their experience, they seek to explain the 'lived experience' of pre-trial processes in their jurisdictions. Furthermore, given the dynamic nature of criminal justice systems and processes, they examine them in an historical context, demonstrating how they have changed in recent years and speculate on how they

---

[1]   S. Karstedt, 'Durkheim, Tarde and beyond: the global travel of crime policies,' in T. Newburn and R. Sparks, *Criminal Justice and Political Cultures*, Cullompton, Willan, 2004, p. 18. For an empirical study of crime policy transfer between the USA and the UK see T. Jones and T. Newburn, *Policy Transfer and Criminal Justice*, Maidenhead, Open University Press, 2007.

1

might develop in the future. In the second part of the book, the authors consider a case study, explaining how suspects arrested and detained in those circumstances are likely to be dealt with in their jurisdiction. By adopting an approach that seeks to understand the ways in which the legal protection of persons suspected of crime works in practice, we hope to develop a nuanced understanding of how the investigative stage of the criminal process operates in a variety of EU jurisdictions, and ultimately to contribute to the development of meaningful policies and processes that will help to ensure the realisation of fair trial rights across the EU.

2.   The EU and European context

The context for this project is the increasingly proactive nature of EU activity in criminal justice, concerning both cross-border and domestic crime. As a result of increased transnational co-operation in criminal matters, those suspected and accused of criminal activity are increasingly the subject of investigative and prosecutorial acts outside their own country, and there will be a growing need for transnational legal assistance. In this process, mutual trust and recognition are the keywords, the guarantees on which co-operation is based.

The Maastricht Treaty (the Treaty on European Union, TEU), which came into force in November 1993, established police and judicial cooperation in relation to terrorism and serious crime within the newly created field of Justice and Home Affairs.[2] The European Union's competence in criminal matters was subsequently strengthened by the 1997 Amsterdam Treaty (amending the TEU) which created an area of freedom, security and justice. Although one of the underlying principles of these structures of co-operation is that they should respect human rights and fundamental freedoms, the emphasis has been upon mechanisms of investigation and prosecution, rather than protection for the accused. Europol provides a basis for police cooperation in connection with serious international crime. Eurojust[3] seeks to support and improve co-ordination between member states in the investigation and prosecution of serious cross-border crime. A proposal for a European Prosecutor was adopted in 2001.[4] The European Arrest Warrant, which came into force in January 2004,[5] provides for the extradition of persons accused of crime or for the

---

[2]   This is in both civil and criminal matters. Examples of the latter include arrangements for extradition, mutual legal assistance and co-operation in the investigation of serious crime such as trafficking in drugs, arms, toxic waste and people. For further information, see the Justice and Home Affairs (JHA) website <http://www.consilium.europa.eu/cms3_applications/showPage.asp?id=249&lang=en&mode=g>.

[3]   Established in 2002, it describes itself as 'a key interlocutor with the European institutions...with a mission to be a privileged partner with Liaison Magistrates, The European Judicial Network and organisations such as the European police office (Europol) and the European Anti-Fraud Office (OLAF)...a legal melting-pot from which subsequent developments to strengthen the European judicial area will be defined.' See the Eurojust website <http://www.eurojust.eu.int/index.htm>.

[4]   See COM(2001)715 final.

[5]   See Council Framework Decision of 13 June 2002 on the European arrest warrant and surrender procedures between member states (2002/584/JHA).

purposes of prosecution in another EU country. And finally, the European Evidence Warrant[6] is designed to make it easier and faster for one member state to obtain evidence, including objects, documents and data, from another.

Recognising that most of the EU criminal justice initiatives had been concerned with law enforcement, the European Commission (the Commission) turned its attention to the need for common standards of protection for those suspected or accused of crime. In 2003 the Commission issued a Green Paper, *Procedural Safeguards for Suspects and Defendants in Criminal Proceedings throughout the European Union*[7] with a view to setting minimum safeguards for suspects and defendants in the EU. Establishing minimum safeguards was described as a 'necessary counterbalance to judicial co-operation measures that [have] enhanced the powers of prosecutors, courts and investigating officers.'[8] This was regarded as an essential element of the policy of mutual recognition since, for mutual recognition to be effective, there has to be mutual trust, not only between member states, but also on the part of legal personnel making decisions in pursuance of mutual recognition policies and legislation. Minimum standards would, in turn, 'highlight the degree of harmonisation'[9] between the criminal justice systems of member states and reinforce the overall policy objective of freedom of movement within the EU.

The key areas identified in the Green Paper as being appropriate for action to create minimum standards were legal advice and assistance; the provision of interpreters; special protection for vulnerable suspects; consular assistance; and knowledge of the existence of rights. Whilst other rights were considered for inclusion, the rights identified were regarded by the Commission as being so fundamental that they should be given priority. Other fair trial rights, specifically those concerning bail and fair procedures for handling evidence, were reserved for separate treatment, the former because it was already the subject-matter of a measure in the mutual recognition programme, and the latter because the subject-matter was so large that it should be covered by a separate programme.[10]

Whilst there was strong support for the proposals from many lawyers and non-governmental organisations, a number of governments objected to the draft framework decision on the grounds that it breached the principle of subsidiarity, was outside the scope of article 31, could result in the lowering of standards (which, it was said, had already been set by the European Convention on Human Rights (ECHR)), and that implementing common standards would be technically difficult. In 2004 the Commission issued a draft *Council Framework Decision on certain procedural rights in criminal proceedings throughout the European Union*. In an attempt to forestall objections, the Commission made it clear that its intention was 'not to duplicate what is in the ECHR but rather to promote compliance at a consistent

---

6   Currently in draft form, the Council of the EU agreed a general approach at its meeting on 1 June 2006. See 11235/06 COPEN 74.
7   Brussels, 19 February 2003, COM(2003) 75f.
8   *Ibidem*, § 1.4.
9   *Ibidem*, § 1.7.
10   *Ibidem*, § 2.6.

standard.'[11] However, a number of governments, including those of the Netherlands and the UK,[12] continued to object to the notion of binding procedural rights in criminal proceedings, questioning the legal basis for EU legislation in this area and its relationship with the ECHR. In response, the Finnish EU Presidency proposed that a Council declaration be adopted as an interim measure, whilst work continued on the text for a framework decision. Significantly, the interim measure was to be non-binding and in respect of those rights that were to be dependent upon a person having been 'charged with a criminal offence' (such as the right to legal advice), that phrase was to be interpreted in accordance with national laws 'while respecting article 6 of the European Convention on Human Rights as interpreted by the European Court of Human Rights.'[13] This approach explicitly 'limits the number and scope of the rights covered and focuses on general standards rather than specifying in detail how the rights should be applied in each member state in view of the different procedural systems.'[14]

The objections reflect, in part at least, the fact that national criminal justice systems within the EU are very diverse, and so too are the ways in which member states consider themselves to have satisfied their obligations to guarantee fair trial rights generally, and to protect the rights of those suspected or accused of crime in particular. They also reflect an unease about importing policies and processes perceived as 'foreign' and, in particular, a tension between different cultural and historical understandings of the criminal process exemplified by the terms 'inquisitorial' and 'adversarial.' However, they also expose an attitude to 'freedom, security and justice' which is informed by the concerns and interests of law enforcement and prosecution agencies rather than those of citizens who may be 'caught up' in the legal processes of other EU jurisdictions. With the increasing movement of persons within the EU, both for employment and other purposes such as leisure, a significant minority of them will increasingly experience the criminal justice systems of other EU jurisdictions as suspects, defendants and as victims of crime. If the creation of an area of freedom, security and justice is to be meaningful and successful it is imperative that mutual trust and recognition, which has been described as 'the cornerstone of judicial co-operation,'[15] is something that is also perceived and experienced by ordinary citizens.

However, the significance and impact of the different legal traditions in the EU cannot be ignored. They are regarded by many as emblematic of national identity, provide the foundation for a range of strongly entrenched institutional and

---

[11]   Draft Council Framework Decision, Explanatory Memorandum, § 9.
[12]   For example, the UK government argued that the provisions should be non-binding, a position that was contrary to the recommendations of the House of Lords Select Committee report: House of Lords, European Union Committee, *Procedural Rights in Criminal Proceedings. Report with Evidence. 1st report of Session 2004-05. HL Paper 28*, London, The Stationery Office Limited, 2005.
[13]   See 9222/06 DROIPEN 34.
[14]   See the press release *Background Justice and Home Affairs Council*, Luxembourg 1-2 June 2006, issued 29 May 2006, p. 4.
[15]   Point 33 – Presidency Conclusions – Tampere European Council 15-16 October 1999.

professional functions and aspirations, and create a prism through which any pan-European criminal justice policies will be refracted. The jurisdictions included in this study represent the three major legal traditions to be found in the EU: common law, inquisitorial, and (post) state-socialist. It is important to conceive of them as traditions, rather than 'systems,' since each has developed, and will continue to develop, in a particular social, political and cultural context.[16] Jurisdictions that are regarded as having the same legal tradition have developed in very different ways, a fact that is amply demonstrated in the various chapters in this book.[17] Nevertheless, in order to understand the different approaches to the investigative stage of the criminal process reflected in this book, and the problems of establishing minimum procedural rights at the investigative stage, it is necessary to describe briefly the broad contours of the three traditions.

3. Three major legal traditions

The common law, adversarial, tradition is based on the notion that the best way of determining guilt or innocence is by contest between two parties, the accuser and the accused – roles now fulfilled by the prosecution (rather than the victim) and the defence. The parties are responsible for the investigation and gathering of evidence pre-trial, and for the selection and presentation of evidence to the court. The judge is not involved in the investigation and at trial plays a relatively passive role, determining questions of law whilst the jury adjudicates on the facts. The trial is the focus of the adversarial model, the point at which the parties present their case and the oral evidence of witnesses is heard, although this may be circumvented if the defendant pleads guilty.[18] This contrasts with the more centralised procedure in the inquisitorial model, where the evidence that comes before the court is not that of two opposing parties, but is the product of an enquiry for which a public prosecutor or investigating judge is responsible. The evidence has already been evaluated and filtered by the prosecutor and/or the judicial officer and there is a sense, therefore, in which the pre-trial process is indeed a form of pre-judgment. In this way, the inquisitorial model places greater emphasis on the pre-trial phase. The trial is not

---

[16]   Whether they are diverging, or converging, or whether a new form of criminal justice process is developing across jurisdictions has prompted considerable academic debate. See, for example, N. Jorg, S. Field and C. Brants, 'Are Inquisitorial and Adversarial Systems Converging?,' in P. Fennell, C. Harding, N. Jorg and B. Swart (eds), *Criminal Justice in Europe: A Comparative Study*, Oxford, Clarendon Press, 1995; P. Duff, 'Changing Conceptions of the Scottish Criminal Trial: The Duty to Agree Uncontroversial Evidence,' in A. Duff, L. Farmer, S. Marshall and V. Tadros, *The Trial on Trial: Volume One*, Oxford, Hart Publishing, 2004; and J. Jackson, 'The Effect of Human Rights on Criminal Evidentiary Processes: Towards Convergence, Divergence or Realignment?,' 68 *Modern Law Review*, 5 2005, p. 737-764.

[17]   For a comparative examination of criminal justice systems see, for example, M. Delmas-Marty and J. Spencer, *European Criminal Procedures*, Cambridge, Cambridge University Press, 2002, and R. Vogler, *A World View of Criminal Justice*, Aldershot, Ashgate, 2005.

[18]   In England and Wales defendants plead guilty in over 95 % of cases.

the focus for the determination of issues, but for the verification and confirmation of an earlier set of data collecting moments.[19]

There is some disagreement amongst comparative lawyers as to whether socialist legal systems constitute a discrete legal tradition.[20] Reichel, for example, believes that it is possible to identify 'distinctions warranting a separate category for a socialist legal tradition,' the key factor being that law is subordinate to state policy, having an economic and educational function.[21] Vogler, on the other hand, at least in the context of the USSR, regards the criminal justice apparatus as a development of inquisitorialism 'adapted for the purposes of the modern totalitarian state.'[22] The focus was the pre-trial investigative process, which was heavily reliant on confessions rather than investigation, with trials being formalised, political, events. The principal function of all participants, including judges and lawyers, was to serve the interests of the state. Since the collapse of the USSR in the late 1980s, many former state-socialist jurisdictions have been heavily influenced by adversarialism, but the direction of reform has varied widely across different jurisdictions.[23] In Vogler's view, whilst constitutionally 'there has been a strong move towards adversariality and due process rights,' at the procedural level there has, for a variety of reasons, been a strong 'desire to entrench a powerful judiciary with broad powers of investigation and control.'[24]

In order to understand the position and experience of those suspected of crime (and indeed of their lawyers), it may be helpful to give a brief account of some of the principle features of the different traditions in their modern context.[25] In England and Wales, a jurisdiction with an adversarial tradition, a person accused of a crime is not, in theory, the passive object of an investigation but is a party to the process of establishing guilt or innocence. This means, again in theory, that they are not obliged to co-operate in the investigation of crime and the determination of guilt but can 'sit back' and see whether the prosecution can establish their guilt by producing sufficient evidence at trial. They can also conduct their own investigations, and call witnesses to give evidence at trial. As a description of the trial process itself, this is still a broadly accurate description, although since 1995 the trial court has been able to draw inferences from the failure or refusal of a person accused of a crime (the defendant) to testify at trial[26] and other recent changes mean

---

[19] For a more detailed discussion of these issues and an account of an inquisitorial-type process in practice (France) see J. Hodgson, *French Criminal Justice: A Comparative Account of the Investigation and Prosecution of Crime in France*, Oxford, Hart Publishing, 2005.

[20] See the brief discussion in P. Reichel, *Comparative Criminal Justice Systems*, New Jersey, Pearson, 4th edition, 2005, p. 123.

[21] *Ibidem.*

[22] R. Vogler, *A World View of Criminal Justice*, Aldershot, Ashgate, 2005, p. 64.

[23] *Ibidem*, p. 186-190.

[24] *Ibidem*, p. 189.

[25] In view of the range of developments in the post-state socialist jurisdictions we concentrate here on jurisdictions with an adversarial or inquisitorial tradition.

[26] Criminal Justice and Public Order Act (CJPOA) 1984, s35, which came into force in 1995, enables the court to draw 'proper' inferences if the defendant fails or refuses to give evidence without good cause. The normal inference is that the defendant has no innocent explanation,

→

that the accused must give the prosecution advance notice of the substance of their defence.[27] However, at the investigative stage the police have extensive powers in relation to a suspect: they can arrest persons suspected of crime; detain them for the purposes of investigation, including by interrogating them; decide whether there is sufficient evidence to charge them with a criminal offence; and decide whether the suspect should be detained or released on bail pending their first court appearance. All of these powers can be exercised without the involvement of either a prosecutor or a judge.[28] Furthermore, lack of co-operation by a suspect (refusing to answer questions or refusing to co-operate with the investigative decisions of the police such as fingerprinting, photographing, searches, taking samples) can have adverse consequences both at the time, because the police may be able to use force, and at trial, when the court may (in effect) treat their silence under questioning as evidence of guilt.[29] In this context, the accused (as a party to the proceedings) has a right to the assistance of a lawyer, who provides a counterweight to the (partisan) police and prosecutor and who, given the high rate of guilty pleas, will normally be the only legally trained person (other than the prosecutor) who determines whether there is sufficient evidence to establish guilt.

In jurisdictions rooted in a more inquisitorial tradition, such as Belgium, Greece, Germany and the Netherlands,[30] the accused is not considered a party to the proceedings in the same way. Central to the criminal process is the notion of an enquiry conducted by a judicial officer, with the suspect as the subject of the enquiry. A distinction should be made in this respect between inquisitorial jurisdictions in the Napoleonic tradition (e.g., France, Belgium, Greece), with its emphasis on a secret investigation by an investigating judge,[31] and other continental criminal jurisdictions (e.g., Germany, the Netherlands, Sweden) where the position of the investigating judge has been abolished or marginalized, with full responsibility for crime investigation being placed on the prosecutor. However, in either case, the investigation of a crime is conceived of as a neutral enquiry conducted by a judicially trained, independent, objective, official. In practice, particularly in those jurisdictions that have dispensed with, or marginalised the role of the investigating judge, there is some recognition that prosecutors may be partisan (or at least may be motivated by prosecutorial objectives), but not to the

---

or none that would stand up to cross-examination. A defendant cannot be convicted on the basis of an inference alone: there must be some other evidence of their guilt (s38(3)).

27   In particular, the disclosure obligations in the Criminal Procedure and Investigations Act 1996 Part I, and in the Criminal Procedure Rules 2005.

28   Although detention without charge beyond 36 hours (or 48 hours in the case of a person arrested under the Terrorism Act 2000) requires authorisation by a court.

29   Under the Criminal Justice and Public Order Act 1994 s34 and ss36 and 37.

30   Whilst Italian criminal procedure has an inquisitorial history, it has undergone a major shift from inquisitorial to adversarial procedure and arguably should now be regarded as having an adversarial basis. See 'The investigative stage of the criminal process in Italy,' in this volume, and W. Pizzi and M. Montagna, 'The Battle to Establish an Adversarial Trial System in Italy,' (Winter) *Michigan Journal of International Law*, 2004, p. 429.

31   Though it should be noted that in practice, even in these jurisdictions, the prosecutor is responsible for the majority of criminal investigations.

extent of changing the essential conception of the criminal process. Again in practice, the police may have extensive powers in relation to suspects but they are, in principle, circumscribed first by the principle of legality, and second by the requirement to seek approval for their actions (either in advance or *ex post facto*) from either a prosecutor or a judge. Since the investigation is 'judicial' and the suspect is a subject of and not a party to the process, the role for a defence lawyer at the investigative stage is relatively limited. The suspect is, in theory, not in need of protection from a 'judicial' enquiry, and there is no need for the lawyer to have any investigative powers. The role of the defence lawyer is, at its highest, to prompt the person conducting the investigation to consider certain lines of enquiry, and to review the legality of the process. In some jurisdictions, the defence is afforded an opportunity to participate in the pre-trial investigation, but in practice this remains limited and difficult to put into effect.

4.   The significance of the investigative stage

Our study focuses on procedural rights at the investigative stage. Whilst comparative studies and popular accounts of criminal justice systems often concentrate on the trial as the most public, and so most apparent, manifestation of the criminal process, there is increasing recognition that an understanding of pre-trial procedures, and particularly the investigative stage, is essential for a proper understanding and evaluation of criminal justice processes. Of particular importance in assessing the value and credibility of evidence produced at trial is an awareness of the processes by which that evidence was created or established – by whom, under what conditions and with what safeguards to ensure reliability? It is also not without significance that in all jurisdictions many more people are subjected to investigative processes – involving arrest or other forms of detention, interrogation, surveillance and other forms of coercive evidence-gathering – than the number who ultimately face trial in a criminal court. Thus for many, the criminal investigation constitutes their experience of the criminal justice system, and serves to inform their own view, and that of their relatives and friends, of whether they have been dealt with fairly and justly.

For the purposes of this study, our working assumption was that whatever legal tradition underlies the criminal justice system of a particular jurisdiction, and irrespective of the formal legal position, there is a *de facto continuum* from investigation to trial, and in this context regulation of the investigative stage of the criminal process is a fundamental part of the regulation of the trial process itself. We maintain that it is not possible to say, in respect of any particular jurisdiction, that the trial satisfies human rights norms unless the investigative stage is also conducted in accordance with those norms. This was implicitly recognised in the draft framework decision on minimum procedural rights, in which a number of the proposed rights, such as the right to legal advice and the special provisions applicable to persons 'entitled to specific attention,'[32] were to apply before or during any initial interrogation by the police.

We accept, however, that our position is not without controversy. As noted earlier, the draft framework decision was not accepted by the governments of a number of member states, although the objections were based largely on arguments concerning the legitimacy of the EU in making binding decisions in this area rather than on any fundamental disagreement about the significance for fair trial of pre-trial processes. Perhaps a greater challenge to our approach, although we would argue that it makes the case for an agreed set of rights applicable at the investigative stage stronger, is the jurisprudence of the European Court of Human Rights (ECtHR). Whilst it has accepted that a fair trial, as guaranteed by article 6, may be vitiated by lack of fairness or by illegality at the investigative stage, this depends on the nature of the unfairness or illegality and its impact on the trial. The fairness of the trial is to be judged by reference to the procedure as a whole, so that if unfairness or illegality at the investigative stage can be adequately compensated for at trial, the procedure as a whole may nevertheless be regarded as fair.[33]

Despite the fact that some governments objected to the draft framework decision on the ground that minimum rights were already guaranteed by the ECHR, and there was no need to duplicate them, the ECtHR has itself been equivocal in determining to what extent procedural rights based on the right to fair trial apply at the investigative stage.[34] This may be illustrated by the approach of the court to the right to legal advice. Article 6(3) of the ECHR states that a person 'charged' with a criminal offence is entitled, *inter alia*, to legal assistance. The ECtHR noted in its judgement in *Murray* v. *UK*[35] that it was not disputed that article 6 applied 'even at the stage of the preliminary investigation into an offence by the police,'[36] and that whilst the right to legal advice was not an unequivocal right, it does normally apply where 'the attitude of an accused at the initial stages of police interrogation... [is] decisive for the prospects of the defence in any subsequent criminal proceedings.'[37] Where it does apply, the right to legal representation arises

---

[32] Defined in article 10(1) of the draft framework decision as persons who cannot understand or follow the content of meaning of the proceedings as a result of their age, mental, physical or emotional condition.

[33] See, e.g., ECtHR 12 May 2000, *Khan* v. *the United Kingdom*, Reports 2000-V at § 34; ECtHR 25 September 2001, *P.G. and J.H.* v. *the United Kingdom*, Reports 2001-IX at § 76; ECtHR 5 November 2002, *Allan* v. *the United Kingdom*, Reports 2002-IX at § 42; ECtHR 11 July 2006, *Jalloh* v. *Germany*, No. 54810/00, at § 95 and ECtHR 18 October 2006, *Hermi* v. *Italy*, No. 18114/02, at § 60.

[34] See e.g. ECtHR 24 November 1993, *Imbrioscia* v. *Switzerland*, A 275 at § 36 and ECtHR 9 June 1998, *Twalib* v. *Greece*, Reports 1998-IV at § 40-43.

[35] ECtHR 8 February 1996, *Murray* v. *UK*, Reports 1996-I.

[36] At § 62.

[37] At § 63. See also ECtHR 6 June 2000, *Averill* v. *UK*, Reports 2000-VI. The compromise approach to minimum procedural rights whereby 'charged with a criminal offence' is to be interpreted by reference to national laws (see text to note 13) could mean that a state in which a suspect is not 'charged' until after police interrogation could argue that, despite this jurisprudence, the right to legal advice does not apply during interrogation that takes place prior to charge.

immediately upon arrest, although a reasonable time is allowed for the lawyer to arrive.[38] However, according to the ECtHR the right to have a lawyer present during police interrogation cannot in general be derived from article 6 (3) ECHR,[39] although in certain circumstances the physical presence of a lawyer can provide the necessary counterbalance against pressure used by the police during interviews.[40]

Such a nuanced exposition of the right to legal advice is not conducive to clear and comparable national regulations or practices, a fact that was demonstrated by Spronken and Attinger's study *Procedural Rights in Criminal Proceedings: Existing Level of Safeguards in the European Union*.[41] They found that all EU states said that provisions exist guaranteeing the right to a lawyer to those accused of crime, and for the appointment of a lawyer where the suspect does not know of one or cannot afford to pay them (although in the latter situation the choice of the suspect is usually restricted), and that this right normally applied at all stages of criminal proceedings. However, there was considerable variation concerning the point in the proceedings at which access to a lawyer is granted, and there was substantial scope for differences in practice across different jurisdictions. For example, nine states responded saying that the right to a lawyer arose 'from the beginning of the proceedings,' or 'from the moment the person is charged,' or 'after the police interview,' responses which, in themselves, reflect widely different approaches to the right to legal advice. The authors concluded that, on the basis of information

---

[38]   ECtHR 8 February 1996, *John Murray* v. *UK*, Reports 1996-I at § 63.

[39]   In *Dougan* (ECtHR 14 December 1999, *Dougan* v. *UK*, No. 44738/98) the ECtHR held: 'Before the Court of Appeal they argued for the first time that the statements made by the applicant to the police should have been declared inadmissible on account of the absence of a solicitor during interview. However the merits of that argument must be tested against the circumstances of the case. Quite apart from the consideration that this line of defence should have been used at first instance, the Court considers that an applicant cannot rely on article 6 to claim the right to have a solicitor physically present during interview.' See also ECtHR 16 October 2001, *Brennan* v. *UK*, No. 39846/98.

[40]   ECtHR 6 June 2000, *Magee* v. *UK*, No. 28135/95 and ECtHR 2 May 2000, *Condron* v. *UK*, No. 35718/97: 'The fact that an accused person who is questioned under caution is assured access to legal advice, and in the applicants' case the physical presence of a solicitor during police interview must be considered a particularly important safeguard for dispelling any compulsion to speak which may be inherent in the terms of the caution. For the court, particular caution is required when a domestic court seeks to attach weight to the fact that a person who is arrested in connection with a criminal offence and who has not been given access to a lawyer does not provide detailed responses when confronted with questions the answers to which may be incriminating.' (§ 60). It should be noted that the Yugoslavia Tribunal acknowledges the right to have a lawyer present during interrogation (Statute of the International Tribunal for the former Yugoslavia art 18(3)) and if the right is violated evidence obtained should be excluded at trial (Decision on the Defence Motion to Exclude Evidence van het Joegoslavie Tribunal in Zdravko Mucic, 2 September 1997, Case No. IT-96-21-T, Trial Chamber II). Further, according to the European Committee for the Prevention of Torture and Inhuman or Degrading Treatment or Punishment, the right to have a lawyer present during police interrogation is one of the fundamental safeguards against ill-treatment of detained persons. See 2nd General Report (CPT/Inf (92)(3), sections 36-38.

[41]   (2005) Brussels: EC DG Justice and Home Affairs, available at <http://arno.unimaas.nl /show.cgi?fid=3891>.

supplied by the states themselves, it was difficult to draw conclusions as to whether legal advice is provided 'as soon as possible,' which was the phrase used in the draft framework decision article 2, and even more difficult to establish whether suspects were entitled to legal advice before answering questions in relation to the alleged offence(s).

5. The research project

The significance of the investigative stage of the criminal process in understanding the ways in which, and the extent to which, national criminal justice systems give effect to fair trial rights led us to focus our research on the legal protection of persons suspected of crime. The different cultural and historical approaches to, and understandings of, the investigative stage of the criminal process and its relationship to other stages, particularly the trial, have serious implications both for EU and national policies, and also for decisions made by legal personnel within the different EU states (which may be particularly relevant in cross-jurisdictional investigations and enforcement). Yet this is an area in respect of which there has been relatively little comparative research and in which information is often not readily available.

The research project, entitled 'Legal protection of persons suspected of crime at the investigative stage in the EU' was carried out during 2005 and 2006. The aim of the research was to examine the nature of the legal protections provided to suspects in a range of EU countries, from both a theoretical and a practice-based perspective. There is a wealth of evidence that practice, and particularly the experience of suspects and their lawyers, is often at variance to the formal legal norms and laws.[42] We were, therefore, particularly concerned to understand not only the formal regulation of the investigative process, but also the ordinary experience of that formal legal position. Thus the objectives of the project were to:

- provide baseline data of pre-trial criminal proceedings in diverse jurisdictions in the EU;
- provide a better understanding of the level of 'parity' between EU states;
- provide a better understanding of what states, legal professionals and others need to do in working towards common minimum standards; and
- to improve standards of laws and practice.

The research was led by four academic lawyers (the editors of this book) from two EU jurisdictions, the Netherlands and England and Wales. Two are also practicing

---

[42]   M. McConville and J. Hodgson, *Custodial Legal Advice and the Right to Silence*, London, HMSO, 1993; M. McConville, J. Hodgson, L. Bridges and A. Pavlovic, *Standing Accused: The Organisation and Practices of Criminal Defence Lawyers in Britain*, Oxford, Clarendon Press, 1994; J. Hodgson, *French Criminal Justice: A Comparative Account of the Investigation and Prosecution of Crime in France*, Oxford, Hart Publishing, 2005; S. Field and A. West, 'Dialogue and the Inquisitorial Tradition: French Defence Lawyers in the Pre-Trial Criminal Process,' 14 *Criminal Law Forum*, 3 2003, p. 261-316.

lawyers, and one a former criminal defence lawyer. The decision as to the countries chosen as subjects for the research was informed by a number of considerations. We wished to reflect the position and dynamics of the two major western European legal traditions, inquisitorial and adversarial (England and Wales, as the prototype of the adversarial tradition), but also those of recent accession states that had formerly been heavily influenced by a state-socialist (and specifically USSR) approach to law and legal regulation (Poland). We also wanted to explore some of the important dissimilarities within the inquisitorial tradition, and particularly the differences in practice between the Napoleonic systems (Belgium and Greece) and others (Germany and the Netherlands), and to investigate the implications for day-to-day practice when an 'adversarial experiment' is conducted in a jurisdiction with an inquisitorial tradition (Italy). The desire to understand the 'lived experience' of criminal justice regulation and processes meant that we wished to include not only academic lawyers in the project, but also lawyers with experience of acting for those suspected or accused of crime.

There were three distinct phases to the research project: preparation of overviews and case studies; an experts' conference; and reflection and revision. In the first, an academic and a practicing criminal lawyer (the experts) in each of the jurisdictions were identified, and they were asked to prepare an overview of the investigative stage of the criminal process in their country, and to prepare a response to a case study. The overview, which was to form the basis of chapters in the first part of this book, was intended to provide a detailed explanation of relevant law and practice in each of the participant countries. In order to deal with the 'gap' between law and practice, the experts were asked in preparing their overviews not only to describe the formal legal basis for investigative stage processes, but also to convey how those processes work on a day-to-day basis. Whilst in some countries, particularly England and Wales, there is a body of empirical research on investigative stage processes and on legal personnel,[43] in most jurisdictions included in this project little, if any, such research is available. Therefore many of the experts, particularly the professional lawyers, had to rely on their own experiences and those of their professional colleagues in describing practice supplemented, where available, by empirical research and other data. In addition, since criminal justice processes are not static, but dynamic, the experts were asked to provide a sense of how those processes are changing.

Investigative stage processes differ as between different jurisdictions, not only in terms of personnel and procedures, but also in terms of the vocabulary applied to certain processes.[44] Whilst allowing for this, in order to facilitate comparison, the experts were asked to prepare their overviews in accordance with a fixed format that covered police powers, suspects' rights and the relationship between the trial

---

[43]   Although much of it was conducted in the late 1980s and early to mid 1990s. See in particular, D. Brown, *PACE Ten Years On: A Review of Research*, Research Study No. 155, London, Home Office, 1997 and M. McConville, A. Sanders and R. Leng, *The Case for the Prosecution*, London, Routledge, 1991. See also the references in note 42.

[44]   See the brief discussion of the meaning of 'charge' in note 37 *supra*. See further the text following note 50 *infra*.

and pre-trial phase. The case study question, prepared by the research team, was designed to explore the ways in which suspects are dealt with at the investigative stage, and to provide a nuanced understanding of how investigative stage processes work in practice. The subject matter of the case study was deliberately relatively mundane, involving a violent incident at a football match in Country A (the experts' own country), in which three different suspects were implicated, one of them being a citizen of another EU country.

The experts' conference was held in Amsterdam, Netherlands, in September 2005. The overviews and case study responses were prepared and circulated in advance of the conference. For each jurisdiction a *rapporteur* from another country was appointed from amongst the experts attending the conference, and they were asked to give a short presentation which, in effect, interrogated the overview and case study response of their assigned jurisdiction, making critical comment and raising questions. In this way, the *rapporteurs* were able to question and expose the assumptions and taken-for-granted meanings that often impede understanding across jurisdictions. The experts from the jurisdiction in question were then able to respond in order to clarify, explain and, sometimes to defend their description and analysis. This exchange led to lively, and sometimes heated, debate which we believe enhanced the process of understanding.

The third phase of the project that took place after the conference, was one of reflection upon and revision of the overviews and case study responses. Building upon the comments from the *rapporteurs* and the ensuing discussion amongst the experts at the conference, the editors provided the expert authors with feedback and comments in order to develop the critical descriptions and analyses which form the basis of this book.

6. Emerging Themes

6.1. *Theory and practice*

As noted earlier, conceptions of the investigative process, and of the respective roles of the judiciary, prosecution, police and suspect (and their lawyers), differ widely as between the different legal traditions represented in this study. However, although the formal structures governing the conduct and supervision of investigations are very different, in practice the differences are often much less pronounced. In most of the inquisitorial jurisdictions in our sample it is assumed that the prosecutor conducts or leads the criminal investigation; the role of the investigating judge in crime investigation has either largely been replaced by the prosecutor, or the position has been abolished altogether. In practice, however, the police often have significant investigative powers, particularly in the case of flagrant or less serious offences, and they often carry out (at least an initial) interrogation of the suspect without the supervision of, or immediate reference to, the prosecutor.[45] Furthermore, the product of such interrogation is normally included in the file, and thus becomes evidence at any subsequent trial. In this respect practice is similar to that in common law, adversarial, jurisdictions in which investigation and interrogation, unsupervised by a prosecutor or judge, is understood to be a police function. Important differences do, however, remain. In the adversarial tradition, once a person has been charged with an offence (which is normally relatively shortly after their arrest and detention by the police), no further interrogation is permitted.[46] In inquisitorial systems, on the other hand, the prosecuting authorities (often, in practice, the police) can continue to interrogate the suspect after charge and continue to do so during the entire period of pre-trial detention, until the decision is made as to whether or not to bring the case to trial.

In many of the jurisdictions there are clear rules governing the rights of suspects (e.g., to legal advice),[47] the conduct of interrogations, and other investigative powers of the police or prosecutor. However, whether they are observed in practice depends, to a large extent, on there being systematic and effective enforcement mechanisms, and in particular the exclusion of evidence obtained in consequence of a breach. Some of the jurisdictions start from the position that illegally obtained evidence is not admissible in evidence (e.g., Italy, Belgium, Germany), whilst others start from the opposite premise (e.g., England and Wales). A third set of jurisdictions distinguish between serious illegality, which should result in exclusion or 'nullity,' and less serious breaches, which do not (e.g., the Netherlands, Greece). However, this is normally tempered either by specific statutory provisions or by the attitude of the courts. Thus in England and Wales, for example, the admissibility of illegally obtained evidence is subject to provisions which prohibit the admission of evidence of confessions which may have been obtained by oppression or in circumstances likely to render them unreliable, and judges have a discretion to exclude other prosecution evidence if it would be unfair to admit it. On the other hand, jurisprudential developments in countries such as Belgium, Germany and the Netherlands have made it less likely that illegally obtained evidence will be excluded, the courts privileging their role in truth-finding over the protection of the rights of the individual.[48] It would be dangerous, therefore, to assume that the formal position regarding the admissibility of illegally obtained evidence reflects practice.

To observe that there is a gap between theory and practice, that is, between the law as it appears in constitutions, criminal codes and legislation, and as it is

---

[45]   Even in Belgium, where the Napoleonic model is more strictly adhered to, it is the police who normally conduct interviews, with interviews being conducted personally by a prosecutor or investigating judge only in exceptional cases.

[46]   Although the British government is currently considering whether to permit post-charge interrogation.

[47]   Although in some, the right does not apply during the course of an initial police interrogation or there is lack of clarity about whether it does apply at this stage.

[48]   In the Netherlands the discretion of the courts to exclude evidence that has been illegally obtained was formalized in the Code of Criminal Procedure, art. 359a in 1995.

interpreted by the courts, is practised by investigative and prosecution agencies and is experienced by suspects and their lawyers, is hardly novel. Yet this truth, and its implications, is central to comparative understandings of criminal procedure and, importantly in the context of this study, to any policy which aims to establish and assure minimum procedural rights that are applicable across jurisdictions. Any instrument for establishing minimum procedural rights that is directed only at formal rights and legal procedure, or in the interpretation of which priority is given to 'respect for the different legal systems and traditions of the member states,'[49] is unlikely to be successful.

6.2. Problems of definition

Even allowing for the problems of translation, different terms may be used to apply to similar factual situations, and similar terms may have different meanings across jurisdictions. In a different but related context, Melossi has argued that translation of criminal policies is impossible since 'generally speaking any term, even the simplest, is embedded within a cultural context, or milieu, that gives it its meaning.'[50] Such difficulties have been placed in stark relief by implementation, and interpretation, of the Framework Decision on the European Arrest Warrant (EAW). Article 1(1) of the framework decision provides that a EAW is a judicial decision issued 'by a member state with a view to the arrest and surrender by another member state of a requested person, *for the purposes of conducting a criminal prosecution* or executing a custodial sentence or detention order' (emphasis added). In England and Wales this was given domestic effect by the Extradition Act 2003, section 2 of which provides that a warrant must be given effect where, *inter alia*, it is issued with a view to a person's arrest and extradition 'for the purpose of being prosecuted for the offence.' The question that had to be considered in *Vey* v. *Office of the Public Prosecutor of the County Court of Montlucon*[51] was whether a warrant issued by a French examining judge for the purpose of conducting a judicial examination satisfied that purpose, or was (in contrast) for the purpose of investigation. If the latter, the EAW procedure would not be available. Despite receiving expert evidence on the issue, the court had considerable difficulty in translating French criminal procedure into the English law context, and in determining for which of the two reasons the warrant had been issued.[52]

---

[49]   As stated in article 1(2) of the Presidency proposal for the text of an instrument on procedural rights in criminal proceedings (see note 13 *supra*).

[50]   D. Melossi, 'The cultural embeddedness of social control: reflections on the comparison of Italian and North-American cultures concerning punishment,' in T. Newburn and R. Sparks (eds), *Criminal Justice and Political Cultures*, Cullompton, Willan, 2004, quoted in T. Jones and T. Newburn, *Policy Transfer and Criminal Justice*, Maidenhead, Open University Press, 2007, p. 162.

[51]   [2006] EWHC 760 (Admin).

[52]   In the event, the court was able to avoid taking a final view on the question because it found the warrant to be defective for other reasons. See also the Supreme Court of Ireland decision in *The Minister for Justice, Equality and Law Reform* v. *McArdle* [2005] IESC 76.

The present study demonstrates that establishing minimum procedural rights at the investigative stage of the criminal process would face similar difficulties. In England and Wales, there is no legal definition of the term 'suspect.' The police have wide discretionary powers to arrest persons suspected of committing a crime, although the word 'arrest' itself is said to be a factual situation involving the denial of liberty rather than a legal term.[53] If the police have decided to arrest a suspect they must normally take them to a police station before interviewing them. Once at the police station, under national law the procedural rights, such as the right to legal advice, and the regulatory requirements, such as the obligation to tape-record interviews, then apply. However, the suspect is not 'charged' (i.e., criminal proceedings are not commenced) until the police have decided that there is sufficient evidence for there to be a successful prosecution, which is normally after they have been interviewed. Once they have been charged, they cannot normally be further interviewed (although the police can continue to carry out other forms of investigation).

Compare this with the position in Poland, where a person does not have the status of 'suspect' until they are officially charged. A person suspected of a criminal offence can be arrested and detained by police for up to 48 hours without being formally charged, and although they cannot be interviewed during that period, they can be 'heard' (i.e., make a 'voluntary' statement), and the police can carry out other investigative acts such as taking fingerprints and samples. However, although they have a right to remain silent during this period, since they have not been charged the police do not have to inform them of this right and nor, in practice, do they have a right to a legally-aided lawyer. In Germany and the Netherlands there is no fixed point at which proceedings are deemed to have commenced. A person should be treated as a suspect if there is strong suspicion that they may have committed an offence, at which point they should be informed of their right to remain silent, but the police have a degree of discretion in determining at what point the evidence is sufficiently strong to treat them as a suspect and an interest in delaying the notification of rights. In Italy, on the other hand, whilst the police have the power to question suspects (although not if they are under arrest), this cannot be done in the absence of a lawyer and if the suspect has not instructed a lawyer the police are under a duty to appoint a duty lawyer.

If, according to the ECHR article 6 or any EU instrument that is developed, the procedural rights or regulatory requirements are expressed not to apply until a person is 'charged' with a criminal offence, and if this is to be interpreted in accordance with national laws, the effect will be different across different jurisdictions. Using another stage of the process as the trigger, such as 'arrest,' would not provide an adequate solution if the intention is, as we would suggest it should be, to ensure the provision of minimum rights to persons who are at risk of prosecution and of having their response to police interrogation (or interrogation by prosecutors or judges) used as evidence at any trial. We have seen, for example, that in a number of jurisdictions persons suspected of a crime may be detained without

---

[53]   Lewis v. *Chief Constable of South Wales Constabulary* [1991] 1 All ER 206.

this being regarded as an 'arrest.' It may be that the trigger for procedural rights should be expressed in a more purposive way, so that it is determined by the consequences that may flow from the action rather than the label applied to it. For example, the right to legal advice could be expressed to apply whenever a person is questioned (or asked to make a voluntary statement) in circumstances where this may lead to criminal proceedings being taken against them and their response or non-response (or their statement) could be used against them in the criminal proceedings.

6.3. Understanding roles and functions

The key legal professionals in the investigative stage of the criminal process are the police (or other law enforcement agency), prosecutor, defence lawyer and, where the role exists, the examining judge. Although sharing the same or similar names, their functions, status, professional relationships and training differ considerably between jurisdictions and so our understandings of their comparable roles must be sensitive to this. This is perhaps clearest when considering the role of the public prosecutor.

In continental legal systems the prosecutor was originally conceived of as a member of the judiciary, albeit one with a special role. As such, the prosecutor was independent of the executive, and irremovable. In some of the jurisdictions included in the study, such as Italy, this is still largely the case although the hierarchical relationships and career structures within ministries of justice are not unimportant in relation to the question of how far individual prosecutors are truly independent. However, in other jurisdictions, such as the Netherlands, justice ministries are increasingly taking responsibility for criminal policy and, in this context, whilst prosecutors remain formally independent, they are coming under increasing pressure to implement criminal policy, placing at risk both their independence and the principle of legality. In England and Wales, where the role of Crown Prosecutor is a relatively modern creation, there has been little formal concern about their independence from the executive, but here too they are increasingly used as an instrument of the government's criminal policies.

Prosecutors in England and Wales have never been conceived of as being part of the judiciary, and until recently have had little or no role in the investigation of crime or the collection of evidence, which in modern times has been regarded as a police function. This is currently undergoing significant change, with prosecutors increasingly advising the police on the course of investigations and taking the decision to commence criminal proceedings. As noted earlier, in many continental jurisdictions the prosecutor has come to replace the investigating judge in having primary responsibility for crime investigation. Whilst in principle their role is a neutral one of 'discovering the truth' there is clear evidence in a number of countries of severe tension between impartial fact-finding and prosecutorial values, and this is particularly so where they are subject to influence from the executive. Poland provides an exception to the general picture of an increasingly strong role for prosecutors, which may be understood in the context of a reaction to its state-socialist history in which prosecutors played an important role in serving the interests of the state. Thus here judicial protection has been strengthened in recent years, and the powers of the prosecutor restricted.[54]

When the role of the Crown Prosecutor was created in England and Wales in the mid- 1980s the government's principle concern was to establish their independence from the police.[55] A clear division of labour between the two was created, with the police investigating crime and taking the decision to commence criminal proceedings, and the prosecutor taking over only once the charge decision had been made. Prosecutors had no supervisory role in respect of the police, and neither did the judiciary. The current developments in the prosecutorial role are likely to cause tensions in relations with the police, and will challenge the professional independence of prosecutors.[56] In jurisdictions with an inquisitorial tradition the role of the police in investigating crime was regarded as being subordinate to that of the prosecutor (or examining judge). However, in those jurisdictions where there is judicial or prosecutorial responsibility for crime investigation, there is now widespread delegation of both investigation and supervisory responsibility to the police (for example, in the Netherlands and Greece), and senior police officers are often deemed to be deputy prosecutors.[57] Such developments provide a particular challenge to those who argue that the judicial role in crime investigation renders unnecessary mechanisms designed to protect the position of the accused.

We were particularly interested in this study in the role of the criminal defence lawyer. At one level it is fairly easy to define the role of the defence lawyer in a way which applies to any of the jurisdictions we examined: to act in the best interests of the client. Although in many jurisdictions the role goes back much further, it is possible to locate this conception of the role in the ECHR article 6 right of a person charged with a criminal offence to defend themselves 'in person or through legal assistance of his own choosing' (art. 6(3)(c)).[58] However, once subjected to scrutiny, this apparently simple conception soon becomes much more complex. In some jurisdictions (e.g., the Netherlands, and England and Wales) the role of the lawyer is directly derived from the right of the accused to defend themselves. As the professional guide for solicitors in England and Wales states, a solicitor 'is under a duty to say on behalf of the client what the client should properly say for himself or

---

54   As discussed below, the runs counter to the trend to move away from a pre-trial judicial role to a greater part for prosecutors in most other European countries. This is unsurprising given the somewhat extreme powers of the Polish prosecutor under communism.

55   Until then prosecutors had normally been employed by the police.

56   See J. Jackson, 'The Ethical Implications of the Enhanced role of the Public Prosecutor,' 9 *Legal Ethics*, 1 2006, p. 35-55.

57   Such developments, however, are always subject to local circumstances. In the Netherlands, for example, the supervisory function of the prosecutor has recently been strengthened in response to a high profile scandal involving misuse by police of their investigative powers, *Evaluatieonderzoek Schiedammer Parkmoord*, TK 2004–2005, 29 800 VI, No. 168 and *Programma versterking opsporing en vervolging*, TK 2004-2005, 30 300 VI, No. 32.

58   Although the point at which this right crystallises is, of course, contested. See text to note 36, *supra*.

herself if the client possessed the requisite skill and knowledge.'[59] In Germany, on the other hand, the defence lawyer is not the defendant's spokesperson, but has an independent role speaking and acting in support of their client. One consequence is that statements of the lawyer are not automatically assumed to be those of the client. Also in Germany, there is disagreement as to whether the lawyer's 'organ of justice' role takes precedence over their role derived from the contractual relationship with the client, a debate which reflects an unresolved tension in many of the jurisdictions in the study and which has many practical implications.

The wider context in which the lawyer operates is also important to their proper role. The right to the assistance of a lawyer at the investigative stage, and particularly to legal advice prior to or during police interrogation, is restricted in many of the jurisdictions (although not in England and Wales or, to a large extent, Italy). Beyond this basic limitation, there are further relevant questions. What right does the lawyer have to information secured during the investigation? To what extent can the lawyer investigate independently and what, if any, investigative powers do they have? Is the lawyer subjected to restrictions regarding to whom they may speak? To what extent, if at all, can the lawyer influence the investigation by the police, prosecutor or judge? In England and Wales, and more recently in Italy, the lawyer is responsible for assembling the defence case independently from the prosecution but has few, if any, powers in this respect and, in legal aid cases, limited resources for doing so. In Germany, the defence may suggest lines of enquiry to the prosecutor or pre-trial judge, but such requests may be refused without reason and with no right of appeal.[60] Where they are granted, neither the suspect nor the lawyer is permitted to be present at any witness interview, whereas in the Netherlands their presence is permitted, when the interview is conducted by the examining judge, provided that it is not contrary to the interests of the investigation, and in Italy the defence lawyer may be present at all formal acts of investigation. Whilst in some jurisdictions a lawyer would be failing in their professional obligation to their client if they did not interview a potential defence witness, in Belgium the lawyer contravenes professional rules if they do so.

6.4. The importance of police interrogation

Whatever the formal position regarding responsibility for the investigation of crime, in most, if not all, of the jurisdictions examined the initial police interrogation is crucial. In England and Wales, it will normally form the backbone of the case against the accused. In countries with an inquisitorial tradition, the rhetoric of the law tends to describe the police investigation as being preliminary, with the more evidentially significant investigation being that conducted by a judge or quasi-judicial officer such as the prosecutor. In most jurisdictions this is wholly at odds with practice, with the majority of cases being dealt with exclusively by the police,

---

[59]   *The Guide to the Professional Conduct of Solicitors*, London, Law Society, 1999, p. 382.
[60]   Cf. the position in France. See Hodgson (2005) note 19 *supra*.

either on their own initiative or under the broad supervision of a judge or prosecutor.

Interviews by the police of persons suspected of crime thus provide the key evidence in most cases other than those that are serious or complex. In inquisitorial jurisdictions the record of the interview is included in the file, and in most such jurisdictions the absence (or abolition) of a hearsay rule enables evidence of police interrogation, including the response (or non-response) of the accused, to be put before the trial court either in documentary form or through the evidence of the interviewing officer. This is also the case in the common law jurisdiction of England and Wales, despite the existence of a hearsay rule. This, of course, has serious implications for the ways in which the suspect is (not) protected during police interviews. In inquisitorial jurisdictions such as Belgium and the Netherlands the suspect enjoys very few safeguards during police interrogation. Yet the evidence secured at this stage is as crucial as that produced by the police in England and Wales where there are safeguards during police interviews such as the right to legal advice, tape-recording, and appropriate adults for vulnerable suspects.

6.5.   *Protecting the rights of the suspect*

Given the significance of the investigative stage of the criminal process in general, and interrogation of suspects in particular, it is important to understand the ways in which the rights and interests of suspects are protected. Protective mechanisms can operate in different ways. First, there are what may be termed procedural rights, that is, rights that are directed at empowering the suspect during the investigative process such as access to legal advice, and to information about the reason for the detention and to the material available to the police or other investigative authority. A second form of protective mechanism is that directed at regulating the process, which may include provisions concerning the length and conditions of detention,[61] measures designed to protect the evidential integrity of the product of the detention, and special measures concerning vulnerable suspects. Thirdly, there are mechanisms that provide protection by opening up the process to persons other than those directly conducting a particular investigation, such as supervision and various forms of accountability.

Most jurisdictions employ some degree of mix although in theory, at least, inquisitorial jurisdictions tend to emphasise the importance of supervision and subsequent review of the legality of the investigative process at the expense of procedural rights. It was noted earlier that in most inquisitorially based systems the right to legal advice is limited during the entire preliminary proceedings, and particularly before and during police interrogations. The right of a person to be informed promptly of the reason for their arrest (and of any charge against them) is guaranteed by article 5(2) of the ECHR, but the effect of this is limited to an extent by the fact that in some jurisdictions various forms of detention are not classified as

---

[61]   See the timelines arrest and pre-trial detention and the comparative overview of the timelines at the end of this book.

arrests. In none of the jurisdictions does the suspect, or their lawyer, have a right of access to investigative material (or the file) during the initial police investigation, although in some (such as Greece) such a right does apply once examination by an investigative judge commences, although in others (such as Belgium) an apparent right to such information at this stage is often denied 'in the interests of the investigation.'

Regulation of the investigation process varies widely. In Belgium, for example, there is no primary legislation governing the detention of suspects, but only a 'complex tangle of secondary legislation, circular letters and internal documents.' In England and Wales, by contrast, most aspects of the investigative process involving the detention of the suspect at the police station are closely regulated by primary legislation and associated codes of practice. The period for which a suspect may be detained by the police on their own authority also varies to a considerable extent. In England and Wales, a suspect may be detained for up to 36 hours without being produced before a court. In Germany, a person may be detained for a maximum of 48 hours,[62] if held under provisional (i.e. non-judicially authorised) arrest, before being produced before a judge. In the Netherlands the equivalent period, amounting to 87 hours, is even longer. In Italy, the police must inform the prosecutor of any detention within 24 hours and the prosecutor must, within the following 24 hours, request a judge to validate the detention. Perhaps surprisingly, given the importance of police interrogation and the developments in technology, in most jurisdictions police interrogations are recorded in writing and normally a verbatim record is not made (although in some jurisdictions the suspect has a right to request this). Only in England and Wales are police interviews routinely tape-recorded, as is prosecutorial questioning in Italy.

As we have seen, and as the various chapters amply demonstrate, supervision by prosecutors and examining magistrates, and accountability to the courts, also varies considerably. How effective are such mechanisms? The independence and effectiveness of prosecutors and judges is affected by a variety of factors including caseload levels, case seriousness, understandings within legal and occupational cultures of what is meant by supervision, the extent of mutual dependency between police and prosecutors/judges, understandings of how investigations should be conducted and what it should achieve (truth, proof, or confession above all else?), and the professional hierarchies within which these personnel operate. In many jurisdictions, although prior authority is required for a wide range of coercive or intrusive investigative measures, such as arrest, search and seizure, the taking of samples, and various forms of surveillance, in practice the police are often able to rely on 'flagrant offence' and 'danger in delay' exceptions that allow them to dispense with authorisation. Even when such exceptions do not apply, and where authorisation is sought, it is rarely refused because the powers are often widely drawn, and the prosecutor or judge will normally base their decisions on information provided exclusively by the police (or prosecutor). This calls into

---

[62]   In fact 47 hours and 59 minutes is the maximum.

question the efficacy of judicial oversight that is often regarded as a sufficient protection in respect of investigative methods.

A further particular concern in this study has been to understand the operation and meaning of the 'right to silence' of the suspect which, although not explicitly part of the article 6 guarantees, has been regarded as a fundamental corollary of the privilege against self-incrimination. All member states claim to respect the right and, furthermore, it is often argued that its existence renders other forms of protection either less important or even unnecessary. In England and Wales, whilst the right continues to exist in principle, its impact as a protective device has been considerably curtailed by legislation that permits a court to draw inferences (amounting, in effect if not in law, to an inference of guilt) from the failure of an accused to tell the police what their defence is during the course of police interrogation.[63] Other jurisdictions do not have similar legislative provisions, and it is often insisted that the right to silence continues to exist. However, in many jurisdictions it is clear, in practice, that if a suspect refuses to co-operate in the investigative process by answering questions or by providing an explanation concerning the allegation, this may well have adverse consequences not only in respect of whether they are found guilty, but also in relation to decisions such as release pending trial. This does not appear to be the case in Italy, but in Belgium, for example, whilst it is legally impermissible for a judge to draw inferences from silence, it appears to be agreed that it will inevitably have some effect on the judge's 'intime conviction.' A further indication of the ambivalent attitude to the right to silence is the fact that in some jurisdictions (e.g. Poland), whilst the right is said to exist there is no obligation on the police to inform the suspect of it, at least at the initial stage. In others, such as the Netherlands and Germany (and formerly in Greece), although the police are under an obligation to tell the suspect of their right to silence, they have devised mechanisms for circumventing this requirement.

6.6. Resourcing legal assistance

A right to the assistance of a lawyer has little meaning if the right cannot be exercised because the suspect cannot afford the lawyer's fees. Article 5 of the draft framework decision,[64] broadly reflecting article 6(3)(c) of the ECHR, provided that the costs of legal advice should be borne by the state in whole or in part if it would otherwise cause undue financial hardship. Cross-jurisdictional comparisons of legal aid provision are difficult for a variety of reasons, and comparison of state expenditure on legal aid is hampered by the difficulties of obtaining comparable data.[65] Similarly, obtaining data on and making meaningful comparison between

---

[63]   See § 3.2 of the chapter on England and Wales for a more detailed consideration of these provisions.

[64]   See note 11 *supra*.

[65]   But see Spronken and Attinger, note 41 *supra*. For consideration of the issues, see C. Tata, 'Comparing Legal Aid Spending: The Promise and Perils of a Jurisdiction-Centred Approach to (International) Legal Aid Research,' in F. Regan, A. Paterson, T. Goriely and D. Fleming, *The Transformation of Legal Aid*, Oxford, Oxford University Press, 1999. See also T. Goriely, C.
→

rates of remuneration for criminal defence lawyers acting in publicly funded cases requires an understanding of the structure of legal professions and of the legal 'market,' as well as of the role of criminal defence lawyers across jurisdictions. Although we present some data on this, and on the ways in which legal professions and professional standards are regulated, we were concerned, in particular, to establish the point in the investigative process (if at all) at which state funded legal advice is available.

In some jurisdictions, the provision of state funding coincides with a right to legal advice during the whole of the investigative stage. This is most obvious in England and Wales where the right to legal advice from the time that an arrested person is first detained in a police station is matched by a free legal aid scheme that is not dependent on the financial resources of the suspect. Similarly, in Italy state funding is available where a person had a right to legal advice, although both the financial limits, and rates of remuneration, are low. However, such arrangements exist in only a minority of the jurisdictions we examined. As we have seen, in many jurisdictions a right to legal advice does not arise during (at least) initial interrogation by the police and applies only at some later stage. For example, in Belgium a suspect only has a right to legal advice after they have been interviewed by the investigating judge. At that point there is a presumption that the arrested person is entitled to legal aid, but only if they are without sufficient means to pay the lawyer, and the financial threshold is strict. Low financial thresholds are also to be found in Greece and the Netherlands. In Germany there is no system of public funding for persons suspected of crime, and the 'compulsory defence' arrangements mean that although an accused may be required to have a lawyer, they must normally pay for their services.

6.7. Challenges to the defence lawyer's role

We saw earlier that conceptions of the proper role of the defence lawyer, when considered at other than a superficial level, is both complex and contested. There is a particular tension between the duty of the lawyer to their client and their obligation to the proper administration of justice, a tension that remains unresolved in most jurisdictions. A theme that emerged during the conference discussion and analysis is the extent to which measures understood to be in the interests of the investigation or the proper administrations of justice can undermine the lawyer-client relationship in a number of different ways. In England and Wales, the legislation permitting inferences to be drawn from the suspect's 'silence' under police interrogation[66] has impacted upon the nature of the relationship and the advice given, causing many lawyers to adopt a more defensive posture when giving advice at the police station, concerned that their professional advice will be

---

Tata and A. Paterson, *Expenditure on Criminal Legal Aid: Report on a Comparative Pilot Study of Scotland, England and Wales, and the Netherlands*, Glasgow, University of Strathclyde, 1997.

[66] See note 63 *supra*.

subjected to the scrutiny of the court.[67] The subsidiary role of the defence lawyer in inquisitorial jurisdictions, when compared to that of the prosecutor or examining judge, coupled with the 'real' (as opposed to the theoretical) consequences of 'silence' of the suspect means that the advice and assistance that they can give to their client is severely circumscribed.

There is also evidence of a large degree of distrust of defence lawyers. The Belgian authorities insist on videotaping lawyer-client consultations for the 'protection' of the lawyer, and in Poland the police can be present during all lawyer-client meetings during the first two weeks of the investigation and can listen to and read all communications between them.[68] In Germany, written communication between a terrorist suspect and their lawyer may be monitored, and the Netherlands has witnessed a number of cases where legally privileged communications between lawyers and their clients have been intercepted by the use of electronic surveillance.[69] In Italy, someone other than the lawyer can determine whether there is a conflict of interest where the lawyer is representing more than one accused. Conversely, in England and Wales the Legal Services Commission, driven by financial considerations, can determine that a number of legally-aided defendants be represented by one lawyer. Thus whilst it has been agreed internationally that lawyers should not be identified with their clients or their clients' causes as a result of discharging their functions as lawyers,[70] in many European jurisdictions defence lawyers, as compared to prosecutors, are not regarded or treated with parity.

6.8. *Conclusions*

There has been, and continues to be, a general trend in jurisdictions with an inquisitorial tradition to move crime investigation away from the more costly and time consuming process of judicial enquiry towards police investigations supervised instead by the public prosecutor. This has been the case in Germany, the Netherlands, Italy (and France) and although the position of the investigative judge in Belgium continues to be invested with great importance, their case-loads mean that most investigative work is delegated to the police.[71] This has significant

---

[67] For an examination of this see E. Cape, 'Rebalancing the Criminal Justice Process: Ethical Challenges for Criminal Defence Lawyers,' 9 *Legal Ethics*, 1 2006, p. 56-79.

[68] Although since prior to 1997 there was only a discretionary right to a lawyer, the current position is regarded as an improvement.

[69] By contrast, in the English case of *R* v. *Grant* [2005] EWCA Crim 1089 covert surveillance of consultations between defence lawyers and their clients at the police station was held to be 'categorically unlawful,' amounting to an abuse of process.

[70] UN Declaration on the Basic Principles on the Role of Lawyers, § 18, adopted by the Eight UN Congress on the Prevention of Crime and the Treatment of Offenders in Havana, Cuba, 7 September 1990 and welcomed by the UN General Assembly in Resolution 45/121 on 14 December 1990.

[71] It is less clear whether this is the case in Greece. Poland, with its very different recent history, is going through a period of transition which means that it is difficult to detect clearly how its criminal justice process will develop.

implications for the protection of suspects in the criminal process, but most jurisdictions have failed adequately to reflect this, in particular, by changing the point at which their rights crystallise to the beginning of the period when a suspect is identified and subjected to some form of detention and/or compulsory examination.[72] This is particularly the case in respect of a right to legal advice supported, where necessary, by an adequate legal aid scheme. On the other hand, the British government looks enviously at the relatively low levels of expenditure on legal aid at the investigative stage in most continental jurisdictions, and the current signs are that it is determined to reduce what it spends on legal aid. At the same time it fails to acknowledge that, historically at least, low levels of legal aid expenditure were counterbalanced by relatively high expenditure on an investigative process in which (relatively expensive) prosecutors and examining judges played the lead role. Whether or not European legal systems are converging[73] there is a danger that without strong minimum pan-European guarantees the lowest common denominators – the inexorable drive to economic efficiency coupled with ever-increasing accretion of investigative powers to the police and other state authorities – will leave those citizens who are suspected of crime without adequate protection.

The draft framework decision on minimum procedural rights, and even more so the Green Paper that preceded it, provided a basis for the creation of real and significant minimum rights across EU jurisdictions. By requiring member states to routinely collect data on key aspects of the criminal process, it also provided a basis for evaluating and monitoring whether these rights were given effect. It was, by no means, a complete panacea. There was certainly room for differing interpretations of who the rights applied to and at what point they applied. Whilst article 1 provided that the rights would apply to suspects from the time that they were informed by 'the competent authorities' that they were suspected of committing an offence, the right to legal advice, for example, was expressed to apply *inter alia* to those '*formally* accused of having committed a criminal offence' (emphasis added). Thus there would still have been scope for states to argue that the right to legal advice did not apply during preliminary detention by the police even if the police could interrogate during that period. The requirement in article 5 that the state bear the cost of legal advice if otherwise it would cause '*undue* financial hardship' (emphasis added) could also have resulted in many poor people going without state aid and, therefore, without the assistance of a lawyer. Nevertheless, they were likely to be far more effective in establishing minimum rights across jurisdictions than the later proposals[74] which identified the arbitrary concept of 'charge' (which was to be interpreted according to national laws) as the point at which the right to legal advice applies and subjected the right to legal aid to an interests of justice test. This study demonstrates not only that the broadly framed text of article 6 of the ECHR is

---

[72]   In France the defence enjoys extensive rights during the enquiry conducted by the *juge d'instruction*, but plays almost no part in the vast majority that are the responsibility of the public prosecutor.

[73]   See note 16, *supra*.

[74]   See note 13, *supra*.

ineffective in establishing a common understanding of and commitment to minimum rights for suspects of crime, but also, given that in most jurisdictions the police routinely detain and interrogate suspects and carry out other coercive methods of investigation, that any European instrument must clearly provide that protective provisions must apply from the first moment that a person is subjected to investigation involving either detention or compulsory questioning or examination.

Finally, this project has had to grapple with the problem that in most jurisdictions there is a paucity of relevant data, and little rigorous, scientific, evidence of how the investigative stage of the criminal process works in practice. In order to monitor whether suspects are treated in a comparable way across jurisdictions there needs to be routinely collected, accessible, data on how many people are arrested or otherwise detained, how many are released with no further action being taken against them and how many proceeded against, how many request and receive the assistance of a lawyer, how long suspects are detained at the various stages of the investigative process, what proportion are minors or otherwise vulnerable, and how many remain silent or confess under interrogation. More than this, in order to understand whether and how principles of fairness and justice are respected across the EU, and whether suspects themselves experience the process as fair and just, further systematic empirical research is urgently required.

7.   Bibliography

The Guide to the Professional Conduct of Solicitors, London, Law Society, 1999, p. 382.

D. Brown, *PACE Ten Years On: A Review of Research*, Research Study No. 155, London, Home Office, 1997.

E. Cape, 'Rebalancing the Criminal Justice Process: Ethical Challenges for Criminal Defence Lawyers,' 9 *Legal Ethics*, 1 2006, p. 56-79.

Caselaw of the ECtHR can be found at the European Court of Human Rights HUDOC Portal: <http://cmiskp.echr.coe.int>, in Series A and after 1 January 1996 in Reports of Judgments and Decisions, both published by Carl Heymans Verlag KG, Köln, Germany.

M. Delmas-Marty & J. Spencer, *European Criminal Procedures*, Cambridge, Cambridge University Press, 2002.

P. Duff, 'Changing Conceptions of the Scottish Criminal Trial: The Duty to Agree Uncontroversial Evidence,' in A. Duff, L. Farmer, S. Marshall & V. Tadros, *The Trial on Trial: Volume One*, Oxford, Hart Publishing, 2004.

S. Field & A. West, 'Dialogue and the Inquisitorial Tradition: French Defence Lawyers in the Pre-Trial Criminal Process,' 14 *Criminal Law Forum*, 3 2003, p. 261-316.

T. Goriely, C. Tata & A. Paterson, *Expenditure on Criminal Legal Aid: Report on a Comparative Pilot Study of Scotland, England and Wales, and the Netherlands*, Glasgow, University of Strathclyde, 1997.

J. Hodgson, *French Criminal Justice: A Comparative Account of the Investigation and Prosecution of Crime in France*, Oxford, Hart Publishing, 2005.

J. Jackson, 'The Effect of Human Rights on Criminal Evidentiary Processes: Towards Convergence, Divergence or Realignment?,' 68 *Modern Law Review*, 5 2005, p. 737-764.

J. Jackson, 'The Ethical Implications of the Enhanced role of the Public Prosecutor,' 9 *Legal Ethics*, 1 2006, p. 35-55.

T. Jones & T. Newburn, *Policy Transfer and Criminal Justice*, Maidenhead, Open University Press, 2006.

N. Jorg, S. Field & C. Brants, 'Are Inquisitorial and Adversarial Systems Converging?,' in P. Fennell, C. Harding, N. Jorg and B. Swart (eds), *Criminal Justice in Europe: A Comparative Study*, Oxford, Clarendon Press, 1995.

S. Karstedt, 'Durkheim, Tarde and beyond: the global travel of crime policies,' in T. Newburn and R. Sparks, *Criminal Justice and Political Cultures*, Cullompton, Willan, 2004, p. 18.

M. McConville, A. Sanders & R. Leng, *The Case for the Prosecution*, London, Routledge, 1991.

M. McConville & J. Hodgson, *Custodial Legal Advice and the Right to Silence*, London, HMSO, 1993.

M. McConville, J. Hodgson, L. Bridges & A. Pavlovic, *Standing Accused: The Organisation and Practices of Criminal Defence Lawyers in Britain*, Oxford, Clarendon Press, 1994.

D. Melossi, 'The cultural embeddedness of social control: reflections on the comparison of Italian and North-American cultures concerning punishment,' in T. Newburn & R. Sparks (eds), *Criminal Justice and Political Cultures*, Cullompton, Willan, 2004.

W. Pizzi & M. Montagna, 'The Battle to Establish an Adversarial Trial System in Italy,' (Winter) *Michigan Journal of International Law*, 429 2004.

P. Reichel, *Comparative Criminal Justice Systems*, New Jersey, Pearson, 4th edition, 2005, p. 123.

C. Tata, 'Comparing Legal Aid Spending: The Promise and Perils of a Jurisdiction-Centred Approach to (International) Legal Aid Research,' in F. Regan, A. Paterson, T. Goriely & D. Fleming, *The Transformation of Legal Aid*, Oxford, Oxford University Press, 1999.

R. Vogler, *A World View of Criminal Justice*, Aldershot, Ashgate, 2005.

Jan Fermon
Frank Verbruggen
Stef De Decker

THE INVESTIGATIVE STAGE OF THE CRIMINAL PROCESS IN BELGIUM

1.   Introduction

Belgium, a small and open multicultural transit country in the heart of Europe, host state for the Union's main institutions, has always taken pride in being a founding member state of the European Union (EU). Belgium's political elite warmly welcomed and eagerly sponsors initiatives at a European Union level. Subsequent implementation often proves more complicated. The difficult internal institutional (a centrifugal de-federalisation process) and political (coalition governments of at least four parties) balance is only one of the explanations. The field of Justice and Home Affairs is no exception to the principled Euro-enthusiasm. On the contrary, successive Belgian governments have been among the few who have been arguing in favour of outright communitarianism ever since the Maastricht negotiations fifteen years ago. Only recently have voices of caution grown stronger, first in civil society and academic circles, later with echoes in the political world. The focus of criticism is usually not 'Europeanisation' as such, but rather the democratic deficit or the policies adopted at the EU level, particularly a perception that excessive stress is put on security, ignoring or downgrading civil liberties and accountability mechanisms in the process. The Belgian criminal law and criminal justice systems are derived from the post-revolutionary French systems. 175 years of independence have since brought many changes and a Belgian touch becomes apparent in the continuous reshaping of the system. A recent example is the introduction of several victim-offender mediation schemes at different stages of criminal procedure, the result of a very active restorative justice movement in Belgium.[1] While such initiatives are welcomed by most, it is too soon to ascertain their overall impact.

In its essence, the investigative stage of the criminal proceedings under Belgian law remains thoroughly inquisitorial.[2] The (French) Code of Criminal

---

[1]   For an overview of the evolution of the restorative justice movement in Belgium, see L. Dupont and F. Hutsebaut, *Herstelrecht tussen toekomst en verleden. Liber Amicorum Tony Peters (Restorative justice between future and past)*, Leuven, University Press, 2001.

[2]   R. Verstraeten, *Handboek strafvordering (Companion to criminal procedure)*, Antwerpen, Maklu, 2005, p. 38; H.-D. Bosly and D. Vandermeersch, *Droit de la Procédure Pénale (Criminal procedure law)*, Bruges, La Charte, 2005, p. 13.

Proceedings (CCP) of 1808, adopted by Belgium on independence in 1830, was a compromise between pre-revolutionary law and a legal model elaborated in the revolutionary process. The trial stage is public and oral and although the presiding judge will search for the truth in an inquisitorial way, many of the principles of adversarial argument apply to the process. For the pre-trial stage, and in particular for the criminal investigation, the mechanisms of the *Ordonnance criminelle* of 1670, as modified by a Decree of 8 October 1789 were restored. The pre-trial stage of the proceedings was a written,[3] non-contradictory[4] and secret[5] one.[6]

The original system presupposed a so-called judicial inquiry (*gerechtelijk onderzoek* in Dutch, *instruction* in French) by an investigating judge (*onderzoeksrechter – juge d'instruction*),[7] under the supervision of the Indictment chamber of the Court of Appeals (*Kamer van Inbeschuldigingstelling – Chambre des Mises en Accusations*). The mighty and powerful investigating judge is an impartial judge, conducting an inquiry in an independent way, looking for both incriminating and exculpatory facts and statements (*à charge et à décharge*). That is supposed to be an important guarantee of a fair treatment of suspects. In practice, this procedure is limited to the most serious cases and to those where very serious infringements of human rights (e.g., arrest warrants, search warrants or wiretapping) are necessary.[8] Most (over 90 %) criminal investigations are called 'preliminary investigation' (*opsporingsonderzoek – information*) conducted by the public prosecution service (*openbaar ministerie – ministère public*). Only in 1998 did this factual situation receive legal acknowledgement in articles 28*bis* and following CCP.[9] When compared to the judicial inquiry, the preliminary investigation remains somewhat under-regulated. Articles 47 and 64 CCP now define the judicial inquiry as a '*subsidiary*' possibility.

---

3   C. Van den Wyngaert, *Strafrecht, strafprocesrecht en internationaal strafrecht (Criminal law, criminal procedure and international criminal law)*, Antwerp, Maklu, 2003, p. 734.

4   H.-D. Bosly and D. Vandermeersch, *supra* note 2, p. 351; R. Verstraeten, *supra* note 2, p. 343 and 396.

5   H.-D. Bosly and D. Vandermeersch, *supra* note 2, p. 353.

6   Constitutional Court, decision No. 1/99, 13 January 1999, *Rev. dr. pén.* 1999, 720 (specifically the considerations under B.5); L. Cornil, 'De la nécessité de rendre à l'instruction préparatoire, en matière pénale, le caractère légal qu'elle a perdu, mercuriale prononcée à l'audience solennelle de rentrée de la Cour d'Appel de Bruxelles, le 15 septembre 1931,' (On the necessity of restoring the legal basis of the investigative stage), *Rev. dr. pén.* 1930-31, p. 811; R. Verstraeten, *supra* note 2, p. 38-39.

7   We will use the notion of '*magistrate*' in its continental meaning, as a concept covering both completely independent judges (members of the Bench) and members of the semi-independent public prosecution service. All magistrates involved in Belgian criminal procedure are therefore professionals.

8   R. Verstraeten, *supra* note 2, p. 251.

9   Initially, the preliminary investigation was not regulated by the CCP and was a 'praetorian construction.' (R. Verstraeten, *supra* note 2, p. 251).

2. Police powers in the investigative stage

2.1. Relations between police, prosecutor and investigating judge

Formally the CCP deals with the judicial police function, not with the police services as institutions in their modern meaning. It vests the judicial police function in investigating judges and public prosecutors. This means that the police officers do not conduct criminal investigations autonomously. They always act under the supervision and responsibility of the public prosecutor or the investigating judge. Nevertheless in both types of investigation prosecutors and investigating judges delegate most of the practical work to the police. The CCP determines a limited number of crucial investigative actions which the investigating judge must personally perform, such as the first interview of a suspect in pre-trial detention or interviews with a witness who wants to remain fully anonymous. The quantity and quality of the control by the magistrates on the police and, conversely, the margins of discretion which the police officers should have while conducting an investigation, has been the subject of a vigorous debate. Since every prosecutor or investigating judge is responsible for a great number of investigations conducted at the same time, effective control of what the police do in criminal investigations is very difficult.[10] The personality, experience and authority of the individual magistrate will, of course, be an important factor with regard to the degree of investigative leadership and supervision that is exercised with regard to police investigators. After a series of real and perceived scandals that shook the public as well as the establishment, the policy has been to 'liberate' magistrates from investigations relating to minor offences, and particularly to limit the number of judicial inquiries, and to shift investigations towards the public prosecution service as much as possible (cf. *infra* nrs. 15-16). Specialisation and training of magistrates is seen as another way of increasing control over the police. The low threshold for victims to act as civil parties and to launch a judicial inquiry on their own initiative means that in practice magistrates do not completely control their workflow. This 'triggering' of judicial inquiries by an investigating judge by civil parties has always been defended as a correction mechanism limiting the broad discretion enjoyed by Belgian prosecutors.

An eternal discussion surrounds the investigating judge. Critics see this crucial institution as an oxymoron. Some judges are criticised by the defence for acting too much as an investigator and not enough as a judge. They must search for the truth, but their human and bureaucratic contacts in day-to-day investigation practice create a seemingly inevitable affinity with the police and the prosecution. An investigating judge who is in an outright and/or continuing conflict with police detective units in their district (or area of specialisation) would cease to function as an investigating judge. On the other hand, the police (and even some prosecutors) deem some investigating judges to be too much judges rather than investigators. They perceive them as being too protective of fundamental rights and as not

---

[10]   H.-D. Bosly and D. Vandermeersch, *supra* note 2, p. 611.

appreciating the price in terms of effective truth-finding and crime-solving. As we already pointed out, a lot depends on the personality, experience, talent and natural authority of the judge.

Recent statutory developments, strongly influenced by domestic case law and the jurisprudence of the European Court of Human Rights (ECtHR), have introduced new rights for the defence and granted it rights at an earlier stage of the proceedings. Legislators acknowledged that the traditional view, that the investigative phase is merely a preparation and that the real issue is the trial phase in which the defence has an established legal position, had become untenable. Many investigations did not lead to a trial, but did seriously affect the lives of people for many years. Furthermore, with the exception of jury trials for the most serious offences, the practical weight of criminal proceedings had clearly shifted to the investigative phase. The actual trial itself has been reduced to a debate on the basis of the case file and on sentencing issues. The 'principle of immediacy' never really ranked high in Belgian criminal court practice. This meant that the legal position of the defence in the investigative phase had to be reinforced.

The general interest in the wellbeing of crime victims has also significantly increased, in Belgium probably more than in many other countries. Consequently, when suspects and defendants were granted extra rights, civil parties and other victims were often granted equal or similar rights.

The reform process has been hastened by the fact that key articles of the European Convention on Human Rights (ECHR), as interpreted by the ECtHR, and of the International Covenant on Civil and Political Rights, are deemed self-executing in Belgium. For example, a decision of the ECtHR[11] led to the introduction, in the Pre-trial Detention Act 1990, of the right of defence lawyers to have access to the case file where a suspect has been arrested. Consultation of the file is possible one or two days before the appearance of the arrested person before the Investigative Chamber of the Court (*Raadkamer – Chambre du Conseil*), which decides on the confirmation of an initial arrest ordered by an investigating judge and on (for most offences) the monthly review of pre-trial detention.

Other important and recent modifications have been made to the CCP by the Statute of March 12th, 1998 '*to improve the criminal proceedings in the stage of the preliminary investigation and the judicial inquiry.*'[12] Unlike the defence, the prosecution service had access to the file at any time during the investigative stage of criminal proceedings and could always request additional investigative measures by the investigating judge. The most important innovation in the Statute of 1998 was to grant other parties (suspects and their lawyers, but also victims or sometimes even

---

[11]   ECtHR 30 March 1989, *Lamy* v. *Belgium,* A 151. The Court ruled that lack of access to the file by the defence lawyer before each session of the Investigative Chamber of the Court (which decides on the confirmation of the initial arrest within 5 days of the arrest), while the prosecutor had full access to all the information at any time, violated art. 5 § 4 of the Convention.

[12]   *Loi relative à l'amélioration de la procédure pénale au stade de l'information et de l'instruction – Wet tot verbetering van de strafrechtspleging in het stadium van het opsporingsonderzoek en het gerechtelijk onderzoek*, published in the Moniteur belge 2 April 1998.

interested third parties) somewhat similar rights. They can now also request the investigating judge to:[13]

-   conduct additional investigations. Refusal by the investigating judge is subject to appeal to the Indictment Chamber of the Court of Appeals, which specialises in the supervision of investigations and inquiries;
-   grant defendants and their lawyers access to the file, with a similar possibility of appeal against a refusal.[14]

All discussions of the effectiveness or abuse of these rights are limited by the total absence of statistics. Nobody really knows how investigating judges react to requests for additional investigations. Many different factors seem to influence the outcome: costs, practical feasibility, the possibilities for the defence to secure access to the requested evidence themselves, the personality of the judge and their (lack of) personal interest in the case. The availability of police officers to conduct the investigation should not, but does play a part. Police reform has weakened the position of investigating judges, compared with that of police chiefs, in respect of the availability and use of police resources for criminal investigative work. Since an investigating judge and the public prosecution service work together very closely, the 'policy' of the latter is another factor to be considered. In some cases, the public prosecution service wants to commit suspects to trial as soon as possible 'to set an example.' In others, they are less keen on doing so.

Important as these reforms may be, they fall far short of putting the prosecution and the defence on an equal footing. After the pre-trial detention has ended, suspects can obtain access to the case file if the investigating judge or the prosecutor-general grants it. The 1998 reform introduced the right to request access, which of course is different from the absolute and unconditional right of access enjoyed by the public prosecution service.[15] Access to the file granted by the investigating judge on the basis of article 61*ter* CCP does not include the right to receive copies, whereas the prosecutor can copy the file at any time. The prosecutor-general does have (under art. 125 of the Royal Decree of 28 December 1950) the discretionary power to allow other parties to take copies of the case file, but no appeal can be lodged against the prosecutor-general's decision.

It is therefore clear that although the inquisitorial model of the pre-trial stage of criminal proceedings has been moderated significantly, its essence remains.[16] Articles 28 *quinquies* (*preliminary investigations*, conducted by the public prosecutor)

---

[13] H.-D. Bosly and D. Vandermeersch, *supra* note 2, p. 747-768; O. Klees and D. Bosquet, 'Essai de synthèse des principaux apports de la loi Franchimont du point de vue des droits de la défense,' *(Overview of the improvements in the rights of the defence after the Franchimont-reform)*, in M. Franchimont (ed.), *Le point sur les procédures, I*, Liège, Formation permanente Université-Palais, 2000, p. 199-221.

[14] Prior to the Statute of 1998, a request for access to a file during the criminal investigation stage could only be made to the prosecutor general (PG). If the PG refused to grant access, they did not have to state their reasons and no appeal was possible.

[15] On the justification and constitutionality of this unequal treatment see *infra* note 79.

[16] H.-D. Bosly and D. Vandermeersch, *supra* note 2, p. 352.

and 57 § 1 al. 2. CCP (*judicial inquiries*, conducted by an investigating judge) still state explicitly that the investigation is secret.[17] The main reason is, of course, that secretiveness is tactically expedient for the investigators. It is also justified by the argument that the privacy of everyone concerned in the investigation, and particularly of suspects who have been cleared by the investigations, victims or other vulnerable persons (like minors), should be protected.

Parliament considered, however, that in a modern, open democracy, absolute secrecy had become unrealistic and improper, especially in high profile cases. It saw proper information provided by official spokespeople as preferable to the previous situation of selective leaks and revelations. Art. 28 *quinquies* of the CCP states in § 1 that the investigation is secret, but in § 3 it allows the prosecutor to inform the press when the public interest requires it. Such press statements should, however, take into consideration the presumption of innocence, the rights of all parties, and the obligation to respect the private life and the dignity of all parties. If possible, the names of the persons involved should not be revealed. Under the equality of arms principle, and in view of the effect public revelations might have for the suspect and the case, § 4 allows the defence lawyer to speak to press under the same conditions if the interest of the client requires it.

Cynics claim that when football club presidents make public statements to express their complete confidence in the coach, this usually means the latter is about to get the boot. Likewise, the Belgian federal parliament, when reshaping the CCP in 1998, purported to support the traditional Belgian choice for a judicial inquiry by modernising it and reinforcing the position of the investigating judge. Yet at the same time, the legislation of the last decade has created all kinds of possibilities to avoid fully-fledged judicial inquiries. It is quite likely that both the burdensome procedures and (especially) the increased adversarial character of the judicial inquiry, has made police detectives and prosecutors even more eager to avoid it if they can. They fear that confidential sources might be exposed, that unsuccessful surveillance operations would be revealed to targets and subsequent surveillance attempts doomed, and that investigative tactics would be revealed. These concerns were taken to heart by the legislators.

Different kinds of hybrid systems were created, under which some judicial intervention is necessary, but without it amounting to a real judicial inquiry. Article 28 *septies* CCP, for instance, created a so-called 'mini judicial inquiry.'[18] The prosecutor conducts the preliminary investigation and the investigating judge is appointed only to issue a warrant (for which they have exclusive competence). Immediately after the execution of the warrant the prosecutor takes over control again. The legislation reduced this form of judicial inquiry to intermezzos in the preliminary investigations by the prosecutor. Normally, the investigating judge retains the possibility of turning the investigation into a full blown judicial inquiry. Given their workload, however, few investigating judges are inclined to do so (see *supra* note 4). Some investigative actions are deemed to be so intrusive that the

---

[17]   R. Verstraeten, *supra* note 2, p. 343 and 379.
[18]   C. Van den Wyngaert, *supra* note 3, p. 787-788; R. Verstraeten, *supra* note 2, p. 337.

investigating judge is obliged to take over the investigation.[19] Consequently, the prosecution service can 'determine' the procedure under which a case is investigated. Only if they want one of these intrusive investigative measures to be taken does the investigating judge takes over the investigation.

In the vast majority of the cases, the emphasis has thus shifted from the investigating judge (an independent and impartial judge) to the magistrates of the public prosecution service. One should not, however, see this as an evolution towards a more accusatorial model. On the contrary, all characteristics of the inquisitorial model apply also to the preliminary investigation conducted by the public prosecutor. As noted earlier, suspects (or civil parties) have fewer rights in a preliminary investigation than they would have in a judicial inquiry. Since they involve less clear or explicit infringements of fundamental rights, the CCP does not deem it necessary to provide for formal proceedings which would allow a person to request access to the file or to ask for additional investigations. Everything happens in a more informal way and the prosecutor has considerable discretion in deciding on the course of the investigation. An investigative or prosecutorial decision by prosecution service magistrates is not subject to any appeal. That means that parties might have to wait until the actual court trial to obtain access to the file and to request additional investigative action.

A major reform of the CCP is currently under discussion in the Lower Chamber of Parliament.[20] The Bill is based on the findings of an Expert Committee on Criminal Procedure. One of the most remarkable innovations is that, if adopted, it will be possible for the defence to obtain access to the case file or to ask for additional investigations in the preliminary investigation conducted by the prosecutor. The 1998 reform had limited that right to judicial inquiries by investigating judges (see *supra* note 9). Members of the public prosecution service have voiced concerns about the proposed reforms. They claim that the experience of post-1998 judicial inquiries shows that most procedural rights were abused by suspects and their lawyers for dilatory reasons. In their opinion, extending those rights to preliminary investigations, where the stakes are usually lower, will

---

[19]   That is, for instance, the case if the public prosecution service wants the investigating judge to issue an arrest warrant (judicial arrest), a search warrant, or a phone-tapping warrant. Also when the prosecution wants to take investigative measures relating to legal professionals, or wants a fully anonymous witness to be interviewed, the investigating judge has to be involved. Finally, the *mini judicial inquiry* cannot be used for two special investigative measures if they concern a private residence: the 'sneak and peek' warrant and the warrant to keep a person under surveillance with technical (i.e. audio-visual) aids. The former is a covert or surreptitious entry warrant, intended for checking the presence of illegal objects or for placing monitoring equipment. It cannot be used for seizing discovered illegal objects (art. 46*quinquies* and art. 89*ter* Sv.) These two special investigative measures were only included in art. 28*septies* CCP after the Constitutional Court had decided that the possibility of by-passing the investigating judge for these special investigative measures was unconstitutional. See *infra* note 49.

[20]   *Wetsvoorstel houdende het Wetboek van strafvordering – Proposition de loi concernant le Code de la procédure pénale*, Parl. St. Kamer 2004-05, No. 51-2138/1, <www.dekamer.be> *(Draft Bill on the Code of Criminal Procedure)*.

increase costs, delays and investigative bureaucracy, and grind the whole system to a halt.[21] As we pointed out before, the complete lack of data makes it impossible to verify their statements.

2.2.   Arrest, limitations on and conditions of detention, and bail[22]

In Belgium a person can be deprived of their liberty on three main grounds: administrative detention, judicial arrest and in order to bring them in for questioning.[23] To begin with, Belgian legislation provides for an autonomous police power of so-called 'administrative detention'[24] (as opposed to the 'judicial arrest' which requires involvement of an independent judge within 24 hours). Persons under administrative detention can be deprived of their liberty up to a maximum of 12 hours, unless the detention is converted into a judicial arrest.[25] The police can use administrative detention in respect of persons who disturb the public peace, although whether someone actually disturbs the peace is wholly at the discretion of the police. This type of arrest is also possible for the dispersal of riots.[26] Every person under administrative arrest can request that a person of their own choosing and who is trusted be informed of the arrest.[27] In practice, however, the police often do not allow direct communication. In most cases, it will be a police officer that delivers the message.

Secondly, the Pre-trial Detention Act 1990 sets out the conditions in which a judicial arrest can be made. When persons are caught in the act, police officers can deprive them of their liberty, but must inform the prosecutor as soon as possible. There is always a prosecutor on standby, around the clock. The prosecutor has to confirm the decision to arrest the person (this usually happens by telephone). The person should be orally informed of this decision. Where a person is not caught in the act, it is for the prosecutor to decide whether the police can deprive a person of their liberty.

In both cases, the maximum duration of police custody is 24 hours. Within 24 hours an investigating judge must interrogate the person and, if this is deemed necessary, issue an arrest warrant (*aanhoudingsbevel – mandat d'arrêt*). If such a warrant has not been notified to the suspect within that 24 hour period, the detained person must be released. The 24 hour period starts when the police actually deprive the suspect of their freedom. The police report must include the exact time and circumstances of the deprivation of freedom, the time when the

---

21	F. Schuermans, 'Donkere wolken boven het Belgisch strafvorderlijk landschap,' (*Dark clouds gathering over the Belgian criminal procedure landscape*), *Panopticon*, 5 2005, p. 39–54.
22	For an exhaustive overview of the Belgian law on pre-trial detention, see B. Dejemeppe and D. Merckx, *De voorlopige hechtenis*, Diegem, Kluwer, 2000.
23	The order to bring someone for questioning will be discussed in the text to note 42.
24	Art. 31 of the Police Function Act 1992.
25	Even after this conversion, the maximum duration of the arrest without the involvement of an independent judge remains 24 hours, starting from the actual deprivation of liberty (art. 32 of the Police Function Act 1992).
26	Art. 22 of the Police Function Act 1992.
27	Art. 31 of the Police Function Act 1992.

prosecutor or the investigating judge were informed of the deprivation of freedom and the decision of the magistrate to place a suspect under judicial arrest. The police report must also note the time when that decision was notified to the suspect. The law does not provide any sanction if these formalities are not respected. The Supreme Court considers that the violation of these formal requirements does not invalidate a subsequent arrest warrant delivered by an investigating judge if all formal requirements of the latter arrest warrant have been met.[28]

Unlike a person in administrative detention, a person under judicial arrest cannot demand that a 'trusted' person be informed of the arrest (see text to note 27). Several authors claim that the suspect should have the same opportunity 'unless it would be detrimental to investigation,'[29] for instance, if there is a belief that the mere issuing of a notice would allow others to escape or evidence to be destroyed.

Article 16 of the Pre-trial Detention Act 1990 sets out the conditions under which an investigating judge can issue an arrest warrant against a person.[30] Several conditions must be met:

- an absolute necessity for public safety;
- an offence punishable with a imprisonment of at least one year;
- if the maximum punishment does not exceed 15 years of imprisonment an arrest warrant can only be issued if there is a serious risk;
  that a further criminal offence would be committed by the suspect, or
  that the suspect would abscond, or
  would destroy evidence, or
  would collude with third persons.

Although the Act specifically states that pre-trial detention cannot be used as a form of immediate punishment or to put pressure on a suspect,[31] it is almost inevitable that the police regard pre-trial detention as a means of obtaining a confession. Furthermore, pre-trial detention allows the police and the investigating judge to conduct their inquiries more conveniently: the suspect is at their 'disposal' in prison, instead of having to be summoned each time for questioning.

If a suspect is available, the investigating judge must interview them before issuing the arrest warrant. The arrest warrant must state reasons, both regarding the serious indications of guilt and as to the absolute necessity for public security to order pre-trial detention. However important these formal requirements may be, their practical value is seriously undermined by the absence of legal assistance during the interview by the investigating judge and the impossibility of contacting a defence lawyer prior to this interview. Many suspects find it hard to assess the exact role of the judge and the difference between that judge and the rest of the machinery of law enforcement, which a suspect at this stage is likely to approach with profound distrust. The combination of time restraints, routine and the fear that

---

[28]   Cass. 12 November 1991, *J.L.M.B.* 1992, p. 470; Cass. 10 November 1993, *J.L.M.B.* 1994, p. 741.
[29]   H.-D. Bosly and D. Vandermeersch, *supra* note 2, p. 423.
[30]   R. Verstraeten, *supra* note 2, p. 501.
[31]   Art. 16 § 1, al. 2 of the Pre-trial Detention Act 1990.

omissions would invalidate the warrants, results in arrest warrants often becoming standardised forms with formal and stereotypical clauses, in which little effort is made to go into the details of the specific circumstances.

The arrest warrant issued by an investigating judge within 24 hours after the deprivation of liberty, must be confirmed by a special section of the Court of First Instance, the Investigative Chamber of Court, within five days.[32]

After this initial confirmation (and unsuccessful appeal), the legality of the detention can no longer be challenged. The same section of the Court should confirm the pre-trial detention every month.[33] Decisions of the Investigative Chamber of the Court are subject to appeal before the Indictment Chamber of the Court of Appeals, which must hear and decide the case within 15 days after the decision of the Investigative Chamber.[34] As the defence will have access to the file two days before every confirmation hearing, this is a way of controlling the progress made by the investigators. If no action was taken following the previous confirmation hearing, the prosecution will be less convincing if they insist that the detention is necessary for the investigation. The prosecution would then have to rely on the necessity of the detention to prevent re-offending in the period before trial. The 2005 modification of the Pre-trial Detention Act 1990 extended the validity of the decision to maintain a suspect in pre-trial detention to three months (instead of one) for the most serious crimes. The intention was to avoid monthly confirmation hearings if there is little chance of the suspect being released. There is no limitation on the number of times the Investigative Chamber or the Indictment Chamber of the Court of Appeals can extend the pre-trial detention as long as a new decision is taken every month (or three months).

Almost 40 % of the Belgian prison population consist of persons in pre-trial detention.[35] Unfortunately, the creation of a power to release suspects 'under certain conditions' has had no noticeable influence on this figure. The authority to end pre-trial detention – either unconditionally, or subject to conditions, possibly with an order to provide a security – rests with both the investigative judge (at any time) and the Investigative Chamber of the Court (during the first confirmation hearing, during the subsequent monthly or quarterly hearings, and when the defendant is committed for trial).[36] It is also possible, when committing a defendant for trial, for the Investigative Chamber of the Court to order that the accused is to remain in pre-trial detention until their trial – the so-called 'committal under arrest warrant.'

If suspects are released 'under certain conditions,' these conditions can vary, but they have to relate to the reasons for which an investigating judge can issue an

---

[32]   Art. 21 § 1 of the Pre-trial Detention Act 1990.

[33]   Art. 22 of the Pre-trial Detention Act 1990.

[34]   Art. 30 § of the Pre-trial Detention Act 1990.

[35]   On 1 March 2005, 3,550 out of 9,375 persons (37,87 %) detained in Belgian prisons were in pre-trial detention. It is unclear how many of these persons were still the object of an investigation, and how many were merely awaiting trial. Source: Justice Department, *Justitie in cijfers 2005*, 20 *(Justice statistics)*, available at
<www.just.fgov.be/cgi_justice/publications/catalog.pl?lg=nl>.

[36]   Art. 35 and 36 of the Pre-trial Detention Act 1990.

arrest warrant, i.e., risk of re-offending, interfering with the evidence, collusion or absconding.[37] The conditions tend to vary from one district to another. For example, the risk of absconding is usually countered by imposing a duty on the accused to present themselves regularly at the local police station; the risk of collusion can be countered by a ban on approaching or communicating with certain persons; for drug addicts the risk of re-offending may be minimised by imposing a treatment condition. Such conditions are valid for a period of three months and should then be renewed. The supervision of these conditions is carried out by the police or officials of the Department of Justice, in a similar way to 'probation officers' in England and Wales.

The suspect can also be ordered to place a certain amount of money into a government account, to serve as a guarantee that the suspect will not abscond. The money is returned at the end of the proceedings provided the suspect was present at all hearings. The Belgian Supreme Court has decided that there is no such thing as an absolute right to be released on bail. Nevertheless, the Investigative Chambers of the Courts have to verify whether the purpose of the pre-trial detention cannot be achieved by releasing someone on bail.[38] The amount is completely at the discretion of the investigating judge or the Investigative Chambers of the Courts.

We noted earlier that one of the justifications for the secret character of the investigation stage in Belgium is the need to protect the honour and the reputation of the suspects.[39] This concern is also reflected in article 35 of the Police Function Act 1992. This article does not allow the police 'to expose unnecessarily an arrested person to public curiosity.' The arrested person cannot be approached by journalists or confronted by the public and should be protected from having their picture taken. The police cannot reveal the identity of arrested persons without prior consent from the judicial authorities.

2.3.   Interrogations

The police do not have the power to apprehend and detain a person for questioning. They can apprehend someone who is caught in the act, but they have to contact the public prosecutor as soon as possible, who decides whether the person will be brought before a judge to be arrested. If the prosecutor decides that pre-trial detention is necessary, they will request an investigating judge to issue an arrest warrant. To be valid, such arrest warrant must be issued within 24 hours of the person being deprived of their liberty.[40]

In general, police officers conduct interviews. In exceptional cases the prosecutor or the investigating judge can conduct the interview personally. For instance, a personal interview by the investigating judge is mandatory prior to

---

[37]   See R. Verstraeten, *supra* note 2, p. 549.

[38]   Cass. 7 May 2003, AR No. P.03.0620.F., <www.cass.be>.

[39]   See text to note 17.

[40]   For the difference between 'deprivation of liberty by the police,' 'judicial arrest' ordered by the prosecutor and 'pre-trial detention' on an arrest warrant issued by an investigating magistrate, see *supra* section 2.2.

issuing an arrest warrant, at least if the person has been detained.[41] Furthermore, the investigating judge can issue an order to bring a suspect in for questioning (*bevel tot medebrenging* – *mandat d'amener*), on the condition that there are serious indications of guilt against them.[42] The order can also be used for unwilling witnesses. After the person has been brought in, it is the investigating judge themselves who have to interview the suspect. The order enables a person to be deprived of their liberty for 24 hours.

Persons who have been interviewed are entitled to a free copy of the police report of the interview, unless a formal decision is taken not to do so (art. 28quinquies and 57 § 2 CCP). This decision can only be made in serious and exceptional circumstances, it must state the reasons for doing so, and service of a copy may be delayed for one month, renewable up to a maximum of three months. Although the requirement to provide a copy of the interview record has its merits, it contributes little to the protection of the integrity of evidence, which relies completely on the integrity of the interviewer. An interviewed person can only dispute the record later but it will be the interviewee's word against that of the interviewer. Most witnesses will not even consult the file containing their statements if they are not suspects or victims themselves. Furthermore, the violation of these formal requirements does not result in sanctions.[43]

At the end of the interview, the interviewed persons can read their statement or have it read out to them by the interviewing officer or magistrate. They must then be asked whether any corrections or additions should be made. Subsequently, they will be invited to sign the statement. In fact, the only way for interviewed persons to show that they do not agree with the content of the record is to refuse to sign. However, this is very exceptional. The refusal of the interviewed person to sign a statement does not stop judges from relying on that piece of evidence if the judges deem it reliable (see *infra* section 4.1).

As a rule, interviews of suspects are not tape or video recorded. Under article 112*ter* CCP the prosecutor and the investigating judge can order the tape or video recording of any interview in criminal proceedings, both of witnesses and suspects. It is, however, used only exceptionally and is meant to protect vulnerable witnesses, rather than the integrity of the statements of suspects for their subsequent use as evidence.[44] Most police stations are not equipped to tape record interviews.

Only one provision of the law protects the evidential integrity of a suspect's statement. Article 47*bis* CCP states that at the commencement of every interview, interviewees should be informed that they can request that their statements, as well as the questions asked, be written down using the exact wording. If no such request is made, the police officer or the magistrate conducting the interrogation will 'reformulate' questions and answers in the report, which very often leads to discussions as to the accuracy of the record at a later stage. Obviously, in this

---

41   Art. 16 § 2 of the Pre-trial Detention Act 1990.

42   Art. 3-15 of the Pre-trial Detention Act 1990.

43   H.-D. Bosly and D. Vandermeersch, *supra* note 2, p. 384; R. Verstraeten, *supra* note 2, p. 271-272.

44   H.-D. Bosly and D. Vandermeersch, *supra* note 2, p. 614; R. Verstraeten, *supra* note 2, p. 267.

process a lot of 'sometimes valuable' information can be lost. In rephrasing, the police officers might mask the fact that the original questions were somewhat insinuating or (mis)leading. On the other hand, the authors of the summary can, to some extent, put certain words into the suspect's mouth. After the interview, the suspect can read through the *procès-verbal* and make alterations. Most suspects content themselves with the summary because they fail to realise the importance that will be attached to the *procès-verbaux* in later stages of the criminal proceedings.

Furthermore, defence counsel cannot be present at interrogations by police or investigating judges.[45] There is, however, one exception to this principle. Article 22 of the Pre-trial Detention Act 1990 stipulates that persons in pre-trial detention can request a summarizing interview. If they file such a request, the investigating judge must conduct the interview in the course of the ten days preceding the monthly review of the pre-trial detention by the Investigative Chamber of the Court. During this interview, an overview of the results of the inquiry is presented and the suspect will be confronted with these results. A real debate is not possible, but defence counsel can make comments and thus have them recorded in the case file.

The degree of protection of the evidential integrity of suspects' statements is therefore low. This is particularly so during the first interviews by police and the investigating judge, when the biggest time-constraints apply to the investigators. In this phase suspects are not allowed to contact their lawyers, so cannot obtain advice as to whether to refuse to sign the record of their interrogation which they feel is not correct. Furthermore, non-suspect witnesses are far less sensitive about the ultimate impact of their statements on the evidence in a case against someone else. They will more easily accept non-literal records of the interview and they are less likely to return to the case file afterwards in order to scrutinise their statements. Often, they will not even know what happened to the case. Yet in practice, the statements of 'neutral' witnesses will often carry a lot of weight as evidence, since statements of suspects and their 'allies' are automatically read with caution and inevitably deemed to be self-serving.

2.4. Coercive methods of investigation

Throughout the regulation of the investigative phase in the CCP, it becomes obvious that judicial intervention is often deemed necessary as a threshold for the infringement of human rights. We noted earlier the position regarding arrest and search, but the same applies to wiretapping, orders to take DNA samples from a suspect who refuses to give such a sample (if necessary, using – minimal – force), the issuing of 'sneak and peek warrants,'[46] or the hearing of anonymous witnesses. On the other hand, the involvement of the independent and impartial judge is often also deemed sufficient and the additional control by the defence in adversarial

---

[45]   A. Sadzot, 'L'égalité des armes et la contradiction dans le procès penal,' (*Equality of arms and adversariality in criminal cases*), in X. (ed.), *Les droits de la défense. Actes du colloque 'Jacques Henry' organisé par la Conférence libre du Jeune Barreau de Liège le 28 mars 1997*, Liège, Editions du Jeune Barreau de Liege, 1997, p. 148. See *infra* section 3.5.

[46]   See *supra* note 19.

procedure thereby rendered unnecessary.[47] When special investigative methods are used, authorisations of magistrates are necessary throughout and it will be the magistrates who will have to perform control over the subsidiarity and proportionality of the operations. They will have to abort operations if those criteria are no longer satisfied. The defence will not have access to the secret reserve of data which has influenced the decision-making process. When the action does not lead to prosecution, nobody outside the law enforcement system is likely to find out what happened or why. If there is a charge, the defence can level criticism afterwards, but this cannot lead subsequent judges to question the legality of the decision of the investigating judge. It should, however, be pointed out that the investigating judge will always act under the control of the Indictment Chamber of the Court of Appeals, which can control the legality of the decisions of the investigating judge. Nevertheless, this censure is not accompanied by effective sanctions and may often amount to no more than a moral victory for the defence.

The traditional idea underlying the CCP was that investigating judges could do whatever they thought necessary to reveal the truth. Only a number of fundamental constitutional rights limited these powers, particularly in the field of personal liberty (arrest) and property (searches, particularly in someone's home). Basically, all investigative methods were allowed unless they were explicitly prohibited. Again, the internationally protected human rights, and particularly articles 6 and 8 ECHR as interpreted by the ECtHR, have pushed the federal parliament to regulate a series of investigative measures and practices (interviewing, DNA, computer data searches etc.). Sometimes regulation is summary, sometimes it is remarkably detailed and extensive.

2.5. Secret investigative measures

The essence of the so-called special investigative measures (infiltration by undercover agents, secret surveillance and active informer management) is the use of ruses (false identities, false pretences, lies, etc.) by investigators. Legalising these 'ruse' methods, which Belgium's case law had already condoned, does not violate the legality principle as such.[48] Judges have so far been quite reluctant to consider law enforcement practices unlawful. It is quite normal for there to be a general presumption that law enforcement officers will act in a lawful way, but the burden of proving unlawful practice should not be too heavy, especially not if law

---

[47] A good illustration can be found in the legal regime of expert investigations. In the pre-trial stage they remain unilateral and without the presence of all parties or adversarial arguments. At the trial stage, case law strongly dictated by a Strasbourg decision on the equality of arms, made adversarial proceedings compulsory. See B. De Smet, *Deskundigenonderzoek in strafzaken (Expert investigations in criminal cases)*, Antwerp, Story-Scientia, 2001.

[48] C. De Valkeneer, *La tromperie dans l'administration de la preuve pénale: analyse en droits belge et international complétée par des éléments de droits français et néerlandais (Trickery and deception in the furnishing of evidence: analysis of Belgian, Dutch, French law and international law)*, Brussels, Larcier, 2000, p. 288.

enforcement agencies have used investigative methods which are treacherous and secretive by nature.

Like its northern neighbour, the Netherlands, Belgium has in the last decade adopted a very explicit regulatory framework for secret investigative methods such as infiltration (undercover policing), secret surveillance, and the use and management of paid informers. Nevertheless, the Constitutional Court has determined that a number of specific aspects of special investigative measures are unconstitutional.[49] Eventually, Parliament adapted the legislation and has granted extra powers of supervision to investigating judges.[50]

3. Rights of the defendant

3.1. Information about suspects' rights

Article 47*bis*, 1., a-c CCP stipulates that all persons who are interviewed, whether as suspect or as witness, should be informed prior to questioning that:[51]

- they can request that all questions asked and all answers given be written down using the precise words that were uttered;[52]
- they can ask that an additional act of investigation be conducted or that a specified interrogation would be conducted;
- their statements can be used as evidence.

As a general rule, the interviewers will add the information mentioned in the next paragraph of the same article 47*bis* CCP, that during the interview, persons may refer to any documents they carry with them. They can request that these documents be added to the file.

Since interviews are normally not tape-recorded,[53] it is very difficult to control the effectiveness of the duty to inform persons of their rights. Every police report

---

[49]   Constitutional Court, decision No. 202/2004, 21 December 2004, <www.arbitrage.be>. On the one hand, the Court had doubts about the possibility for the prosecution service to by-pass the investigating judge, by means of a 'mini judicial inquiry,' for two special investigative measures: the sneak and peek warrant (see *supra* note 19) and the warrant to keep someone under surveillance with technical aids. On the other hand the Court was critical of the inadequate supervision over the so-called 'confidential case file' (e.g. containing the names of undercover agents or descriptions of infiltration tactics).

[50]   The amending legislation has been rushed through Parliament to meet the ultimatum (31 December 2005) set by the Constitutional Court: *Wet 27 december 2005 houdende diverse wijzigingen van het Wetboek van strafvordering en van het Gerechtelijk Wetboek met het oog op de verbetering van de onderzoeksmethoden in de strijd tegen het terrorisme en de zware en georganiseerde criminaliteit*, published in the *Moniteur Belge*, 30 December 2005 (*Statute modifying the Code of Criminal Procedure and the Code of Civil Procedure, extending investigative powers in cases of terrorism and organised crime*).

[51]   H.-D. Bosly and D. Vandermeersch, *supra* note 2, p. 381; R. Verstraeten, *supra* note 2, p. 267 and 269.

[52]   See the text preceding note 45.

[53]   See text to note 44.

will start with the pre-formatted text of article 47*bis* CCP, but it is hard to find out if and how the information has effectively been given and if it has been properly understood.[54] Every once in a while, the issue of lawyers being allowed to assist at witness interviews is raised, and Council of Europe reports (like the CPT's) have periodically suggested it. However, the proposals do not seem to attract much support. The police and some prosecutors fear it will affect the effectiveness of interviews.[55] A distrust of lawyers remains a strong feature of police institutional culture, particularly in the specialised investigative units.

3.2. *The Right to silence and caution*

Case law has recognised the right to silence, with clear reference to article 14.3 of the International Covenant on Civil and Political Rights and article 6 ECHR as interpreted by the ECtHR.[56] However, police detectives are under no obligation to inform persons who are about to be interviewed that they have the right to remain silent.[57]

Suspects or defendants also have the right to remain entirely passive and have no obligation to cooperate with the judicial authorities.[58] In principle, a 'passive' attitude should have no negative consequences for defendants. However, at the pre-trial stage the lack of co-operation is very often used as an argument for detaining the accused. If suspects are unco-operative, prosecutors will point out that they must be prevented from destroying or manipulating evidence, from colluding with other people, and may even argue that the suspect is more likely to abscond. All of these are grounds to prolong pre-trial detention. In theory, the passive nature, or the complete absence, of suspects does not liberate investigating magistrates from the obligation to act in a balanced way, looking for both incriminating and exculpatory data. In practice, especially in *in absentia* proceedings, neither the police nor the magistrates have a tendency to invest a lot of energy in the search for exculpatory evidence on their own initiative. The role of the defence seems to be crucial in drawing their attention to favourable elements or to pointing out of weaknesses in the prosecution case. At the trial stage, the lack of co-operation can be considered by the judge as an absence of reasonable explanation for the suspect's behaviour. In a system where the intimate conviction of the judge is decisive (see *infra* section 4), this can lead to very serious consequences.

---

[54] H.-D. Bosly and D. Vandermeersch, *supra* note 2, p. 382-383.

[55] A high ranking member of the federal prosecution service told Parliament that access to lawyers in the hours after arrest would be detrimental to the effectiveness of law enforcement in terrorism and organized crime cases. Only in the first hours after they have been deprived of their liberty are suspects 'confused' enough to make statements, at a time when they have not had enough time to concoct stories and organize alibis.

[56] Court of Appeals Antwerp 30 January 1992, *R.W.* 1991-92, p. 891; Court of Appeals Antwerp 11 November 2001, *R.W.* 2002-03, p. 464; H.-D. Bosly and D. Vandermeersch, *supra* note 2, p. 27 and 543.

[57] H.-D. Bosly and D. Vandermeersch, *supra* note 2, p. 617; C. Van den Wyngaert, *supra* note 3, p. 599.

[58] H.-D. Bosly and D. Vandermeersch, *supra* note 2, p. 25.

3.3. The Right to an interpreter

Under article 47*bis* § 5 CCP three possible alternatives are open if persons who are being interviewed express themselves in a different language than the language of the proceedings: they can give a written statement in their own language; their statements can be written down in their own language; or a sworn translator can assist them. Questions relating to the language used during proceedings and the rights of suspects to express them in a different language, and eventually to be assisted by a sworn translator, are rather well established. Historical and political sensitivity about linguistic rights is very high in trilingual Belgium and the use of languages in proceedings has been stipulated in the Languages Act 1935 in a very detailed way.[59]

The absence of a (polyglot) defence lawyer during interviews by the police or investigating magistrate, and the lack of audio or video recording, render any effective control of the quality of the translation during interrogations at the pre-trial stage impossible.[60]

3.4. The Right to be informed about the charge and existing evidence[61]

Article 5.2 of the ECHR requires that suspects be informed promptly, in a language which they understand, of the reasons for their arrest and the charges against them. As far as the initial 24 hour period of a suspect's deprivation of liberty is concerned, the Belgian law on criminal proceedings does not contain requirements or formalities 'translating' this requirement of art 5.2. It has, however, to be noted that the ECHR is self-executing. At the stage of the deprivation of the suspect's liberty by the police no formal charges will have yet been brought. They will, however, receive a copy of the police interview report if they request it. The report will mention the type of offence, although the description given of the suspected offence is not binding.

At the later stages of the pre-trial phase a distinction has to be made between the preliminary investigation and the judicial inquiry. If only preliminary investigations are conducted (i.e., there is no judicial inquiry), the prosecutor will only bring formal charges at the end of the investigation, by issuing a direct summons for trial.[62] The suspect will therefore not be formally charged with any offence until they receive the summons.

In the case of a judicial inquiry, the point at which formal proceedings are commenced depends on whether or not the investigating judge issues an arrest

---

[59]   Loi concernant l'emploi des langues en matière judiciaire – Wet van 15 juni 1935 op het gebruik der talen in gerechtszaken, published in the Moniteur belge, 22 June 1935; H.-D. Bosly and D. Vandermeersch, supra note 2, p. 102-121; R. Verstraeten, supra note 2, p. 271.

[60]   However, at the trial stage the sworn translator is very often present in the Court, but unless the defence explicitly asks for a complete translation, they will not translate the complete proceedings but only the questions asked by the Court of the defendant and their answers.

[61]   R. Verstraeten, supra note 2, p. 492-496.

[62]   Art. 182 CPP; H.-D. Bosly and D. Vandermeersch, supra note 2, p. 555.

warrant, placing the person in pre-trial detention. When an arrest warrant is not deemed necessary, the investigating judge does not have to bring charges at this point of the investigation. Charges can also be brought against a suspect later, either during an interview or even by written notification (in practice a letter sent to the suspect informing them that charges are brought).[63] There is no obligation for the investigating judge to hear suspects before bringing formal charges against them (except when charges are brought at the same time that an arrest warrant is issued).[64] If the prosecutor requests the investigating judge to issue an arrest warrant, the suspect will be interviewed by that investigating judge. The investigating judge will then have to decide whether they formally charge (*in verdenking stellen – inculper*) the suspect. The charges will be registered in the report of the interview by the investigating judge. They are based on indications that the suspect has committed the offence and are temporary; they can be altered if additional data (e.g. aggravating circumstances, subsequent death of the victim) emerges in the course of the inquiry. If need be, additional charges can also be brought in the course of the inquiry.

A charge is an obvious pre-condition for the issuing of an arrest warrant by the investigating judge.[65] The law also requires that the suspect should be interviewed before an arrest warrant can be issued. During that interview, the judge must inform the suspect of the charges and of the possibility of an arrest warrant being ordered and pre-trial detention being ordered. Suspects will be able to state their position on the issue. This means that all arrested suspects in Belgium are brought before and can speak to a judge within 24 hours. This is considered to be a deterrent against physical abuse by the police in the risky phase immediately following the deprivation of liberty. Without prior access to a lawyer, it is doubtful whether foreign suspects will realise who the judge is and to what extent they can report irregularities by the police to that judge. Normally police officers transport the suspect to and from the judge's office.

In principle, investigating judges must formally inform suspects of the charges as soon as they are convinced that serious indications of guilt exist. However, it is for them to decide whether and when this condition is met. The official notification of the charges triggers a number of rights of the defence, such as the right to request access to the file, the right to ask for additional investigations, the right to ask for a 'summary interrogation' in the presence of the defence lawyer, etc.[66] Many practitioners are therefore under the impression that some investigating judges delay the moment of formal charge as long as possible, be it for tactical or bureaucratic motives, thus preventing suspects from effectively exercising their rights. Such a practice undeniably violates the legality principle, but as the law provides no sanctions, suspects are somewhat defenceless. They can always make an application for review to the Indictment Chamber of the Court of Appeals

---

63   R. Verstraeten, *supra* note 2, p. 427-428.
64   H.-D. Bosly and D. Vandermeersch, *supra* note 2, p. 619 and 621.
65   The interview should concern the criminal facts of which the person is suspected as well as the possibility of an arrest warrant being issued. See section 2.2 *supra*.
66   Art. 61*ter* and *quinquies* CPP.

(which can charge the suspect itself) and they can eventually claim in the later stages of the procedure (Investigative Chamber or trial chamber of the Court, cf. *infra* nrs. 73-75) that the unlawful behaviour and inherent violation of the rights of defence should be sanctioned by declaring the prosecution inadmissible altogether. Courts have, however, been extremely lenient on alleged foul play and the prosecution has very rarely been sanctioned by inadmissibility.[67] Usually they will give the investigating judge a broad margin of appreciation and unjustifiable delays will not be considered to be a violation of the right to a fair trial, as they can be remedied by subsequent rebuttal or additional inquiry.

The charges notified by the investigating judge are temporary and merely indicative. Ultimately, the formal charges are brought by the prosecutor at the end of the judicial inquiry. At that time, the investigating judge will transfer their file to the prosecutor. The latter will formulate a demand to a special section of the Court (the Investigative Chamber of the Court) to commit the person to the Criminal Court on specific offences. The Investigative Chamber of the Court (or at the second degree a similar section of the Court of Appeals, the Indictment Chamber) will decide on what charges the suspects will stand trial as defendants. At this stage the prosecutor can indict persons who were not formally charged earlier by the investigating judge.

The requirement of article 5.2 ECHR seems to be met, as in normal conditions suspects will receive copies of the reports of the police interview as well as interviews by the investigating judge. In any case they will receive official notification of the arrest warrant. At the end of the preliminary investigation suspects will receive a summons setting out the charges brought against them. At the end of a judicial inquiry they will receive the decision of the Investigative Chambers with the same information. These documents inform defendants of the reasons for their arrest and the charges brought against them.

3.5. Legal assistance

Suspects have a general right to be assisted by a lawyer, but in case of arrest, only after the interview by the investigating judge which precedes the issuing of an arrest warrant. The debate between the suspect and the Judge regarding the decision whether to issue an arrest warrant is only adversarial to the extent that the suspect themselves will be able to argue that the warrant should not be issued when interviewed by the investigating judge.[68] In a decision of 14 December 1999 the Belgian Supreme Court (*Hof van Cassatie – Cour de Cassation*) decided that article 14, sub. 3 b and d of the International Covenant on Civil and Political Rights and article 6, sub. 3 c of the ECHR do not apply to interviews during the investigative stage of the criminal process.[69] The Supreme Court emphasized that the trial in its entirety

---

[67]   Cass. 2 October 2002, *Rev. dr. pén.* 2003, p. 125.
[68]   The Bill currently debated in parliament would change this (see *supra* note 20).
[69]   Cass. 14 December 1999, *Arr. Cass.* 1999, No. 678, <www.cass.be>.

has to be fair. Only if a violation of the ECHR during the investigative stage would jeopardize the fairness of the procedure as a whole can one invoke the ECHR.

From a practical point of view, this means that contact between lawyers and their detained clients will only be possible in prison approximately 24 hours after the initial deprivation of liberty by the police. There is one exception, in fast track, summary proceedings (supposed to lead to 'quick trials' and not often used), where a suspect is interviewed by the public prosecutor instead of an investigating judge and contact with the lawyer was possible. Such fast track trials are used at the discretion of the prosecutor when further investigations (preliminary investigation or judicial inquiry) appear to be unnecessary.

At a hearing in Parliament, members of the Bar applauded the Bill (No. 51-2138) which would increase access to lawyers for persons who have been detained, but admitted to being completely unprepared for a system under which most lawyers would have to be on stand-by and have a far more flexible agenda than they currently do. No study, not even an assessment of the impact of the proposals on the legal aid system, has been made. The Justice Minister's plans for legal aid reform have received a cold shoulder from the Flemish Bar. Whereas the possibility of consulting with a lawyer of choice is as warmly greeted by the Bar as it is contested by police and prosecution service, few seem to want to spend public defender money on lawyers who would be assisting clients throughout all interviews. Many seem to fear that the additional bureaucracy would be disproportionate in view of the expected benefits. The inquisitorial system rests on trust in the investigating judge, the public prosecutors and the police. Supervision by magistrates should guarantee that abuse by the police does not occur.

3.6. Legal aid

The investigating judge must inform suspects subject to an arrest warrant that they have the right to choose a lawyer.[70] If the person detained does not choose their own lawyer, the investigating judge must inform the Dean of the Bar association, who will then immediately appoint a lawyer. A similar provision is applicable when the public prosecutor conducts a similar interrogation in the context of fast track summary proceedings.[71]

Indigent suspects can make a request to the investigating judge for the appointment of a duty lawyer.[72] The investigating judge must immediately transfer such a request to the bureau for legal assistance organised by the bar. Fortunately, a Royal Decree of 18 December 2003 put in place a presumption that all persons who have been arrested would benefit from free legal aid unless it is proven that they are not without means. In practice, the duty lawyer will have to discuss with the arrested person their financial position in order to find if the strict income limits are met. The duty lawyer will be paid on the basis of a number of points they earn for

---

70   Art. 16 § 4 of the Pre-trial Detention Act 1990.
71   Art. 216*quater* CCP.
72   Art. 184*bis* al. 2 CCP.

every case, the number of points attainable for the legal intervention being set out within the relevant law. In criminal cases, hearings or client/lawyer contacts will be taken in consideration. No points will be granted for the time needed to study and prepare a file. If the case is simple, that is not a major problem, but it can lead duty lawyers in more complicated cases not to prepare and study the file to the extent necessary in order to conduct an effective defence. Furthermore, the amount a duty lawyer receives for every point they 'earn' varies every year and is not known in advance. Compared to the time needed to accomplish an act that will lead to earning 'a point,' the amount allocated is far lower than the normal fee that lawyers would receive in a privately paid case. If the indigent detainee does not speak a language understood by any lawyer, the State will pay for an interpreter for a maximum of three hours.

3.7. *The Right to disclosure*

As noted earlier, the basic model for the investigative stage of the criminal process is still inquisitorial, with the secret nature of the investigation as a corollary (art. 28quinquies and 57 § 1 al. 2 CCP). Both the inquisitorial principle and the accompanying secrecy are deemed incompatible with a disclosure obligation on the police, the prosecutor or the investigating judge.[73] The powers of unilateral action inherent in inquisitorial proceedings entail, of course, a general obligation for investigators to act in a lawful way when gathering evidence. This legality principle, binding all parties, was considered to be a general principle of law, but has now been included explicitly in the CCP.[74] However, it is not really clear how far it extends, what protection it offers to suspects,[75] or what the appropriate sanction is for breaches (exclusion of evidence, disciplinary or civil liability of the officers, of the authorities, etc.?).[76]

Throughout the whole investigative phase, the prosecution has significantly more access to the evidence than the defence. Whether conducted by the prosecutor or by the investigating magistrate, the former always has permanent access to the file. This allows the public prosecutor to ask for investigative initiatives (without it being binding on the investigating judge or the Indictment Chamber) at any time and therefore to actively influence the course of the inquiry. For all kinds of decisions of the investigative judge (such as the decision to lift pre-trial detention or the freezing of assets), the judge has to notify the prosecutor and the decision does

---

[73]   Exceptions are, of course, a possibility since an investigating judge can grant access to the file. The fact that partial access can be granted is an illustration of the absence of an obligation to 'disclose.' Another exception is the possibility for the defendant and their lawyer to have access to the file of the investigation 24 or 48 hours before the monthly detention hearings in the Investigative Chamber of the Court or the Indictment Chamber of the Court of Appeals.

[74]   Art. 28*bis* § 3 al. 3 CPP and art. 56 § 1 al. 2 CPP.

[75]   A suspect will probably not be able to invoke unlawful behaviour against other suspects or against witnesses, unless it affects them personally.

[76]   The uncertainty about the sanction has even increased since the Supreme Court decision concerning the exclusion of illegally obtained evidence: see *infra* note 88.

not become effective until the period for appeal by the prosecutor with the Indictment Chamber has elapsed. Appeal by the public prosecutor usually suspends decisions which are favourable to defendants.

As we already pointed out, the opportunity for the defence to have very limited access to the case file was only established in 1998. Furthermore, defence lawyers cannot assist their clients during interview by the police, the public prosecutor or the investigating judge,[77] while the public prosecutor has the right to be present at any interview. When the investigating judge visits the *locus in quo* for any reason, the public prosecutor must accompany them.[78] The judge may decide that the suspect should also be there, but the defence lawyer is never allowed to be present. The exception to the general rule, clearly under the influence of Strasbourg case law,[79] is the procedure for the hearing of anonymous witnesses, under which the investigating judge is present with the witness, and the defence and prosecution are able to suggest questions via telecommunication links.[80]

3.8. Juveniles

The legal position of juveniles (those less than 18 years old) is determined by the Child Protection Act 1965.[81] Their cases are dealt with according to completely different procedures before a Juvenile Court. In exceptional cases involving minor offenders older than 16, the Juvenile Court can decide to remit the case to be dealt with under the normal criminal justice process. Under the influence of Strasbourg case law, minors can no longer be detained in a prison.[82] Since 2002 they are remanded to secure accommodation by virtue of a Juvenile Court order.

4. The impact of the investigative stage on the trial

4.1. The relationship between the investigative stage and the trial phase

The investigative phase has a very important influence on the trial phase. The latter will basically consist of a contradictory discussion of the evidence that has been collected in the pre-trial phase. The judges in the trial phase will have full access to the file that has been created in the pre-trial phase. A combination of everything that they have read in the file and what they have heard during the hearings at the trial stage will constitute the 'evidence' on which judges should base their decisions. Statements made by witnesses in the pre-trial phase, for example, will be considered as evidence even when the witness is not heard again by the Court in the trial

---

[77]   Exceptions are the 'summary interrogation' by the investigating judge and interrogations by the prosecutor in a fast track proceeding.
[78]   Art. 62 CCP.
[79]   ECtHR 30 October 1997, *Van Mechelen a.o.* v. *The Netherlands*, Reports 1997-VII.
[80]   Art. 86*ter* CCP.
[81]   *Loi relative à la protection de la jeunesse – Wet betreffende de jeugdbescherming*, published in the *Moniteur belge*, 15 April 1965.
[82]   ECtHR 29 February 1988, *Bouamar* v. *Belgium*, A 129.

phase. The only exception to this is proceedings in the Assizes Court, a jury court, in which the proceedings are oral. In such cases the jury will not have access to the file of the investigation in advance and, therefore, all witnesses will be heard during the Court hearings.

Typical of the judicial inquiry system in Belgium is the fact that the law provides for extensive judicial review in the pre-trial stage. The Indictment Chamber of the Court of Appeals, a panel of three judges, supervises the judicial inquiry and deals with appeals against certain decisions by the investigating judge. Sometimes an extra, technical, appeal to the Supreme Court is possible on points of law. When special investigative measures have been used in a preliminary investigation by the public prosecution service, there is still a judicial review by the Indictment Chamber of the Court of Appeals.[83]

When the investigating judge deems their inquiry complete, they will remit the file to the prosecution service, which will subsequently formulate the indictment. The prosecutor can indict persons against whom no formal charges were brought earlier by the investigating judge. They can even add charges that were not part of the judicial inquiry but which, in the opinion of the prosecutor, result from the information in the case file.[84]

After a phase in which parties can require additional investigative acts or after those requests have been executed or denied, the case will be brought before the Investigative Chamber of the local criminal court. It will have to decide whether there is sufficient evidence to commit the suspects for trial in the criminal court. It does so after an adversarial debate behind closed doors. Suspects have the right to be present, but there is no obligation. The Investigative Chamber commits the suspects for trial or decides there is no case to answer. In 1998, parliament wanted this stage to be used by the judges to 'clean' the file by eliminating procedural acts or documents that were 'null and void.' On the one hand, the issue was of one of procedural economy. The sooner all parties have a decision on the validity of certain contested investigative acts, the better: why conduct an extensive and expensive trial if in the end the judge has to establish an initial nullity, for instance, an initial search conducted without the necessary warrant, which undermines the whole case? Public reaction to some notorious mistrials or acquittals influenced this choice for an early vetting. On the other hand, the measure was also said to protect suspects. Under the former system, the trial judge was supposed to ignore the elements that were null and void, but they remained in the file and might in practice influence the decision. Under the new regime, they disappeared from the file and were put in a sealed envelope, thus excluding 'unconscious' influence.

After long discussions, it was agreed that suspects could not be compelled to invoke a process which would nullify proceedings at the pre-trial stage 'or forever hold their tongue.' They have the fundamental right to raise procedural or evidentiary issues when they deem it necessary. The fact that they could or might

---

[83]   Art. 235*ter* CCP.

[84]   Since the investigating judge had no mandate with regard to those offences, no additional acts of inquiry can be requested.

have known about a procedural error from the outset does not prevent them from raising it for the first time in the trial phase. The process economy does, however, justify the position that if a party has raised the issue in the pre-trial phase and the judges (if necessary, the Appeals or Supreme Court judges) have decided on validity, the same issue cannot be raised at the trial stage. The rights of the defence under article 6 ECHR were, however, invoked to argue that trial parties who had not been involved at the pre-trial stage retained the right to raise the issue of nullity. A particular complication can be envisaged when illegally obtained evidence which has been excluded at the request of one suspect might be exculpatory for another suspect who was not involved in the procedure at the time that the evidence was excluded. This happened in a very high-profile trial, and the Constitutional Court quashed legislation that had been adopted to prevent 'excluded evidence' for being reintroduced at trial.[85]

The Investigative Chamber or (if there is an appeal against its decision[86] or if it orders committal for jury trial in the Assizes Court) the Indictment Chamber of the Court of Appeals decides the charges for which the defendants will stand trial. On points of law a subsequent appeal to the Supreme Court is possible. The qualification given at committal is not definitive, with the exception of the existence of mitigating circumstances. In Belgium, mitigating circumstances usually serve as a procedural device to avoid jury trials, which are seen as excessively burdensome and expensive for many crimes that would require a jury trial without the mitigation. If the trial court considers changing the charge, it must inform the defendant of this intention to enable them to put forward their argument on this issue.

When only preliminary investigations have been conducted, if need be with the intermezzo of a mini-inquiry by an investigating judge (see *supra* note 18), there will be no judicial control at the end of the investigation. The public prosecution service will decide whether the case should go to trial. Victims can also decide to take the case to a trial court by a direct summons of the defendant. In such cases, the trial court will have to control the legality of investigative actions contained in the file. Direct summons is, however, not possible for the most serious crimes, which will always go through the pre-trial judicial vetting process. Finally, there is an

---

85   Constitutional Court, decision No. 86/2002, 8 May 2002, *R.W.* 2002-03, p. 290, <www.arbitrage.be>. After the murder of very well known veterinary inspector who had been fighting the so-called 'meat mafia,' the hit man first named certain persons as the ones who had ordered the killing. This confession had been part of a sworn statement under French criminal procedure rules, which led the Belgian judges to conclude it could not be used in evidence because it violated the privilege against compelled self-incrimination. In subsequent statements the hit man indicated other people as his 'clients.' When the latter were effectively prosecuted, they wanted to invoke the first statement to challenge the reliability of the hit man's statements. Eventually, they were allowed to do so, but they failed to convince the jury and were convicted.

86   The prosecutor and the civil party can base their appeal both on the facts and on the law if the Chamber refuses committal. Suspects can only appeal on points of law. If they are committed to the criminal court, they will be able to raise factual issues there. If they are not committed, they lack the necessary interest in appealing.

important exception to the general rule on preliminary investigations. If certain special investigative methods have been used, there is still a judicial review by the Indictment Chamber of the Court of Appeals. These are dealt with behind closed doors, rather than in open court at trial. The control concerns the legality, rather than the appropriateness, of the methods used.

The courts cannot base their decision on evidence that has not been subjected to rebuttal by the defence. This right of the defence is considered to be an integral part of the right to a fair trial under article 6 ECHR. Here, the trial phase contrasts sharply with the investigative phase. If the prosecution were to reveal certain information to the judges, but not to defence, then the judges cannot rely on that information. The investigating judge can, on the contrary, sometimes be informed of certain secret information which is never revealed to the defence.

4.2. Exclusion of illegally obtained evidence

Belgium has very few rules of evidence. The system is based on the 'intimate conviction' of the judge as to the facts, and the judge is normally a professional judge although sometimes a jury is instructed by a judge. It is perfectly possible for a judge to attach more importance to a witness statement than to a confession.[87] However, this free assessment does not allow the judge to distort the content of the procès-verbaux. For example, a judge cannot 'alter' a witness statement, but they can dismiss it as unreliable. A judge has to believe that the guilt of the defendant has been established beyond reasonable doubt. Specific exceptions are rare and often of recent making, such as the Strasbourg-inspired prohibition on basing a conviction exclusively or to a decisive extent on the statements of anonymous witnesses (art. 189bis CCP).

When, during the pre-trial investigations, the rules have been bent or breached the crucial issue is whether and how this will be punished. Belgium had a longstanding tradition of excluding illegally obtained evidence, even applying a 'fruits of the poisonous tree' doctrine. The Supreme Court had, however, limited its impact. It has stated, for instance, that the prosecution should not be punished by suppression of the evidence if a private person, without a link to the authorities, had committed the illegalities. A remarkable Supreme Court decision of 14 October 2003 overturned established case law.[88] Subsequent Supreme Court decisions confirmed this new line and refined it. As result, judges are only allowed to exclude illegally obtained evidence in three circumstances:

- if the legislation explicitly provides nullity if a formality is not met;
- if the reliability of the evidence has been tainted;
- if the use of the evidence violates the right to a fair trial.

---

[87] R. Verstraeten, *supra* note 2, p. 875.
[88] Cass. 14 October 2003, *T. Strafr.* 2004, p. 129, with comment by P. Traest.

As very few rules are explicitly protected (by a Belgian statute or an international treaty) by nullity in case of a breach, illegal actions by investigators will normally not lead to exclusion of the evidence obtained as a consequence of their action.

5. The Role of the defence lawyer

The general model of the investigative stage of the criminal process in Belgium is, as has been noted, inquisitorial, and the series of new rights for defendants and civil parties does not fundamentally alter the model. This strongly affects the position of the different parties to the proceedings. In the Belgian inquisitorial model of the investigative phase equality of arms, read into article 6 ECHR by the ECtHR, means that there is some balancing rather than real equality.[89] Parties in criminal proceedings are in fact anything but equal. The prosecution is not a 'trial party' comparable to the defendant or the civil party. The Constitutional Court has recognised on repeated occasions the specific position of the public prosecution service, stating that the fundamental difference between the prosecutor and the defendant is that the first is representing the public interest while the latter is representing a personal interest.[90] The Court has confirmed the traditional vision of the public prosecution service as the guardian of the interests of society[91] and has ruled that, therefore, the fact that the public prosecutor has some extensive powers, denied to the other trial parties in the investigative phase, does not violate the Constitution, read in the light of international human rights instruments.[92] The prosecutor holds a predominant position during the whole of the criminal proceedings, from the start of the investigation to the execution of sanctions. They can use methods of investigation and procedures to which no other party in the trial has access. Like the police and judges, prosecutors are bound by the secrecy obligation and illegal revelation of secrets amounts to a criminal offence. A specific offence of revelation of investigative secrets was introduced by the Statute of 1998 which applies to other parties (for instance victims) who have been granted access to the file and who abuse this right, for instance, by selling the story to the press.

---

[89] A. Sadzot, *supra* note 45, p. 136.

[90] The public prosecution service has a special function in an inquisitorial system, as representative of the general interest, and for that reason it cannot be considered to be a party in the same way as suspects or civil parties who defend a personal interest. The Constitutional Court concludes that consequently the regime's more favourable treatment of the public prosecution service does not violate the constitutional principle of equality (Decision 58/98 of 27 May 1998, <www.arbitrage.be>).

[91] F. Close, 'Et le parquet?,' (*And what about the public prosecution service?*), in X. (ed.), *Les droits de la défense en matière pénale – Actes du colloque des 30-31 mai – 1er juin 1985*, Liège, Editions du Jeune Barreau, 1985, p. 97.

[92] Constitutional Court, decision No. 82/94, 1 December 1994, *Rev. dr. pén.* 1995, p. 276 with comment by Renders; *R.W.* 1994-95, p. 224 with comment by R. Declercq; Constitutional Court, decision No. 22/95, 2 March 1995, *Rev. dr. pén* 1995, p. 656 with comment by H.-D. Bosly. See for a similar development on the situation of the civil party: Constitutional Court, decision No. 43/95, 6 June 1995, *J.L.M.B* 1995, p. 1560.

Suspect(s) themselves do not commit an offence when they reveal data from the file as they are not bound by any secrecy obligations.

The role of the defence lawyer in the investigative phase of the criminal process was initially conceived as a marginal one. We pointed out that the undeniable evolution towards a more active role for the defence is very recent. At an important meeting on the rights of defence organised in 1985 by the Liège Bar Association, the president of the Bar said that the 'inventory of the non-rights of defence in Belgium is surprising,'[93] and another eminent jurist made a contribution under the title: 'The lawyer, a phantom?'[94] This outcry has contributed to the recent modification of the law (for instance the Statute of 1998 and the Pre-trial Detention Act 1990), which have somewhat adjusted the imbalance between prosecution and defence. Nevertheless, the inquisitorial and secret nature of the pre-trial phase entails that the respective positions of defence and prosecution remain very different. The defence has no right to participate actively in the investigations. This is a corollary of the principle of the secrecy of the investigation. The defence cannot be in contact with witnesses and a fortiori cannot interview them. The role of the defence is limited to communicating available information to the investigating judge (in a judicial inquiry) or to the public prosecutor (in preliminary investigations), and to request that additional investigative action be taken.

As explained above, defence lawyers have no access to their clients during the (often crucial) first 24 hours after the arrest. During this period the prosecutor leads the investigations and is informed in detail by the police about the evolution of the case. The evidence gathered during this period is no less evidence than evidence collected afterwards; sometimes prosecutors and judges even deem information obtained in this period as more reliable on the basis that suspects are caught by surprise and do not have time to make up a story (with the help of their lawyers). There is general acknowledgement that the pre-trial phase has a decisive influence on the trial stage, as the evidence on which the trial is based is precisely the file that has been composed in the investigations of pre-trial phase (see *supra* section 4.1). The important role of the defence lawyer in the accusatory trial phase cannot compensate for the relative absence of the defence lawyer during the investigation.

Belgium realises that the weight of the inquisitorial pre-trial stage on the criminal procedure 'as a whole,' compared to that of the adversarial trial phase, has significantly increased. It has adjusted its laws to this state of affairs by reinforcing to a certain extent the situation of suspects, especially where they have been deprived of their liberty. It has also added some adversarial ingredients to the judicial inquiry, but without altering its fundamentally inquisitorial nature. The defence is allowed to make some 'pitches,' but the magistrates ultimately retain enormous discretion in their conduct of the investigation. To check that power, the Belgian legislators rely on supervision by (other) judges, whose intervention can

---

[93]   J. Henry, 'Rien que la parole,' in X. (ed.), *Les droits de la défense en matière pénale – Actes du colloque des 30-31 mai – 1er juin 1985*, Liège, Editions du Jeune Barreau, 1985, p. 11.

[94]   F. Piedboeuf, 'L'avocat phantome?,' (*The lawyer, a phantom?*), in X. (ed.), *Les droits de la défense en matière pénale – Actes du colloque des 30-31 mai – 1er juin 1985*, Liège, Editions du Jeune Barreau, 1985, p. 57-78.

often be prompted by the defence, rather than on an active defence standing on equal footing with the prosecution. The position of the defence is even weaker in the preliminary investigations conducted by public prosecution magistrates, which constitute the bulk of all criminal investigations. Defence lawyers, rightly or wrongly, are still seen as having a disturbing influence rather than as constructive contributors to a balanced finding of the (judicial) truth. The enormous trust which the Belgian law, in complete harmony with the Strasbourg Court, places in magistrates in general and in judges in particular, would be more convincing if it were accompanied by a less lenient supervision and more effective sanctioning system if those people abuse the trust society puts in them and bend or break the rules.

6. List of abbreviations

J.L.M.B.   *Jurisprudence de Liège, Mons et Bruxelles* (Case law of Liège, Mons and Brussels)

Parl. St.   *Parlementaire Stukken* (Reports of Parliamentary proceedings)

Rev. dr. pén.   *Revue de Droit pénal et de criminologie* (Criminal law and Criminology Review)

R.W.   *Rechtskundig Weekblad* (Legal Weekly)

T. Strafr.   *Tijdschrift voor strafrecht: jurisprudentie, nieuwe wetgeving en doctrine voor de praktijk* (Criminal Law Review: case law, legislation, and jurisprudence)

7. Bibliography

H.-D. Bosly & D. Vandermeersch, *Droit de la procédure pénale (Criminal procedure law)*, Bruges, La Charte, 2005.

Caselaw of the ECtHR can be found at the European Court of Human Rights HUDOC Portal: <http://cmiskp.echr.coe.int>, in Series A and after 1 January 1996 in Reports of Judgments and Decisions, both published by Carl Heymans Verlag KG, Köln, Germany.

F. Close, 'Et le parquet?,' (And what about the public prosecution service?), in X. (ed.), *Les droits de la défense en matière pénale – Actes du colloque des 30-31 mai – 1er juin 1985*, Liège, Editions du Jeune Barreau, 1985, p. 91-131.

L. Cornil, 'De la nécessité de rendre à l'instruction préparatoire, en matière pénale, le caractère légal qu'elle a perdu, mercuriale prononcée à l'audience solennelle de rentrée de la Cour d'Appel de Bruxelles, le 15 septembre 1931,' (On the necessity of restoring the legal basis of the investigative stage), *Rev. dr. pén.*, 1930-31, p. 809-823.

R. Declercq, *Beginselen van strafrechtspleging (Principles of criminal procedure)*, Antwerp, Kluwer, 2003.

B. Dejemeppe & D. Merckx (eds), *De voorlopige hechtenis (Pre-trial detention)*, Antwerp, Kluwer, 2000.

B. De Smet, *Deskundigenonderzoek in strafzaken (Expert investigations in criminal cases)*, Antwerp, Story-Scientia, 2001.

C. De Valkeneer, *La tromperie dans l'administration de la preuve pénale: analyse en droits belge et international complétée par des éléments de droits français et néerlandais (Trickery and deception in the furnishing of evidence: analysis of Belgian, Dutch, French law and international law)*, Brussels, Larcier, 2000.

L. Dupont & F. Hutsebaut, *Herstelrecht tussen toekomst en verleden. Liber Amicorum Tony Peters (Restorative justice between future and past)*, Leuven, University Press, 2001.

J. Henry, 'Rien que la parole,' in X. (ed.), *Les droits de la défense en matière pénale – Actes du colloque des 30-31 mai – 1er juin 1985*, Liège, Editions du Jeune Barreau, 1985, p. 11-13.

O. Klees & D. Bosquet, 'Essai de synthèse des principaux apports de la loi Franchimont du point de vue des droits de la défense,' (Overview of the improvements in the rights of the defence after the Franchimont-reform), in M. Franchimont (ed.), *Le point sur les procédures, I*, Liège, Formation permanente Université-Palais, 2000, p. 199-221.

F. Piedboeuf, 'L'avocat phantome?,' (The lawyer, a phantom?), in X. (ed.), *Les droits de la défense en matière pénale – Actes du colloque des 30-31 mai – 1er juin 1985*, Liège, Editions du Jeune Barreau, 1985, p. 57-78.

A. Sadzot, 'L'égalité des armes et la contradiction dans le procès penal,' (Equality of arms and adversariality in criminal cases), in X. (ed.), *Les droits de la défense. Actes du colloque 'Jacques Henry' organisé par la Conférence libre du Jeune Barreau de Liège le 28 mars 1997*, Liège, Editions du Jeune Barreau de Liege, 1997, p. 129-180.

F. Schuermans, 'Donkere wolken boven het Belgisch strafvorderlijk landschap,' (Dark clouds gathering over the Belgian criminal procedure landscape), *Panopticon*, 5 2005, p. 39-54.

C. Van den Wyngaert, *Strafrecht, Strafprocesrecht en internationaal strafrecht in hoofdlijnen (Criminal law, criminal procedure and international criminal law)*, Antwerp, Maklu, 2003.

R. Verstraeten, *Handboek strafvordering (Companion to criminal procedure)*, Antwerp, Maklu, 2005.

Ed Cape
Jacqueline Hodgson

THE INVESTIGATIVE STAGE OF THE CRIMINAL PROCESS IN ENGLAND AND WALES

1.   Introduction

Criminal procedure in England and Wales is rooted in the adversarial tradition. There is no investigating judge and although there is a public prosecutor they have almost no pre-trial supervisory role. Investigation is carried out by the police, although they may instruct experts in the course of their enquiry. Police investigation is regulated by a number of key pieces of legislation, the most important being the Police and Criminal Evidence Act (PACE) 1984. The custody officer plays a key role in regulating the detention of suspects and ensuring their overall welfare. They authorise the initial and continuing detention and questioning, are responsible for informing the suspect of their rights and for ensuring their effective exercise (e.g. contacting a solicitor if required), as well as assessing whether special arrangements must be made for the suspect's protection, for example, the attendance of an interpreter or an appropriate adult. The defence lawyer may advise the suspect at the police station and may be present during the police interrogation of their client, but they have no access to the case file during this period. At the end of the suspect's detention, the police may charge[1] or release them, or bail them to return to the station at a later date. If the suspect is charged, the file is passed on to the Crown Prosecution Service (CPS) who will decide whether to continue with the prosecution. If the suspect is not charged (or notified that they may receive a summons), the matter is closed. Thus until recently the police have played a crucial gate-keeping role, as the prosecutor would only be aware of cases where the police have decided to charge. This has also meant that there has been no effective external scrutiny of cases in which no police charges were brought. However, recent legislation has modified this procedure, so that prosecutors will in future take the decision whether or not to charge a suspect in all

---

[1]   The 'charge' is the formal process by which prosecution is commenced. This is the normal way in which prosecution is commenced although there is a second method, normally used in the case of minor offences, which is by a summons issued by a magistrates' court.

but the most minor offences, and are likely to become increasingly involved in advising the police on their investigations.

Once a prosecution has started (i.e., when the person has been charged or summoned), the defendant is entitled to a copy of the prosecution evidence.[2] Previously, the defence were also entitled to inspect any additional material held by the police – information gathered in the course of the investigation that did not support the prosecution case (known as unused material), but which, of course, may assist the defence. Although a number of miscarriages of justice were only discovered as a result of post-conviction inspection of unused material, restrictions are now placed on the defendant's ability to consult it. In order to access unused material that has not been disclosed, the defence must now disclose an outline of its case in order to demonstrate the relevance of such additional disclosure. This is, of course, difficult, as one cannot request information that one does not know exists. The prosecutor is placed in the rather strange position, in an adversarial procedure, of being responsible for assessing what material they hold that might be of relevance to the defence.

Recent reforms have tended to encourage, if not coerce, the defence to participate in the police investigation. Adverse inferences may be drawn from an accused's 'silence' at the police station or in court and pre-trial disclosure of evidence by the defence is also increasingly required. Whilst the pre-trial resolution of evidential issues makes sense (at least in theory) within a more inquisitorial procedure, it is problematic within an adversarial one. In addition, the defence role itself is undermined as it becomes increasingly difficult for defence lawyers to give vigorous and confidential advice, and the defence is effectively required to participate in the construction of the prosecution case.

There is no constitutional court in England and Wales, but citizens may petition the European Court of Human Rights (ECtHR) and, since the passing of the Human Rights Act 1998, the European Convention on Human Rights (ECHR) is directly enforceable in domestic courts. A court does not have the power to strike out legislation which it considers to be incompatible with the ECHR, but it must read legislation in a way that is compatible or, where this is not possible, it must issue a declaration of incompatibility. There is then a fast track procedure in place to amend the legislation accordingly, although the government is not obliged to change the law so that it is compatible with the ECHR.

2.   Police Powers in the Investigative Stage

2.1.   *Relations between police, prosecutors and defence*

Principle responsibility for investigating crime and arresting suspects rests with the police. There are other agencies that have investigative powers, and a few of them

---

[2]   The precise entitlement depends upon whether the case is to be tried in a magistrates' court or the Crown Court, but generally the defendant is entitled to copies of the statements of prosecution witnesses.

also have powers of arrest (in particular, HM Revenue and Customs), but generally it is the police who decide who to arrest, what crimes to investigate, and how to investigate those crimes.[3] There is no external supervision or accountability to a judicial officer or public prosecutor.[4] Until 1985, cases were prosecuted by the police who employed lawyers to act on their behalf. The Prosecution of Offenders Act 1985 established the Crown Prosecution Service (CPS) as a prosecution service independent of the police. The CPS determines whether or not to continue a prosecution commenced by the police. Until recently, the police enjoyed sole discretion over whether or not to charge a suspect, thus controlling completely which cases were passed to the CPS for prosecution and which would be discontinued without any need for CPS involvement. During the past few years the government has given the CPS increased responsibility for taking decisions about charge, and in the future they, rather than the police, will take most charge decisions other than in respect of minor crimes.[5] However, prosecutors have no investigative powers nor, generally, authority over or responsibility for police investigations. They can advise or suggest lines of enquiry, but they cannot require or forbid the police to investigate further. A judge can issue a warrant for arrest in certain circumstances, but in practice most arrests are made by the police without warrant. Detention of suspects by the police without charge beyond certain periods of time requires judicial authorisation,[6] as do some (but not all) police searches of property. However, judges have no role in determining the course of criminal investigations and they do not supervise criminal investigations in any direct way.

The investigative stage of the criminal process is primarily regulated by PACE which came into force 20 years ago following fierce political and legal debate and concern about the role of the police in miscarriages of justice. PACE established a regulatory structure governing police powers and suspects' rights from arrest through to the formal commencement of criminal proceedings, and also established evidential rules governing the admissibility of confession and other prosecution evidence. It is supplemented by Codes of Practice which set out more detailed provisions governing, for example, searches of property, the treatment of suspects at police stations, identification procedures and the recording of police interviews.[7] The Codes do not have direct legislative force, and whilst the police and other law enforcement officers must have regard to their provisions, breach of any provision of a Code does not render the officer liable to any criminal or civil proceedings.[8] However, a breach may be taken into account in criminal or civil proceedings, and

[3]   Although in the case of offences involving serious fraud, the Serious Fraud Office has extensive investigative powers and has responsibility for prosecution.
[4]   Most prosecutions are conducted by the Crown Prosecution Service, although a number of other institutions have prosecution responsibilities and powers, normally circumscribed by reference to particular types of crime, e.g., the Serious Fraud Office, and HM Revenue and Customs.
[5]   Criminal Justice Act (CJA) 2003 Part 4 and Sch 2.
[6]   Police and Criminal Evidence Act (PACE) 1984 ss43 and 44.
[7]   In January 2006 a further Code of Practice, on police powers of arrest, was introduced.
[8]   PACE 1984 s67.

may (but does not necessarily) lead to the exclusion of confession evidence on the grounds of oppression or unreliability,[9] or the exclusion of any prosecution evidence on the grounds of unfairness.[10] If evidence is excluded the trial court must not take it into account in determining guilt or innocence.

The suspect may have a defence lawyer present during their detention and interrogation in police custody (discussed below in section 3), but they do not have access to the case file (i.e. they have no right to disclosure of the evidence in the hands of the police) and have no right to participate in the investigation in the sense of requiring investigative acts to be carried out. As noted earlier, there is a move towards a more coerced form of participation in the form of requiring the suspect to answer police questions, or risk adverse inferences being drawn at trial if they do not do so.

2.2. Arrest and detention

The police and other law enforcement officers have a variety of powers to detain people temporarily without arresting them. The most important of these is the power to stop and search a person on suspicion that they are in possession of stolen or prohibited articles or, where a senior officer has given authority on the grounds that it would be expedient for the prevention of acts of terrorism, anyone in the area covered by the authorisation.[11] The police and other law enforcement officers have a wide range of arrest powers in respect of any offence, principally governed by PACE 1984 s24.[12] Most powers of arrest require the officer to have reasonable suspicion that an offence has been, is being, or is about to be, committed, and in addition the officer must believe that arrest is necessary for one or more of a number of reasons set out in s24. In principle, the reasonable suspicion and necessity requirements are a due process safeguard, but in practice they provide only a minimal safeguard against arbitrary arrest.

---

[9]   PACE 1984 s76.

[10]   PACE 1984 s78.

[11]   See PACE 1984 Part I, Terrorism Act 2000 s44, Criminal Justice and Public Order Act 1994 s60 and s60AA. Official figures show that about 750,000 stop and searches are conducted under theses powers each year, although this is almost certainly an underestimate. It was held in *R (Gillan and another)* v. *Commissioner of Police for the Metropolis and another* [2006] UKHL 12 that detention properly conducted under these powers does not normally engage the European Convention on Human Rights article 5. In addition, customs officers also have wide powers to stop people who are crossing national borders.

[12]   Powers of arrest were significantly changed in January 2006. For an account of police powers of arrest see E. Cape, *Defending Suspects at Police Stations,* London, Legal Action Group, 5th ed., 2006, ch. 2. For critical accounts of arrest powers see A. Sanders and R. Young, *Criminal Justice,* Oxford, Oxford University Press, 3rd ed., 2006; F. Belloni and J. Hodgson, *Criminal Injustice: An Evaluation of the Criminal Justice Process in Britain,* Basingstoke, Macmillan, 2000, and research discussed therein. About 1.3 million arrests are carried out each year.

Once a person has been arrested, they must normally be taken to a police station as soon as practicable,[13] a requirement designed to ensure that the police do not circumvent the 'protective provisions' of PACE 1984 (such as the right to legal advice), most of which only apply at the police station. On arrival at a police station, the arrested person must be taken before a custody officer who must decide whether or not the person should be detained. Detention without charge should be authorised only if there is not, at that initial stage, sufficient evidence to charge the arrested person with a criminal offence and if the officer believes that detention is necessary to secure or preserve evidence or to obtain evidence by questioning.[14] It was recognised by those who designed the PACE structure that detention in a police station amounted to a gross incursion upon a person's liberty which should only be interfered with if other methods of dealing with the person were not available or appropriate. The role of custody officer was regarded as key to protecting the rights of suspects, both at the initial stage of determining whether a person should be detained and throughout their detention. In practice, the protective role of custody officers has been more limited, and the courts have effectively sanctioned the routine detention of arrested suspects.[15] Custody officers rarely, if ever, refuse to authorise detention of a suspect arrested for an offence.

When detention is authorised, the custody officer is required to open a custody record, a written or, more usually, an electronic record of the key features of a suspect's detention.[16] Custody records are designed to make the detention process transparent, and open to scrutiny after the event. Whilst they have, to an extent, been successful in achieving this aim, there is concern that they are completed in a 'self-serving' way to give the appearance of legality and conformity with procedural rules.[17] Defence lawyers must be given access to their client's custody record whilst at the police station, and are entitled to a copy of the complete record following charge.[18] However, their utility has been limited somewhat following recent statutory changes as a result of which the custody officer does not

---

[13]   PACE 1984 s30(1). Under recent legislation, as an alternative to taking an arrested person to a police station, the police officer can grant the arrested person 'street bail' requiring them to attend a police station at a future date (PACE 1984 s30 as amended by Criminal Justice Act 2003 s4).

[14]   PACE 1984 s37. The provisions are similar where a person is arrested under the Terrorism Act 2000, although a more senior officer must take the decision.

[15]   For a review of the research, see D. Brown, *PACE Ten Years on: a Review of the Research*, Home Office Research Study 155, London, Home Office, 1997, ch. 4. See also *R* v. *McGuinness* [1999] Crim LR 318 and *Al Fayed and others* v. *Commissioner of Police for the Metropolis and others* [2004] EWCA (Civ) 1579.

[16]   Code of Practice C § 2.1. For a complete account of the rules regarding custody records, see E. Cape, *supra* note 12.

[17]   As a custody officer commented in early research on PACE 1984, 'If it's not in the custody record, it didn't happen.' K. Bottomley, *et al.*, *Safeguarding the Rights of Suspects in Police Custody*, unpublished paper presented to the British Criminology Conference, Bristol, 1989.

[18]   PACE Code C § 2.4.

have to record on the custody record property that is taken from the suspect on arrival at the police station.[19]

2.3.   Duration and review of detention; bail

Detention without charge is initially limited to 24 hours from the time of arrival at the police station, although where the suspect is detained for an indictable offence[20] this may be extended by a senior police officer for up to a further 12 hours. At the expiration of this period, the suspect must be charged or released unless a magistrates' court grants a warrant of further detention, which may be initially for up to a further 36 hours and, on re-application, for a further period up to a total of 96 hours from first arrival at the police station. In order to extend detention the senior officer or magistrates' court must be satisfied that it is necessary in order to secure or preserve evidence or to obtain evidence by questioning. Detention without charge beyond 36 hours is relatively rare, although where an application is made to a magistrates' court, a warrant of further detention is rarely denied.[21]

A person in police detention must have their detention reviewed periodically in order to determine whether continued detention is justified. The first review must be carried out no later than six hours after detention is first authorised, and then at intervals of no more than nine hours. Prior to charge, the review must be conducted by a middle-ranking officer (a police inspector), who must be satisfied that the grounds for detention continue to be satisfied. If they are not, the suspect must be taken before a custody officer with a view to them being either charged or released. Before making a decision, the review officer must give the suspect and/or their lawyer the opportunity to make representations. Research evidence tends to suggest that reviews are relatively ineffective in the sense that review officers rarely, if ever, decide that continued detention is not justified, although there is some evidence that reviews do sometimes result in the reviewing officer encouraging the investigation officers to speed up their investigation.[22]

The decision whether there is sufficient evidence to charge a suspect with a criminal offence rests formally with the custody officer, rather than the officer in charge of the investigation. The question of when the decision must be made has been the matter of some controversy.[23] Although PACE s37 provides that a decision about charge must be made when a custody officer decides that there is sufficient evidence to charge (thereby bringing interviewing to an end), the courts have

---

[19]   Criminal Justice Act 2003 s8, amending PACE s54.

[20]   An indictable offence is an offence that may be tried in the Crown Court, and includes most assaults, theft, burglary, robbery, most sexual offences, and most drugs offences.

[21]   Statistics on length of detention without charge are not routinely collected, but a relatively small proportion of suspects are detained without charge for more than 24 hours. Almost all applications for a warrant of further detention are granted. See Home Office, 'Arrests for Notifiable Offences and the Operation of Certain Powers under PACE,' *Home Office Statistical Bulletin*, 18 2004, London, Home Office.

[22]   See D. Brown, *supra* note 15, ch. 4.

[23]   See E. Cape, 'Detention Without Charge: What Does "Sufficient Evidence to Charge" Mean?,' *Criminal Law Review*, 874 1999.

supported a broad interpretation of this provision, and the current version of Code C permits the police to continue interviewing until they are satisfied that they have asked all the questions they wish to ask, irrespective of whether there is sufficient evidence to charge.[24] Until recently, it has also been the custody officer's responsibility to decide what offence(s) the suspect should be charged with but, as previously explained, in future a prosecutor will normally take this decision other than in minor cases. To facilitate this, prosecutors are increasingly being located within police stations during office hours, with 'on call' facilities being set up for other times. As an alternative to prosecution, the custody officer may formally caution a suspect (known as a 'simple caution' which is, in effect, a formal admonishment). Alternatively, as a result of recent legislation, prosecutors have the power to impose a conditional caution which can, for example, require some form of reparation or other action to be taken by the offender.[25] Both forms of caution require the consent of the offender, but if they do not consent they can be prosecuted in the usual way.

Where a person is charged with a criminal offence, the custody officer must decide whether they are to be granted bail pending their first court appearance in accordance with criteria set out in PACE 1984 s38. Under these criteria bail may be denied if the custody officer has doubts about the identity or address of the suspect, or has reasonable grounds for believing that detention is necessary to prevent them committing further offences or interfering with the administration of justice, or is necessary to ensure that they appear in court. If bail is denied, the person must normally be produced in court within 24 hours. If bail is granted, which in practice is frequently the case, the first court appearance will normally take place within two days. Bail may be unconditional or subject to conditions, such as residence at a specified address, to keep away from witnesses, or a curfew. Although the police have the power to require a surety or security (e.g. the deposit of a passport or driving licence), this is relatively rare.

2.4. Police interview

Interviews of suspects must normally only be conducted at a police station and, in practice, in a formal interview room. Code of Practice C sets out detailed rules about the conditions of interviews, and their maximum length. Most interviews must be recorded on audio-tape, and where these facilities are not available, must normally be contemporaneously recorded in writing.[26] The recording of interviews has largely, although not completely, eliminated disputes over what was said by a suspect in police interviews. At trial, the prosecution will frequently adduce a transcript of the tape-recorded interview as evidence, and either prosecution or

---

[24] Code C § 11.6, and see *R* v. *McGuinness* [1999] Crim LR 318 and *R* v. *Howell* [2003] Crim LR 405.

[25] Criminal Justice Act 2003 Part 3, and see the Conditional Cautioning Code of Practice. Recent legislation, the Police and Justice Act 2006, gives prosecutors the power to impose a financial penalty as part of a conditional caution.

[26] Code E and Code C section 11.

defence can apply to have the tape-recording itself played to the court. It has been recognised by the courts that a tape-recording can convey important information that is not evident from a transcript.[27] Once a person has been charged with an offence, they must not normally be further interviewed about that offence by the police.[28]

Evidence of a confession obtained by oppression cannot be used by the prosecution at trial, but there are few detailed rules on the proper limits of interviewing. Code of Practice C does provide that the police must not use oppression to obtain answers in interview, and further provides that they must not offer inducements to confess, e.g., the offer of bail. However, police interviewing provides an important opportunity for the police to 'construct a case' favourable to the prosecution[29] and some degree of coercion is accepted by the courts.

The police have the power to interview any potential witness that they wish. They do not have formal powers to require co-operation, but there are ways in which they can 'encourage' co-operation, which may include arrest where their (wide) powers of arrest are available. Interviewing witnesses who are not suspects is largely unregulated, which is a matter of continued concern, and in particular there are no formal rules about the recording of witness interviews.

2.5. Coercive methods of investigation

The police have extensive and wide-ranging powers to gather and secure evidence in respect of suspected criminal offences. Police powers to take fingerprints, photographs and non-intimate samples[30] have increased throughout the past decade so that they may now be taken as a matter of routine from anyone who is in police detention.[31] Information so obtained can be held indefinitely whether or not the person from whom they are taken is charged with and/or convicted of an offence, and may also be checked against relevant databases (known as speculative searches) to check for evidence of involvement in other crimes. Intimate samples (i.e. a sample from a body orifice other than the mouth – which is non-intimate for these purposes) may be taken with the authority of a middle-ranking officer (an inspector) if satisfied that it would tend to confirm or disprove involvement in an offence.[32] Powers to conduct personal searches are also extensive, although powers

---

[27]   See, in particular, *R v. Paris, Abdullahi and Miller* (1993) 97 Cr App R 99. For a review of research on recording of interviews see D. Brown, *supra* note 15, p. 144.

[28]   Code C § 16.5. However, the government is consulting on whether this rule should be changed, in order to allow post-charge interviewing.

[29]   M. McConville, A. Sanders and R. Leng, *The Case for the Prosecution*, London, Routledge, 1991, and J. Baldwin, 'Police Interview Techniques: Establishing Truth or Proof?,' 33 *British Journal of Criminology*, 3 1993, p. 325.

[30]   A non-intimate sample is a sample of hair (other than pubic hair), a sample taken from a nail or under a nail, a swab taken from any part of the body (including from the mouth, but not other body orifices), saliva and a skin impression (PACE 1984 s65(1)).

[31]   PACE 1984 ss61, 63, 63A, 64 and 64A.

[32]   PACE 1984 s62.

to carry out an intimate search (i.e. a search of a body orifice) are more limited.[33] Powers to search property depend, in part, on whether the property concerned is occupied or controlled by a person under arrest. Broadly, where a person is under arrest, property that they were in at the time of arrest or immediately before, or property that they occupy or control, may be searched for evidence in respect of the offence for which they are under arrest and, in some cases, other offences as well.[34] Where a person is not under arrest, the police have power to search property in order to arrest a person for an indictable offence,[35] and the police have a range of powers to search property for evidence on the authority of a judge.[36] With the exception of the latter, all of the other powers may be exercised without approval of either a prosecutor or a judge. Where the property of a person under arrest is searched, they have no right to be present whilst the search is conducted.

Visual identification procedures are regulated by PACE Code of Practice D. Generally, where one or more witnesses has identified a suspect, but does not personally know them, and the suspect denies being the person that the witness claims to have seen, an identification procedure must be held unless this is not practicable or it would serve no useful purpose in proving or disproving whether the suspect was involved in committing the offence.[37] The normal identification procedure is a video identification in which the suspect is shown together with at least eight other people who as far as possible resemble the suspect in age, height, general appearance and 'position in life.' The conduct of video and other identification procedures is closely regulated by Code D, although breach of the provisions will only lead to exclusion of the evidence of identification obtained if a judge decides to exclude it under PACE 1984 s78 (see above). Voice identification is becoming more prevalent as relevant technology develops. The regulation of voice identification is less well developed, although the Home Office is moving towards more meaningful regulation.

One of the features of the common law tradition in England and Wales was that in their evidence gathering activities, the police were permitted to do anything unless it was prohibited by law. Where those activities involved interference with privacy, this approach conflicted with the requirements of, in particular, article 8 of the ECHR and the jurisprudence of the ECtHR. Thus regulation of covert surveillance activities of the police is of relatively recent origin, and is now principally governed by the Regulation of Investigatory Powers Act (RIPA) 2000.[38] Interception of telecommunications for the purpose of the investigation of crime is

---

[33]   PACE 1984 ss54 and 55.
[34]   PACE 1984 ss18 and 32, but only if they were arrested for an indictable offence.
[35]   PACE 1984 s17. In recent years pressure has been mounting to change this rule in order to permit such material to be admitted in evidence.
[36]   See, in particular, PACE 1984 Part II and Code of Practice B.
[37]   Code of Practice D § 3.12.
[38]   See E. Cape, *Regulation of Investigatory Powers Act 2000 Current Law Statutes* (Annotated Edition), London, Sweet and Maxwell, 2000. Reprinted in RIPA 2000, *Related SIs and Codes of Practice*, London, Sweet and Maxwell, 2005. Other legislation governing surveillance includes the Intelligence Services Act 1994 and the Police Act 1997.

generally only lawful if the Secretary of State for Home Affairs (a government minister) grants authority, which they may only give if it is necessary in the interests of national security or for the purpose of preventing or detecting serious crime.[39] A peculiarity of English and Welsh law is that information obtained by such interception cannot be used as evidence.[40] Other forms of covert surveillance, and the use of informants (known as covert human intelligence sources), is subject to internal authorisation by the police, and authorisation may only be given if certain conditions are satisfied and, in so far as it interferes with the right to private life, it is necessary and proportionate. The product of these forms of surveillance are admissible in evidence at trial. Although covert surveillance of consultations between suspects and their lawyers is not prohibited by RIPA 2000, the courts have held that it is unlawful.[41]

2.6. Terrorism powers

Whilst PACE 1984 regulates the detention and treatment of people arrested for any criminal offence, including a specific terrorist offence, the Terrorism Act 2000 empowers the police to arrest a person who they have reasonable grounds for suspecting to be a terrorist.[42] This avoids the need to justify an arrest by reference to a specific terrorist offence, and it gives the police greater powers than they have under PACE.[43] Access to legal advice may be delayed for up to 48 hours and in certain circumstances the police may insist that any consultation between the suspect and their lawyer is conducted in the sight and hearing of a police officer. The maximum period of detention without charge is initially 48 hours, but this may be extended by a designated judge up to a total of 28 days.[44] Reviews of detention must be conducted at not more than 12 hourly intervals.

3. Rights of the defendant

3.1. Information about the suspect's rights

On detaining a suspect, the custody officer must tell them that they have a right to have someone informed of their arrest, that they have a right to free, independent, legal advice and that they have a right to consult the PACE Codes of Practice. In

---

[39]   RIPA 2000 s5 'Serious crime' is defined as an offence for which an adult without previous convictions could reasonably be expected to be sentenced to three years' imprisonment or more, or where the conduct involves the use of violence, results in substantial financial gain or is conduct by a large number of persons in pursuit of a common purpose (RIPA 2000 s81(2) and (3)).

[40]   RIPA 2000 s17.

[41]   R v. Grant [2005] EWCA Crim 1089.

[42]   Terrorism Act 2000 s41(1). 'Terrorist' is defined in the Terrorism Act 2000 s11 and s12.

[43]   Detention of a person arrested on suspicion of being a terrorist is governed by the Terrorism Act 2000 Sch 8.

[44]   The maximum period was increased from 14 days by the Terrorism Act 2006.

addition, the suspect must be given a written notice setting out these rights and information about the arrangements for obtaining legal advice, the right to a copy of the custody record, and the caution (see below). The custody officer must then ask the suspect if they want legal advice and, if so, make arrangements for the lawyer to be contacted without delay.[45]

PACE and Code of Practice C contain detailed rules on the treatment of suspects, including the physical conditions of detention, the provision of meals, routine inspection visits and medical treatment.[46]

3.2. Right to silence and the caution

There is normally no legal obligation on a suspect to provide information to the police at the investigative stage.[47] However, failure by a suspect, on being questioned by the police or on being charged, to disclose to the police facts on which they rely in their defence at trial can lead to adverse inferences being drawn at trial if the court decides that it would have been reasonable for them to have done so.[48] The police must warn suspects of this when they arrest them and when they interview them by reading out a caution in the following terms:

> 'You do not have to say anything. But it may harm your defence if you do not mention when questioned something which you later rely on in Court. Anything you do say may be given in evidence.' (Code C § 10.5)

Whilst a person cannot be convicted on the basis of inferences without supporting evidence,[49] failure to disclose relevant facts to the police can mean that they could be convicted of an offence in circumstances where the other evidence would not, in itself, be sufficient to establish guilt beyond reasonable doubt. For example, where a person is being tried for an offence of assault, and the only witnesses are the complainant and the accused, in determining whether the accused is guilty, the court could infer from the fact that they did not tell the police that they acted in self-defence that they are not telling the truth when they put forward this defence at the trial.

This places suspects, and the lawyers who advise them, in a difficult position in deciding what information to give to the police since it may be difficult, or impossible, to determine at the investigative stage whether inferences would be drawn at trial and what the consequences of such inferences would be. Evidence suggests that the legislation on inferences from silence has led to fewer suspects

---

[45] Code C § 3.1-3.5.

[46] See especially Code of Practice C sections 8 and 9. Similar provisions relating to persons detained under the Terrorism Act 2000 are contained in Code of Practice H.

[47] In some circumstances, mostly involving companies and financial services, refusal to co-operate with investigators by providing information is a criminal offence. However, evidence obtained from compulsory disclosure cannot normally be used as evidence in a criminal trial of the person providing the disclosure.

[48] CJPOA 1994 ss34, 36 and 37.

[49] CJPOA 1994 s38(3).

remaining 'silent' at the investigative stage,[50] although it has also led defence lawyers to develop strategies such as handing in prepared statements to the police, followed by refusal of the suspect to answer police questions.[51]

Overall, the legislation on inferences from 'silence' and the subsequent jurisprudence has resulted in a 'normative expectation' that suspects will answer police questions.[52] Whilst, traditionally, formal criminal proceedings do not start until a suspect has been charged with a criminal offence, the legislation has transformed the police interview 'into a formal part of the proceedings against an accused,' but without the due process safeguards that apply at trial.[53] Thus, contrary to the normal characterisation of the criminal process in England and Wales as being adversarial, the police have increasingly been given significant inquisitorial powers that can be used to the adversarial advantage of the prosecution at trial.

3.3. Right to an interpreter

The custody officer must determine whether or not the suspect requires an interpreter and if they do, arrange for one to attend as soon as practicable in order that the suspect can be told of their rights in a language that they understand.[54] The suspect should not be interviewed without an interpreter unless this poses any of the risks set out in Code C § 11.1 (e.g. interference with evidence, harm to others).[55] Suspects who are foreign nationals may also consult with someone from their High Commission, Consulate or Embassy. Where a bilateral consular agreement has been signed, the Consulate must be informed of the suspect's detention unless the suspect is a political detainee.[56]

---

[50]   See T. Bucke, R. Street and D. Brown, *The right of silence: the impact of the Criminal Justice and Public Order Act 1994,* Home Office Research Study 199, London, Home Office, 2000. For further discussion, and specifically of the methodological problems in counting the incidence of 'silence' see M. McConville and J. Hodgson, *Custodial Legal Advice and the Right to Silence,* RCCJ Research Study No. 16, London, HMSO, 1993, p. 174.

[51]   It was accepted in *R* v. *Knight* [2003] EWCA Crim 1977 that handing a written statement to the police does amount to mentioning the facts that are set out in the statement, which has the effect of preventing inferences from being drawn.

[52]   See R. Leng, 'Silence pre-trial, reasonable expectations and the normative distortion of fact-finding,' *International Journal of Evidence and Proof,* 5 2001, No. 4, p. 240. In a number of recent cases the Court of Appeal has held that inferences from silence can be drawn even where the suspect was genuinely relying on legal advice. See *R* v. *Howell* [2003] Crim LR 405, *R* v. *Hoare and Pierce* [2004] EWCA Crim 784, and *R* v. *Beckles* [2005] 1 All ER 705.

[53]   J. Jackson, 'Silence and proof: Extending the boundaries of criminal proceedings in the United Kingdom,' *International Journal of Evidence and Proof,* 5 2001, No. 3, p. 173.

[54]   Code C § 3.5 (c)(ii) and 3.12. This is also the case for hearing impaired suspects. Guidance note 3B states that notices should be available in Welsh, and the main ethnic minority and principal European languages.

[55]   Code C § 13.

[56]   Code C § 7.

3.4. Right to be informed about the reason for arrest

It is a general principle that the police must explain to the suspect the reason for their arrest, and if they fail to do so the arrest is rendered unlawful.[57] This information need only provide an indication of the offence and when and where it was committed, and the police are not required to disclose the basis for their suspicion. At the police station, the custody officer must set out in the custody record the reasons for the arrest and must inform the suspect as soon as practicable of the grounds on which detention is authorised.[58] This requirement does not extend to requiring the record to show the details of any evidence held by the police.

3.5. Legal assistance

All people who are arrested and held in custody by the police are entitled to consult a solicitor (i.e. a lawyer) in private at any time during their detention.[59] This applies whether or not the suspect is a British citizen. This means that, in addition to consulting a solicitor at the police station prior to a police interview, a suspect is also entitled to have a solicitor present when they are being interviewed by the police. Access to a solicitor may be delayed for up to 36 hours on the authority of a superintendent (a senior police officer), but the circumstances in which they can grant such authority are limited.[60] Except where access to a lawyer has been delayed under these provisions, once a suspect has requested legal advice they cannot normally be interviewed until they have received advice.[61] Although statistics on legal advice are not routinely collected, about 40% of suspects request legal advice.[62]

Although the defence lawyer is able to consult extensively with their client, they are not permitted access to the file of evidence, nor may they play any part in the police investigation. As noted earlier, the defence case is constructed

---

[57]   Christie v. Leachinsky [1947] AC 573 and PACE s28.

[58]   PACE 1984 s37 and Code C § 3.4.

[59]   PACE s58.

[60]   The grounds for refusing this right are that the officer has a reasonable grounds for believing that evidence or persons will be harmed, other suspects will be alerted, the recovery of property will be hindered or the recovery of drug trafficking money or a confiscation order will be frustrated. The case of R v. Samuel [1988] QB 615, makes it clear that custodial legal advice is a fundamental right and should only be delayed in exceptional circumstances. Research in the late 1980s found that delay was authorised in about 1 % of cases, but later research found no cases where a request for legal advice had been formally refused. See Bucke and Brown (n50), p. 23. However, there is evidence from the late 1980s that the police use ploys to discourage suspects from requesting, or pursuing requests for, legal advice. See A. Sanders, L. Bridges, A. Mulvaney and G. Crozier, Advice and Assistance at Police Stations and the 24 Hour Duty Solicitor Scheme, London, Lord Chancellor's Department, 1989.

[61]   Code C § 6.6.

[62]   There was a rising trend throughout the late 1980s and the 1990s, and research conducted in 1995/96 found the request rate to be 40 %. See T. Bucke and D. Brown, In police custody: police powers and suspects' rights under the revised PACE codes of practice, Home Office Research Study 174, London, Home Office, 1997.

independently of the prosecution and whilst the suspect is required increasingly to participate in the police enquiry, they have no right to ask that certain investigative acts be carried out.[63]

3.6. Legal Aid

Legal advice is available free to people arrested and held in police custody,[64] and is not subject to a means test, although it may only be provided free by a solicitor with a contract with the Legal Services Commission or by a Public Defender.[65] The costs of legal advice at the investigative stage cannot be recovered from the suspect even if they are subsequently prosecuted and convicted of an offence. A suspect may choose their own solicitor, but to cater for suspects who do not know of a solicitor, or where their chosen solicitor is not available, there is a national police station duty solicitor scheme designed to ensure that legal advice is always available. The contracting arrangements require solicitors' firms to take part in the duty solicitor scheme and, in addition, most solicitors' firms operate an out-of-hours call-out scheme for their own clients.

3.7. Right to disclosure

With regard to disclosure at the investigative stage, there is a significant difference, both in law and in practice, between the respective obligations of the police (and prosecution) and the accused. In section 3.2 it was seen that a suspect may suffer adverse consequence at trial if they do not tell the police what their defence is going to be. The disclosure obligations on the police are, by contrast, very limited. As noted in section 3.4, a person who is arrested must be told the grounds for their arrest and, if detained, must be informed of the grounds for their detention. Beyond this, the police are under no legal obligation to inform a suspect of any evidence that they have.[66] The only exception is where the police propose to hold an

---

[63] Contrast this with the model of pre-trial defence participation in France, discussed in J. Hodgson, *French Criminal Justice: A Comparative Account of the Investigation and Prosecution of Crime in France*, Oxford, Hart Publishing, 2005, ch. 4.

[64] It is also available free to 'volunteers,' i.e. persons who attend the police station voluntarily in connection with the investigation of an offence.

[65] Most legal aid criminal defence lawyers are in private practice, but the government has been piloting a Public Defender Service which currently has eight offices. Legal aid expenditure on police station advice and assistance currently costs about £ 180 million per annum, and as a result of concern about expenditure, a series of measures intended to reduce expenditure are currently being implemented. Although all persons arrested and detained at police station will continue to have a right to free legal advice, in some cases it is limited to advice on the telephone only, and their choice of lawyer may be limited.

[66] This was confirmed in *R v. Imran and Hussain* [1997] Crim LR 754. See also *R v. Thirlwell* [2002] EWCA Crim 2703. In *R v. Ara* [2001] 4 All ER 559 the Divisional Court did impose a limited disclosure obligation on the police, but only to the extent of disclosing the contents of a previous police interview of the suspect so that the suspect's lawyer could advise about whether to consent to a caution (as an alternative to prosecution).

identification procedure, such as a video identification parade, in which case they must disclose the description given by any witness who is to attend the procedure.[67]

In practice, the police frequently do disclose to suspects and their lawyers some information about the evidence that they have, although this depends on the nature of the case and the attitude of the police officers concerned. An important factor affecting the police decision on disclosure is the law relating to inferences from 'silence.' A court can only draw an inference from the suspect's 'silence' if it would be reasonable to expect them to have disclosed facts relating to their defence to the police. The Court of Appeal has decided in a number of cases that failure by the police to disclose to the suspect information about the evidence that is available to them can mean that it would not be reasonable to expect the accused to have disclosed their defence to the police.[68] However, even very limited information may be enough to render unreasonable a decision by the suspect not to disclose relevant facts to the police. Some police forces have a policy, particularly in more serious cases, of pursuing a strategy of 'phased disclosure' designed to release information gradually in response to the suspect's answers to questions in the police interview, and to seek to ensure that inferences will be drawn if the suspect fails to provide full disclosure of their defence. In any event, it is normally impossible for the suspect, or their lawyer, to be confident that the police have disclosed all relevant evidence.

3.8. Special protection of juveniles and other vulnerable persons

As part of their role in ensuring the welfare and appropriate treatment of those detained, the custody officer must determine whether the suspect is, or might be, in need of medical treatment, and whether they require help with documentation, an interpreter, or an appropriate adult.[69] Where a suspect is a juvenile (i.e. under 17 years of age) or is, or may be, mentally disordered or otherwise mentally vulnerable, the custody officer must arrange for an appropriate adult[70] to attend the police station, and the suspect must normally only be interviewed in their presence.[71] The appropriate adult is normally a parent, guardian or social worker, and must not be a police officer or a person employed by the police.[72]

---

[67]   PACE Code of Practice D § 3.1.
[68]   See *R* v. *Condron* [1997] 1 WLR 827, and *R* v. *Argent* (1997) 2 Cr App R 27.
[69]   Code of Practice C § 3.5.
[70]   Code C § 11.17 states that if an appropriate adult is present at a police interview they must be told that they are not expected to act simply as an observer, and that the purpose of their presence is to advise the person being interviewed, to observe whether the interview is being conducted properly and fairly, and to facilitate communication with the person being interviewed.
[71]   See further J. Hodgson, 'Vulnerable Suspects and the Appropriate Adult,' (November) *Criminal Law Review*, 1997, p. 785-95 and E. Cape, *supra* note 12, ch. 11.
[72]   Code C § 1.7.

4.   Impact of the investigative stage on the trial

In the vast majority of cases, over 90 %, the defendant pleads guilty, and as a result evidence is never disclosed to or scrutinised by a court. This fact reinforces both the importance of the investigative stage, since it will frequently determine the outcome of the case, and the significance of the role of the defence lawyer, since in most cases they will be the only legally trained person, other than a prosecutor, who assesses whether there is sufficient prosecution evidence to establish the guilt of the accused.

If the accused pleads not guilty, the prosecution and defence decide what evidence to put before the court and, in line with adversarial theory, judges have almost no role in determining what evidence should be put before the court, and only a limited residual role in deciding how witnesses should be questioned.[73] In general, any relevant information that is obtained at the investigative stage can be put before the court, subject to certain evidential rules such as the rule against hearsay evidence. In most trials the prosecution will call police witnesses to give evidence of what was said in the police interview(s) and sometimes they will play the audio-recording of the interview(s) to the court. The prosecution can also use physical evidence obtained from the defendant such as fingerprints, DNA samples and photographs, and can adduce evidence of identification obtained from an identification procedure conducted at the police station or from CCTV. In addition, they can adduce evidence from witnesses which, under the principle of orality, must normally be given at the trial by the witness in person.[74]

The general rule regarding the admission at trial of evidence that has been obtained illegally or in an unfair way is that it is admissible.[75] However, this is subject in particular to two evidential rules. First, although evidence of a confession[76] made by the accused is normally admissible at trial,[77] if the accused suggests that it was obtained by oppression or in circumstances likely to render it unreliable, then it is not admissible unless the court is satisfied beyond reasonable doubt that it was not so obtained.[78] This potentially provides a powerful safeguard against police misconduct in securing confessions, although courts are sometimes reluctant to exclude evidence of confessions under these provisions. Confession evidence has, for example, been excluded where the police interviewed a man with learning difficulties for 13 hours spread over five days in a manner that was bullying and verbally threatening,[79] but not in a case where the police were 'rude

---

73   *R* v. *Hulusi and Purvis* 58 Cr App R 378.
74   There are exceptions where the parties agree (Criminal Justice Act 1967 s9), or where, for a variety of reasons, a witness is unavailable (Criminal Justice Act 2003 s116). There are also a number of special provisions for vulnerable witnesses enabling them to give evidence by live television link or, in some cases, by pre-recorded video.
75   *R* v. *Sang* [1980] AC 402.
76   Defined by PACE 1984 s82(1) as including 'any statement wholly or partly adverse to the person who made it, whether made to a person in authority or not and whether made in words or otherwise.'
77   PACE 1984 s76(1).
78   PACE 1984 s76(2).
79   *R* v. *Paris, Abdullahi and Miller* (1993) 97 Cr App R 99.

and discourteous.'[80] The mere fact that a suspect was withdrawing from the effects of drugs at the time of the police interview may not be treated by the courts as rendering a confession unreliable, but such a confession may be excluded if the police deliberately denied such a suspect access to a doctor.[81]

The second major evidential rule gives judges a discretion to exclude any prosecution evidence (including evidence of confession) if, having regard to all the circumstances including the circumstances in which it was obtained, they are satisfied that the admission of the evidence would have such an adverse effect on the fairness of the proceedings that it ought not be admitted.[82] Judicial approaches to this rule vary considerably, but generally prosecution evidence should be excluded if it was obtained as a result of a significant and substantial breach of procedural rules and admission of the evidence would have a serious adverse effect on the fairness of the trial.[83] For example, evidence has been excluded where a suspect was wrongly denied access to legal advice before being interviewed by police,[84] but in a similar case the Court of Appeal decided that the trial judge was right not to exclude evidence where the accused knew what their rights were.[85]

5. The role of the defence lawyer

In the early years following the introduction in 1986 of the statutory right to legal advice at the investigative stage, there was evidence that the quality of provision was relatively poor.[86] Solicitors' firms[87] regularly used unqualified or semi-qualified staff to provide advice at police stations and there was confusion about the proper role of defence lawyers, particularly in police interviews. The evidence suggested that defence lawyers were frequently passive, unwilling to challenge the police, and often identified with police objectives and values. The Royal Commission on Criminal Justice, reporting in 1993,[88] was critical of the legal profession in this respect and this, amongst other things, prompted a series of initiatives and developments which are still relevant today.

---

[80]   *R v. Emmerson* (1991) 92 Cr App R 284.

[81]   *R v. Crampton* (1990) 92 Cr App R 369.

[82]   PACE 1984 s78.

[83]   *R v. Walsh* (1989) 91 Cr App R 161, and *R v. Keenan* (1989) 90 Cr App R 1. For an analysis of these provisions see P. Mirfield, *Silence, confessions and improperly obtained evidence*, Oxford, Clarendon, 1997; S. Sharpe, *Judicial Discretion and Criminal Investigation*, London, Sweet and Maxwell, 1998.

[84]   *R v. Samuel* (1988) 87 Cr App R 232.

[85]   *R v. Alladice* (1988) 87 Cr App R 380, and see also *R v. Dunford* (1990) 91 Cr App R 150. For a discussion of this case see J. Hodgson, 'Tipping the Scales of Justice: The Suspect's Right to Legal Advice,' *Criminal Law Review*, 1992, p. 854.

[86]   See McConville and Hodgson, *supra* note 50; M. McConville, *et al.*, *Standing accused: The Organisation and Practices of Criminal Defence Lawyers in Britain*, Oxford, Clarendon, 1994 and D. Brown, *supra* note 15, ch. 6.

[87]   The lawyers' profession is divided into solicitors and barristers, but generally barristers play no role at the investigative stage of the criminal process.

[88]   Royal Commission on Criminal Justice, *Report*, Cm 2263, London, HMSO, 1993, p. 35.

A number of steps were taken to clarify the role of defence lawyers in advising clients at police stations and to improve quality. Code of Practice C was amended so that it contained a positive description of the defence lawyer's role, as follows:

'The solicitor's only role in the police station is to protect and advance the legal rights of their client. On occasions this may require the solicitor to give advice which has the effect of the client avoiding giving evidence which strengthens a prosecution case. The solicitor may intervene in order to seek clarification, challenge an improper question to their client or the manner in which it is put, advise the client not to reply to particular questions, or if they wish to give their client further legal advice.'[89]

The solicitors' professional body, the Law Society, published Standards of Performance, which set out in detail the scope of the solicitor's role at the police station and the standard to which it should be performed[90] and this was, in effect, adopted by the Legal Aid Board which had responsibility for administering the legal aid scheme. In addition, the selection mechanism for duty solicitors was improved.

In order to deal with the problem of non-qualified staff providing police station advice, the Law Society and the Legal Aid Board jointly introduced an accreditation scheme for non-solicitors, which required police station advisers to meet minimum standards, and assessed candidates by an innovative form of assessment involving a self-critical portfolio of cases worked upon, a written knowledge-based test, and a role-play (known as a critical incidents test) designed to assess relevant skills. Research evidence demonstrated that this led to an improvement in standards,[91] and the accreditation scheme has since been extended to all trainee solicitors who advise at police stations, and duty solicitors, and more recently to all defence solicitors providing state funded police station services. The Legal Services Commission (which took over responsibility for legal aid from the Legal Aid Board) is currently developing peer review as a mechanism for assuring and improving standards, although it should be noted that pressure on legal aid funding is currently placing these improvements at risk.

One important factor that has not been addressed is that of the investigative powers of defence lawyers. As noted earlier, the police have extensive investigative powers but only limited obligations of disclosure, especially at the investigative stage of the criminal process. Defence lawyers can carry out their own investigations and interview any potential witnesses, but they have no formal powers in this respect and, in practice, public funding for defence investigation is limited. Normally, investigation by defence lawyers consists of little more than the interview of witnesses who are willing to co-operate.

---

89   Code C Note for Guidance 6D.
90   The current Standards of Performance are available at <http://www.lawsociety.org.uk //documents/downloads/panelsclasproceduresv12004.pdf>.
91   L. Bridges and S. Choongh, *Improving Police Station Legal Advice*, London, The Law Society and the Legal Aid Board, 1998.

6.   Bibliography

A. Ashworth & M. Redmayne, *The Criminal Process*, Oxford, Oxford University Press, 3rd ed., 2005.

J. Baldwin, 'Police Interview Techniques: Establishing Truth or Proof?,' 33 *British Journal of Criminology,* 3 1993, p. 325.

F. Belloni & J. Hodgson, *Criminal Injustice: An Evaluation of the Criminal Justice Process in Britain*, Basingstoke, Macmillan, 2000.

K. Bottomley, *et al.*, *Safeguarding the Rights of Suspects in Police Custody*, unpublished paper presented to the British Criminology Conference, Bristol, 1989.

L. Bridges and S. Choongh, *Improving Police Station Legal Advice*, London, The Law Society and the Legal Aid Board, 1998.

D. Brown, *PACE Ten Years on: a Review of the Research, Home Office Research Study 155*, London, Home Office, 1997.

T. Bucke and D. Brown, *In police custody: police powers and suspects' rights under the revised PACE codes of practice*, Home Office Research Study 174, London, Home Office, 1997.

T. Bucke, R. Street and D. Brown, *The right of silence: the impact of the Criminal Justice and Public Order Act 1994*, Home Office Research Study 199, London, Home Office, 2000.

E. Cape, 'Detention Without Charge: What Does "Sufficient Evidence to Charge" Mean?,' *Criminal Law Review,* 874 1999.

E. Cape, *Regulation of Investigatory Powers Act 2000 Current Law Statutes* (Annotated Edition), London, Sweet and Maxwell, 2000.

E. Cape, 'Assisting and Advising Defendants Before Trial,' in M. McConville & G. Wilson (eds), *The Handbook of The Criminal Justice Process*, Oxford, Oxford University Press, 2002.

E. Cape, 'The Rise (and Fall) of a Criminal Defence Profession,' *Criminal Law Review,* 401 2004.

E. Cape, *Defending Suspects at Police Stations*, London, Legal Action Group, 5th ed., 2006.

D. Clark, *The Investigation of Crime*, Oxford, Oxford University Press, 3rd ed., 2004.

R. Ede & E. Shepherd, *Active Defence,* London, Law Society, 2nd ed., 2000.

J. Hodgson, 'Tipping the Scales of Justice: The Suspect's Right to Legal Advice,' *Criminal Law Review,* 1992, p. 854.

J. Hodgson, 'Vulnerable Suspects and the Appropriate Adult,' (November) *Criminal Law Review,* 1997, p. 785.

J. Hodgson, *French Criminal Justice: A Comparative Account of the Investigation and Prosecution of Crime in France,* Oxford, Hart Publishing, 2005, ch. 4.

J. Jackson, 'Silence and proof: Extending the boundaries of criminal proceedings in the United Kingdom,' *International Journal of Evidence and Proof,* 5 2001, No. 3, p. 173.

R. Leng, 'Silence pre-trial, reasonable expectations and the normative distortion of fact-finding,' *International Journal of Evidence and Proof,* 5 2001, No. 4, p. 240.

M. McConville, A. Sanders & R. Leng, *The Case for the Prosecution,* London, Routledge, 1991.

M. McConville & J. Hodgson, *Custodial Legal Advice and the Right to Silence,* London, HMSO, 1993.

M. McConville, J. Hodgson, L. Bridges & A. Pavlovic, *Standing Accused: The Organisation and Practices of Criminal Defence Lawyers in Britain,* Oxford, Clarendon, 1994.

P. Mirfield, *Silence, confessions and improperly obtained evidence,* Oxford, Clarendon, 1997.

A. Sanders, L. Bridges, A. Mulvaney & G. Crozier, *Advice and Assistance at Police Stations and the 24 Hour Duty Solicitor Scheme,* London, Lord Chancellor's Department, 1989.

A. Sanders & R. Young, *Criminal Justice,* Oxford, Oxford University Press, 3rd ed., 2006.

S. Sharpe, *Judicial Discretion and Criminal Investigation,* London, Sweet and Maxwell, 1998.

E. Shepherd, *Police Station Skills for Legal Advisers: Accreditation Manual and Practical Reference,* London, Law Society, 3rd ed., 2004.

M. Zander, *The Police and Criminal Evidence Act 1984,* London, Sweet and Maxwell, 5th ed., 2005.

Thomas Weigend
Franz Salditt

THE INVESTIGATIVE STAGE OF THE CRIMINAL PROCESS IN GERMANY

1.   Introduction

The main source of criminal procedure law in Germany is the Code of Criminal Procedure (CCP). The CCP dates from 1877. It has since frequently been revised and amended, but its main structure has remained in place. German criminal procedure law generally follows the 'inquisitorial' approach, which means that the court is ultimately responsible for finding relevant facts and collecting incriminating as well as exonerating evidence. In the pre-trial phase, the former investigating judge has, however, been replaced by the public prosecutor (*Staatsanwalt*, literally: State's attorney), who the law casts in a similar neutral position by requiring them to collect evidence both in favour and to the detriment of the suspect's interests (§ 160 § 2 CCP).

The German Constitution (Basic Law, BL) of 1949 also has a significant impact on criminal procedure law. With few exceptions,[1] the Constitution does not grant suspects and defendants specific rights, but article 20 § 3 BL declares that the executive as well as the judiciary is bound by the law and by statutes. Basic tenets of criminal procedure law, such as the presumption of innocence and the privilege against self-incrimination, are deemed to be inherent in the principle of the 'rule of law' (*Rechtsstaatsprinzip*).

The Constitution, moreover, guarantees certain individual rights that are likely to be infringed in the criminal process, such as the secrecy of telecommunications (art. 10 BL) and the inviolability of the home (art. 13 BL). 'Inviolability' in this context means that the citizen has the right to keep their home or telecommunications private and that the state must not intrude into the protected spheres. In addition to these specifically protected areas of privacy, a general right of privacy is inferred from the protection of the dignity of the person (art. 1 § 1 BL)[2]

---

[1]   According to art. 101 BL, exceptional courts are prohibited and no person can be brought before a court the jurisdiction of which has not been established in advance. Art. 103 BL entitles every person to be heard in court, and art. 104 BL grants *habeas corpus* protection against deprivation of liberty without a judicial warrant.

[2]   Art. 1 § 1 BL reads: 'The dignity of the person is sacrosanct. It is the duty of all State powers to respect and protect it.'

in connection with the right of every person to develop their personality (art. 2 § 1 BL). This general right of privacy includes, for example, a right not to have one's private speech recorded on tape[3] and not to have one's private diaries read.[4] The fact that privacy rights are deemed 'inviolable' should not, however, be taken at face value. The state is absolutely precluded from encroaching on the intimate details of people's lives; it would thus be impermissible, even for the purpose of detecting serious crime, to install a hidden microphone under the bed of a married couple.[5] Such intrusion would be deemed to violate human dignity, which is probably the only value absolutely protected under the Basic Law. But beyond that core area, the German constitution itself specifies circumstances under which, for example, the secrecy of telecommunications or the privacy of the home can be limited if a statute so provides (see art. 10 § 2, art. 13 § 2 – 5 BL). Even personal privacy is not immune to restriction. Although the constitution contains no specific provision in that respect, the Federal Constitutional Court has ruled that privacy rights can be superseded by other important interests, such as an effective judicial process.[6] According to long-standing jurisprudence of the Federal Constitutional Court, the executive can infringe a human right guaranteed by the constitution only if three conditions have been met: the act in question must be apt to secure a legitimate objective; the act must be the least intrusive means to secure that objective; and the infringement must not be out of proportion to the importance of the objective sought.

The Federal Constitutional Court,[7] located in Karlsruhe, has jurisdiction in all matters concerning individual rights granted by the Constitution. Any person who feels that their constitutional rights have been violated or unlawfully abridged by an act of the executive or judiciary can, after having exhausted the ordinary judicial remedies, appeal to the Federal Constitutional Court. That court, therefore, frequently rules on issues of criminal procedure law.

The European Convention on Human Rights (ECHR) was incorporated into national law in 1952. The ECHR does not have constitutional status but is treated as an 'ordinary' statute. Although the Federal Constitutional Court does not have formal jurisdiction to decide on the compatibility of State acts or court judgements with the ECHR, the Federal Constitutional Court does take that document, as well as the jurisprudence of the European Court of Human Rights (ECtHR), into account when interpreting parallel provisions of the German Constitution or of national criminal procedure law. Since the German Constitution lacks specifics in matters of criminal procedure and is hence quite flexible in that regard, there are no obvious conflicts between the text of the ECHR and German constitutional law. In fact, the traditional assumption had been that national German law comprises all guarantees of the ECHR, and more. This assumption has been shattered by a few cases

---

3   See 34 *Entscheidungen des Bundesverfassungsgerichts* 379.
4   See 80 *Entscheidungen des Bundesverfassungsgerichts* 367.
5   See 109 *Entscheidungen des Bundesverfassungsgerichts* 279.
6   See, for example, 80 *Entscheidungen des Bundesverfassungsgerichts* 367.
7   Most German States also have constitutional courts, but they do not have jurisdiction over individual complaints.

Germany has recently lost before the ECtHR, for example, concerning the permissible duration of pre-trial custody[8] and the right of a suspect to inspect the file when they wish to challenge pre-trial custody.[9] In recent years, German courts have increasingly looked to the Strasbourg jurisprudence when deciding on relevant issues of German criminal procedure law, but they have not always followed the relevant jurisprudence of the ECtHR.[10]

The presumption of innocence is not explicitly guaranteed in the Code of Criminal Procedure, but article 6 § 2 ECHR is directly applicable law in Germany. The presumption of innocence is recognized as a guiding principle of constitutional status preventing state agencies from treating a mere suspect as being guilty of a crime and thus precluding, for example, the imposition of pre-trial custody as a means of punishment. According to the majority view, the presumption of innocence does not apply to the media. Police and prosecutors should, nevertheless, refrain from disclosing the personal data of suspects before trial unless there is a special legitimate public interest in the alleged offence or in the identity of the suspect (as when a prominent politician is suspected of a criminal offence).

2. Police powers in the investigative stage

2.1. Relations between prosecutor, police and defence

According to § 152 and § 160 CCP, any criminal investigation is conducted by the public prosecutor's office.[11] In reality, prosecutors rarely perform investigative measures but leave that to the police. Only in serious cases, especially those arousing the interest of the public and the media, or those falling within the expertise of specialised prosecutors' offices (that exist, for example, in relation to economic crime), is the prosecutor likely to take the more active role suggested by the legal allocation of authority, actively working with the police and supervising their investigations. The police are organised independently of the prosecutor's office – they report to the Ministry of the Interior rather than the Ministry of Justice – but they are obliged, in the criminal process, to carry out requests and orders of the prosecutor (§ 161 § 1 CCP). In routine cases, however, prosecutors are unlikely to even know that there is an ongoing investigation before the police have concluded it and deem the case 'solved.' The police rely on their authority to take

---

8   ECtHR 5 July 2001, *Erdem* v. *Germany*, No. 38321/97.
9   ECtHR 13 February 2001, *Lietzow* v. *Germany*, No. 24479/94.
10   See, e.g., 45 *Entscheidungen des Bundesgerichtshofes in Strafsachen* 321 (1999) (discussing at length the decision of the ECtHR in *Teixeiro de Castro* v. *Portugal* concerning the violation of fair trial by use of an *agent provocateur*. The German court found a reduction of sentence to be sufficient compensation for the entrapped defendant).
11   § 152 § 1 CCP provides that the public prosecutor's office is called upon to file criminal accusations; and § 160 § 1 CCP obliges the prosecutor's office to investigate the facts whenever it has learned of the suspicion that a criminal offence may have been committed. The Code of Criminal Procedure refers to the 'public prosecutor's office' (*Staatsanwaltschaft*), which is conceived of as an institution acting through its – interchangeable – employees. In the text, we will instead use the shorter expression 'prosecutor.'

the immediately necessary first steps in an investigation (§ 163 § 1 CCP), stretching the concept that includes all investigatory measures not requiring special judicial authorization.

Germany no longer has the office of investigating judge (*Untersuchungsrichter*), which existed until 1975.[12] A specially designated judge (called *Ermittlungsrichter*, or Judge of the investigation) of the local court of the community in which the act of investigation is to be carried out is in charge of authorizing investigatory measures that invade the liberty or private sphere of individuals, e.g., searches, seizures, pre-trial detention and surveillance of telecommunications. The *Ermittlungsrichter* can also interrogate the suspect as well as witnesses and inspect real evidence before trial (with a view to conserving the results of these acts for the trial), but they can do so only on the prosecutor's request. The police normally[13] cannot approach the *Ermittlungsrichter* directly but have to ask the prosecutor to file the requisite motion.

Defence lawyers, to the extent they become active before trial, will mainly deal with the prosecutor, asking for inspection of the case file. The police, although they actually put together the file, cannot grant the defence inspection. The defence can also request the prosecutor (but not the judge) to take additional evidence, but the prosecutor will do so only if they deem the evidence in question relevant at this stage of the proceedings.

2.2. *Arrest and Pre-trial Custody*

In Germany, the arrest of a suspect (i.e., the seizing and taking of the suspect to the police station or courthouse) is not the normal method of initiating the criminal process. A suspect's personal liberty can, in principle, be restricted only when that is necessary to ensure their presence at the trial.[14] Only the Judge of the investigation (or the trial court after a formal accusation has been filed) can impose pre-trial custody. The main grounds for ordering pre-trial custody are danger of flight and danger of unlawful tampering with evidence (§ 112 CCP).[15] 'Danger of flight' is often assumed when a suspect has no permanent residence or resides abroad, or if the suspect has a strong incentive to flee from the jurisdiction because the offence carries a stiff sentence. 'Tampering with the evidence' can be expected if a suspect has a strong interest, e.g., to conceal or destroy incriminating documents or to induce witnesses to falsely testify on their behalf. Making a full confession is often deemed to remove any incentive to tamper with evidence, and thus may lead to release from custody.

12　The *Untersuchungsrichter* was abolished because it was deemed to duplicate and inhibit the investigation, which had in fact been taken over by the prosecutor in the great majority of cases.

13　Except in cases of emergency (§ 165 CCP).

14　A trial cannot normally be held in the absence of the defendant (§ 230 § 1 CCP).

15　Persons suspected of having committed certain serious offences, such as murder or aggravated arson, can be held in pre-trial custody even in the absence of specific grounds (§ 112 § 3 CCP).

If one of the grounds for pre-trial custody exists or the identity of a suspect is not known, the police (or any private citizen, who can perform a so-called citizen's arrest if a member of the public catches an offender in the act of committing a crime, § 127 § 1 CCP) can provisionally arrest a suspect without a judicial warrant. The police can hold the suspect until the end of the following day[16] and can use that time to interrogate the suspect and to look for additional evidence.[17] Before the end of the day following arrest, the police must either release the suspect or bring them before the Judge of the investigation (§ 128 sec. 1 CCP).[18] The judge must inform a relative of the suspect, or a person of their confidence, of the fact that they have been placed in custody (art. 104 § 4 BL, § 114b CCP). The judge then holds a hearing with the suspect present. The Judge informs the suspect of the criminal acts of which they are suspected and grounds on which the prosecutor has applied to have them placed in pre-trial custody (§ 114a CCP). On the basis of this hearing, the judge determines whether there exist sufficient grounds for issuing a custody warrant (*Haftbefehl*) to keep the suspect in custody while the prosecutor's investigation continues. No formal accusation has been made at this point.[19]

2.3. Interrogation

Suspects can be summoned to appear before a public prosecutor (§ 163a § 3 CCP) as well as before a judge (§§ 133, 162 CCP) before trial. In either case, the suspect is obliged to appear but need not make any statement beyond providing identification. The police can approach any person and ask questions but cannot compel a suspect (or anyone else) to appear or even to speak to them; any conversation the suspect may have with the police is to be entirely voluntary. Police summons forms do not emphasize this fact but tend to create the impression that a police summons must be complied with. Because many people are unaware of their right to silence, the Code of Criminal Procedure provides that the police as well as a prosecutor or judge must, in advance of any interrogation,[20] inform a suspect of

[16]   The maximum period of police detention without judicial authorization is thus 47 hours and 59 minutes, if a suspect is arrested at 12:01 a.m.
[17]   See *Bundesgerichtshof* Judgement of 17 November 1989 in 10 *Neue Zeitschrift für Strafrecht* 195 (1990) (declaring that the police need not present the suspect to the judge as soon as possible but can use the time provided by the Code to conduct further enquiries).
[18]   If the suspect has been arrested outside the jurisdiction of the Judge of the investigation, a local judge provisionally examines the identity of the suspect and the legitimacy of the warrant, making contact with the Judge of the investigation if necessary (§ 115a CCP).
[19]   Only when the prosecutor determines that they have collected all necessary information and evidence will they decide whether to file a formal accusation. A suspect can thus spend several months in custody while the investigation continues, and sometimes that the suspect will later be released without a formal accusation ever having been filed.
[20]   There is some dispute as to what exactly constitutes an 'interrogation.' The courts require a certain amount of formality for an interrogation. It is not uncommon for police to 'talk with' a suspect or witness informally before initiating a formal interrogation by giving the proper warnings of the right to remain silent. It is not entirely clear whether information obtained in the course of such informal 'talks' can later be introduced as evidence, but generally a suspect
→

their right to remain silent (§§ 136 § 1, 2nd sent. 163a § 4 CCP). If the suspect has not been made aware of their right to remain silent, any ensuing statement is inadmissible at trial unless the defendant explicitly or tacitly consents to its use.[21] If the suspect, after receiving the required information, states that they do not wish to make a statement the interrogator can, in any manner they find appropriate, explain to the suspect that making a statement may be advantageous, but the interrogator must not exert any verbal or other pressure on the suspect to make them change their mind. No adverse inference may be drawn from the fact that the suspect refused to make a statement;[22] this means that silence cannot be used as an indication of guilt, nor can it be regarded as a factor aggravating a forthcoming sentence, if there is eventually a conviction.[23] (For the right to a lawyer, see 3.6, *infra*).

The Code of Criminal Procedure specifically prohibits the use of certain means of interrogation; this prohibition applies to interrogation of suspects as well as witnesses (§§ 69 § 3, 136a CCP). Whenever one of the prohibited means has been employed in an interrogation its results cannot be used as evidence even if the interrogated person subsequently gives their consent (§ 136a § 3 CCP). Prohibited means of interrogation include physical abuse, psychological torment, hypnosis, sleep deprivation, administering drugs, deceit and illegal threats and promises. Courts have broadly construed the prohibition on using such means; for example, a confession elicited by a false statement on the part of the police that they already had sufficient incriminating evidence against the suspect has been ruled inadmissible because of 'deceit.'[24]

Interrogations are not routinely tape-recorded or documented on videotape, although the Code mentions this option with respect to witnesses (§ 58a CCP). Normally the police draft a written protocol of the interrogation, and the suspect reads and signs it. The protocol goes into the prosecutor's file. Although the transcript of a police or prosecutorial interrogation cannot be read into evidence at the trial,[25] the presiding judge can confront the defendant with their prior statements by reading the transcript directly to the defendant. It is also possible to hear the interrogating officer as a (hearsay) witness[26] as to the contents of the statement made by the suspect or witness.

Non-suspects can be summoned to testify before a public prosecutor or a judge (§§ 133, 161a § 1 CCP), and can be physically compelled to appear. If they refuse to testify without having a legal privilege they can be fined and even held in

---

can block the introduction of any evidence they have given to a police officer before they were informed of their rights.

21 See 38 *Entscheidungen des Bundesgerichtshofes in Strafsachen* 214.

22 The fact that a suspect *selectively* answers the questions put to them can, according to the courts, be used in evaluating the overall credibility of their statements if their responses indicate evasiveness rather than mere inadvertence.

23 A confession is, by contrast, often cited as a factor in mitigation by sentencing courts.

24 See 35 *Entscheidungen des Bundesgerichtshofes in Strafsachen* 328.

25 Confessions contained in the protocol of a *judicial* interrogation can be used as documentary evidence at trial even against the defendant's will (§ 254 § 1 CCP).

26 In German evidence law, there is no general rule against admitting hearsay evidence.

custody, for a maximum period of six months, until they fulfil their obligation to testify (§ 70 § 2, 3, § 161a § 2 CCP).

2.4. Coercive Methods of Investigation

The public prosecutor responsible for conducting the pre-trial investigation needs, with few exceptions, judicial authorisation for any investigatory measure infringing upon a citizen's liberty or privacy rights. This applies especially to any deprivation of liberty, such as arrest or pre-trial custody, but also to invasions of personal privacy, legally protected communications and private homes. For such measures, including examination of a person's body, searches, seizures, wiretaps and surveillance of conversations, the prosecutor is obliged to apply to the Judge of the investigation (see 2.1, *supra*) for prior authorization. The judge normally determines the permissibility of the measure *ex parte*, that is, without hearing from the suspect or their lawyer, because in most cases the measure (for example, an arrest or a search for contraband) could be frustrated if the suspect was made aware of it before it is carried out. The judge does not have discretion but must issue the order if its legal requirements have been met. Judicial search warrants must precisely identify the suspected offence, the persons and objects to be searched as well as the items (pieces of evidence or objects to be confiscated as contraband or illegally acquired gains) the search is designed to discover. This requirement, frequently neglected in practice, is meant to protect citizens from unlimited invasions of their personal belongings, homes and places of business.[27]

Prior judicial authorization of arrest, searches, seizures, examinations of the body and telecommunications surveillance[28] may be dispensed with when there is a 'danger in delay,' that is, where the purpose of the measure would be frustrated if it had to be postponed until a judge has had the opportunity to act. Surveys have shown that the vast majority of searches and seizures are conducted where the 'danger in delay' clause is invoked. The Federal Constitutional Court has criticized this practice and has required the police to precisely document the reasons for acting without judicial authorization; if the police could easily have waited until a judge was available and falsely claimed exigent circumstances, a search or seizure conducted without judicial warrant is deemed unconstitutional.[29] The Federal Constitutional Court has not yet ruled on whether the unconstitutionality of a search results in the inadmissibility of its results. At present, it is unlikely that a

---

[27]   Prosecutors have sometimes applied for and obtained a judicial search and seizure warrant and then kept it 'in reserve' only to use it much later. This practice has been condemned by the Federal Constitutional Court as violating the basic idea of judicial review. The Court declared that a search warrant automatically loses force after six months; *Bundesverfassungsgericht, Neue Juristische Wochenschrift* 1997, p. 2165.

[28]   With respect to surveillance of telecommunications and of conversations outside a home, provisional measures cannot be taken by the police but only by the prosecutor, and they lose force after three days; §§ 100b § 1, 100f § 2 CCP.

[29]   See 103 *Entscheidungen des Bundesverfassungsgerichts* 142. The Federal Constitutional Court has also called for the creation of judicial standby services, permitting judicial review of requests for intrusive investigation methods even at night and on weekends.

court would exclude evidence acquired without a necessary warrant unless the police had acted in blatant disregard of the law.[30]

If an object has been seized without prior judicial authorization, the affected citizen can subsequently petition the court for a determination of the lawfulness of the act, and if the seizure was not legal the object must be returned (§ 98 § 2 CCP). The courts have, by analogy, extended this rule to other instances of infringements of individual rights by the police or prosecutors acting without a warrant, for example, searches and examinations of the body.

It should be noted, however, that prior judicial authorization of intrusive acts of investigation has little practical effect. Because the judge must decide on the basis of the police report alone and does not usually hear the affected citizen they have little reason to refuse to issue a warrant requested by the prosecutor. Only if it is blatantly evident that there are no grounds for suspecting a crime or that the warrant sought is overbroad in scope will a judge deny the prosecutor's request.

2.5. Secret Investigative Methods

The Code of Criminal Procedure of 1877 provided for the interception of mail (§§ 99, 100 CCP). Consequent to the development of other methods of secretly obtaining information, the Code has since been amended several times to allow for the surveillance of telecommunications (§ 100a CCP), for the installation of hidden microphones (§§ 100c, 100f para.2 CCP), for video surveillance (§ 100f § 1 CCP) and for the activities of undercover police officers (§ 110a-110e CCP). In addition to examining the body of a suspect (§ 81a CCP) or another person (§ 81c CCP), the Code permits the use of samples of body fluids or body parts to analyse a suspect's DNA (§ 81e CCP). Some of these measures (e.g., examination of the body) are permitted in any criminal investigation if needed to supply evidence; others, especially the surveillance of telecommunications and conversations, are limited to certain categories of serious offences specifically listed in the Code. They all require judicial authorisation.[31]

2.5.1. Wiretaps

Surveillance of telecommunications is permissible under the following conditions:

- there must be some suspicion, based on facts, that a person has committed or has attempted to commit one of several offences specifically listed in § 100a CCP. The list includes serious offences ranging from murder and high treason to extortion, arson, drug offences and money laundering;

---

[30]   For an example of such a case, see the district court decision Landgericht Osnabrück in: 11 *Strafverteidiger* 152 (1991).

[31]   An exception is the use of undercover police agents, which can be authorised by the public prosecutor. However, if the undercover agent is to pursue an individualised suspicion or is expected to enter a person's private home, judicial authorisation is required (§ 110b CCP).

- an investigation of the offence by means other than telecommunications surveillance would be impossible or significantly more difficult;
- surveillance is ordered by the Judge of the investigation or, after a formal accusation has been filed, the trial court. If delay would jeopardize the success of the measure, the public prosecutor can order surveillance for a period of three days; after that time, surveillance must cease unless a judicial order has been issued. Normally, a prosecutor will directly apply to the judge for authorisation to conduct surveillance.

Generally only telephone lines used by the suspect can be placed under surveillance. If the suspect uses other persons' telephones or employs others to relay messages on their behalf these other persons' telephones can also be placed under surveillance. Surveillance can be ordered for a maximum of three months, but the order can be renewed if its prerequisites continue to exist. There is no absolute time limit for telephone surveillance, but the judge may question the legitimacy of continuing the measure if the prosecutor cannot show results after several months.

Through these conditions, the legislature has sought to limit the scope of telecommunications surveillance. The number of wiretap orders has nevertheless risen steadily over the years, partly owing to the greater number of telephones (especially mobile phones) in use. In 2004, judges ordered 30,000 telephone connections to be placed under surveillance (as compared with 5,000 in 1995).

Telecommunications surveillance is usually conducted automatically, that is, any conversation on the tapped telecommunications connection is recorded on tape. If the legal prerequisites for surveillance have been met the tape can later be used as evidence at trial.[32] Sometimes the tapes reveal evidence of offences other than those for which surveillance had been authorized, or of offences committed by other persons. Such 'chance finds' can be used as evidence if they relate to one of the offences listed in § 100a CCP (cf. § 100b § 5 CCP).

2.5.2. Surveillance of Live Conversations

In 1992, surveillance of conversations by using hidden microphones was introduced as a measure to combat the perceived threat of organized crime. This measure was originally limited so that surveillance of homes or business premises was not permitted. In 1998, the CCP was amended to cover audio-surveillance of homes and business premises, though under narrow restrictions. In 2004, the Federal Constitutional Court ruled that, even in light of these restrictions, the statute violated the constitutionally guaranteed core of personal privacy in the home[33] and voided critical parts of this legislation. A new version of the relevant § 100c CCP, introduced in 2005, still permits surveillance within private homes by the use of a

---

[32] There has been some debate as to whether tapes can also be used as evidence when the wiretap was conducted illegally, for example without a proper judicial order. The prevailing view prohibits such use at least if the police or other authorities consciously violated the law; cf. 31 *Entscheidungen des Bundesgerichtshofes in Strafsachen* 304.

[33] See 109 *Entscheidungen des Bundesverfassungsgerichts* 279.

hidden microphone. The law now limits this measure to a list of felonies and requires suspicion of a 'particularly serious' case of a listed offence. Surveillance can be authorised, by a three-judge panel of the district court, only when there is no reason to expect that it will cover conversations of core personal privacy; the law declares that conversations about past or future crimes do not belong to that protected 'core' sphere. Surveillance must immediately be stopped when a conversation touches upon the 'core' private sphere (§ 100c § 5 CCP), and protected 'core' conversations, if recorded, cannot be used as evidence and must immediately be deleted. It is not very likely that this extremely complicated legislation will prove feasible in practice; it may well lead to limiting surveillance to places of business and other semi-public places.[34]

2.6. Special Powers in Cases of Suspected Terrorism or Organised Crime

German criminal procedure law avoids reference to the vague term 'organised crime.' Special rules exist, however, for cases in which someone is suspected of belonging to or supporting a terrorist organisation as defined in § 129a Penal Code.[35] Based on that suspicion, the Judge of the investigation can authorize not only wiretaps and the use of hidden microphones (§ 100a § 1 No. 1c, § 100c § 2 No. 2 CCP) but also the search of complete buildings (§ 103 § 1, 2nd sent. CCP), the installation of checkpoints on public streets (§ 111 CCP) and the storing of data collected at border checks (§ 163d § 1 CCP). Written communication between a terrorist/terrorism suspect and their defence lawyer can be monitored (§ 148 sec. 2 CCP), and under certain circumstances any contact between the suspect and the outside world (with the exception of a special court-appointed lawyer) can be interrupted (§§ 31-38 *Einführungsgesetz zum Gerichtsverfassungsgesetz*[36]).

3. Rights of the Defendant

3.1. Information about Suspect's Rights including Right to Silence

There is no fixed point or formal act to commence criminal proceedings. The Code provides that an investigation must be initiated when there are sufficient facts to indicate that a crime has been committed (§ 152 § 2 CCP). An investigation can be (and often is) initiated before any individual suspect is known; it is, in other words, crime-related and not necessarily individualized. In the course of an investigation, various persons can become suspects and later lose that status. A person must be

---

[34] According to § 100c§ 4, 2nd sent. CCP, conversations in places of business or enterprise are, as a rule, not deemed 'core' private.

[35] According to § 129a Penal Code, terrorist organisations are characterized by their intention to commit homicide, genocide or kidnappings, or certain other offences with the special purpose of terrorising a population or of compelling a state agency or an international organisation to do an act or to refrain from doing an act.

[36] These provisions were in 1977 inserted into the Introductory Law to the Court Organisation Code of 1877.

treated as a suspect (rather than a mere witness) when there is a strong suspicion that they may have committed a criminal offence.[37] The police may have an interest in continuing to treat a 'suspicious' person as a witness, and they have some (limited) discretion in that regard. As soon as suspicion arises or gains sufficient strength, the police must inform the person what offence they are suspected of as well as of their rights as a suspect. These rights include the right to remain silent (see 2.3, *supra*) and the right to consult with a lawyer before interrogation. The suspect must also be informed of the possibility of submitting a written statement, of the right to suggest that evidence be taken on their behalf, and of the availability of victim/offender reconciliation services (§ 136 § 1 CCP).

3.2. The Right to an Interpreter

For persons who do not speak sufficient German, the court appoints an interpreter for any interrogation or court hearing (§ 185 Court Organisation Act). The same applies to translating written documents to the extent that their knowledge is necessary for the suspect or defendant to make use of their procedural rights (§ 187 § 1 Court Organisation Act). Regardless of the outcome of the proceedings, the costs of interpreters and translators are borne by the state.

3.3. The Right to Bail

Under German law, there is no general right to bail. Under the principle of proportionality the court must, however, consider whether it is possible to release a person from pre-trial custody under conditions that guarantee their continuing presence for further investigation and trial (§ 116 CCP). These conditions can (and often do) include a monetary surety. If custody has been based on the risk that the suspect may destroy or tamper with evidence, a condition of provisional release can contain an obligation not to contact certain individuals (§ 116 § 2 CCP).

3.4. Right to be Informed about the Charge

At the first interrogation, a suspect must be informed about what acts or occurrences the proceedings relate to and what provisions of the criminal law they are alleged to have violated (§ 136 § 1, 1st sent. CCP). Different opinions exist as to whether the suspect must continually be advised of changes in the offences of which they are suspected. There is, in any event, no obligation to inform the suspect of the available evidence (but see the right of the suspect to inspect the prosecution file, 3.7 *infra*).

---

[37]   See 38 *Entscheidungen des Bundesgerichtshofes in Strafsachen* 214 at 228.

3.5.   Legal Assistance

The defence has no duty to participate in any way in the prosecutor's pre-trial investigation. One of the most important tasks for a defence lawyer before trial is to gather information on the case, and at this stage the main source of information will be the client. Prior to trial, when the suspect is interrogated either by the Judge of the investigation or the prosecutor,[38] the lawyer has a right to be informed of the time of the interrogation, to be present and to ask questions (§ 168c § 1, 5, § 163a § 3 CCP). They also have a right to participate at judicial interrogations of witnesses before trial (§ 168c § 2, 5 CCP). Such interrogations rarely occur, but when they do they usually concern critical witnesses whose testimony the prosecution wishes to preserve for trial. The defence lawyer, nevertheless, remains free to ignore the invitation to attend such interrogations.

The fact that the Code of Criminal Procedure does not expressly grant the defence lawyer a similar right to be present at police interrogations has been interpreted by the courts as a denial of a right of attendance.[39] Because the suspect need not make any statement to the police, they can insist on having their lawyer present if the police want to interview them. Suspects lacking experience with the criminal justice system are usually not aware of this option, nor do they know that they can refuse to talk to the police and still submit a written statement to the prosecutor. There is, however, no right to be interviewed in person by a prosecutor, and prosecutors in routine cases leave the task of interviewing suspects and witnesses to the police unless they have a special interest or reason to get involved. A suspect has, in any event, a right to consult with a lawyer before they submit to police interrogation, and the police must inform the suspect of that right (§ 136 § 1, 2nd sentence, § 163a § 4 CCP). If this information has not been given, or if the police have denied access to a lawyer, any statement made by the suspect in an ensuing interrogation is inadmissible at trial.[40] The right to consult with a lawyer does not mean that an indigent suspect must have a lawyer appointed at this time and, therefore, a suspect who wishes to consult with a lawyer at this early time must normally pay the lawyer's fees from their own funds,[41] and most suspects do not hire a lawyer before talking with the police.

Although the Code of Criminal Procedure does not mention it, defence lawyers have a right to conduct their own investigations. The defence can even

---

[38]   The right to have a lawyer present at *prosecutorial* interrogations was introduced in 1975. Before that time, lawyers could only participate at *judicial* interrogations, the results of which could easily be transferred into the trial; interrogations by police and prosecutors were, by contrast, regarded as merely 'preparatory' acts of information-gathering without immediate evidentiary value.

[39]   It is of interest to note that a *witness* has the right to have a lawyer present during any interrogation (see 38 *Entscheidungen des Bundesverfassungsgerichts* 105 at 115 [1974]). This applies also (and especially) when the witness might incriminate themselves.

[40]   See 47 *Entscheidungen des Bundesgerichtshofes in Strafsachen* 172.

[41]   In most cities, there are free defence lawyer hotlines for arrested suspects. Even in the absence of such a service, many lawyers accept calls to intervene on behalf of indigent arrestees, expecting later to be appointed as defence lawyer by the court.

summon witnesses and experts at the trial when the court has refused to subpoena them (§ 220 CCP). In that case, the defence must make known to the court and the prosecution the name and address of the witness to be summoned in advance of the trial (§ 222 § 2 CCP).[42] The defence lawyer is not precluded from interviewing witnesses before trial, even if they are expected to later testify at the trial, but there is no legal obligation for any person to talk to a defence lawyer. The defence lawyer can conduct other enquiries as well, and they can employ private detectives and experts, but they have no compulsory authority nor can they request a judicial warrant. They cannot, for example, enter premises without the owner's permission. Defence investigations are thus limited to obtaining information offered voluntarily. Some defence lawyers are, moreover, wary of speaking with prospective witnesses lest they create the appearance of influencing the witness. The costs of any investigation by the defence must almost always be borne by the defendant – a fact that also limits the feasibility of far-reaching defence investigation.

A theoretically more promising alternative is for the defence to suggest to the prosecutor or the Judge of the investigation that they take certain evidence that may help the defence case (§§ 163a § 2, 166 CCP). However, the prosecutor or judge will only comply with such request if they deem the suggested evidence relevant to the investigation. A refusal to hear evidence suggested by the defence does not require reasons and cannot be appealed. If the prosecutor follows the defence lawyer's suggestion and interrogates a witness, neither the suspect nor the lawyer has a right to be present and may only later learn what the witness has said. In contested cases, therefore, it is tactically advantageous for the defence to let the prosecutor's investigation run its course and to defer filing motions for exculpatory evidence to the trial. At the trial, a defence motion to hear additional evidence can be overruled by the court only on narrow legal grounds (§ 244 § 3, 5 CCP; see below).

Toward the end of the pre-trial phase, the defence lawyer will often try to persuade the public prosecutor to dismiss the case instead of filing an accusation. Defence lawyers often negotiate with prosecutors over the possibility of dismissing the case in exchange for the client paying a sum of money (§ 153a CCP); or if that fails they may try to persuade the prosecutor to file a penal order (a written draft judgement to be signed by the court; § 407 CCP) rather than a formal accusation resulting in a trial. The defence can also address the court at the 'intermediate' stage when the court examines whether there is sufficient evidence to take the case to trial, but in most cases the defence remains passive at that stage of the proceedings.

---

[42] In practice it is very rare for the defence to summon its own witnesses. If they do, the defence must offer the witness a cash advance for their witness fee and travel expenses. Defence counsel will usually request the court to call additional witnesses if they have an interest in having them testify. The court will have to comply with such a request unless the offer of witness testimony is redundant, irrelevant or otherwise inappropriate (cf. § 244 § 3 CCP; see text at 4.1, *infra*). If that is the case, the court need not hear the witness even if they have been summoned by the defence.

3.6. Compulsory Defence and Legal Aid

§ 137 CCP provides that a suspect can make use of the services of a lawyer at any time. A suspect – as is the case for any client – must, in principle, pay for their lawyer's services from their own funds. Only if the suspect is acquitted[43] will the suspect be reimbursed by the state for the lawyer's legal fees.[44] Given the fact that the great majority of criminal suspects do not have significant funds available, only a minority will be able to hire a lawyer.

Germany does not have a system of legal assistance for indigent defendants. There exists, however, a system of 'compulsory defence.' If a defendant is charged with a serious offence (with a statutory minimum of one year's imprisonment) or for some other reason faces a severe sanction, if they have spent at least three months in pre-trial custody, or if for some personal reason they lack the capacity to conduct their own defence, the trial cannot take place without a lawyer for the defence (§ 140 CCP). In any of those situations, it would be regarded as inherently unfair to even permit the defendant to conduct their own defence without professional support. The defendant will, therefore, be given a lawyer even if they do not want one, and the suspect must pay that lawyer's fees if convicted provided they have the financial means to do so. It is unusual for defendants in serious cases to refuse to co-operate with a lawyer appointed for them by the court, but if they do there is no ready solution for this conflict.

In situations where a professional defence is compulsory the suspect or defendant can hire any defence lawyer admissible under § 137 CCP. If the suspect fails to do so, either because they are unwilling to hire a lawyer or unable to pay the lawyer's fee, the presiding judge of the trial court appoints a lawyer, usually from among the lawyers practising locally with some experience in criminal cases. Before choosing a lawyer, the presiding judge must give the defendant an opportunity to nominate a lawyer to be appointed, and the presiding judge must comply with the defendant's choice unless there is good reason not do so, for example, because the nominated lawyer resides in a distant place and is therefore unable to attend an extensive trial (§ 142 § 1 CCP). In practice, suspects often approach a lawyer on their own initiative and later, being unable to pay the fee, petition the court to appoint that lawyer for them.

While a suspect can hire a lawyer at any time, court appointment of a defence lawyer, as a rule, occurs only after the public prosecutor files the accusation and a copy has been served on the defendant (§ 141 § 1 CCP). This means that there is no

---

43   If the defendant is acquitted on one or more of several criminal acts charged, the State must pay part of the attorney's fees and other necessary expenses (§ 465 § 2 CCP). The same applies if the defendant had asked for investigation of a particular issue, and the investigation discovered facts favourable to the defendant.

44   Defence lawyers' fees are regulated by statute (*Rechtsanwaltsvergütungsgesetz* - Lawyers' Fees Act - of 2004). In practice, many defence lawyers demand payment beyond the limits indicated by the Lawyers' Fees Act. This practice is legal provided that the client has agreed to the lawyer's fee in advance by written contract (§ 4 Lawyers' Fees Act). An acquitted defendant will, however, be reimbursed to the extent of the statutory fees.

general right to have a lawyer appointed in the investigation phase of the process. The prosecutor[45] is obliged, however, to request the judge to appoint a lawyer during that phase when it becomes evident that the suspect will need one, for example, when a critical witness is to be interrogated by the Judge of the investigation and the suspect will be precluded from attending (§ 141 § 3 CCP).[46]

An appointed lawyer has the same rights and duties as a lawyer hired by the defendant. They cannot, however, simply withdraw from the case if their views about trial tactics conflict with those of the defendant. Only if mutual confidence between the defendant and their lawyer is non-existent or has been seriously undermined will the presiding judge dismiss the lawyer and appoint another. Since the lawyer is obliged to preserve professional secrecy they may, however, find it difficult to apply for dismissal.[47]

3.7. Right to Disclosure

The defence lawyer's most powerful tool for gathering information on the case is the right to inspect the case file of the prosecution (which is in fact the police file). According to § 147 § 1 CCP, the defence lawyer[48] has a right to inspect the file as well as pieces of real evidence which the prosecutor will have to give to the court before trial. The prosecutor as well as the police are duty-bound to include in the file whatever information their investigation has produced, regardless of whether it favours the prosecution or the defence. Police files must not be 'edited' for the purpose of defence inspection, but they need not contain material that bears no relevance to the eventual charges, e.g., leads to persons whom the police later cleared of suspicion. In practice, police sometimes attempt to keep out of the file some highly sensitive information (e.g., names of secret police informers).

The defence inspection right exists, in principle, at any time during the investigation. The prosecutor can, however, refuse inspection before the investigation has been closed to the extent that disclosure of sensitive information could jeopardize the investigation (§ 147 § 2 CCP). The background of this rule is the fact that the defence lawyer can (and according to the majority view, must) inform their client of information obtained through inspection of the prosecutor's file. The lawyer is permitted to (and as a rule will) give a copy of the file to their client. It is left to the lawyer's discretion, however, in what manner they inform their client of the relevant facts.

---

[45] According to the majority view, the suspect cannot directly file a motion with the presiding judge to have a lawyer appointed before an accusation has been filed, nor can the presiding judge do so on their own motion.

[46] See 46 *Entscheidungen des Bundesgerichtshofes in Strafsachen* 93 (2000).

[47] Changing defence lawyers during trial is disruptive because the new lawyer can demand sufficient time to prepare for the defence, delaying the progress of the trial (cf. § 145 § 3 CCP).

[48] The right to inspect the file is limited to the lawyer. The defendant, personally, can only ask the prosecutor for copies from the file, and the prosecutor has some discretion with respect to such requests (§ 147 § 7 CCP).

If there is reason to believe that an individual suspect might interfere with the investigation, for example, by putting pressure on witnesses to change their testimony or to refrain from testifying in court, the prosecutor has a strong interest in withholding from the suspect relevant information on the results of the investigation. Since the prosecutor cannot control the flow of information between the defence lawyer and their client the prosecutor's only option is to keep the file secret, even from the lawyer, until the investigation has been closed and an accusation has been filed with the court.[49] As a rule, a suspect who has confessed to the crime will not have a motive to interfere with the investigation and in that case the prosecutor will, therefore, not block defence inspection of the file.[50] The prosecutor's decision to temporarily keep the file secret can be challenged by the defence only on very limited grounds (§ 147 § 5, 2nd sent. CCP). After the investigation has been closed, the inspection right of the defence lawyer is absolute. There is no corresponding right on the part of the prosecutor to obtain disclosure of information the defence may have gathered.

3.8.   Special Rules for Juveniles

With respect to pre-trial procedure, there exist only a few special rules concerning suspects who, due to their age (between 14 and 20 years), come under the jurisdiction of the juvenile court. Any pre-trial interrogation of the suspect has to be conducted by the prosecutor or the presiding judge of the juvenile court if the alleged offence is serious enough to warrant imprisonment (§ 44 Juvenile Court Act — *Jugendgerichtsgesetz*). 'Compulsory defence' (see 3.6, *supra*) applies whenever a juvenile younger than 18 years has been placed in pre-trial custody (§ 68 No. 4 Juvenile Court Act), and in cases where participation of a defence lawyer is not compulsory the court can at any time appoint a person to act as the juvenile's friend (*Beistand*) in court, who can speak on behalf of the juvenile (§ 69 Juvenile Court Act).

3.9.   Special Rules in Terrorism Cases

Written communication between a terrorist/terrorism suspect and their defence lawyer can be monitored (§ 148 sec. 2),[51] and under certain circumstances any contact between the suspect and the outside world (with the exception of a special

---

[49]   Some parts of the file must be immediately disclosed to the defence lawyer; this applies to transcripts of interrogations of the suspect and to statements of expert witnesses (§ 147 § 3 CCP).

[50]   This will often be different when there are several suspects involved unless all have confessed.

[51]   Monitoring must be done by a judge who is not involved in the investigation or adjudication of the case in question, and the judge must not disclose what they have discovered except in order to *prevent* commission of a serious offence (§ 148a CCP).

court-appointed lawyer) can be interrupted (§§ 31-38 *Einführungsgesetz zum Gerichtsverfassungsgesetz*).[52]

4. The impact of the investigative stage on the trial

4.1. Pre-trial and Trial Stages

The criminal process is divided into two main parts, the pre-trial investigation conducted by the public prosecutor and the trial conducted by the court. The prosecutor is obliged by law not only to investigate incriminating circumstances but also to collect evidence tending to exonerate the suspect (§ 160 § 2 CCP).

At the end of the investigation process, the prosecutor must determine whether to charge the suspect with an offence. The prosecutor is legally obliged to do so if sufficient evidence for conviction is available (§ 170 § 1 CCP), although the prosecutor can dismiss even a provable case of lesser seriousness when there is no public interest in prosecution or the suspect has made a 'penance payment' imposed by the prosecutor (§§ 153, 153a CCP). When charges have been filed the trial court will review the prosecutor's file and determine whether there is sufficient cause to make the defendant stand trial. At the same time, the defence lawyer can demand to inspect the prosecution file (§ 147 CCP).

Since the function of the pre-trial investigation is only to help the prosecutor determine whether or not to bring criminal charges, the court's judgement can generally be based only on evidence introduced at the trial. There are, nevertheless, connections between the pre-trial phase and the trial. The court can, for example, introduce as trial evidence tapes of telephone conversations obtained by legal surveillance measures conducted before trial, and any other real or documentary evidence discovered before trial.

The written protocol of the police or prosecutorial interrogation of a defendant or witness is not usually admissible as documentary evidence at the trial (§ 250 CCP). The interrogating officer can, however, testify as a hearsay witness as to what the defendant or witness had said. If the officer does not remember, the court can read the transcript of the interrogation in order to refresh the officer's memory. The transcript of pre-trial testimony given before a judge can be used as documentary evidence at trial if the witness is no longer readily available or if all parties agree (§ 251 § 2 CCP).[53] In practice, the defence does not usually agree to have transcripts read in court so that in most contested cases 'live' witnesses appear and can be interrogated by the parties.

At the trial, the defence lawyer has the right to request the court to call additional witnesses and expert witnesses if it is thought that this information will

---

[52] These provisions were inserted into the Introductory Law to the Court Organisation Code of 1877 in 1977.

[53] A confession made by the defendant before a judge can be introduced even without the defendant's agreement. The same applies to other recorded declarations of the defendant that contradict their trial testimony (§ 254 CCP).

be helpful to the client. This is a powerful weapon in the hands of the defence because the court cannot deny such request except for specific reasons listed in the Code (§ 244 § 3, 5 CCP); these reasons cover cases in which the proposed evidence would be evidently redundant or irrelevant. The fact that the defence can thus 'impose' upon the court evidence favourable to its cause may explain the fact that it has a relatively weak position before trial.

4.2. *Exclusion of illegally obtained evidence*

Evidence at the trial stage is the court's evidence, because it is the court that is responsible for collecting all evidence it needs to arrive at a judgement (§ 244 § 2 CCP).[54] 'Exclusion' of evidence in the German system thus does not mean that the court rejects evidence offered by a party; rather, the court must knowingly cast aside relevant information that it is aware of (from the prosecutor's file) when it finds and explains the judgement. In light of the importance of determining the true facts of the case, German courts are reluctant to exclude evidence unless the gravity of the procedural violation clearly outweighs the interest in proper fact-finding.

There are few specific statutory rules on the exclusion of illegally obtained evidence. According to § 136a § 3 CCP, when police or other interrogators have used prohibited means[55] any ensuing statement is inadmissible, and information from protected private conversations obtained through hidden microphones must not be used as evidence (§ 100c § 5, 3rd sent. CCP). Similarly, a suspect's statement cannot be used against their will[56] if they have not been advised of their right to remain silent before the interrogation.[57] Objects seized illegally must be returned to the rightful possessor and are thus unavailable as evidence unless the court can obtain them legally in time for the trial. In all other cases of improper evidence gathering (for example, illegal searches, wiretaps or examinations of the body), courts determine on a case-by-case basis whether the evidence obtained can be used in court. The courts tend to err in favour of using tainted evidence because they regard exclusion as an assault on their primary task of 'finding the truth' and of basing the judgement on the 'true' facts. Based on that reasoning, the Federal Court of Appeals has, for example, declared admissible the statement of a witness made before a judge before trial in circumstances where the defendant had been unable to question the witness because they had been excluded from the interrogation and no

---

[54] Parties, and in particular the prosecution, *suggest* evidence before and possibly during the trial. Yet the court is in no way limited by their suggestions but can and must summon witnesses or issue warrants to obtain documents or real evidence to the extent necessary to fulfil its task of 'finding the truth.' The court actively seeks evidence based on the information contained in the file or unfolding at the trial.

[55] See 2.3-2.6, *supra*.

[56] In this and other instances, the courts require the defence lawyer to make a timely motion to exclude in court; otherwise the defendant's right to have the evidence excluded will be deemed waived.

[57] See 38 *Entscheidungen des Bundesgerichtshofes in Strafsachen* 214.

lawyer had been appointed for them.[58] Similarly, the courts permit the fruits of illegal wiretaps (as well as of other illegal measures) to be used as evidence,[59] and they do not require exclusion where there was only a 'technical' violation of the law.[60] By contrast, blatant and arbitrary violations of legal prescriptions tend to be sanctioned by exclusion of the evidence obtained through the measure in question.[61]

5. The role of the defence lawyer

5.1. Qualification

Defence lawyers can be licensed attorneys or law teachers at public universities[62] (§ 138 CCP). A suspect or defendant can choose anyone from these two groups to be their lawyer, but at the trial the suspect cannot have more than three hired lawyers at any given time. In order to avoid conflicts of interest, co-defendants must have different lawyers (§ 146 CCP).

5.2. Role within the Justice System

Defence lawyers are regarded as organs of justice, but they must be exclusively devoted to the interests of their client. The defence lawyer is not the defendant's spokesperson or legal representative in court — their statements are therefore not automatically regarded as having been made by the defendant - but must be seen as an independent attorney speaking and acting in support of the defendant. A defendant who has a lawyer is not precluded from making statements in court and from personally interrogating witnesses (cf. § 240 § 2 CCP). The exact legal nature of the relationship between the defence lawyer and their client is a matter of dispute in German legal literature. The majority view places greater emphasis on the lawyer's role as an organ of justice than on the lawyer's contractual duties toward their client; the minority view regards the client/lawyer contract[63] as paramount but sees

---

[58]   See 46 *Entscheidungen des Bundesgerichtshofes in Strafsachen* 93 (2000). The Court ruled, however, that the evidentiary value of the witness' statement was reduced and could not be used to convict the defendant unless there was corroborating evidence.

[59]   See 32 *Entscheidungen des Bundesgerichtshofes in Strafsachen* 68 (1983). The taped conversation itself cannot be used as evidence when the wiretap was performed without proper judicial or prosecutorial authorization.

[60]   E.g., telephone surveillance conducted after the period authorised by the judge had ended; 44 *Entscheidungen des Bundesgerichtshofes in Strafsachen* 243 at 249-250 (1998); taking of a blood sample by a non-approved physician in violation of § 81a CCP; 24 *Entscheidungen des Bundesgerichtshofes in Strafsachen* 125 (1971). See also *Bundesverfassungsgericht* in: 22 *Strafverteidiger* 113 (2002) ruling that a wrongful search does not make seizure of an object found illegal if the search could have been conducted with a proper warrant.

[61]   When the police circumvented the judicial warrant requirement and recorded a telephone conversation between a police informer and a suspect, the ensuing evidence was declared inadmissible; 31 *Entscheidungen des Bundesgerichtshofes in Strafsachen* 304 (1983).

[62]   The number of law teachers actively involved in legal defence work is small.

[63]   This view has some difficulty in explaining the legal position of the court-appointed lawyer.

the lawyer's obligation to carry out their client's wishes as limited by the general notion that illegal or immoral obligations cannot be imposed by contract (§§ 134, 138 Civil Code).

5.3. Regulations and Limitations

To the extent that they are licensed lawyers (and not law professors), defence lawyers are subject to the supervision and discipline of the organised bar, to which every lawyer must belong. The bar is organised at the district court level and maintains its own disciplinary system based on federal statute (Federal Lawyers Act, *Bundesrechtsanwaltsordnung*). In practice, it is rare for a lawyer to be disciplined for malfeasance at or before trial.

5.4. Professional Standards and Restrictions

Defence lawyers must do everything legally permissible to help their client's cause. It is generally for the client to define their interest in the case. For example, if the client wishes to keep secret the fact that they have had mental problems the defence lawyer must not bring that issue up even if it might work in their client's favour. Trial tactics are generally the province of the lawyer, but they must take their client's wishes into account. If there is serious disagreement, the lawyer should withdraw from the case.

Although the lawyer should be zealous in the interests of the client, they must draw the line at actively misleading the court. They must not ask the court to call witnesses who they know will lie, and they must not present to the court documents they know to be forged. If the defendant wishes to make a statement in court that the lawyer knows or assumes to be false, the lawyer cannot stop the defendant from doing so (because it is the defendant's personal decision to make a statement), but the lawyer should refrain from referring to the client's statement as being proof of the facts claimed by the defendant. It would, however, be impermissible for the lawyer to disclose the fact that their client has told lies in court.

A lawyer has an absolute duty of secrecy and must not disclose any information received from the client, or otherwise obtained in connection with the case, to the court or anyone else unless the client has authorized them to do so.[64] The defence lawyer has an unlimited right to have unsupervised contact with their client even if the suspect is in pre-trial custody (§ 148 § 1 CCP). Conversations between the defence lawyer and their client must neither be overheard by jail staff nor recorded or wiretapped. Only if the client is suspected of being a member of a terrorist organisation can written communication between the lawyer and client be monitored, with judicial authorization (§§ 148 § 2, 148a CCP).

---

[64] In the criminal process, defence lawyers can refuse to testify on any information obtained in their professional capacity (§ 53 § 1 No. 2 CCP).

6. Conclusion

On the whole, the rights of suspects and defendants are adequately protected in the German system, and reports of serious overreach by law enforcement personnel are comparatively rare. The traditionally strict separation between the pre-trial and trial stages has protected the trial from pre-trial violations' spilling over into the trial and judgement phase. But this separation is weakening,[65] and it may become more and more important to protect the suspect's rights, including their right to secure evidence in their favour, during pre-trial investigation. This need engenders a strong interest in providing a professional defence not only at the trial level but from the very beginning of criminal proceedings – an interest only imperfectly served by the present organisation of the legal defence in Germany, which lacks a system of legal aid functioning in the early stages of the investigation.

7. Bibliography

Handbooks and Commentaries in German

W. Beulke, *Strafprozessrecht*, Heidelberg, C.F. Müller, 8th ed., 2005.

Caselaw of the ECtHR can be found at the European Court of Human Rights HUDOC Portal: <http://cmiskp.echr.coe.int>, in Series A and after 1 January 1996 in Reports of Judgments and Decisions, both published by Carl Heymans Verlag KG, Köln, Germany.

H.H. Kühne, *Strafprozessrecht*, Heidelberg, C.F. Müller, 6th ed., 2003.

L. Meyer-Gossner, *Strafprozessordnung, Gerichtsverfassungsgesetz, Nebengesetze und ergänzende Bestimmungen*, Munich, C.H. Beck, 48th ed., 2005.

G. Pfeiffer (ed.), *Karlsruher Kommentar zur Strafprozessordnung*, Munich, C.H. Beck, 5th ed., 2003.

P. Rieß (ed.), *Löwe-Rosenberg Grosskommentar StPO* (8 vols.), Berlin, de Gruyter, 25th ed., 2005.

C. Roxin, *Strafverfahrensrecht*, Munich, C.H. Beck, 25th ed., 1998.

H.-J. Rudolphi, *Systematischer Kommentar zur Strafprozessordnung und zum et al. Gerichtsverfassungsgesetz*, Munich, Luchterhand, 3rd ed., (Looseleaf).

---

[65]   For example, the list of documents that can be read out at the trial *in lieu of* hearing the declarant in person has been lengthened over the years and has recently been extended to any protocol or declaration documenting an act of police investigation other than an interrogation (§ 256 § 1 No. 5 CCP).

Publications in English

M. Bohlander, 'Legal advice in criminal proceedings in the Federal Republic of Germany,' *Criminal Law Forum*, 3 1992, p. 401-418.

R. Frase & T. Weigend, 'German Criminal Justice as a Guide to American Law Reform: Similar Problems, Better Solutions?,' *Boston College International and Comparative Law Review*, 18 1995, p. 317-360.

B. Huber, 'Criminal Procedure in Germany,' in J. Hatchard, B. Huber & R. Vogler (eds), *Comparative Criminal Procedure*, London, British Institute of International and Comparative Law, 1996, p. 96-175.

H.-H. Kühne, 'Germany,' in C. van den Wyngaert (ed.), *Criminal procedure systems in the European Community*, London, Butterworths, 1993, p. 137-162.

S.C. Thaman, *Comparative Criminal Procedure: A Casebook Approach*, Durham NC, Carolina Academic Press, 2002.

T. Weigend, 'Germany,' in C.M. Bradley (ed.), *Criminal Procedure. A Worldwide Study*, Durham NC, Carolina Academic Press, 1999, p. 187-216.

T. Weigend, 'Criminal Procedure: Comparative Aspects,' in J. Dressler (ed.), *1 Encyclopedia of Crime & Justice*, New York NY, Macmillan, 2nd ed., 2002, p. 444-457.

Zinovia Dellidou

THE INVESTIGATIVE STAGE OF THE CRIMINAL PROCESS IN GREECE

1.   Introduction

Criminal procedure in Greece has undergone various changes within the last decade or so as a result of legislative and case law developments. These have resulted in the modification of some of what were previously considered as its fundamental characteristics.[1] Most of the legislative developments have been fuelled by a desire to accelerate the delivery of criminal justice. In doing so these provisions have often led to uncertainty and lack of coherence (making it necessary to introduce more changes) and have even encroached on the rights of suspects or defendants.[2] On the other hand, some of the developments in the courts' jurisprudence have been in the direction of ensuring greater respect for those rights, often in line with the developments in the jurisprudence of the European Court of Human Rights (ECtHR).[3] The balance, as recently achieved, is arguably in favour of protecting the rights of suspects and defendants.

The first effort to formulate a codified system governing criminal matters in modern Greek history was in 1823. This system was later replaced by the Penal Law of 1833 and the 1834 Penal Procedure Act. The latter was the work of George Ludwig von Maurer, one of the legal advisors to the German king Otto.[4] The Greek

---

[1]   For example, with regard to the principle of 'legality' or mandatory prosecution governing the initiation of criminal proceedings by the Attorney General. See P. Tsiridis, *The New Legislation for the Acceleration of Criminal Proceedings*, Athens-Komotini, Ant. N. Sakkoulas Publishers, 2005, p. 50 for a discussion of the changes recently introduced.

[2]   For example, following the changes introduced by law 3346/2005 temporary detention may now be ordered not only for felonies but also with regard to the misdemeanour of reckless manslaughter of a number of persons.

[3]   See the Supreme Court jurisprudence regarding the use of the suspect's pre-trial testimonies under section 3.2 below. The Supreme Court (*Areios Pagos*) hears appeals on points of law from most of the lower criminal courts.

[4]   Broadly based on the text of the French '*Code d'Instruction Criminelle,*' Maurer's Code was also greatly influenced by one of his works on the ancient German trial. See N.K Androulakis, *Fundamental concepts of the criminal trial*, Athens-Komotini, Ant. N. Sakkoulas Publishers, 1994, p. 40. The link with the German tradition is still evident today. Modern German
→

law of criminal procedure currently in force is mainly contained in the 1951 Code of Penal Procedure[5] (CPP) as last amended in 2003 and 2005.[6] These latest amendments entitled 'On the acceleration of criminal procedure,' aim to achieve efficiency and avoid delays in the delivery of criminal justice. Other sources of criminal procedure include: a) the 1975 Constitution, amended in 1986 and 2001, guaranteeing freedoms the non-respect of which may result in criminal sanctions; b) the European Convention on Human Rights, ratified by legislative decree 53/1974. Article 28.1 of the Greek Constitution guarantees that foreign conventions signed by the government are superior to any contrary legal enactment; and c) the Code of Traffic Regulations, the Statute on Judicial Organisation, the Military Code and other special penal procedural provisions contained in various legal enactments.

The Greek penal procedure system currently in use has been characterised as a 'mixed' system of criminal justice.[7] Unlike the civil trial where the pre-trial stage is run by the parties, the criminal pre-trial stage is mainly governed by State functionaries conducting both investigation and prosecution. These tasks are entrusted to distinct and mutually interdependent officials who are legally protected against interference and influence by the executive or by private persons. This aims to introduce objectivity and impartiality to the process of gathering and evaluating the evidence produced by the police and the investigating judge as well as to the decisions depending on them.[8] There is extensive use of the written form and, generally, secrecy and lack of publicity. This stage of the proceedings is also generally characterized by the lack of confrontation between the parties. The pre-trial stage can thus be said to be generally governed by principles of the 'inquisitorial' perspective.

The trial stage is, on the other hand, held to be governed by the principles of publicity, orality,[9] immediacy and, in general, open party confrontation.[10] The

---

doctrine and jurisprudential developments are often cited by academics and practising lawyers. This is also the case, but to a lesser extent, with the French and Italian legal traditions.

5   For a discussion of the influences on this Code, see the *Introductory Report to the 1950 Code* and A. Bouropoulos, *Interpretation of the Code of Penal Procedure*, Athens-Thessalonica, Nik. A. Sakkoulas Publications, 1951.

6   The amendments were introduced by Law 3160/2003 FEK 165A/30 June 2003 and Law 3346/2005 FEK 140A/17 June 2005 respectively.

7   See D.D. Spinellis, 'Criminal Law and Procedure,' in K.D. Kerameus and P.I. Kozyris (eds), *Introduction to Greek Law*, Deventer/Athens, Kluwer/Sakkoulas, 2nd ed., 1988, p. 355.

8   For example, the decision to arrest, remand in custody, or commit to trial. See L. Tsoureli, 'Human Rights in Pre-Trial and Trial Procedures in Greece,' in J.A. Andrews (ed.), *Human Rights in Criminal Procedure, A Comparative Study*, The Hague, Martinus Nijhoff Publishers, 1982, p. 213. Article 87 of the Constitution guarantees the independence and impartiality of the judicial authorities and applies to both judges and prosecutors. Enjoying functional and personal independence in carrying out their work means that they are not bound by any directive, order or intervention emanating from other authorities. Article 28 CPP guarantees the independence of those in charge of initiating the criminal prosecution from all other authorities and the courts.

9   The relevant evidence is introduced into the trial orally so that all participants are aware of it and in a position to respond. See also under section 4.1.

conduct of the oral hearing is entrusted to the trial court which has been diligently kept out of the pre-trial stage and which will eventually pronounce judgement on the case on the basis of the arguments made and the evidence put before it by the parties. It is not bound by the dossier prepared at the pre-trial stage, nor must the dossier be in any way determinative of its final judgement.

The criminal courts in Greece are classified according to the severity of the offences they can try and the stage of the proceedings. The classification of the offence is also important for the pre-trial stage since it determines both the steps that will be taken and the parties who will be involved in carrying out the pre-trial investigation. Article 18 of the Penal Code divides criminal offences into: felonies, misdemeanours and petty offences. A felony is any offence punishable by life imprisonment or a term ranging from five to twenty years (art. 52 of the Penal Code); a misdemeanour is any offence punishable by imprisonment or by pecuniary sanction or by confinement in a reformative institution (art. 53 Penal Code: the custodial penalties here range from ten days to five years). A petty offence is any act punishable by jail or by a fine (art. 55 Penal Code: the jail sentence can range from one day to one month). Children and adolescents are tried before the juvenile courts.

Greek criminal procedure is based on the principle of the search for the substantive/objective truth. Unlike civil trials, where only the evidence produced by the parties will form the basis of the court's judgment, in criminal cases all evidence has to be searched for and examined since the court's final judgment must not be limited by the quantity and quality of the evidence produced by either the Attorney General or the defendant and the other parties involved.[11] With regard to pre-trial procedure the principle is enunciated in article 239.2 CPP which provides that those responsible for carrying out the investigation are required to examine all evidence pointing towards both the guilt and innocence of the accused person. This objective results in a series of rights and obligations for the participants which are discussed further in the rest of the chapter.

2. Powers of the Investigating Authorities at the Pre-trial Stage

2.1. Relations between police, prosecutor and investigating judge

As previously noted, the categorisation of the offence is of importance for the course that the pre-trial investigation will take. The common thread is that a judicial officer, the Attorney General, is always involved in the process regardless of the nature or seriousness of the offence. They may be involved from the beginning (i.e. the moment the *notitia criminis* is received) or as soon as practicable in the case of flagrant offences (i.e. offences where the defendant is detained whilst allegedly committing the offence or no later than the end of the day following its commission - i.e. within a maximum of forty-eight hours from its alleged commission).

---

10   See N. K Androulakis, *supra* note 4, p. 371-376.
11   *Ibidem*, p. 157.

The previous formulation of article 43.1 CPP put in place the principle of 'legality' with regard to the commencement of criminal proceedings: the Attorney General of the misdemeanours court was generally obliged to institute criminal proceedings as soon as an offence was reported to them,[12] unless the report was obviously unfounded in law or in substance, in which case she would file it and present a copy to the Attorney General of the Court of Appeal.

In the case of petty offences or minor misdemeanours (those triable before the one-member misdemeanours court), if there exist indications of guilt, the Public Prosecutor or Attorney General[13] (respectively) may summon the accused directly before the trial court. In the case of other offences criminal proceedings may, depending on the circumstances of the case, be commenced in one of three ways: the Public Prosecutor or Attorney General may order a summary investigation, or an ordinary investigation, or may summon the accused directly before the trial court.

Before 2003, the Attorney General of the Misdemeanours Court also had the option of carrying out a preliminary inquiry, in order to establish the weight of the information received, avoiding the commencement of proceedings where reports of an offence having been committed were clearly unsubstantiated. The purpose of the ordinary or summary investigation (which would follow the preliminary inquiry) was to collect the evidence necessary to allow the Attorney General or the judicial council to decide whether there was a prima facie case against the accused (art. 239.1 CPP). Following the amendments introduced by law 3160/2003, they are now obliged to carry out a preliminary inquiry before initiating criminal proceedings in the case of felonies or serious misdemeanours, i.e. those that will be tried by the three-member Misdemeanours Court (art. 43.1 CPP).[14] The purpose of the preliminary inquiry is to establish whether or not there is sufficient evidence to commence criminal proceedings. If the authorities have already identified a suspect he or she, though not yet charged (but who is a potential defendant), can be required to attend and give explanations before them. The preliminary inquiry can last for up to four months, and can be ordered by the Attorney General of the Misdemeanours Court (art 31 CPP), of the Court of Appeal or of the Supreme Court

---

[12]   Whether by the police, a citizen, the victim, or an official report issued by another authority. The Attorney General has discretion whether to prosecute the following: a) offences committed by under age offenders, b) offences involving a defendant already serving a sentence more severe than any possible punishment the new prosecution may entail or c) offences discovered as a result of reporting an instance of blackmail, where, by reporting it, the victim lays themselves open to the discovery of an offence they have previously committed themselves (art. 44-45A CPP).

[13]   The Attorney General (*Eisaggeleas*) in Greece has judicial training, and is regarded as a judicial officer. In relation to petty offences the duties of the Attorney General are exercised by a public prosecutor (*Dimosios Katigoros*), who is normally a higher-ranking police officer (although if none is available the duties of the public prosecutor are carried out by a judge of the petty offences court).

[14]   There will be no preliminary inquiry if an *ex officio* summary investigation or internal administrative investigation has already taken place producing sufficient evidence to commence criminal proceedings.

(art 35 CPP),[15] who can either carry it out in person or order others to do it. The Attorney General of the Misdemeanours Court may order the general or specialised officers to conduct the enquiry, whilst the Attorney General of the Court of Appeal can order the Deputy Attorney Generals of that court to carry it out on their behalf.[16] If it is carried out by the Attorney General of the Misdemeanours Court, and in exceptional circumstances, the enquiry can be extended for a further period of four months following approval by the Attorney General of the Court of Appeal (see art. 31 CPP). In such cases, a criminal prosecution will commence only if there is sufficient evidence following the preliminary inquiry. It would appear, therefore, that in the case of more serious offences, the principle of 'legality' is giving way to the principle of 'opportunity' with regard to the commencement of criminal proceedings.[17] Following the preliminary enquiry the Attorney General may, depending on the circumstances, summon the accused directly before the trial court or order a summary or ordinary (main) investigation.

An ordinary investigation is compulsory when the suspected offence is a felony or a serious misdemeanour with regard to which restrictions on personal liberty may be imposed (art. 246 and 282 CPP).[18] It is performed by the investigating judge, a judge of first instance in the Misdemeanours Court.[19] Following a written request from the Attorney General, they are obliged to examine the case and carry out all investigations necessary for the discovery of the truth e.g. collect information, examine witnesses, hear the accused, order experts reports, etc. They also decide (in agreement with the Attorney General) on any coercive measures to be taken during the pre-trial stage, such as temporary detention or restrictive conditions.[20] The investigating judge is restricted by the Attorney General's mandate, as described in the investigation request: whilst they may conduct the investigations freely, they may only investigate the offence specified in it.[21] They may collect evidence with respect to the suspect and to all potential co-suspects and accomplices, but not with respect to offences other than those mentioned in the request. If, during the course of the investigation, it appears that another offence has also been committed the investigating judge must inform the Attorney General, who issues a new order. At the end of the investigation, the investigating judge will inform the parties as to the findings and send the file to the Attorney General.

---

[15]   Although the article mentions all three Attorney Generals, there has been criticism as to what the proper role of the AG of the Supreme Court should be. See A.X. Papadamakis, *Penal Procedure: Theory-Practice-Jurisprudence*, Athens-Thessalonica, Sakkoulas Publications, 2006, p. 230.

[16]   See art. 33-35 CPP.

[17]   See P. Tsiridis, *supra* note 1, p. 49-50.

[18]   See section 3.4 below.

[19]   Following an opinion of the Council or the President of the Court and recommendation by the Attorney General of the Court of Appeal, the investigating judge is appointed for a period of two years by presidential decree.

[20]   If there is a disagreement, the decision is referred to the Judicial Council.

[21]   When the Attorney General lays the charge, initiating criminal proceedings, they must specify the nature of the offence committed (A. X. Papadamakis, *supra* note 15, p. 249). The final determination is, however, made by the investigating judge.

Following the provisions on the obligatory preliminary inquiry introduced by law 3160/2003, there has been a grey area regarding the need for a summary investigation.[22] A summary investigation, like a preliminary inquiry, is directed at the discovery of sufficient evidence verifying the commission of an illegal act following a brief exploration of the circumstances, and may be followed, if necessary, by an ordinary investigation (art. 243-245 CPP). It is ordered by the Attorney General of the Misdemeanours Court who may require general or specialised investigating officers[23] to carry out any investigative act necessary to fully dispose of their duty.[24] The general investigating officers can be either Judicial Officials, who are magistrates, or Police/Administrative Officials who are either police officers above a certain rank or other public sector employees appointed by specific laws.[25] It cannot take longer than six months, although this period can be extended by four months in exceptional circumstances on approval of the Attorney General of the Court of Appeal (art. 243.4 CPP). Article 244 CPP provides that a summary investigation is not necessary if a preliminary inquiry has already taken place. It appears that a summary investigation will now be ordered for misdemeanours triable by the three member Misdemeanours Court only in exceptional circumstances, e.g. if there is sufficient evidence of an offence having been committed but the perpetrator remains unknown or it is necessary to take their testimony.[26]

The *ex officio* summary investigation, however, remains. In cases of urgency, such as flagrant offences where delay can lead to loss of evidence, investigating officers (usually the police) can initiate an *ex officio* summary investigation on their own without a request by the Attorney General, provided that they inform the Attorney General as soon as possible. Only police officers of the rank of sergeant or above, or Police Academy graduates, can carry out acts of pre-trial investigation, such as interrogating the suspect, during the course of this investigation.

If the Attorney General decides that there is no need to lay charges (following an *ex officio* summary investigation or because a brief examination of the indictment demonstrates that it was unfounded in law or substance), the case does not have to continue. In this case the Attorney General may file it and inform the Attorney General of the Appeal Court of the reasons why the criminal prosecution should not be commenced. Before 2003, once criminal proceedings had been instituted, the Attorney General had no power to discontinue proceedings in the event that they concluded that there was not enough evidence against the defendant. The judicial

---

[22]   See P. Tsiridis, *supra* note 1, p. 96.
[23]   The difference being whether they can investigate *any* illegal act or only those offences specified by law. Directors of the port authorities are general investigating officers. Specialised officers include: health officers within their sphere of responsibility, customs officers and all public sector employees regarding the offence of illegal trade, the higher rank fire service employees regarding the crime of arson etc.
[24]   See articles 13 and 33-35 CPP.
[25]   See article 33 CPP. Only judicial officials can carry out house searches.
[26]   See A. X. Papadamakis, *supra* note 15, p. 260.

council was the only authority competent to discontinue the case.[27] Under the new law, the Attorney General can file the complaint following the preliminary inquiry or an internal administrative investigation, or even following the institution of criminal proceedings in case of a minor misdemeanour (i.e. one that will be tried by the one-member misdemeanours court). In this case the Attorney General must give a reasoned opinion why it is considered that the case should not be proceeded with. In all other cases, once a criminal charge has been laid or an ordinary investigation commenced, the charges can no longer be discontinued. The Attorney General may only submit the file to the judicial council with a request for acquittal.

It is clear, therefore, that the judiciary plays a major part in pre-trial investigation. Even where they do not directly conduct an investigation, they are responsible for supervising it.

2.2. *Arrest and detention*

The Greek Constitution and the Code of Penal Procedure make provision for arrest and detention. Article 6.1 of the Constitution provides that there can be no arrest or imprisonment without a properly justified judicial warrant (except where the person is caught whilst committing the act).[28] The warrant is issued by the investigating judge (after receiving the Attorney General's opinion) or the judicial council, and must be presented at the time of arrest. According to articles 276.2 and 282.3 CPP, an arrest warrant can only be issued in respect of offences for which temporary detention can be ordered. Generally, therefore, arrest warrants are only available in respect of suspected felonies. However, following the amendments introduced by law 3346/2005, detention can now also be ordered with regard to the misdemeanour of reckless manslaughter where there are more than two victims e.g. traffic accidents, ship accidents, etc., which are to be tried before the three-member Misdemeanours Court. A judicial warrant is not required for the purpose of arrest in respect of 'flagrant offences,' i.e. where the person is caught whilst committing the act or soon afterwards.[29] In such cases, the relevant investigating officers (usually the police) are obliged to arrest the person involved. Any citizen who is present during the commission of the act also has the right to arrest (art. 275.1 CPP).

Where a person has been arrested, they must be taken before the competent Attorney General within twenty-four hours from the time of arrest, or within the shortest possible transfer time if the arrest took place outside the area of the investigating authorities (art. 279.1 CPP). If the offence is a felony or if an arrest warrant has been issued, the Attorney General must refer the person to the investigating judge (art. 279.1. CPP). With regard to flagrant offences, however, it was noted earlier that this period can be longer than twenty-four hours. According

---

[27] The Judicial Council is a chamber of the Misdemeanours Court (first instance) or the Court of Appeal (at appellate level) composed of three professional judges. It deliberates in camera and is the authority competent to decide whether a case should go to trial or be dismissed without one.

[28] Art. 276.1 CPP is similarly worded.

[29] Art. 242 CPP.

to article 243.2 CPP the police should attempt to carry out the *ex officio* summary investigation, which means that they are required to carry out a first examination of the accused and record their testimony.[30] In such cases, once the accused is taken before the Attorney General they may be committed for trial on the same day or the following day (art. 418 CPP). The Attorney General may order the defendant's detention until the trial takes place, i.e. for a maximum of twenty-four hours from the moment the defendant appeared before them (art. 419 CPP). If the oral hearing cannot take place within the above time limits, the Attorney General must bring the defendant before the investigating judge who must decide, within a maximum of twenty-four hours, whether temporary detention should be ordered. Once the oral hearing starts, the defendant may ask for a three-day delay in order to prepare their defence, and the court will then decide on whether the defendant should be detained for this period. The court may also delay the hearing for a further period of not more than fifteen days in order to obtain further evidence or call other witnesses or co-accused to testify. In that case, the court will decide *ex officio* on whether the defendant should be detained until the hearing (art. 423 CPP).

The investigating judge must either issue a warrant of imprisonment or release the suspect within three days from the time the suspect was first brought before them. There can be an extension for a further two days, following a request by the arrested person or in case of '*force majeure*' confirmed by a decision of the competent judicial council. At the expiry of this period, the person must be immediately released (art. 6.2 and 6.3 of the Constitution).

In addition to the power of arrest, the police have the power to stop and ask anyone to produce evidence of their identity. The person asked is obliged to produce their identity card or other means of identification, under penalty of imprisonment.[31]

2.3. Police interview

The role of the police is particularly important during the course of an *ex officio* summary investigation. In practice, the Attorney General is normally informed by means of a fax that an offence was committed and that the investigation is in progress. Having carried out the arrest, the police must compile an arrest report.

The person who is the subject of an *ex officio* investigation enjoys all the rights guaranteed to defendants (art. 105 CPP). The Police Code of Conduct[32] also specifies that police officers must immediately inform the person of the reason for their arrest and detention along with the charges against them, their rights and the procedure to be followed. This information must be given in a language the person understands through an interpreter or by the best means available. They must also ensure the suspect is allowed to immediately contact by telephone or any other means available any person they wish or the consular authorities of their country in order

---

30 N. K. Androulakis, *supra* note 4, p. 268.
31 This power was included in art. 157 of Law 2458/1953.
32 Presidential Decree 254/2004, FEK 238A/3 December 2004.

to inform them of the reason for and the place of arrest (Police Code of Conduct, art. 3c). The grant of legal assistance to the detainee must be facilitated and their immediate and unobstructed communication with counsel ensured (art 3.d). The police are responsible for the protection of the detainee's health, ensuring their immediate medical care in case of need and for providing them with the opportunity to be examined by a doctor of their choice (art. 3 h).

Everything that occurs during the course of the suspect's examination must be recorded in writing. There is, however, no tape-recording of interviews of suspects. All reports must be signed by the police officer compiling them and another judicial officer, or, if none is present, by two witnesses (art. 150 CPP). The report must include the place, date and time it was compiled as well as the names and addresses of those present. It must record in detail the defendant's statements and specify whether they were prompted by questions asked or whether they were voluntary. The statement must be read out to the defendant, who will be asked to sign it. A refusal to sign must be clearly recorded on the statement (art. 151 CPP). Once the police have finished their questioning, they will submit the file to the Attorney General who may summon the defendant to court to be tried on the same day or the day following.

2.4. Coercive methods of investigation

There have been extensive changes to coercive methods of investigation in recent times, especially with regard to DNA samples and the use of undercover methods (discussed in the following section). The direction of change is to increase police investigative powers and to require suspects to submit to procedures which would previously have been unlawful or permissible in respect of a very limited range of offences. The primary justification for the extension of such powers had been the need for adequate powers to deal with terrorism and criminal organisations under article 187 and 187A PC. However, the inclusion of a wide range of offences under these articles raises concern about the potential extent of these investigative methods.[33]

The power to conduct a search of premises is only available during the pre-trial investigation of a felony or misdemeanour. Searches may be carried out either in the course of an ordinary investigation following the commencement of criminal proceedings by the Attorney General (art. 243.1 CPP), or before a criminal charge is laid, i.e. in the course of an *ex officio* summary investigation of a flagrant offence where delay might lead to loss of evidence (art. 243.2 CPP). A search of premises is not permitted during the course of a preliminary inquiry[34] and if carried out would be unlawful and absolutely invalid.[35]

---

[33]   See, *inter alia*, E. Simeonidou-Kastanidou, 'Law 2928/2001 "on the protection of the citizen from unlawful acts of criminal organisations"', *PoinDik*, 2001, p. 698.

[34]   A. X. Papadamakis, *supra* note 15, p. 234.

[35]   Case AP 1328/2003 *P.Chr* 2004, p. 341.

Where the power of search is available, it is permitted only where there are reasonable grounds to believe that it would facilitate or ensure: a) confirmation that a crime has been committed, b) the discovery or arrest of the perpetrator, or c) the confirmation/revelation or restoration of the damage caused (art. 253 CPP). Premises used without lawful permission to play illegal games or for prostitution can be searched during the night.[36] A night search of premises is also permitted in order to arrest a person under an arrest warrant or a person caught while committing the act. Article 254 CPP provides that searches of premises may only be carried out by the Attorney General, the investigating judge, justices of the peace, a judge of the petty offences court or, if none of them is available, high ranking police officers. The person carrying out the search is required to be accompanied by at least one investigating officer. If the search is carried out by police officers they should, therefore, ask a judicial officer to be present (art. 255 CPP), under penalty of nullity.[37] A home search must always be conducted in the presence of a representative of the judiciary (art. 9.1 of the Consitution).The owner of the premises to be searched is invited to be present during the course of the search (art. 256 CPP). If the owner is inside the premises and refuses to allow entry, force may be used to enter the premises. Once the search has been conducted, a report must be given to the owner if they request it.

Searches of the person are subject to the same pre-conditions as other searches (art. 253 CPP, see above). Moreover, art 257 CPP specifies that a personal search of the defendant may only be conducted where the person in charge of the investigation considers that it is useful for ascertaining the truth. A female can only be searched by another female. The personal search of a person who is not a suspect can only be carried out where there is serious and grounded suspicion or absolute need. Personal searches should, as far as possible, be carried out in such a way as not to offend the person (art. 257.1 CPP).

The taking and analysis of DNA samples has been included in the CPP as a means of proof following the introduction of law 2928/2001.[38] According to article 200A CPP (introduced by this law), the judicial council can order a DNA analysis when there are serious indications that a person has committed a felony by using violence, or a sexual crime, or is part of or a founding member of a criminal or terrorist organisation.[39] The law does not expressly require the consent of the person from whom the sample is to be taken. However, it is not clear whether, where consent is refused, the use of force to take a sample is lawful. The person

---

[36]   Between 20.00 and 06.00 from the beginning of October to the end of March and between 21.00 and 05.00 from the beginning of April to the end of September.

[37]   See Judicial Council of Misdemenours Court of Herakleion 261/2005 in *PoinDik*, 2006, p. 42-45. Art. 255 CPP provides that, in the absence of a judicial officer, the town mayor can be asked to be present. The express requirement of art. 9.1 of the Constitution, that a judicial officer be present, however, makes that provision obsolete.

[38]   Although this is widely known as the anti-terrorism law, it introduces a number of changes to the CPP and the PC relating to offences committed by criminal organisations not confined to terrorism.

[39]   As amended by Law 3251/2004, FEK 127A/9 July 2004.

responsible for taking the sample must notify the defendant that their refusal will be evaluated at trial.[40] In 2002 the Judicial Council of the Misdemeanours Court of Thessalonica[41] held that whilst the taking of a DNA sample may violate human dignity, it is a lawful violation because of the need in very serious offences to strike a balance between human dignity and the public interest. The constitutional principle of proportionality must therefore be respected where consent is refused.[42]

2.5. Secret methods of investigation

The regulation of secret investigative methods, such as interception of communications,[43] infiltration, pseudo-purchase, and the use of audio-visual means of surveillance, was first introduced into the Code of Penal Procedure by law 2928/2001 which added a new article 253A CPP.[44] This deals with investigative acts relating to terrorist activities[45] or the activities of criminal organisations[46] consisting of three or more persons, and only if the following conditions of necessity and proportionality are satisfied: a) there are serious indications that criminal acts contrary to article 187 and 187A PC have been committed, and b) the uncovering of the criminal organisation or the terrorist activities is otherwise impossible or extremely difficult (see art. 253A § 2).

These forms of investigation are only permitted on the authority of the competent judicial council following an application by the Attorney General. However, in cases of extreme urgency they can be authorised by the Attorney General or the Investigating Judge, who must then refer their decision to the judicial council within a period of three days. Any material or information uncovered can only be used for the purposes indicated by the judicial council, unless it decides otherwise.[47] With regard to infiltration, article 253A specifies that the only acts allowed are those considered absolutely necessary to uncover crimes that the members of the criminal organisation have already agreed to commit.

---

[40] G. Siaperas, 'Human consent to the taking and analysis of genetic material (DNA),' *PoinDik*, 2005, p. 1457.

[41] Decree no 69/2002, *PoinDik*, 2002, p. 276. *Ibidem*, p. 1455.

[42] G. Siaperas, *supra* note 40, p. 1458 and 1460.

[43] Specifically regulated by articles 4 and 5 of Law 2225/1994 and Presidential Decree 47/2005 adopted on the basis of art. 9 of Law 3115/2003.

[44] Even though such methods had already been (and are still) available, by means of special penal laws with regard to, for example, drugs related offences (Law 1729/1987) or offences committed by police officers (Law 2713/1999) or other serious offences specified by art. 4 of Law 2225/1994 (see art. 253A § 1 and 5 CPP).

[45] Under art. 187A of the Penal Code.

[46] I.e. an offence under art. 187 of the Penal Code. For an attempt at defining what is meant by a 'criminal organisation' see Judicial Council of the Court of Appeal of Thessalonica 93/2006, *PoinDik*, 2006, p. 412-419 with comments by E. Kastanidou-Simeonidou who notes a tendency for a wide definition in previous years.

[47] According to art. 370A § 3 of the Penal Code, the use of material obtained by unlawful interception of communications or audio-visual surveillance incurs a minimum penalty of one year's imprisonment.

In addition to the circumstances referred to above, interception of communications is also be permitted where it is in the interests of national security (art. 19.1 of the Constitution), and in investigations concerning a number of felonies (and one misdemeanour) as specified in article 4 of Law 2225/1994 (as amended by art. 12 of Law 3115/2003).

3. Rights of the suspect or defendant

3.1. Information about suspect's rights

Those arrested by the police must be given a leaflet containing information on their rights, which is available in a number of languages.[48] These leaflets are also displayed in all detention areas of police stations. Police guidelines also provide that those detained by the police must be informed orally and in writing about the reason for arrest, the place of detention and their rights.

During a summary investigation, the investigating officers must give the defendant at least 48 hours notice that their testimony is required. The investigating officer must inform the defendant of their rights (according to art. 103 CPP) and prepare the relevant report in writing (art. 273.2 in conjunction with art. 103 and 104 CPP). After the defendant has been informed of their rights and before giving any testimony, the defendant may ask for a delay and obtain copies of the documents contained in the case file. The investigating officer must inform the defendant in detail and with clarity about the content of the accusation (art. 273.2 CPP). However, in practice, the information given is often very basic, which means that it is difficult for the defendant to answer the accusation properly.[49] This could, in theory, lead to invalidity according to article 171.1.d CPP. At the end of the summary investigation and before its transmission to the Attorney General, the case file must be made available to the defendant. Otherwise, absolute invalidity occurs which will extend to the act by which the defendant is summoned to court.[50]

A failure to respect the rights of the person under investigation during the preliminary inquiry will also lead to absolute invalidity of the acts carried out at this stage of the proceedings (art. 171.1 d and b).

3.2. The right to silence

Article 273.2 recognises the defendant's right to silence before the investigating authorities. This right arguably forms part of the general right of personality recognised under article 5.1 of the Constitution,[51] giving it a basis independent from

---

[48] Those leaflets have been translated into French, English, Italian, German, Spanish, Arabic, Turkish, Albanian, Russian, Bulgarian, Romanian, Serbian and Polish.

[49] See A. X. Papadamakis, *supra* note 15, p. 263.

[50] *Ibidem*, p. 266.

[51] Art. 5.1 provides that: 'Everyone has the right to freely develop his personality and participate in the social, economic and political life of the country as long as he does not infringe the rights of others and does not violate the provisions of the Constitution or the

→

the provisions of the Code and meaning that it cannot be removed by a later legislative provision. No adverse consequences can result from the silence of the accused. A defendant also has the right to submit their testimony in writing. In this case, those in charge of the investigation can ask any questions necessary to clarify the content of the defendant's testimony, and such questions will be set out in the report that the investigator compiles. The defendant can refuse to answer such questions (art. 273.2. CPP) and no adverse consequences should result.

However, in practice the right to silence may be undermined in a number of ways. Article 273.2 CPP clearly recognises that a defendant has a right to silence. According to the old formulation of article 72 CPP, a defendant is any person who the Attorney General has formally charged, or who a criminal act is attributed to at any stage of the pre-trial investigation, or whose name appears on the indictment, complaint, or report of the criminal act. Despite the relative clarity of the provision, a grey area existed in practice regarding the stages of the pre-trial procedure where the person was investigated without having been formally charged, i.e. the *ex officio* summary investigation and the preliminary inquiry. Until 1996 persons caught in the act could be denied the rights of defendants (such as the right to be informed of the documents of the investigation or to ask for a delay before giving testimony) if those carrying out the investigation believed that exercising these rights would be disadvantageous to the investigation and the discovery of the truth (*ex* art. 105 CPP). The only right that could not be denied was the right to be assisted by a lawyer.

The police, however, resorted to a technique that facilitated their investigations and removed the right of access to a defence lawyer. They examined the suspect as a 'witness,' without requiring them to take an oath, although the law provided that only defendants should be examined unsworn. Being examined as a 'witness' meant that they were not allowed to consult with a defence lawyer before being questioned, neither did the right to silence apply to them. Although a witness has the right not to incriminate themselves (art. 223.4 CPP), article 225.2 indent 2 of the Penal Code obliges a witness to answer questions, refusal being punishable with a maximum sentence of one year's imprisonment. The normal police practice would be to question the 'witness' once, or more than once, and then ask them to testify as a 'defendant,' essentially affirming their previous unsworn testimony which would form the basis of the police pre-trial file.

The Supreme Court was called to examine whether these unsworn testimonies could be presented to and evaluated by the trial court. Whilst testimony secured by such a device had previously been permitted, a change in the law in 1996 made it compulsory for everyone questioned by the police under an *ex officio* investigation to be given the full spectrum of rights allowed to defendants. Testimony obtained contrary to this obligation would be null and void, and would not to be taken into account by the court. However, the new article 105 and 31.2 CPP provided that testimony obtained in this way had to remain in the Attorney General's office and

moral values.' See also art. 2.1 of the Constitution which provides that 'The respect and protection of human value is a primary obligation of the State.'

not be placed before the trial court, but there was no express provision that taking it into account would nullify the proceedings. In 1999 the Supreme Court held, referring to the European Court of Human Rights decision in *Murray* v. *UK*,[52] that this would lead to the proceedings being annulled since it violated the rights of the defence, in particular the right to silence and the privilege against self-incrimination.[53]

In the following years, a number of efforts to limit the effects of this judgment were noted in the jurisprudence of the Supreme Court.[54] For example, an effort was made to limit it to *ex officio* questioning by the police for flagrant offences, distinguishing this procedure from an investigation following the opening by the Attorney General of criminal proceedings (*in rem*). It was held that in the latter case, that the testimony of witnesses, who may later be charged as defendants, should be admissible in court to be evaluated freely by it.[55]

The Supreme Court has, however, recently re-affirmed its 1999 decision by holding (in Full Court Composition)[56] that even though article 31.2b CPP does not expressly provide that reading and evaluating testimonies secured in this way nullifies the proceedings, reliance on such testimony violates the defendant's right to silence and privilege against self-incrimination, which are essential aspects of the right to a fair trial guaranteed by article 6. ECHR and article 223.4 CPP. This applies to the *ex officio* police summary investigation, the ordinary or summary investigation, and the preliminary inquiry. Where an administrative investigation is conducted under the new article 43 CPP, which equates an administrative investigation with a criminal preliminary inquiry and which permits the Attorney General to take the case directly to court should sufficient evidence of guilt emerge, witness testimonies obtained should be considered null and void for the purposes of criminal proceedings.

Following the amendments introduced by law 3346/2005, article 72 CPP now gives the quality of defendant to anyone 'who the Attorney General has formally charged and anyone who the criminal act is attributed to at any stage of the pre-trial investigation.' At the same time, article 31.2 CPP clearly guarantees that the person required to give explanations under a preliminary inquiry, 'Has the right to appear with counsel, refuse in all or in part to provide explanations and receive a forty-eight hour delay in order to provide them....'

3.3.   The Right to an interpreter

Article 233 CPP provides for the right to an interpreter. An interpreter is to be appointed by those carrying out the pre-trial investigation or those presiding over the oral hearing, during the examination of the defendant, the civil party or a witness. According to article 234 CPP, certain people must be excluded from being

---

52   ECtHR 8 February 1996, *Murray* v. *UK*, Reports 1996-I.
53   See A.P. (Full Court), No. 2/1999, *NoB* 1999, p. 90 and *P. Chr.* 1999, p. 811.
54   See A.P. (Section F, in camera) No. 710/2003, NoB 2004, p. 98-99.
55   A.P. (Section F, in camera) No. 92/2004 NoB 2004, p. 1033.
56   A.P. (Full Court) 1/2004, *PoinDik*, 2004 p. 917-919.

an interpreter: the defendant him or herself, the civil party, legal counsel, a witness, an expert or technical advisor, the judge involved in the criminal trial, the attorney general and the court secretary.

Defendants, suspects or witnesses must be informed of their right to an interpreter. This information is contained in the Report compiled by the person carrying out the investigation which the defendant/suspect has to sign at the end of the procedure. The violation of this right will lead to absolute nullity under article 171.1.d CPP.

3.4. Detention and bail

Pending their first court appearance, defendants may be temporarily detained or released on bail, which may be unconditional or subject to restrictive conditions. Restrictive conditions are only permissible if, during the course of the pre-trial investigation into the commission of a felony or a serious misdemeanour,[57] there are serious indications of the defendant's guilt. Conditions must be directed at ensuring that the defendant will be present during the course of the pre-trial investigation or at trial and will submit themselves to the execution of the court decision (see art. 296 and 282 CPP). Conditions can include the payment of a security, an obligation for the defendant to present themselves before the investigating judge or other authorities at regular intervals, or to keep away from or avoid contact with certain people, or a prohibition on living in or moving to a certain place or on leaving the country (art. 282.2 CPP). Breach of a condition may result in the person being placed in temporary detention (see art. 282.4 CPP and 298 CPP).

Until 2005, temporary detention could only be ordered in respect of a defendant accused of a felony, where there were serious indications regarding their guilt. Following the amendments then introduced, it can now also be ordered with respect to the misdemeanour of reckless manslaughter of two persons or more (Law 3346/2005). Temporary detention can be ordered instead of restrictive conditions when the defendant has no known address or has taken steps to facilitate an escape or has in the past been a defaulter or been found guilty of aiding another to escape or for breaching residence restrictions. It may be ordered where, taking into account the circumstances of the offence of which they are accused and/or their past conduct, the authorities consider that they are likely to commit further offences if they are released.

The temporary detention order is issued by the investigating judge after receiving the Attorney General's agreement in writing. The Attorney General must hear the defendant and their counsel before expressing their opinion to the investigating judge. In case of disagreement between the Attorney General and the investigating judge, the decision is made by the judicial council (art. 283.1 CPP).

According to the Constitution (art. 6.4) and the CPP (art. 287), the maximum periods of detention pending trial are one year in respect of a felony and six months in the case of a misdemeanour. These periods can be extended in exceptional

---

57   One that incurs a penalty of at least three months imprisonment. See art. 282.1 CPP.

circumstances by the judicial council for a further six and three months, respectively. Detention must be reviewed after six months. If the pre-trial investigation has not been completed, the investigating judge must inform the Attorney General of the Court of Appeal of the reasons for the delay and must submit the case file to the Attorney General of the Misdemeanours Court. The latter submits the dossier to the Judicial Council of the Misdemeanours Court, which is competent to make the decision about continued detention after receiving the Attorney General's opinion. Prior to 2005, the defendant was notified five days before the hearing to enable written defence submissions to be made to the Council. The Council could, at its discretion, invite the defendant to appear and present their views in person or through counsel. Following the 2005 amendments, it will be the norm to invite the defendant to be present at the hearing.[58] If there is no extension of the detention period the defendant must be released (art. 287.3 CPP).

3.5. *The right to be informed about the reason for arrest and the existing evidence*

Following the amendments to the preliminary inquiry introduced in 2005, the person invited to give explanations has the right to request copies of the case-file (not simply the indictment but all documents already included in the dossier). The person in charge of the preliminary inquiry must inform the suspect of these rights. If the defendant is denied the rights guaranteed by article 31 § 2 CPP, this constitutes an absolute invalidity, which the suspect/defendant must bring to the attention of the judicial council before they are irrevocably summoned to court (under art. 176 CPP).

   Moreover, according to article 101.1 CPP, the investigating judge must inform a defendant about to give a testimony of the content of the accusation against them and of all the documents relating to the investigation. The defendant or the defendant's lawyer may study these documents and, upon written request, make copies at their own expense. If the ordinary investigation takes longer than a month, the defendant is allowed to exercise the abovementioned rights once a month. Each time, the investigating judge must file a report alongside the defendant's testimony (art. 101.2 CPP). The same rights are available to a defendant who is subject to a summary investigation or an *ex officio* summary investigation (art. 104 and 105 CPP).

3.6. *Legal assistance*

The defendant's right to be assisted by a lawyer in person during every act of the pre-trial investigation (including when making a statement to the investigating authorities) is guaranteed in the Greek Code of Penal Procedure (art. 100.1 CPP),[59]

---

[58]   See art. 12 of Law 3346/2005.
[59]   The Defendant is generally allowed a twenty-four hour delay before any act of pre-trial investigation to that effect (art. 102 CPP).

116

which provides that the parties may be present with a maximum of two lawyers (art. 96 CPP). Article 100.4 CPP provides that a defendant's right to communicate with counsel cannot be denied. A defence lawyer must be appointed *ex officio* to a defendant appearing before the investigating judge during an ordinary investigation (art. 100.3. CPP). The right to appear with counsel is guaranteed in article 100 § 1, 2 and 4, and this also applies during the summary investigation.[60] However, the right to *ex officio* appointment for defendants appearing before an investigating judge during an ordinary investigation (guaranteed by art. 100.3 CPP) is not included in article 104 CPP, which deals with summary investigations. Similarly, article 105 provides that during an *ex officio* summary investigation the person under investigation has all the rights mentioned above, but without reference to the right to have counsel appointed by the authorities.

While the Code does not prevent the suspect or defendant from being assisted by counsel, the lack of an obligation to appoint one *ex officio*, in the circumstances described above, adversely affected indigent suspects and defendants since legal aid was generally available only when there was a requirement for counsel to be appointed *ex officio*.[61] Article 20 of the Greek Constitution,[62] which guarantees the right to be heard, along with the jurisprudence of the European Court of Human Rights, reinforces the argument for *ex officio* appointment in these cases.[63] The introduction, in 1999, of the new article 96A CPP where there was, for the first time in the Code, express mention of a lawyer being present during the summary investigation seemed to settle this point. The new legal aid legislation has, however, taken this reference away, and it does not expressly provide for legal aid during the *ex officio* summary investigation at the police station. The police must, however, inform the suspect/defendant of their right to be assisted by counsel.

With regard to the preliminary inquiry, suspects' rights of access to legal advice have been somewhat undefined. As the person investigated at this stage has not yet been charged, it was held that the criminal prosecution had not yet commenced. The suspect was thus not to be allowed the rights given to defendants, in particular the right to defence counsel.[64] This issue was dealt with following the introduction of law 3160/2003 which, as noted earlier, made the preliminary inquiry compulsory for felonies and serious misdemeanours that will be tried by the three-member misdemeanours courts. Under the new article 31.2 CPP, the person in question is examined unsworn and has the right to consult and appear with

---

[60]   Expressly mentioned in art. 104.1 dealing with the defendant's rights during the summary investigation.

[61]   For further discussion see the section 3.7.

[62]   Article 20 provides that: '1. Everyone has the right to lawful protection by the courts and can develop before them his views on his rights or interests as provided by the law. 2. The right of the interested person to be heard applies also with regard to any administrative act or measure taken against their (his) rights or interests (author's translation).'

[63]   See, *inter alia*, A. X. Papadamakis, *supra* note 15, p. 267.

[64]   N. K. Androulakis, *supra* note 4, p. 230, who stressed, however, that the testimony given at this stage should remain in the Attorney General's office.

counsel. They also have the right to silence and can ask for a forty-eight hour delay before giving their explanations.

The right to legal advice is thus now guaranteed although the *ex officio* appointment is again not provided for. The legislature recognised that the changes introduced to the preliminary inquiry have enhanced the need for defence counsel's presence in order to guarantee the defendant's rights.[65] It should be noted, however, that under the new article 43.1 CPP, there is now no need for a preliminary inquiry if, following an internal administrative investigation, sufficient evidence is produced to commence criminal proceedings. Linking administrative with criminal proceedings in such a way makes it crucial to ensure that defence rights are guaranteed during the course of the former.

3.7.   Legal Aid

As previously noted, Greek law requires the authorities responsible for the conduct of both the pre-trial and trial stages to appoint defence counsel *ex officio* in certain cases to an unrepresented defendant. The cases in which *ex officio* appointment is expressly provided for in the Code[66] include, for example, a felony trial (art. 340, 344 and 348 CPP), a misdemeanor trial when the defendant was caught in the act, and a defendant's examination before the investigating judge. In most cases, *ex officio* appointment is subject to the defendant's express request. There are, however, no other conditions to be fulfilled regarding this appointment. There is, for example, no 'means' test regarding the applicant.

Where a lawyer is to be appointed *ex officio*, the court or investigating judge appoints the lawyer from a list especially compiled for that purpose by the local Bar Association. Only practising lawyers can be appointed as legal representatives. The unrepresented defendant has to accept the appointment made by the court and cannot choose their own lawyer. Following legislative developments introduced in 1999[67] and 2004,[68] lawyers appointed *ex officio* are remunerated from state funds.[69] A

---

[65]   For example, under the amended art. 244 CPP, a case can now be taken directly to court, following the preliminary inquiry, if there is sufficient evidence that a misdemeanour was committed.

[66]   The president of the first instance court assigns counsel to an unrepresented defendant tried for a felony, regardless of whether the defendant asked for the appointment (art. 340.1 CPP). The Appeal Court appoints counsel to an unrepresented defendant, tried for a felony, if the latter so requests (art. 376 CPP). Under article 402 CPP, the same applies for cases tried by the mixed criminal courts. An accused tried for a felony, who having appeared in court must leave because of a health problem or other reasons, continues to be represented by their lawyer or appoints another lawyer to represent them in their absence (art. 344 and 348 CPP). A defendant caught while committing a flagrant act is appointed a counsel during the misdemeanour trial if the defendant so requests (art. 423 CPP). The investigating judge or the court appoints a lawyer to a defendant who must undergo a psychiatric evaluation (art. 200 CPP). The president of the appeals court will appoint a lawyer during the discussion of an extradition request, should the person concerned so request (article 448.1 CPP). The violation of these provisions leads to absolute nullity.

[67]   Art. 96A CPP as introduced by art. 17 of Law 2721/1999.

[68]   Law 3226/2004 FEK 24A/4 February 2004.

defendant appearing before the investigating judge, who does not have a lawyer, will be therefore have a defence lawyer appointed to assist them irrespective of their financial means.

In addition to the provisions for *ex officio* appointment, there is now provision for defence counsel to be appointed to defendants charged with misdemeanours 'who do not have the financial means to appoint a lawyer themselves'. Appointment in these cases is, therefore, made subject to a 'means test.' Although the criteria for indigence were left unspecified in the 1999 legislative changes, a financial limit has now been introduced by law 3226/2004. Legal aid will be available to those whose annual family income is less than two-thirds of the lowest annual income set by the National General Employment Contract Agreement (art. 1.2).[70]

The new legislation also clarifies that legal aid will be provided for the trial hearing for those tried for misdemeanours before the three-member Misdemeanours Courts for offences carrying a minimum of six months prison sentence (art. 7.2.b Law 3226/2004). There is currently no legal aid provision for the pre-trial stage regarding these offences. Cases tried before one-member Misdemeanours Courts are excluded from legal aid provision both pre-trial and at trial. Moreover, while a combined reading of the previous article 96A (introduced in 1999 but repealed in 2004) provisions seemed to include legal aid during the *ex officio* summary investigation, the new legislation makes no provision for that.

3.8.   The Right to disclosure

As noted earlier, a person who is arrested must be immediately told the grounds for their arrest. Following the amendments introduced in the preliminary inquiry in 2005, a person asked to give explanations to the authorities can ask to be informed of all the contents of the case-file up to that point before offering the required explanations. Moreover, they can refuse to answer all or part of the questions put to them (art. 31.2 CPP).

The pre-trial stage is, however, said to be run according to the principle of secrecy. The pre-trial investigation procedure generally remains secret from the parties, including the defendant, who is informed about the contents of the investigation file only when called to testify before the investigating judge. It is at this stage that the defendant can copy all documents contained in the file and ask for a forty-eight hour delay before giving their testimony (art. 101.1 and 102 CPP).

[69]   See Decision no 64762/2004 of the Minister for Economy and Economics and the Minister of Justice FEK 888B/15 June 2004 estimating the funds required for legal aid during 2004 to be approximately € 500,000 and around € 3,500,000 for the following years. According to the Ministry of Justice official data, the final expense for 2004 amounted to € 729,323, the amount for the period between January and July 2005 amounted to € 329,794. This covers lawyers' remuneration for both civil and criminal legal aid.

[70]   See art. 1.2 of Law 3226/2004. The legislator's intention was to bring within the legal aid provisions pensioners, unemployed persons and those occasionally employed. The limit set at the moment is less than € 5,800.

The Attorney General, on the other hand, has a right to be informed of the process of the investigation at any time (art. 31 CPP).

The accused has a right to silence before the investigating judge and no adverse inferences may be drawn from silence. The accused is, however, invited to present the proposed defence in as full a manner as possible (art. 273.2 and 274 CPP). According to article 274, the person carrying out the pre-trial investigation must investigate with due care and diligence every incident that the defendant has referred to in the stated defence, if this is useful in order to ascertain the truth. The system, therefore, encourages disclosure on both sides at this point in order to resolve any issues at the pre-trial stage. Moreover, both the defendant and the civil party have the right to know the content of the Attorney General's proposal before its submission to the Judicial Council (art. 308.2 CPP). The defendant and the civil party can submit a memorandum with their comments and answers.

If the defendant's request for notification of the proposal is not complied with, this will lead to the annulment of the proceedings (art. 171.1.d CPP). Refusing the civil party's request does not have the same result. This inequality between the defendant and the civil party arguably demonstrates that guaranteeing the defendant's rights against the investigating authorities is paramount at the investigative stage.[71]

3.9. *Special protection of juveniles and other vulnerable persons*

In Greek law those between the age of eight and eighteen years at the time the alleged criminal act was committed are considered to be juveniles.[72] Children between the age of eight and thirteen years old cannot be convicted of a criminal offence, although they may be made the subject of reformative or therapeutic measures (art. 122, 123 and 126.1 of the Penal Code). Children over thirteen but under eighteen years can be convicted of an offence, but may only be given a custodial sentence (which results in detention in a special juvenile centre) if that is considered necessary to prevent them from committing further offences.

Juveniles appear before juvenile rather than adult courts (see art. 7 and art. 113 CPP). In the Court of Misdemeanours in Athens, Thessalonica, Patras and Piraeus the Attorney General of the Court of Appeal appoints a specific Attorney General (as well as a substitute) to deal with criminal proceedings relating to juveniles (art. 27.1 CPP). Misdemeanours Courts appoint one of their investigating judges to deal specifically with offences allegedly committed by juveniles (see art. 33.3.b and art. 4.2a CPP).[73]

Article 239 CPP provides that a social report on the juvenile, consisting of information on their family, educational, psychological and ethical background

---

71   See the following Supreme Court Decisions: A.P. (Section E, in camera) No. 334/2002, *NoB* 2002, p. 1519 and A.P. (in camera), No. 737/2002, p. 1755; A.P. (in camera) No. 213/2003, *NoB* 2003, p. 1285; A.P. (in camera) No. 650/2003, *NoB* 2004, p. 90.

72   The maximum age changed from 17 to 18 years with the introduction of Law 3189/2003 FEK 243A/21 October 2003.

73   A. X. Papadamakis, *supra* note 15, p. 257.

must be compiled as part of the pre-trial investigation. The investigating judge can, but is not obliged to, order a report and investigating judges often omit to request a report during the pre-trial investigation. It is, however, normally prepared for the oral hearing. Temporary detention may be imposed on juveniles only if they are above thirteen years and are accused of a felony punishable by a minimum sentence of ten years (art. 282.5 CPP as amended by Law 3189/2003).

The police must ensure that they treat both juveniles and other vulnerable groups with respect. According to the Police Code of Conduct, police officers must take special care with regard to vulnerable groups and ensure that the conditions of detention guarantee the security, health and respect of the arrested person. With regard to juveniles they must try, as far as possible, to keep them separate from adults. Should the person under arrest need medical attention, the police must provide it immediately, allowing the person to be examined by a doctor of their choice (art. 3.h Code of Conduct).

4. The impact of the investigative stage on the trial

4.1. The principles of 'immediacy' and 'orality' and the use of pre-trial statements

As there is no guilty plea procedure in Greece,[74] if there is sufficient evidence to justify taking a case to court, the evidence will be scrutinised by the judicial authorities at the oral hearing irrespective of whether the accused admits the offence. This, therefore, guarantees that pre-trial investigation work will be evaluated by the judiciary in order to assess whether the evidence is sufficient to establish the guilt of the accused. If the evidence is considered to be insufficient to either commence criminal proceedings or take the case to court the case will, depending on its nature and the stage of the proceedings, either be filed by the Attorney General or dismissed by a decision of the judicial council.

While the Greek criminal trial is said to be run according to 'adversarial' principles, the judge's role is not that of an umpire. The judge is permitted to actively examine the witnesses, the accused and the third parties. The judges, who will already have had access to the pre-trial case dossier, will be aware of the evidence contained in it. Their role is central in determining how the trial will develop and how witnesses will be questioned. The presiding judge in Misdemeanours Courts, for example, will normally commence the proceedings by asking questions first,[75] with the aim of clarifying the parts of the dossier they are not satisfied with. The other judges (if not a single judge court) may ask additional questions and the Attorney General may then ask her own questions.

The emphasis placed on the pre-trial dossier is a point of difference from classical adversarial theory. The fact that judges will sometimes interrupt defence

---

[74] A confession is one of the means of proof which will be freely evaluated by the court (art. 178 CPP).

[75] This is almost always the case in one-member misdemeanours courts.

questions or their line of argument saying that 'there is no point in this question, this is all contained in the case file (dossier)'[76] highlights the confidence placed in the pre-trial investigation work and offers an explanation for the reluctance to allow extensive adversarial-type defence involvement in the oral hearing. This judicial attitude, however, also arguably goes against one of the fundamental principles underlying the oral procedure and the evidence presented at trial, i.e. the principle of 'immediacy.' This suggests a preference for the evidence that is closest to the judge (that with which she came into immediate and personal contact) and can create a reason for annulling the proceedings.[77]

The principle of 'orality' requires that all documents the Court takes into consideration to reach its decision have to be publicly presented during the trial hearing. However, if one considers the limited role of the defence during the pre-trial stage of the compilation of the 'dossier,' the greater the role attributed to the dossier by the court (by limiting defence attempts to re-evaluate the evidence presented in it), the less effectively defence rights are being protected.

4.2. The exclusion of illegally or unfairly obtained evidenced

Article 179 CPP provides that all forms of evidence are allowed in the criminal process. Article 177 CPP introduces the principle of 'moral' rather than 'legal' proof, which allows the judge to reach a verdict through a free evaluation of the evidence before them. That allows the judge to pronounce someone as innocent despite the accused having already confessed. It also delimits the freedom introduced by article 179 CPP by providing that evidence that has been obtained unlawfully must not be taken into account in deciding on the defendant's guilt or innocence, or the sentence. Moreover, article 19.3 Constitution (introduced in 2001) provides that the use of any evidence that has been obtained in contravention of the provisions relating to the secrecy of communication, the collection and use (especially by electronic means) of personal data, or by violation of a person's home and private and family life, will be prohibited. While the prohibition of article 19 is absolute, that introduced by article 177.2 CPP[78] provides for an exception in the case of felonies punishable by life imprisonment. In such cases, unlawfully obtained evidence can be used if the court gives a reasoned opinion on the matter. The Greek courts have held that the defendant can use evidence obtained illegally if this is the only means of proving their innocence.

Article 170 and 171 CPP deal with those breaches of the rules of criminal procedure which may result in annulling the particular act and acts relating to or resulting from it. Two types of nullities are distinguished: relevant and absolute nullities. The more serious violations of the procedure rules, in particular those

---

76 This comment was noted during the fieldwork research in criminal courts for the completion of my PhD thesis. I observed one defence counsel who told the court that if they were to decide on the basis of the dossier then there was no point in the oral hearing.

77 See also D.D. Spinellis, 'Recent Trends in the Greek Criminal Proceedings: Limiting or Expanding the Rights of the Accused?,' *Temple Law Review*, 1989, p. 1269.

78 This provision was introduced by Law 2408/1996.

relating to the defendant's fundamental rights, are subject to absolute nullities. For example, if the procedure relating to the court's composition, the initiation of criminal proceedings by the Attorney General or the appearance, representation and legal assistance of the defendant and the exercise of their rights are not respected, this will result in the nullity of these acts and those that depend on them. Acts that are deemed invalid will have to be repeated in a lawful way if this is considered necessary and is possible (art. 176 CPP).

The absolute nullities relating to the pre-trial stage have to be brought to the attention of the relevant authorities, at the latest, before the decision is irrevocably made that the case be taken to court (art. 173 CPP). Otherwise, they are deemed to have been 'cured' or 'covered', i.e. the voidable procedural act has recovered full legal effect (art. 174 CPP). The courts have, however, recently accepted that reading in court the pre-trial testimony of the defendant which was taken in contravention of article 31.2 and 105.2 CPP, can lead to nullity even if the nullity had not been brought to the authorities' attention at the pre-trial stage. So, for example, the assertion that the defendant's confession was obtained by oppression can be made at the oral hearing since this evidence has been obtained by unlawful means. A confession obtained by oppression is also treated as a 'non-existent' act in the legal sense since it lacks its fundamental feature, i.e. it is not the result of the defendant's free will.[79] Similarly, a confession obtained without the defendant having had the opportunity to consult a lawyer means that the act of examination will be invalid and the confession will be treated as unlawfully obtained evidence.

The Greek Supreme Court has recently placed emphasis on the necessity for the oral hearing to provide an opportunity for truly adversarial proceedings protecting the rights of the defence. It held[80] that reading in open court the absent prosecution witness' pre-trial statements and evaluating them when making the final judgment deprived the defendant of their right to cross-examine prosecution witnesses, as part of the right to defend oneself guaranteed under article 6.3.d of the ECHR and article 14.3.e of the ICCPR. This makes the procedure void and will create a reason for annulling the court's decision. These judgments have, however, placed emphasis on the defendant's attitude during the trial process holding that, if the defendant and/or their lawyer do not object to the witness testimony being read, there is no reason for annulling the proceedings.[81] This, arguably, enhances the need for the defence lawyer to be present, and requires them to play a more pro-active part.

Whilst the admission of hearsay evidence is contrary to the principle of adversarial proceedings, since the defendant and the Court are not able to cross-examine witnesses on it,[82] article 224 CPP allows the court to freely evaluate this evidence. This is consistent with the principle enunciated in article 179 CPP, that all

---

[79] P. Brakoumatsos, 'Procedural invalidities and their "cure" stages,' *PoinDik*, 2005, p. 737.

[80] A.P. (Section F) No. 1566/2003, *NoB* 2004, p. 643.

[81] See; *inter alia*, A.P. No. 636/2002, *NoB* 2002, p. 1755; A.P. (Section F) No. 1605/2002, *NoB* 2003, p. 727; A.P. No. 1790 and 1803/2003, *NoB* 2004, p. 643. This is the case even if the court did not verify whether the witness' absence was justified (see A.P. No. 922/2003, *NoB* 2004, p. 91).

[82] See N.K. Androulakis, *supra* note 4, p. 126.

means of evidence are acceptable. Hearsay witnesses must, however, name their source of information. Otherwise, their testimony is not taken into account.

5.   The role of the defence lawyer

The organization of the Greek criminal justice system, in which State officials control, to a large extent, the criminal justice processes both pre-trial and at trial, necessarily affects the role of the defence lawyer. This has been justified on the basis that the presence of judicial officers in the process guarantees the required level of both objectivity and fairness.

The lawyer's role has, however, been seen to be crucial with regard to a number of practices developing despite established principles of the criminal justice process. The strong judicial presence in the trial, in the form of both judges and the Attorney General, should have been enough, for example, to ensure respect for the principle of 'immediacy,' which requires that the statements of absent witnesses may not be read in court. The gradual erosion of this principle, however, now requires an even stronger defence counsel willingness to object to this practice even when the court is willing to proceed by reading these statements. Respect for the defendant's rights necessarily passes through to their lawyer. Even though the court is also meant to play this role, it has arguably sometimes treated it as secondary to the principle of the search for the truth. It is in keeping this balance that the defence lawyer's role becomes important. The prominent role of the judge, the extensive presence of the Attorney General and the often heavy reliance on the pre-trial dossier, create a situation where the defence may be sometimes be required to act under 'hostile circumstances.'

The judicial supervision of the pre-trial investigation is meant to give the system the required levels of objectivity and fairness. Practices relating to the investigation of flagrant offences, whereby the police are required to perform all actions thought necessary on their own initiative in order not to lose important evidence and to inform the Attorney General as soon as possible, make this supervision posterior to the actual investigation. As noted earlier, the *ex officio* appointment of defence counsel is not required in such cases.[83]

The presence of judicial officers at the pre-trial stage and their extensive powers of deciding how to proceed with the investigation often reduce the defence lawyer's role to that of requesting the authorities to carry out the sort of investigations the defence thinks necessary, but the final decision always rests with the investigating authorities. Because of the investigating authorities' obligation to search for all the evidence, however, the defence is invited to present anything that supports its case so that it may be further investigated. It may then be considered to be to the defendant's advantage to present all the evidence it has at that stage so that the search can be complete and possibly lead to the judicial council not referring the case to trial.

---

[83]   It is, however, provided for during the trial which is normally arranged for the following day; a three-day delay can be requested (and is generally given) to prepare one's defence.

As for defence counsel carrying out their own investigations, it has been suggested that this is necessary in order to deal with the problem of the investigating authorities' heavy workload, which may lead them to conclude their investigative acts once they are satisfied they have a strong case against the accused.[84] Financial and time considerations may, however, limit the defence lawyer's willingness or ability to carry out their own investigation. Their powers of effective action may also be limited by the fact that they are not aware of the evidence available until the defendant is invited to present themselves to the authorities to give their testimony.

Defence lawyers are required to strike a balance between acting in their client's interests and not obstructing the work of the investigative authorities. Certain provisions of the Code of Lawyers emphasize their role as contributing to the discovery of the truth and upholding the law, while at the same time providing that they must perform all acts necessary to represent and defend their client freely and without obstructions.[85] Article 233 PC provides that a lawyer who intentionally harms the interests of their client may be punished by up to three years' imprisonment. At the same time, various practices and legislative developments have required them to become more adversarial towards the judicial investigators. The practice, for example, of including the defendant's pre-trial testimonies in the case-file submitted to the court,[86] requires a degree of vigilance on counsel's side in order to defend their client's rights effectively. It requires counsel to challenge the contents of the dossier and the judicial decision to include and/or use them. This may be more difficult to accomplish in a system governed by the presumption of objectivity in respect of the work carried out by the judicial authorities. This mix of a more pro-active adversarial-type defence attitude before a more interventionist-type court, which may still consider objections as a direct challenge to its authority, arguably requires a fine balance to be struck by Greek lawyers. The existence of the right to silence, on the other hand, makes both the lawyer's and the defendant's place more straightforward since no adverse inferences can lawfully be drawn nor can there be an examination of the reasons for the suspect acting on the advice of their lawyer.

The Greek system arguably recognizes the importance of the defence lawyer's role in criminal justice since it expressly provides for the *ex officio* appointment of a lawyer in the circumstances referred to earlier. Only qualified lawyers are allowed

---

[84]   A.I. Konstantinidis, *The place of defence counsel in the criminal trial*, Athens-Komotini, Ant. N. Sakkoulas Publishers, 1992, p. 51.

[85]   Art. 46 and 39.1 of the Code of Lawyers respectively. See also art. 30 of the Code of Ethics which provides that lawyers '….have the right and the obligation to defend with vigour and consistency their views, to confront the opposing views of the Attorney General, the judges or the representatives of the Authorities and to strive to prove their client's innocence or the soundness of the views of the party they support and generally to strive with all legal means towards the discovery of the truth and the correct interpretation and application of the law.'

[86]   According to the Supreme Court (A.P. No. 622/2003, *NoB* 2004, p. 90.), this will not cause the proceedings to be annulled if the evidence is not read or evaluated by the court and does not interfere with its judgment.

to assist suspects and defendants at the pre-trial stage. The situation regarding the right to legal aid has certainly improved in the last few years. There is now provision for lawyers to be paid out of public funds for work done. The availability of legal aid is, however, still quite limited since the 'means' test, operating in cases other than those of *ex officio* appointment, is very strict. Moreover, as previously noted, legal aid is not available for the stage of *ex officio* summary investigation by the police nor during the pre-trial summary investigation of misdemeanours to be tried by the one or three-member Misdemeanours Court, leaving many defendants, who may be in need of legal advice, unrepresented.

6.   List of abbreviations

A.G.	Attorney General
A.P.	Areios Pagos (Supreme Court)
CPP	Code of Penal Procedure
FEK	Fillo Ephimeridas tis Kiberniseos (Government Official Journal)
NoB	Nomiko Bima (Law Review of the Athens Bar Association)
PC	Penal Code
P. Chr	Poinika Chronika (Journal of Penal Law)
PoinDik	Poiniki Dikaiosini (Journal of Penal Justice)

7.   Bibliography

In Greek

N.K. Androulakis, *Fundamental concepts of the criminal trial*, Athens-Komotini, Ant. N. Sakkoulas Publishers, 1994.

X. Argyropoulos, 'The Institutional role of defence counsel in the criminal trial,' in *Proceedings of 1st International Conference of the Greek Association of Penal Law Practitioners, The Institutional role of defence counsel in the criminal trial - Tradition and Perspectives*, Athens-Komotini, Ant. N. Sakkoulas Publishers, 1998.

Chr. Bakas, *The pre-trial stage of the criminal trial*, Athens-Komotini, Ant. N. Sakkoulas Publishers, 1995.

A. Bouropoulos, *Interpretation of the Code of Penal Procedure*, Athens-Thessalonica, Nik. A. Sakkoulas Publications, 1951.

P. Brakoumatsos, 'Procedural invalidities and their "cure" stages,' *PoinDik*, 2005, p. 733-738.

Caselaw of the ECtHR can be found at the European Court of Human Rights HUDOC Portal: <http://cmiskp.echr.coe.int>, in Series A and after 1 January 1996 in Reports of Judgments and Decisions, both published by Carl Heymans Verlag KG, Köln, Germany.

Th.I. Dalakouras, *Penal Procedure*, Athens-Komotini, Ant. N. Sakkoulas Publishers, 2003.

G. Kalfelis & L. Margaritis, *Penal Procedure, Special Procedures, Flagrant offences and summary proceedings*, Athens, Nomiki BiBliothiki, 1998.

A. Karras, *Penal Procedural Law*, Athens-Komotini, Ant. N. Sakkoulas Publishers, 1998.

A.I. Konstantinidis, *The place of defence counsel in the criminal trial*, Athens-Komotini, Ant. N. Sakkoulas Publishers, 1992.

L.P. Limberopoulos, *Nullities in penal procedure*, Athens-Komotini, Ant. N. Sakkoulas Publishers, 1993.

G.A. Mangakis, *Defence Counsel – A paradoxical achievement of civilisation*, Athens-Komotini, Ant. N. Sakkoulas Publishers, 1992.

A.X. Papadamakis, *Penal Procedure*, Athens-Thessalonica, Sakkoulas Publications, 2006.

G. Siaperas, 'Human consent to the taking and analysis of genetic material (DNA),' *PoinDik*, 2005, p. 1451-1460.

E. Simeonidou-Kastanidou, 'Law 2928/2001 on the protection of the citizen from unlawful acts of criminal organisations,' *PoinDik*, 2001, p. 694-699.

P. Tsiridis, *The New Legislation for the Acceleration of Criminal Proceedings*, Athens-Komotini, Ant. N. Sakkoulas Publishers, 2005.

In English

K.D. Kerameus & P.J. Kozyris (eds), *Introduction to Greek Law*, Deventer, Kluwer/Sakkoulas, 1988.

D.D. Spinellis, 'Criminal Law and Procedure,' in K.D. Kerameus & P.I. Kozyris (eds), *Introduction to Greek Law*, Deventer/Athens, Kluwer/Sakkoulas, 1988.

D.D. Spinellis, 'Recent Trends in the Greek Criminal Proceedings: Limiting or Expanding the Rights of the Accused?,' *Temple Law Review*, 1989, p. 1261-1279.

L. Tsoureli, 'Human Rights in Pre-Trial and Trial Procedures in Greece,' in J.A. Andrews (ed.), *Human Rights in Criminal Procedure, A Comparative Study*, The Hague, Martinus Nijhoff Publishers, 1982.

Giulio Illuminati
Michele Caianiello

THE INVESTIGATIVE STAGE OF THE CRIMINAL PROCESS IN ITALY

1. Introduction: the criminal process in the Italian system: the choice for an accusatorial model

1.1. *The Separation between investigation and trial. The orality principle provided for by the Constitution in the criminal process*

Notwithstanding its inquisitorial traditions, since 1988 Italy has had a new Code of Criminal Procedure (the 1988 Code), modelled on the adversarial system typical of common law jurisdictions.[1] After World War II, and especially since the end of the 1950s, scholars increasingly criticised the Code which was considered to be a remnant of the inquisitorial model inherited from the fascist era of the 1930s. The post-war Constitution of the Italian Republic, established in 1948, was the starting point for the rights movement in the field of criminal law and criminal procedure. Protection of the rights of the accused soon became a political issue. The initial effects of this ideological paradigm shift was that some of the reforms improved the rights of the defence, in particular by permitting the accused's lawyer to participate in the actions performed by the investigating judge. After more than twenty years of political pressure, academic studies and Parliamentary debate, the 1988 Code replaced the modified 'old system' with a Code derived from the adversarial model.

As a consequence of the reform the new Code distinguishes between the investigation and the trial phase. Most of the information collected in the first phase of the proceedings – the investigation – is inadmissible as evidence at trial. The new Code is based on the premise that the probative value of evidence is affected by the manner in which it is collected. The drafters of the Code believed that the best

---

[1]   See E. Amodio and E. Selvaggi, 'An Accusatorial System in a Civil Law Country: The 1988 Italian Code of Criminal Procedure,' *Temp. L. Rev.,* 1989, p. 1211; W.T. Pizzi and M. Montagna, 'The Battle to Establish an Adversarial Trial System in Italy,' *Mich. J. Int'l L.,* 2004, p. 429; G. Illuminati, 'The Frustrated Turn to Adversarial Procedure in Italy (Italian Criminal Procedure Code of 1988),' *Wash. U. Global Stud. L. Rev.,* 2005, p. 567. On the distinction between inquisitorial and accusatorial system, specifically referring to the Italian criminal pro-cess, see G. Illuminati, 'Accusatorio e inquisitorio (sistema),' in *Enciclopedia Giuridica Treccani,* 1988, vol. I, p. 1 *et seq.*

method for proving the facts and discovering truth is a context in which opposing viewpoints are present. As a consequence, the only evidence on which a decision can be based is the evidence received orally at trial, involving the form of cross-examination inspired by the Anglo-American system of criminal procedure.[2] The symbol of the separation between the trial phase and the investigative phase is the 'double-dossier system,' distinguishing it from the single investigative dossier that characterized the old system prior to 1988. During the investigative stage of criminal proceedings all records of evidence are collected in an investigative dossier. At the end of the investigation, this dossier is set aside and is available only to the parties, who can use it to prepare for trial or to challenge a witness' credibility during their trial testimony.[3] The trial judge will never see the investigative dossier. Instead, the trial judge is given a completely new dossier, the trial dossier, which only contains the evidence collected during trial, and the evidence which is objectively impossible to reproduce in court (*corpus delicti*, wiretappings, records of searches performed by the police, records of prior convictions of the accused).[4]

Compared to the 1930 Code, the 1988 Code had a completely different profile. In the first years after the adoption of the new Code, it was clear that the newly introduced system had not been completely accepted by the actors within the criminal justice field, especially by the judiciary.[5] As a result of this cultural hostility to the 1988 reform, two divergent legal strands developed simultaneously. Whilst many new provisions of the 1988 Code were nullified by the Constitutional Court,[6] which restored the old system through its decisions (thus frustrating the strict separation introduced by the 1988 Code between the investigative and trial stages), other provisions were interpreted and applied by the judges in a way more consistent with the inquisitorial rather than with the accusatorial model.

After some years of the judiciary not accepting the new code, the Constitutional Act 2 of 1999 saw Parliament modifying article 111 of the Constitution to restore the accusatorial model whilst retaining the principles of both the adversarial and accusatorial systems which were deemed to correspond to the principles of a fair trial. After the 1999 reform, article 111 of the Constitution stated that evidence in criminal cases should only be heard in court, in front of the parties and an impartial judge. The only legitimate exceptions that allow for any substantive use of evidence collected outside of the trial are where presenting such

---

2   G. Giostra, 'Contraddittorio,' in *Enciclopedia Giuridica Treccani*, 2001, vol. II, p. 1 *et seq.*; G. Ubertis, 'La ricerca della verità giudiziale,' in G. Ubertis (ed.), *La conoscenza del fatto nel processo penale*, Milano, Giuffrè, 1992, p. 2 *et seq.*

3   See G. Illuminati, 'Giudizio,' in G. Conso & V. Grevi (eds), *Compendio di procedura penale*, Padova, Cedam, 2003, p. 644 *et seq.*

4   See C. Cesari, *L'irripetibilità sopravvenuta degli atti d'indagine*, Milano, Giuffrè, 1999, p. 9.

5   See M. Panzavolta, 'Reforms and Counter-Reforms in the Italian Struggle for an Accusatorial Criminal Law System,' *N.C. J. Int'l L. & Com. Reg.*, 2005, p. 577- 595; G. Illuminati, 'The Frustrated Turn,' *supra* note 1, p. 573.

6   In Italy, any provision of law can be submitted to the Constitutional Court for review to determine whether this law is consistent with or in violation of the Constitution (article 134 of the Italian Constitution).

evidence at trial would, in general, be worthless or impossible.[7] As a consequence of the constitutional reform, Parliament reintroduced the prohibition placed on the use of the investigative records at trial, except for disqualifying witnesses. At the same time, one of the central pillars of the accusatorial system, the prohibition on the use of police officers' testimony concerning statements collected during the investigation, was restored.[8] Finally, the Code now establishes that a decision can never be based on evidence of a witness who has refused to subject their testimony to the scrutiny of the court. No out-of-court statements of a witness who fails or refuses to attend the trial can be used to establish guilt.[9]

1.2. *Exceptions to the accusatorial model*

Despite the choice of the accusatorial model, the 1988 Code did retain some features of the traditional continental model. One such feature is the legality principle, which the drafters incorporated throughout all criminal proceedings. According to the Constitution, the prosecutor is obliged to take action in criminal cases: the principle of legality applies strictly. No matter how minor the offence,[10] the law allows the prosecutor no discretion on whether to prosecute, nor can the prosecutor suspend or withdraw the action, which must always end in a judicial decision. Another feature preserved in the Code is the judge's power to introduce evidence when they cannot decide the case on the evidence submitted at trial. In such a situation, the judge may introduce evidence unilaterally or ask the parties to submit evidence on certain specific issues. This power can only be exercised at the conclusion of the parties' case.[11] A further important feature of the traditional inquisitorial system that was maintained by the 1988 reform is that there is no jury in criminal proceedings. Fact-finding remains in the hands of professional judges.

---

7   See M. Panzavolta *supra* note 5, p. 609; G. Giostra, *supra* note 2, p. 1 *et seq.*

8   F. Caprioli, 'Palingenesi di un divieto probatorio. La testimonianza indiretta nel funzionario di polizia nel rinnovato assetto processuale,' in R. Kostoris (ed.), *Il giusto processo tra contraddittorio e diritto al silenzio*, Torino, Giappichelli, 2002, p. 59; G. Illuminati, 'La testimonianza della polizia giudiziaria sul contenuto di dichiarazioni non verbalizzate,' *Cassazione Penale*, 2003, p. 660.

9   P. Ferrua, 'La regola d'oro del processo accusatorio,' in R. Kostoris (ed.), *Il giusto processo tra contraddittorio e diritto al silenzio*, Torino, Giappichelli, 2002, p. 11; P.P. Paulesu, 'Volontaria sottrazione al contraddittorio,' in *ivi*, p. 125 *et seq.*

10 G. Illuminati, 'The Role of the Public Prosecutor in the Italian System,' in J.P. Peter Tak (ed.), *Tasks and Powers of the Prosecution Services in the EU Member States*, Nijmegen, Wolf Legal Publishers, 2004, p. 308-310; M. Caianiello, *Poteri dei privati nell'esercizio dell'azione penale*, Torino, Giappichelli, 2003, p. 14-20.

11 See P. Ferrua, 'I poteri probatori del giudice dibattimentale: ragionevolezza delle Sezioni Unite e dogmatismo della Corte Costituzionale,' *Rivista Italiana Diritto e Procedura Penale*, 1994, p. 1073; G. Spangher, 'L'articolo 507 c.p.p. davanti alla Corte Costituzionale: ulteriore momento nella definizione del 'sistema accusatorio' compatibile con la Costituzione,' *Giurisprudenza Costituzionale*, 1993, p. 919; G. Illuminati, 'Ammissione e acquisizione della prova nell'istruzione dibattimentale,' in P. Ferrua *et al.*, *La prova nel dibattimento penale*, Torino, Giappichelli, 2005, p. 92-98.

The sole exception is the '*court of assise*,' a hybrid panel composed of six lay judges and two professional judges, which deals with major crimes. Moreover, judges' must always give written reasons for their decisions.[12] Both the prosecutor and the accused have a right of appeal.

Since the adoption of the Constitution in 1948, prosecutors are members of the judiciary and are guaranteed the same independence and tenure as judges. Both are classified as *magistrati* (judicial officers), and both are selected by the same competitive process of examination and are able to move, at their request, from one function to the other.[13] This 'objective' concept of the role of the prosecutor is also a relic of the inquisitorial system. It is significant that the most representative association of criminal lawyers, the so called Penal Chamber (*Camera Penale*), is now conducting a high profile political campaign to lobby Parliament to put in place measures that will separate prosecutors from the judiciary. The rationale for this proposal is that under the 1988 Code the prosecutor and defence are in an adversarial relationship, and 'equality of arms' requires that prosecutors must not be institutionally treated as members of the judiciary. Otherwise, there is a risk of a *de facto* unequal relationship between prosecution and defence at trial since the judiciary are, in most cases, more keen to sustain the arguments of the former for reasons relating to professional culture.

1.3. Alternative means for resolving criminal cases inspired by the inquisitorial model

In order to make the accusatorial system sustainable, the 1988 Code provides alternative methods of resolving criminal cases. The first alternative is called 'application of punishment at the request of the parties' (*applicazione della pena su richiesta delle parti*) and bears some resemblance to the plea-bargaining model found in the United States of America.[14] Under this procedure, the defendant and the Prosecutor agree on a penalty, but without a guilty plea. The penalty is reduced by up to one-third of the normal level of punishment. The judge must conduct a rapid review of the investigative file to ensure that there is no clear indication of innocence within the records. The judge should also verify – as a consequence of the legality principle – that the penalty is consistent with the nature of the crime.

Another alternative is the 'abbreviated trial' (*giudizio abbreviato*) in which, at the request of the defendant, the judgment is made on the basis of the investigative

---

12 See. F.M. Iacoviello, *La motivazione della sentenza penale e il suo controllo in cassazione*, Milano, Giuffrè, 1997, p. 9 *et seq.*

13 Some restrictions on the ability to move from one function to the other were introduced by Legislative Decree 5 April 2006 No. 160.

14 G. Lozzi, 'Il giusto processo e i riti speciali deflativi del dibattimento,' *Rivista italiana di diritto e procedura penale*, 2002, p. 1165 *et seq.*; D. Vigoni, *L'applicazione della pena su richiesta delle parti*, Milano, Giuffrè, 2000.

files.[15] In other words, the defendant waives the right to trial, receiving a reduction of one-third of the normal penalty.

A third alternative, 'proceeding by penal decree' (*decreto penale di condanna*), may occur where the accused is charged on the basis of records contained in the investigative dossier, following a prosecutor's written request. The judge's decision is made in camera, and in the absence of the parties,[16] and the penalty may be reduced up to one-half. This form of proceeding, strongly inquisitorial, is available only if the proposed penalty is a fine. The defendant may contest the judge's decision, in which case a regular trial will take place, but the defendant loses the opportunity to receive a penalty reduction and can even receive a custodial sentence.

If we look at such alternative proceedings as a means of making the system sustainable (which was the intention of the legislature), we must recognize that they have not been particularly successful. The number of indicted persons who agree to such methods of case disposal is not sufficient – about one third nationally – to ensure the efficiency and the celerity of the criminal justice system. Italy indeed has not yet solved the issues relating to what is a 'reasonable delay' in criminal proceedings, as provided for by the European Convention of Human Rights.

2. Police powers in the investigation phase

2.1. The relation between the Prosecutor and the police

Inspired by the adversarial model, as previously stated, the task of undertaking the criminal investigation rests with the Prosecutor. Despite its inquisitorial tradition, the Italian criminal procedure system does not make provision for an investigating judge. Thus the investigative phase is conducted mainly by the Prosecutor, and by the police under their direction. In this stage of the proceedings, a judge (the judge for the preliminary investigation – *giudice per le indagini preliminary*), intervenes only in exceptional cases where a restriction of fundamental rights is involved.[17] This judge, however, does not have control of the investigation (for this reason they are also called a 'judge without a file'). On the contrary, they are a mere judge *ad acta*. In other words, they are involved only in relation to specific acts, and at the request of the parties (usually, at the request of the prosecutor).

To guarantee the independence of the prosecutor, the Constitution provides that the police, whilst investigating a criminal case, act under the control of the prosecutor even though, from an administrative point of view, all police institutions are part of the executive.[18] The police bodies acting under the control of the

---

15   See R. Orlandi, 'Giudizi speciali,' in G. Conso and V. Grevi (eds), *Compendio di procedura penale*, Padova, Cedam, 2003, p. 580 *et seq.*; F. Zacchè, *Il giudizio abbreviato*, Milano, Giuffrè, 2004, p. 61.

16   See M. Caianiello, 'Art. 459,' in G. Conso and V. Grevi (eds), *Commentario breve al codice di procedura penale*, Padova, Cedam, 2005, p. 1658 *et seq.*

17   See 2. 2 *infra*.

18   G. Illuminati, *supra* note 10, p. 308-310.

prosecution are called *sezioni di polizia giudiziaria* (judicial police sections). Once the commission of an offence is discovered, the police must report it to the prosecutor without delay.[19] In theory, the police are partially independent of the prosecutor only in the first stages of the investigations, until the prosecutor has taken over the case. The Code (article 348 § 3) provides that after the communication of the *notitia criminis* (information of the existence of a crime) to the prosecutor the police are under the supervision of the prosecutor, who may order the police to carry out specific investigative acts, such as summoning and questioning suspects, witnesses and victims, or who may give binding orders. The police must promptly inform the prosecutor of the activities undertaken and of the results of their investigations. In fact, when investigating the *notitia criminis* and conducting on-site investigations, the police can act without the control of the prosecutor. In practice the police have a broad discretion in cases of minor or middle importance. In the ordinary course of the investigations, the prosecutor provides only superficial supervision of the police action. It is up the police, *de facto*, to set the agenda during the investigations, asking the prosecutor to issue the orders they need. Only in major cases does the prosecutor exercise any real control over the work of the police, actually directing the investigations.[20]

2.2. Arrest

The Italian Constitution recognizes the right to personal freedom. It can be limited only by judicial order, and in the specific cases provided for by the law;[21] moreover, every decision regarding personal freedom can be appealed to the Court of Cassation (article 111, § 7 of Italian Constitution). In case of 'flagrancy,' the police may arrest a person but they must, within 24 hours, inform the prosecutor of the arrest (who may then interview them), and transfer the person from the police station to jail. The prosecutor must, within the following 24 hours, request a judge to validate the arrest. If, within 96 hours from the arrest, a judge does not endorse the validity of the arrest, the arrested person must be immediately released.

The 1988 Code decrees that pending the proceedings, the judge for the preliminary investigation may order the detention of the suspect, or other such coercive measures, to be undertaken at the request of the prosecutor, provided probable cause is established. In addition, detention pending trial may be authorized if this is necessary in order to protect the gathering of the evidence, to prevent the escape of the suspect, or to prevent the suspect from committing further crimes.[22] In the case of the most serious crimes – those which may involve terrorism,

---

19   See L. D'Ambrosio and P.L. Vigna, *La pratica di polizia giudiziaria*, Padova, Cedam, 1998, p. 176; A. Nappi, *Guida al codice di procedura penale*, Milano, Giuffrè, 2004, p. 216-217.

20   See G. Illuminati, *supra* note 10, p. 308 *et seq.*

21   See D. Negri, *Fumus commissi delicti. La prova per le fattispecie cautelari*, Torino, Giappichelli, 2004, p. 205 *et seq.*

22   See F. Cordero, *Procedura penale*, Milano, Giuffre, 2004, p. 472-474; V. Grevi, 'Misure Cautelari,' in G. Conso and V. Grevi (eds), *Compendio di proceudra penale*, Padova, Cedam, 2003, p. 351.

organized crime or trafficking in hard drugs – detention is the normal practice except where, in some specific cases, house arrest is considered more appropriate.[23] Where the judge authorises the detention of the suspect pending the trial, they must interrogate them within five days of the suspect being effectively detained.[24] If the time limit of five days is not observed, the suspect must be immediately released. The judge must also interrogate the suspect at an 'arrest validation' hearing.[25]

The defendant may appeal decisions made by the judge of the preliminary investigations which limit their personal freedom, at the first instance to the Tribunal (*tribunale del riesame*)[26] and then (or directly, if the defendant prefers), to the Court of Cassation.

2.3. The interrogation of the suspect

Despite their subordination to the prosecutor, the police enjoy some autonomous powers during the investigative stage, and they may summon and question witnesses and the suspect.[27] In this case, the suspect has a duty to make themselves available to the police, but has the right to remain silent. Questioning of the suspect cannot be conducted by a police officer in the absence of a lawyer: if the suspect has not instructed one, the police must appoint a duty lawyer. Questioning of the suspect by the police is not permitted if the suspect is under arrest or subject to detention. Unlike the prosecutor's interrogation, the police are not obliged to disclose the facts relating to the offence for which the suspect is under investigation, nor to give details of the evidence gathered so far.[28] Nevertheless, the police have a duty to inform the person to be questioned of the ongoing criminal investigation. The police must make a written record of the questions asked of the suspect and the answers received.

If the prosecutor intends to interrogate the suspect they must summon the person, by writ, giving notice to their counsel at least 24 hours in advance (except for cases of justified urgency). Generally, this notice requirement is respected by prosecutors because unjustified delay in the communication of the notice leads to invalidity of the interrogation. If the suspect has not yet instructed a lawyer, the

---

23   See 2.6 *infra*.
24   In other words, a suspect can be placed in custody on only written information. The judge is not obliged to see the suspect before issuing the detention order.
25   Following an arrest, the prosecutor may decide to interrogate the suspect before the 'arrest validation' hearing, that is, before the judicial interrogation. However, because of the strict time limits governing the arrest validation hearing, this power is rarely exercised, and only in most serious cases. In any case, the provisions of the Code concerning interrogation of the suspect before the prosecutor apply, *mutatis mutandis*, at the interrogation before the judge.
26   M. Ceresa Gastaldo, *Il riesame delle misure coercitive nel processo penale*, Milano, Giuffrè, 1993, p. 35; V. Grevi, *supra* note 22, p. 432.
27   A. Scaglione, *L' attività ad iniziativa della polizia giudiziaria*, Torino, Giappichelli, 2001, p. 91 *et seq.*
28   M. Ceresa Gastaldo, *Le dichiarazioni spontanee dell'indagato alla polizia giudiziaria*, Torino, Giappichelli, 2002, p. 69 *et seq.*; A. Morgigni, *L'attività della polizia giudiziaria*, Milano, Giuffrè, 2002, p. 460.

prosecutor must appoint a duty lawyer and simultaneously inform them of the intended interrogation. The summons must contain an explanation of the facts in respect of which the suspect is under investigation, and it may also indicate the information that has already been gathered by the prosecutor. In practice, it is unusual for the summons to contain any reference to the evidence available to the prosecutor; more usually, the prosecutor communicates the available evidence at their discretion at the beginning of the interrogation.[29] Although it is mandatory for the prosecutor to give notice to the suspect's lawyer, the presence of the lawyer at the interrogation is not mandatory.[30] The interrogation of the suspect must be recorded in writing (*verbale*), including all the questions posed by the prosecutor and the answers given by the suspect. If the suspect is under arrest, the interrogation must be audio or video-recorded. This requirement is, in practice, strictly observed.

2.4.   Coercive methods

The prosecutor can summon and question witnesses, interrogate the suspect, order a search of premises and seizure of the *corpus delicti* or other items related to the *corpus delicti*. However, in many cases, the actual performance of such acts is delegated by the prosecutor to the police.

When it is necessary to seek the *corpus delicti* or other objects pertaining to the crime, the prosecutor has the power to issue an order to search the premises of the suspect or of other persons, and to seize what might be relevant to the investigation. In exceptional cases the police may conduct autonomous searches of premises and of the suspect (in case of urgency, flagrancy or at the moment of the arrest of the suspect). In these circumstances the police must, within 48 hours, transmit the file of the searches conducted and seizures sanctioned by the prosecutor, who must validate them within the subsequent 48 hours.

Finally, under article 349 § 2-*bis* and article 354 § 3, the police may take a DNA sample from a suspect. Following a judgment of the Constitutional Court,[31] the taking of blood samples for the purpose of testing has been forbidden.

2.5.   Secret investigative methods

The right to privacy of communications is recognized by the Italian Constitution. However, the judge of the preliminary investigations may, at the request of the prosecutor, allow the interception of private communications by the police. Authorisation may only be granted when there are reasonable grounds to believe that a crime is being committed, or has been committed. Furthermore, interception of communications is only permitted if there is an absolute necessity for this mean

---

29   See O. Mazza, *L'interrogatorio e l'esame dell'imputato nel suo procedimento*, Milano, Giuffrè, 2004, p. 148.
30   F. Cordero, *supra* note 22, p. 803-804.
31   Constitutional Court, judgment 9 July 1996, No. 238.

of investigation to be used.[32] If communications are intercepted in cases not permitted by the Code, the consequent information gained may not be used as evidence, either during the preliminary phase of the proceeding[33] (for instance, for for the purposes of an order to limit the personal freedom of the suspect, or to seize their property), or at trial.

Despite the strict provisions of the Code, interception of communications can be authorized by the judge in many circumstances, not only in the most serious cases but also in investigations of only 'average' seriousness. The judge for the preliminary investigation will usually authorize requests for interception because the authorization is given *inaudita altera parte* (the defence, of course, is not informed of the prosecutor's request) and is based only on the evidence and argument presented by the prosecutor. Moreover, the prosecutor is not obliged to disclose to the judge all of the investigative information available to them, but only those facts which are relevant and which demonstrate probable cause for the issuance of the warrant.

The prosecutor may give permission to the police to conduct undercover investigation, including simulated purchase of drugs and the like, in cases involving drug trafficking, organized crime and national or international terrorism.

2.6. *Terrorism and organized crime*

The investigation of suspected terrorism and 'organized crime' are normally subject to the ordinary rules of procedure, except where different provisions apply. Investigations can often last for two years whilst, usually, the maximum period of investigation sanctioned by the Code is 18 months.[34]

In criminal cases involving terrorism or organized crime, wiretapping is more readily available than in investigations involving other forms of crime. As noted above, in 'ordinary' investigations, interception of communication is permitted, with the consent of the judge, only when it is 'absolutely necessary' for the purpose of the investigation, and where there are 'serious reasons to believe that a crime has been committed'. However, in investigations of terrorism and organized crime, interception is permitted if it is merely 'necessary' for the purposes of the investigation, and provided there are 'sufficient reasons to believe that a crime has been committed.' Other particular provisions were approved for undercover police investigations, after 11 September 2001, which were intended to make it easier for

---

[32]   The Code permits not only the tapping of the suspect's telephone, but also any other telephone line if this is likely to produce useful information. A. Camon, *Le intercettazioni nel processo penale*, Milano, Giuffrè, 1996, p 77-78.; E. Aprile and F. Spiezia, *Le intercettazioni telefoniche e ambientali: innovazioni, tecnologie e nuove questioni giuridiche*, Milano, Giuffrè, p. 9 *et seq.*

[33]   L. Filippi, *L'intercettazione di comunicazioni*, Milano, Giuffrè, 1997, p. 90 *et seq.*; F. Ruggieri, *Divieti probatori e inutilizzabilità nella disciplina delle intercettazioni telefoniche*, Milano, Giuffrè, 2001, p. 16.

[34]   The Code establishes a maximum period for the investigation even where the suspect is not in custody.

the investigation and enforcement agencies to collate large amounts of information. Finally, in the field of personal freedom, the Code makes it easier to authorize detention of the defendant pending the proceedings. Indeed, prison detention is always presumed necessary, in lieu of any other measures, when a person is charged with offences related to terrorism or organized crime and there is probable cause as well as one of the specific exigencies mentioned earlier.

3.   Rights of the defendant during investigations

3.1.   *The right to be informed of being a suspect*

The right to be informed of being under investigation in the criminal proceeding is the first and, probably, the main right recognized by the Code, as it affects the applicability of all other rights. It implies the duty of the police, the prosecutor and the judge, to communicate to a person the fact that they are a suspect.[35] The Code decrees that the prosecutor must give notice of the proceedings to all interested parties from the first act of investigation at which counsel has the right to be present. The main acts which counsel has the right to attend are the interrogation of the suspect, the inspection, the confrontation between the suspect and another person, and search and the seizure. In addition, at their first appearance before the judicial officers, the police or the prosecutor must formally inform the suspect of their position in the proceedings.[36] Moreover, the prosecutor must, from the first act of investigation at which the counsel has the right to be present, give written notice to the suspect of their rights in the criminal proceedings. The notice must contain the name of the counsel appointed *ex officio* (where relevant) and must mention the main rights of the defence in the proceedings; moreover, it must explain the legal conditions under which the State will pay for the expense of legal assistance. The prosecutor must also inform the suspect of their right to hire a lawyer: if the suspect does not instruct counsel, a lawyer must be appointed *ex officio*. If a person who is interrogated as a witness gives self-incriminating statements, the prosecutor or the police must stop the interrogation and warn them that, as a consequence of the statements rendered, an investigation may begin against them. The person must also be notified that they have the right to appoint counsel. Any statement given prior to that moment cannot be used against them although it may be used against other persons involved (article 63 § 1 of the Code). If the police or the prosecutor fail to give the information required by the law, the statements obtained cannot be used against anyone in any criminal proceeding (article 63 § 2). This provision applies

---

[35]   As said above, the right to be informed to be a suspect has a different content with regard to the questioning by the police and the interrogation before the prosecutor: only in the latter case the judicial officer has to communicate the fact for which the person is involved in the proceeding, while in the former the right provided by the code involves just the juridical qualification of the charge, but not the fact.

[36]   O. Mazza, *supra* note 29, p. 36.

even where the police or the prosecutor interrogate the suspect without informing them of their position in the proceedings.[37]

3.2. The Right to silence and caution

Where a suspect is summoned, either by the police, the prosecutor or the judge, in order to be questioned or interrogated, they have the duty to present themselves and to give to the investigating authority their personal particulars. Before questioning the suspect, the police, the prosecutor or the judge must warn the suspect of the right to remain silent and of the fact that, if a statement is made regarding other persons, the suspect will become a witness in relation to those facts: in these cases, the defendant loses the right to silence regarding the facts given relating to others. However, even in this case, the defendant can maintain the right to remain silent in relation to the charges brought against them (article 64 § 3).[38] Failure to give the caution required by law renders the statements gathered inadmissible as evidence.[39] The rationale for these rights is that a person must be able to decide their own attitude towards authority when they are under suspicion in a criminal proceeding. On some occasions, this is the reason why the Court of Cassation has declared inadmissible the evidence of statements gathered by undercover police operations.[40] Following the same arguments, the Court of Cassation has also refused the admission in evidence of police testimony as to statements made by the suspect to undercover police officers.[41]

3.3. The right to an interpreter

The appointment of an interpreter is authorized by the Code for every person charged or under investigation in criminal proceedings who does not speak Italian. Ignorance of the Italian language must be specifically verified, and cannot be presumed from the fact that the person is not an Italian citizen.[42] The duty to assign

---

[37] G.P. Voena, 'Soggetti,' in G. Conso and V. Grevi (eds), *Compendio di procedura penale*, Padova, Cedam, 2003, p. 94; R. Kostoris, 'Art. 63,' in M. Chiavario (ed.), *Commento al nuovo codice di procedura penale*, Torino, Utet, 1990, vol. I, p. 325.

[38] The distinction between facts involving the suspect's involvement and fact relating to the involvement of others is, in practice, quite problematic. A statement regarding another person may have consequences, or give rise to inferences, regarding acts performed by the person making the declaration. It is not unusual, in the case law, that where a clear distinction appears impossible or at least quite difficult, the judge decides to acknowledge to the accused the right to remain silent not only in respect of the questions regarding the specific charges brought against the suspect, but also in respect of those concerning other persons whose responsibility is connected with the suspect.

[39] On the other hand the Code also provides that, when a person questioned as a witness gives self-incriminating statements, the police, the prosecutor or the judge must stop the interview and inform the person that investigations might be initiated against them. See *supra* § 3.a.

[40] Cass., 31 March 1998, Parreca, *Cassazione penale*, 2000, p. 965.

[41] It must be noted that any testimony on the defendant's statements during the proceedings is forbidden: article 62 of the Code. See note 40 *supra*.

[42] Cass. 12 February 2003, Liu Xon Fei, *Guida al Diritto*, 2003, vol. 26, p. 80.

an interpreter is recognized from the first investigative act that the defendant has the right to attend. The solution worked out in the case law on the subject is not satisfactory, since it is not easy for a person to prove that they do *not* speak a language. In practice, suspects or accused persons are sometimes not provided with an interpreter even if they do not understand Italian or, at least, if they do not have a good understanding of the Italian language. The costs of the interpreter are met by the State. In addition, the Code provides for the translation of the indictment where the prosecutor decides to bring the case to the trial. Violation of the duty to appoint an interpreter makes the act performed null (but does not imply the nullity of subsequent acts). Despite the fact that the interpreter acts as an assistant to the lawyer, the interpreter may not be appointed by the defendant, but only by the court. As a result, the interpreter may face a challenge (from the defendant) for either incapacity or incompatibility. The defendant also has the right to the translation of the act in a language that they understand.[43]

3.4. The right to bail or the right to be released on conditions pending trial

In the Italian system there is no provision for a right to be released on bail or on some similar condition. The detained suspect or accused may, however, request another appearance before the same judge who issued the detention order, or they can appeal to the tribunal, but only on the basis that the conditions for detention are not satisfied. In other words, the suspect or the accused may challenge the decision if the evidence presented by the prosecutor is not sufficient to establish a reasonable belief that the suspect or the accused has committed the crime or, more frequently, that the evidence is not sufficient to establish the presence of any of the specific exigencies required for the detention of a person in a criminal proceeding[44] and a less restrictive measure (e.g., house arrest) is more appropriate.

3.5. Right to counsel

From the first act of the investigations in which the defendant may be assisted by a counsel, the prosecutor must appoint counsel *ex officio* and communicate their name to the suspect, informing them in writing of the main rights of a person under suspicion in a criminal proceeding.[45] The duties of the lawyer appointed by the prosecutor, by the police or by the judge, cease if and when the accused instructs their own lawyer. The lawyer appointed *ex officio* has the same powers, rights and

---

43 The Court of Cassation, in plenary session, decided in two different cases that this right has to be applied to all the acts communicated to the suspect or to the indicted person; Cass. Sez. Un., 24 September 2003, Zalagaitis, *Cassazione penale*, 2004, p. 1563; Cass. Sez. Un., 31 May 2000, Jakani, *Cassazione penale*, 2000, p. 3255.

44 See *supra*, 2.2.

45 Article 369-*bis* c.p.p. of the Code. See on this subject M. Scaparone, 'Indagini preliminari e udienza preliminare,' in G. Conso and V. Grevi (eds), *Compendio di procedura penale*, Padova, Cedam, 2003, p. 494; S. Ciampi, 'A proposito del nesso tra informazione sul diritto di difesa e avviso di conclusione delle indagini,' *Cassazione penale*, 2004, p. 3305 *et seq.*

duties as one appointed by the accused. In general, no influence is exerted by the police or by the prosecutor on the work of the lawyer appointed *ex officio*. The lawyer is formally appointed by the judicial authority, from a list prepared in advance by the bar association. It may happen, however, that the lawyer appointed by the prosecutor, the police or the judge is not, in practice, as strongly motivated as one appointed by the defendant. This fact may lead the lawyer to decide not to raise juridical or factual issues that may appear in some way 'unpleasant' to the prosecutor or the judges. However, this is not the rule, and in general lawyers appointed *ex officio* are not influenced in any way by the police, the prosecutor or the judge.

During the investigative phase counsel has, in some circumstances, the right to be informed when the police or the prosecutor are going to carry out an investigative act which the lawyer has the right to attend; in others, the presence of the lawyer is necessary in order for the act to be valid. As noted earlier, the questioning of the suspect by the police cannot be conducted in the absence of counsel. Where an interview is conducted by the prosecutor, counsel only has the right to be informed in advance, and they may not attend the interrogation (although in practice, this rarely happens). When the prosecutor issues an order to search premises and seize anything related to the crime, counsel does not have the right to be informed in advance, but may participate in the act. Generally, when the law does not provide for information to be made available in advance, counsel has the right to inspect the records of the acts performed by the police or by the prosecutor, and to make a copy of them.[46]

Following arrest by the police counsel, whether appointed by the arrested person or by the prosecutor, must be promptly informed of the arrest (article 386 § 2 of the Code) and of the date of the arrest validation hearing before the judge (article 390 § 2 of the Code).[47] If the arrested person gives their consent, the police must immediately inform their family of their arrest. Once counsel has been appointed, the accused has an absolute right to meet their lawyer at any time. In particular, the Code provides for a full right of access by counsel to an accused who is detained during the proceedings. Despite the fact that the right of access to legal assistance is plain and, in principle, may not be limited by the authorities, during the investigative phase the judge may, at the request of the prosecutor, delay access to counsel for up to five days (article 104 § 3 of the Code) if specific and exceptional

---

[46]   P. Felicioni, *Le ispezioni e le perquisizioni*, Milano, Giuffrè, 2004, p. 210; G. Tranchina, 'Le indagini preliminari e l'udienza preliminare,' in D. Siracusano *et al.* (eds), *Diritto processuale penale*, Milano, Giuffrè, 2004, vol. II, p. 131.

[47]   Despite the clear words of the Code, the jurisprudence determines that only the failure to communicate the date of arrest validation hearing before the judge may render the arrest a nullity. A delay in, or failure by, the police to communicate promptly the fact of the arrest to counsel does not result in any consequence regarding the validity of the arrest. See Cass., 14 January 2000, Sljivic, *Cassazione penale*, 2001, p. 2402; Cass., 30 Jaunary 1992, Lucariello, *Archivio della nuova procedura penale*, 1992, p. 588. It is not possible to say how often in practice the police delay or fail to communicate promptly to the counsel the arrest of their client. However, it is in some ways significant that the Court of Cassation has had to decide, more than once, on the validity of such police (mis)behavior.

circumstances occur, for instance, where there is a fear that evidence may be tampered with or where there is more than one defendant in the same case. The prosecutor also has a similar power to delay access to the lawyer until the time when the arrested person is presented before the judge. Taking into account the fact that the arrest validation hearing must be held within 96 hour from the time of arrest, the prosecutor cannot prevent communication between counsel and the arrested person beyond that period. However, this power of delay ordinarily has significant consequences for the result of the arrest validation hearing (the main purpose of which is the interrogation of the arrested person by the judge) since the person may be taken before the judge without having had an effective consultation with their lawyer. The case law demonstrates that the interrogation of the arrested person who had not had the opportunity to consult with their lawyer does not result in annulment.[48]

As a result of the Bill of 7 December 2000, No. 397, Parliament introduced the power that allows defence counsel to conduct parallel investigations. The defence counsel, or appointed assistant, may now run private investigations and collate written results, the records of which may be introduced at any stages of the proceedings. In particular, the lawyer has the right to contact persons who might have information relating to the facts of the crime and ask them to make a statement. There is no duty to provide a statement, but in cases of refusal, counsel may ask the prosecutor or the judge to summon the person to be questioned, a request with which they must comply. If the witness agrees to speak to the lawyer, their declarations may be recorded using the same forms as used by the prosecutor or the police. Alternatively, the witness may provide a written statement in which the known facts are described and counsel may produce this document to the investigating judge after having authenticated the witness's comments and allegations and having set out the context and authenticity of the statement given. The records of the lawyer's investigations (including those of the statements collected) may be used at trial or in the decisions taken in the investigation in the same manner as those collected by the prosecutor or the police.

The defendant's or the victim's lawyer may, with the authorization of the judge, have access to private premises, and the result of such access may be recorded by counsel and produced at trial as evidence.

3.6. The availability of legal assistance

In Italy there is a distinction between the concept of counsel appointed by the law and counsel remunerated by the State. On one hand, counsel is appointed by the court (or, during investigations, by the prosecutor or the police, at the first act at which the suspect has the right to be assisted) when the suspect or the accused is

---

[48]   Cass., 12 October 1994, Agostino, *Giurisprudenza italiana*, 1996, II, p. 97; Cass., 18 October 1995, Canonizzo, CED Cass., No. 203316.

not able to hire their own.[49] On the other, counsel is paid by the State when the suspect or the accused cannot afford the expense of a criminal proceeding (specifically, when their annual income is under € 9,296.22).[50] Despite this funding distinction, the suspect or accused may have their legal expenses met by the State even if they instruct the lawyer; at the same time, counsel appointed by the court are remunerated by the person assisted, and the State covers the expenses of the defence in a complementary way, that is only when the defendant can not afford them.[51] Thus, when appointed by the court, the law requires the lawyer who wants to be paid by the State to prove that their client cannot afford the expenses of legal assistance. The problem with this system is that when the annual income of the defendant is slightly above the financial limit the lawyer appointed by the court must carry out every step to obtain payment from the client, including sueing their client, and the lawyer may ask the State to cover their fee only if every legal effort has failed. It is easy to see and understand that the obligation of counsel to collect their fees from an almost indigent client makes it difficult to build a confidential relationship between the Court appointed counsel and the client.

The distinction between the concept of mandatory appointment of counsel and that of free access to legal assistance does have one advantage: the indigent accused may choose and hire the lawyer they prefer and they are not obliged to accept the one appointed by the court. However, in practice, the fee paid by the State to counsel under the legal aid scheme is not very high. For example, in a simple case (involving no more than 3-5 trial hearings), the average fee is around € 1,000-1,500. This is much lower than that claimed by a privately instructed practitioner in the same case (which can be expected to be not less than € 4,000-5,000). It follows that the possibility, for indigent persons, of instructing their counsel of choice is only a theoretical option. The lawyer contacted by an indigent accused may well refuse to accept the case because they are aware that the fees paid by the State will be much lower than in privately paid cases.

There is another problem connected with the inadequate remuneration of legal aid counsel. Lawyers appointed *ex officio* often lack the necessary training and experience to prepare a good defence. Since 2001, the law has required local bar associations to organize and control the training of the lawyers who are eligible and included on the Court list. However, the services of counsel appointed *ex officio* rarely reach the same standard of quality as those of privately paid lawyers. It is possible to say that sometimes the same lawyer works in a different manner when engaged by a privately paying client than when appointed by the court. The right to mandatory legal assistance and to free legal assistance works differently in juvenile

---

[49] A. Giannone, *Riflessioni sulla riforma*, in *Soggetti deboli e giustizia penale* (Miscellaneous), Torino, Giappichelli, 2003, p. 1 *et seq.*; F. Della Casa, 'Soggetti,' in G. Conso and V. Grevi (eds), *Compendio di procedura penale*, Padova, Cedam, 2003, p. 142 *et seq.*

[50] For every dependent relative the eligibility level is increased by € 1,032.91. However, if the applicant lives with other relatives, their income is also taken into account (article 74 and 92 of President of the Republic Decree 30 May 2002, No. 115).

[51] Or if the suspect or the accused is untraceable. In Italy, as is well known, trial *in absentia* is permitted.

criminal proceedings. In such cases the law provides that the lawyer appointed by the court is to be paid by the State in all cases. The State may then recover the expenses sustained from the person assisted if they are able to afford them, i.e. if the annual income of the family unit is over the limit mentioned above.

3.7. Disclosure

In general, criminal investigations are kept secret (known as the 'investigative secret'). At the end of the investigation, the prosecutor is obliged to formally notify the defendant that the investigations are complete and, among other considerations, that the defendant may have access to the investigative file and make copies of the records contained therein. After this communication, the defendant may ask for a further interview with the prosecutor. The defendant may also produce evidence collected by their counsel or request the prosecutor to carry out further investigations. The formal notification of the conclusion of the investigations is mandatory, and failure by the prosecutor to issue it affects the indictment subsequently filed against the accused, causing it to be nullified. A failure by the prosecutor to accede to a request by the accused for a further interrogation has the same effect.[52]

The accused does not normally have a right of access to the investigative file before the end of the prosecutor's inquiries. However, the Code exceptionally allows the accused or their counsel to assist the investigative acts carried out by the prosecutor or by the police even if they have no right to be informed of their completion in advance. Moreover, when the judge issues a warrant involving the restriction of a fundamental right, such as the right to personal freedom or to secrecy of communication, the accused has, at any stage of the proceeding, a recognized right of access. In cases of preventive detention or other coercive measures, the accused has the right to consult the file with regard to the elements of the investigation that the judge considers relevant in making their decision. When interception of communications is ordered, the accused, at the end of the interception activities, can check the result of the operation and challenge the relevance and the admissibility of the recorded conversations gathered through the interception.

3.8. Diversion in juvenile cases

When the suspect or the accused is a juvenile (from 14 to 18 years old), the alternative proceedings set out earlier[53] are not available, but instead, specific measures are provided by the law. In the case of minor offences, the prosecutor may ask the judge not to prosecute the suspect. If, on the other hand, the prosecutor has

---

[52] G. Frigo, 'L'indagine difensiva da fonti dichiarative,' in L. Filippi (ed.), *Processo penale: il nuovo ruolo del difensore*, Padova, Cedam, 2001, p. 206; A. Furgiuele, 'Colloqui ed assunzione di dichiarazioni,' in M. Ferraioli (ed.), *Il nuovo ruolo del difensore nel processo penale*, Milano, Giuffrè, 2002, p. 155.

[53] See *supra*, 1.3.

promoted the criminal proceedings, the judge may acquit the accused at the preliminary hearing. Another means of diversion is probation: the judge may suspend the criminal process for the purpose of evaluating the behavior of the indicted person for a certain period of time with the assistance of the State social services. At the end of the period determined by the judge, if the evaluation of the social services is positive, the judge may acquit the defendant on this basis. Finally, if the juvenile has no previous criminal record and it is likely that they will not commit further crimes, the judge may acquit the accused for this reason.

3.9. Restrictions on the rights of the defence in cases of terrorism and/or organized crime

As was observed earlier, in the Italian system, the investigation file is not admitted as evidence at trial, and all the witnesses have to testify orally before the judge, and they may be cross-examined. However, in cases involving alleged terrorism or organized crime there is an important divergence from the ordinary procedure, since out-of-court statements are permitted as evidence at trial. In cases of terrorism, the law limits the parties' right to proof at trial whenever the witnesses have already given their statements in the course of the investigation before a judge (*incidente probatorio*).[54] The same limitations apply where the witness has already testified in other connected proceedings in which the admission of evidence was requested (although the right to confrontation must have been granted). In these circumstances a new examination of the witness at trial is permitted only when the parties intend to ask new questions: in other words, the witness's examination is inadmissible if it is based on the same facts on which a statement has already been given before trial but, on the contrary, is admissible only if the parties intend to pose questions on new facts, or if a new examination is necessary on the basis of specific exigencies (article 190 *bis* of the Code).[55]

Furthermore, as noted in 2.6 *supra*, in terrorism and organized crime investigations, the circumstances in which interception of communication is permitted are wider than for 'ordinary' investigations. Specifically, it is permitted when it is simply 'necessary' to carry out the investigation, and where there are 'sufficient,' but not 'serious,' reasons to believe that a crime has been committed.

In case of alleged terrorism or organized crime the detention of the suspect pending the proceeding is, in practice, almost an absolute rule. In general, when it is necessary to apply some restrictive measures involving personal freedom, the judge is asked by the law to authorize detention only if no other measure is suitable, as an

---

[54]   The so-called *incidente probatorio* may be granted by the judge where there is a serious risk that the testimony will not be reproduced at trial. In this case, the statement of the witness is given during the pre-trial phase, before the judge for the preliminary investigations, with the same cross-examination method that applies at trial.

[55]   A. Bernasconi, 'Il diritto al contraddittorio,' in R. Kostoris (ed.), *Il giusto processo tra contraddittorio e diritto al silenzio*, Torino, Giappichelli, 2002, p. 110. Evidence by anonymous witnesses is not permitted in the Italian System.

extrema ratio.[56] However, where a case involving terrorism and organized crime is under investigation this presumption is replaced by advice contained within article 275 § 3, which states that the judge must authorise detention of the suspect unless there are clear reasons not to adopt such a course of action.

4. Impact of the investigative stage on the trial: actual relevance of the investigative phase in the Italian Criminal Process

4.1. The principle of immediacy

Despite the orality principle provided for by article 111 of the Italian Constitution,[57] some exceptions to the hearsay rule are provided for by the 1988 Code within the ordinary trial process, which permits in particular the substantive use at trial of witness statements collected during the investigation. Generally, prior statements are available only for the purpose of undermining the witness's credibility, and not for proving the facts thereby asserted. However, the Code provides for specific exceptions, for example, where an examination is impossible for objective reasons independent of the party's will, when the witness has been threatened or evidence has been tampered with, and when both parties agree.[58]

The above considerations should reinforce the importance of the investigative phase in the criminal process in the Italian system, notwithstanding the aim of the reforms introduced since 1988. The Prosecutor has the duty, based on the legality principle, to investigate every *notitia criminis,* and to collect all relevant information relating to the case. In other words, as the Constitutional Court has asserted,[59] the investigation must be complete. The strictness of the rule against hearsay defined by the Code is modified or diluted by the many exceptions. In particular, where an alternative means of resolving a criminal case is chosen,[60] the decision of the judge will be based on the investigative file.

4.2. Exclusion of illegally or unfairly obtained evidence

Article 191 of the Code states that evidence which is obtained in violation of a prohibition established by law cannot be used at any stage of criminal proceeding.

---

[56]   The Code provides for a variety of measures which in some way limit personal freedom: a prohibition on leaving Italian territory, a requirement to stay away from some specific municipality, or the duty to reside in some specific municipality, the obligation to go periodically to a police office, the obligation to leave the family house, house arrest, or detention. The latter is conceived by the Code, usually, as an *extrema ratio,* and the judge, in issuing a detention order, is obliged to explain why no other measure was considered appropriate for the suspect.

[57]   See *supra,* 1.1 and 1.2.

[58]   See F. Cordero, *supra* note 22, p. 695-720.; P.P. Paulesu, *Giudice e parti nella 'dialettica' della prova testimoniale,* Torino, Giappichelli, 2002, p. 236.

[59]   *Corte costituzionale,* judgment 28 January 1991, No. 88, in <www.giurcost.org>.

[60]   See *supra,* 1.3.

A party may seek to exclude any evidence obtained by illegal methods at any stage of the proceeding. Inevitably, the interpretation of specific provisions has given rise to different legal solutions. For example, there is a much debate regarding the meaning of the term 'prohibition' adopted by the Code. For example, does it include so-called 'implicit prohibitions,' the occurrence of which may be deduced from an affirmative proposition (as where the law provides that a certain operation is admissible *only* if a specific formality is complied with)? Moreover, it is not clear what the law means by the words 'established by law.' In particular, there is a conflict of interpretation between those who consider that it only refers to procedural law, and others who believe that it includes a prohibition under the substantive criminal law. In many instances there is no doubt regarding the application of the rule, for example, when an order for the interception of communication was issued despite the lack of the lawful conditions.[61] Another fundamental provision in this field prohibits the use of any statement obtained in a way that might limit the freedom of self-determination, or influence the way the facts are remembered or evaluated (article 188 of the Code).[62]

There are some uncertainties regarding the admissibility of evidence obtained as a result of an illegal search. The solution provided by the Supreme Court is to allow the use of such evidence when it constitutes the *corpus delicti*, and to forbid the admission of any other element gathered by an illegal search. This solution, as may be seen, permits the judge to use the most relevant pieces of evidence that the police or the prosecutor might find as a consequence of a search even if illegal. At the same time, it is possible to say that in some way the principle of fairness in the conduct of the investigation is preserved.

5. The role of the defence lawyer

5.1. Self-perception of criminal lawyers

Under the pre-existing Code of Criminal Procedure, there is no doubt that the criminal lawyer was a sort of *plaidoyant*, that is, a subject whose function was to adduce some arguments based on the evidence gathered by someone else (the investigating judge or the prosecutor). All of the evidence gathered during the investigative phase was considered to be admissible at trial, as in the inquisitorial model derived from the *Code Napoléon*. In this sense we can say that under that pre-existing Code the lawyer's role could be described as a 'process controller.'

After more than 15 years since the adoption of the new Code, inspired by the accusatorial model, it is possible to say that criminal lawyers increasingly tend to perceive themselves as adversaries (even if they maintained their role of criminal process controller). In other words, they are aware of the possibility of conducting

---

[61]   See *supra*, 2.5.
[62]   M. Nobili, 'Art. 188,' in M. Chiavario (ed.), *Commento al nuovo codice di procedura penale*, Torino, Utet, 1990, vol. I, p. 396; L. Scomparin, *La tutela del testimone nel processo penale*, Padova, Cedam, 2000, p. 3 *et seq.*

investigations and to build at trial a different and personal strategy, in contrast to the one presented by the prosecutor. This new perception of their role was not without political consequences. As mentioned in the introduction to this chapter, defence lawyers are asking that the public prosecutor become a real party in the criminal process instead of a kind of magistrate. This is a consequence of a change in the dynamics of the criminal process ushered in by the incorporation of adversarial proceedings.

5.2. *Statutory regulations and limitations*

Focusing on the role of defence lawyer in the Italian system, and with reference to the technical features outlined in the preceding paragraphs, it is worth mentioning that lawyers as a class are quite influential, both at the political and the social level. The first reason for this is that in Italy there are significant numbers of lawyers, possibly more than 140.000 nationally. Lawyers are organised into bar associations that are sited in every Tribunal district (*Consigli dell'Ordine degli Avvocati*), and each district bar association constitutes a local 'cell' of the National Bar Association (*Consiglio Nazionale Forense*). These local institutions, which represent the National Bar Association at the district level, are recognized by the State in many laws. Criminal lawyers are generally associates of the Penal Chamber (*Camera Penale*), a private association organized both at national and at district level. The Penal Chamber has in practice exercised a role in the reforms of the last ten years in the field of criminal law and procedure, notably during the legislative drafting phase of the proposed Constitutional reform of article 111. The Penal Chamber is not recognized as a public institution by the law, it is merely a private law association, and its influence operates only *de facto*, but many of its higher representatives sit in the Italian Parliament.

There are numerous rules regulating the conduct of lawyers during criminal proceeding, both in the Code of Criminal Procedure and in the deontological code of professional behaviour. Regarding the rules contained within the Code, the most important are articles 106 and 107. The first states that a lawyer cannot defend more than one accused when there is the possibility of a conflict of interests. When a conflict of interests arises after the lawyer has begun to carry out their functions, they must resolve the matter. If the lawyer fails to act, the judge must consider the matter and issue a decision to settle the case. During the investigation the same power is given by the Code to the prosecutor. Article 107 states that when a lawyer refuses to accept instructions in a case, or renounces it, the lawyer must continue to act until a new appointment is made by the accused or by the court.

5.3. *Professional standards and restrictions*

There is a deontological code of professional behaviour, issued by the National Bar Association, and there is also a code of professional behaviour for criminal lawyers, drafted by the Penal Chamber. However, only a violation of the former may give rise to a disciplinary proceeding before the local Bar Association. The disciplinary sanctions adopted by the local Bar Association as a consequence of 'deontological misbehaviour' may be appealed before the National Bar Association and, at the ultimate level, before the Court of Cassation. Despite the strict rules of the Code of Criminal Procedure and of the deontological code, it is rare for a lawyer to be sanctioned by the Bar Association or, if a lawyer is punished, for the sanction to be serious. In particular, it is rare for 'deontological misconduct' by a lawyer to result in the Bar Association banning the lawyer from continuing within the profession. The reason for this is, of course, political and social in nature. In other words, there is something of an unwritten corporate stance that establishes the customary outcome. Normally, only a criminal conviction will result in deletion from the Bar Album and a prohibition on the person exercising their profession (at least for some years, in minor cases).

In particular, it is not usual for very serious sanctions to be applied if there has been a violation of the lawyer's duty to keep confidential the information received from the client or regarding the client (article 9 of the deontological code of professional behaviour). Moreover, the disclosure of confidential information is tolerated as lawyers may 'defend' the client in the mass media even if this entails violation of the confidentiality rule (article 18 of the deontological code of professional behaviour).

6. List of abbreviations

Am. J. Comp. L.	American Journal of Comparative Law
Cass.	Italian Court of Cassation
CED Cass.	Informatics archive of the Italian Court of Cassation
Const.	Italian Constitution
ivi	in the same contribution just mentioned in the same footnote
Mich. J. Int'l L.	Michigan Journal of International Law
N. Car. J. Int'l L. & Comm. Reg.	North Carolina Journal of International Law and Commercial Regulation
et seq.	following pages
Temp. L. Rev	Temporary Law Review
Wash. U. Global Stud. L. Rev.	Washington University Global Studies Law

Review

Yale J. Int'l L.   Yale Journal of International Law

7.   Bibliography

E. Amodio & E. Selvaggi, 'An Accusatorial System in a Civil Law Country: The 1988 Italian Code of Criminal Procedure,' *Temporary Law Review*, 1989, p. 1211.

E. Aprile & F. Spiezia, *Le intercettazioni telefoniche e ambientali: innovazioni, tecnologie e nuove questioni giuridiche*, Milano, Giuffrè, p. 9 *et seq.*

A. Bernasconi, 'Il diritto al contraddittorio,' in R. Kostoris (ed.), *Il giusto processo tra contraddit-torio e diritto al silenzio*, Torino, Giappichelli, 2002, p. 110.

M. Caianiello, *Poteri dei privati nell'esercizio dell'azione penale*, Torino, Giappichelli, 2003.

M. Caianiello, 'Art. 459,' in G. Conso & V. Grevi (eds), *Commentario breve al codice di procedura penale*, Padova, Cedam, 2005, p. 1658 *et seq.*

A. Camon, *Le intercettazioni nel processo penale*, Milano, Giuffrè, 1996, p 77-78.

F. Caprioli, 'Palingenesi di un divieto probatorio. La testimonianza indiretta nel funzionario di polizia nel rinnovato assetto processuale,' in R. Kostoris (ed.), *Il giusto processo tra contraddittorio e diritto al silenzio*, Torino, Giappichelli, 2002, p. 59.

M. Ceresa Gastaldo, *Il riesame delle misure coercitive nel processo penale*, Milano, Giuffrè, 1993, p. 35.

M. Ceresa-Gastaldo, *Le dichiarazioni spontanee dell'indagato alla polizia giudiziaria*, Torino, Giappichelli, 2002.

C. Cesari, *L'irripetibilità sopravvenuta degli atti d'indagine*, Milano, Giuffrè, 1999.

S. Ciampi, 'A proposito del nesso tra informazione sul diritto di difesa e avviso di conclusione delle indagini,' *Cassazione penale*, 2004, p. 3305 *et seq.*

G. Conso & Zagrebelsky V. (eds), *Pubblico ministero e accusa penale: Problemi e prospettive*, Bologna, Zanichelli, 1979.

G. Conso & V. Grevi (eds), *Compendio di procedura penale*, Padova, Cedam, 2003.

G. Conso & V. Grevi (eds), *Commentario breve al codice di procedura penale*, Padova, Cedam, 2005.

F. Cordero, *Ideologie del processo penale*, Milano, Giuffrè, 1966.

F. Cordero, *Procedura Penale*, Milano, Giuffrè, 2001.

L. D'Ambrosio & P.L. Vigna, *La pratica di polizia giudiziaria*, Padova, Cedam, 1998, p. 176.

F. Della Casa, 'Soggetti,' in G. Conso & V. Grevi (eds), *Compendio di procedura penale*, Padova, Cedam, 2003, p. 142 *et seq.*

M.L. Di Bitonto, *Profili dispositivi dell'accertamento penale*, Torino, Giappichelli, 2004.

P. Felicioni, *Le ispezioni e le perquisizioni*, Milano, Giuffrè, 2004, p. 210.

P. Ferrua, 'I poteri probatori del giudice dibattimentale: ragionevolezza delle Sezioni Unite e dogmatismo della Corte Costituzionale,' *Rivista Italiana Diritto e Procedura Penale*, 1994, p. 1073.

P. Ferrua, 'La regola d'oro del processo accusatorio,' in R. Kostoris (ed.), *Il giusto processo tra contraddittorio e diritto al silenzio*, Torino, Giappichelli, 2002, p. 11.

L. Filippi, *L'intercettazione di comunicazioni*, Milano, Giuffrè, 1997, p. 90 *et seq.*

G. Frigo, 'L'indagine difensiva da fonti dichiarative,' in L. Filippi (ed.), *Processo penale: il nuovo ruolo del difensore*, Padova, Cedam, 2001, p. 206.

A. Furgiuele, 'Colloqui ed assunzione di dichiarazioni,' in M. Ferraioli (ed.), *Il nuovo ruolo del difensore nel processo penale*, Milano, Giuffrè, 2002, p. 155.

A. Giannone, *Riflessioni sulla riforma*, in *Soggetti deboli e giustizia penale* (Miscellaneous), Torino, Giappichelli, 2003, p. 1 *et seq.*

G. Giostra, 'Contraddittorio,' in *Enciclopedia Giuridica Treccani*, 2001, vol. II, p. 1 *et seq.*

E. Grande, 'Italian Criminal Justice: Borrowing and Resistance,' *American Journal of Comparative Law*, 2000, p. 228.

V. Grevi, 'Misure Cautelari,' in G. Conso & V. Grevi (eds), *Compendio di proceudra penale*, Padova, Cedam, 2003, p. 351.

F.M. Iacoviello, *La motivazione della sentenza penale e il suo controllo in cassazione*, Milano, Giuffrè, 1997.

G. Illuminati, *La presunzione d'innocenza dell'imputato*, Bologna, Zanichelli, 1979.

G. Illuminati, 'Il nuovo dibattimento: l'assunzione diretta delle prove,' *Foro italiano*, 1988, p. 357.

G. Illuminati, 'Accusatorio e inquisitorio (sistema),' in *Enciclopedia Giuridica Treccani*, 1988, vol. I, p. 1 *et seq.*

G. Illuminati, 'La testimonianza della polizia giudiziaria sul contenuto di dichiarazioni non verbalizzate,' *Cassazione Penale*, 2003, p. 660.

G. Illuminati, 'Giudizio,' in G. Conso & V. Grevi (eds), *Compendio di procedura penale*, Padova, Cedam, 2003, p. 644 *et seq.*

G. Illuminati, 'The Role of the Public Prosecutor in the Italian System,' in J.P. Peter Tak (ed.), *Tasks and Powers of the Prosecution Services in the EU Member States*, Nijmegen, Wolf Legal Publishers, 2004, p. 308-310.

G. Illuminati, 'The Frustrated Turn to Adversarial Procedure in Italy (Italian Criminal Procedure Code of 1988),' *Washington University Global Studies Law Review*, 2005, p. 567.

G. Illuminati, 'Ammissione e acquisizione della prova nell'istruzione dibattimentale,' in P. Ferrua *et al.*, *La prova nel dibattimento penale*, Torino, Giappichelli, 2005, p. 92-98.

R. Kostoris, 'Art. 63,' in M. Chiavario (ed.), *Commento al nuovo codice di procedura penale*, Torino, Utet, 1990, vol. I, p. 325.

G. Lozzi, 'Il giusto processo e i riti speciali deflativi del dibattimento,' *Rivista italiana di diritto e procedura penale*, 2002, p. 1165 *et seq.*

G. Lozzi, *Lineamenti di procedura penale*, Torino, Giappichelli, 2003.

O. Mazza, *L'interrogatorio e l'esame dell'imputato nel suo procedimento*, Milano, Giuffrè, 2004.

A. Morgigni, *L'attività della polizia giudiziaria*, Milano, Giuffrè, 2002, p. 460.

A. Nappi, *Guida al codice di procedura penale*, Milano, Giuffrè, 2004.

D. Negri, *Fumus commissi delicti. La prova per le fattispecie cautelari*, Torino, Giappichelli, 2004, p. 205 *et seq.*

M. Nobili, *Il principio del libero convincimento del giudice*, Milano, Giuffrè, 1974.

M. Nobili, 'Art. 188,' in M. Chiavario (ed.), *Commento al nuovo codice di procedura penale*, Torino, Utet, 1990, vol. I, p. 396.

M. Nobili, *Scenari e trasformazioni del processo penale*, Padova, Cedam, 1998.

R. Orlandi, 'Giudizi speciali,' in G. Conso & V. Grevi (eds), *Compendio di procedura penale*, Padova, Cedam, 2003, p. 580 *et seq.*

M. Panzavolta, 'Le letture di atti irripetibili al bivio tra "impossibilità oggettiva" e "libera scelta",' *Cassazione penale*, 2003, p. 3974.

M. Panzavolta, 'Reforms and Counter-Reforms in the Italian Struggle for an Accusatorial Criminal Law System,' *North Carolina Journal of International Law and Commercial Regulation*, 2005, p. 577.

P.P. Paulesu, 'Volontaria sottrazione al contraddittorio,' in *ivi*, p. 125 *et seq.*

P.P. Paulesu, *Giudice e parti nella 'dialettica' della prova testimoniale*, Torino, Giappichelli, 2002, p. 236.

W.T. Pizzi & L. Marafioti, 'The New Italian Code of Criminal Procedure: The Difficulties of Building an Adversarial Trial System on a Civil Law Foundation,' *Yale Journal of International Law*, 1992, p. 1.

W.T. Pizzi & M. Montagna, 'The Battle to Establish an Adversarial Trial System in Italy,' *Michigan Journal of International Law*, 2004, p. 429.

F. Ruggieri, *Divieti probatori e inutilizzabilità nella disciplina delle intercettazioni telefoniche*, Milano, Giuffrè, 2001, p. 16.

A. Scaglione, *L' attività ad iniziativa della polizia giudiziaria*, Torino, Giappichelli, 2001.

M. Scaparone, 'Indagini preliminari e udienza preliminare,' in G. Conso & V. Grevi (eds), *Compendio di procedura penale*, Padova, Cedam, 2003, p. 494.

L. Scomparin, *La tutela del testimone nel processo penale*, Padova, Cedam, 2000, p. 3 *et seq.*

D. Siracusano *et al.* (eds), *Diritto processuale penale*, Milano, Giuffrè, 2004.

G. Spangher, 'L'articolo 507 c.p.p. davanti alla Corte Costituzionale: ulteriore momento nella definizione del 'sistema accusatorio' compatibile con la Costituzione,' *Giurisprudenza Costituzionale*, 1993, p. 919.

G. Tranchina, 'Le indagini preliminari e l'udienza preliminare,' in D. Siracusano *et al.* (eds), *Diritto processuale penale*, Milano, Giuffrè, 2004, vol. II, p. 131.

G. Ubertis, 'La ricerca della verità giudiziale,' in G. Ubertis (ed.), *La conoscenza del fatto nel processo penale*, Milano, Giuffrè, 1992, p. 2 *et seq.*

D. Vigoni, *L'applicazione della pena su richiesta delle parti*, Milano, Giuffrè, 2000.

G.P. Voena, 'Soggetti,' in G. Conso & V. Grevi (eds), *Compendio di procedura penale*, Padova, Cedam, 2003, p. 94.

F. Zacchè, *Il giudizio abbreviato*, Milano, Giuffrè, 2004, p. 61.

Ties Prakken
Taru Spronken

THE INVESTIGATIVE STAGE OF THE CRIMINAL PROCESS IN THE NETHERLANDS

1.   Introduction

The Dutch Code of Criminal Procedure (CCP), which was enacted in 1926, sought to promote adversarial proceedings and individual rights of the suspect[1] and was intended to put an end to the situation in which the suspect was deprived of legal protection during preliminary investigations. In practice, as a result of the case law of the Supreme Court, the traditional, inquisitorial practice has been given room to continue, to the detriment of suspects' rights. Following the European continental tradition, Dutch criminal justice contains many inquisitorial elements. Criminal proceedings are an investigation into the actual truth under the supervision of the investigating, prosecuting and judicial authorities, a process in which defence counsel figures only marginally. Direct applicability of the European Convention on Human Rights (ECHR) has slightly improved adversarial processes, for instance in respect of the right of the accused to question witnesses.[2] However, although the investigation at trial is now more adversarial in nature, it is barely a forum for uncovering the truth. Rather, it serves to assess and review the file of the preceding investigation into the facts.[3]

Originally, at the investigative stage of the criminal process, the CCP provided for a police investigation for uncomplicated cases, and a preliminary judicial investigation (*gerechtelijk vooronderzoek*) in respect of more serious cases. In the latter, the investigating judge, who led the preliminary judicial investigation, was obliged to direct it in an objective way, protecting the rights of the suspect and third parties

---

[1]   In some jurisdictions different terminology is used, depending on the particular stage of the procedure. To prevent confusion we use the term suspect as a general term for persons under investigation including the accused and suspects.

[2]   ECtHR 20 January 1989, *Kostovski* v. *The Netherlands*, A 166; ECtHR 23 April 1997, *Van Mechelen* v. *The Netherlands*, Reports 1997-III; ECtHR 10 November 2005, *Bocos-Cuesta* v. *Netherlands*, No. 5478/00.

[3]   As a result of case law of the Supreme Court police records containing hearsay evidence are admissible in court, HR 20 December 1926, *NJ* 1927, 85.

and balancing these rights against the needs of the prosecution. However, in 1983 the Supreme Court accepted that a police investigation could be conducted simultaneously with the preliminary judicial investigation led by the investigating judge.[4] As a consequence, in practice the prosecution only turned to the investigating judge if a prior authorisation was needed for an investigative measure.

In 2000 two pieces of legislation were enacted that drastically changed the original character of the investigative stage of criminal procedure, the Act on Covert Investigative Powers and the Act on Revision of the Preliminary Judicial Investigation.[5] Important secret investigative methods were introduced (or, more accurately, legalised), and simultaneously the primary responsibility for investigation was given to the public prosecutor, who is supposed to control the police. In addition, greater investigative powers were given to the police and the prosecutor, powers that do not require the prior authorisation of the investigating judge. Only far-reaching coercive powers, for example, the search of a private dwelling, still require prior authorisation of the investigating judge or have to be conducted by them.[6] As a result the principle role of the investigating judge is largely limited to giving consent for the most intrusive, coercive and secret methods of investigation. Other than in some very serious cases, the investigative judge is no longer the director of the investigative stage. Their role is principally that of controller of the legality, but not the necessity, of the use of investigative measures. The decline of the preliminary judicial investigation, in which the suspect had formalized rights, has increased the marginalization of the position of the defence in the investigative stage. The prosecution is now the most powerful organ in the criminal process, not only in individual cases, but also in relation to criminal policy. The power of the prosecutor not to prosecute if the general interest so requires – the principle of discretionary powers – has evolved towards a system of criminal policy in the hands of a hierarchical and bureaucratic public prosecution office under the control of the minister of justice.

2. Police Powers in the Investigative Stage

2.1. Relations between police, prosecutor, investigating judge and defence

In the Netherlands, the criminal trial process is dominated by the investigative stage. The police have extensive investigative powers and the evidence gathered by the police and recorded in the file can be used as evidence at trial (see also 4.1 *infra*). At the investigative stage the public prosecutor is responsible for the actions of the police and officially heads the investigation, and the police must obey the public

---

[4]   HR 22 November 1983, *NJ* 1984, 805.

[5]   *Wet bijzondere opsporingsbevoegdheden* (Act on Covert Investigative Powers), 27 May 1999, *Stb.* 1999, 245 and *Wet herziening GVO* (Act on Revision of the Preliminary Judicial Investigation), 27 May 1999, *Stb.* 1999, 243.

[6]   Prior judicial authorization can, however, often be postponed if delay would be detrimental to the investigation.

prosecutor's orders. One of the purposes of the Covert Investigative Powers Act 2000, passed following a scandal involving abuse of powers by the police, was to increase the prosecutor's control of the police. The powers that the police and public prosecutor have under the CCP are regulated by guidelines drawn up by the Board of the Procurator-General (*College van Procureurs-Generaal*), who is responsible for the prosecution service. These guidelines are binding on public prosecutors in each court district. Prosecutors who have a more senior position in the hierarchy can give official commands to lower ranks. The hierarchically organized public prosecution service is responsible to the Minister of Justice and to Parliament. Over time the role of the prosecutor has developed from that of an independent magistrate towards one that is part of the executive. Although prosecutors are still expected to be objective and to safeguard the rights and interests of the suspect, they have in practice become 'crime fighters,' without a predominant concern for the rights and interests of the defence. This is exacerbated by the fact that many powers of the prosecutor under the CCP may be delegated to an assistant public prosecutor, who in practice is a high ranking police officer who liaises between the police officers conducting the investigation and the public prosecutor.[7] In some circumstances, the CCP enables the assistant public prosecutor to replace the public prosecutor. This means in practice that, depending on the latitude the prosecutor is willing to give to the police, many investigative powers assigned to the public prosecutor are in fact delegated to the police.

Prior to 2000, defence lawyers had frequent contact with the investigating judge concerning ongoing investigations and could influence the investigation. Since the preliminary judicial investigation has become an exception, this is now more difficult. If the defence want certain investigations to be carried out, they are dependent on the prosecutor. On the other hand, the possibility of negotiating with the prosecution has increased in practice, especially in the field of financial crime where plea-bargaining is rather common.

2.2. Arrest and preliminary detention

2.2.1. Arrest and first period of questioning

A person may be stopped by the police if there is a reasonable suspicion that they have committed a criminal offence. The police can request the person to provide their personal data (*staande houden*).[8] If a person is caught in the act of any offence, any citizen has the power to stop and hold them in order that they are brought, without delay (through the police), before a public prosecutor or assistant public prosecutor.[9] In practice this course of action is used by store detectives and security officers who sometimes even lock up suspects until the police arrive. In cases where

---

[7]   Art. 154 CCP determines which police officers can be designated as assistant prosecutors by the Minister of Justice.

[8]   Art. 52 CCP.

[9]   Art. 53 CCP.

a person is not caught in the act, arrest (*aanhouding/arrestatie*) may be ordered by a public prosecutor or assistant public prosecutor, but only in the case of a criminal offence for which the law allows detention on remand.[10] Detention on remand is permitted for those offences that can be punished with four years or more imprisonment,[11] in addition to a series of listed offences. Persons who have been arrested in respect of a suspected offence may be held for questioning at a police station for a maximum period of six hours, not including the time between midnight and 9:00 am – in other words, for a maximum period of 15 hours (*ophouden voor onderzoek*).[12] During these first 15 hours the prosecutor is normally not involved.

2.2.2. Police custody

Both the public prosecutor and the assistant public prosecutor can order that a person, who is suspected of a criminal offence for which the law allows detention on remand, is held in police custody (*inverzekeringstelling*) for a further period of three days if the interests of the investigation so requires.[13] During this period of police custody questioning of the suspect can continue. This period can be extended by another three days on the authority of the prosecutor. However, the suspect must be brought, within the period of three days and 15 hours after arrest, before the investigating judge, who tests the lawfulness of the detention.[14] If the investigating judge concludes that the detention is unlawful, the suspect must be released immediately. In practice, detention during the first three days and 15 hours is based on a decision of the assistant public prosecutor. The prosecutor has little or no concern with the detention in this phase of the investigation.

Normally a suspect is only brought before the investigating judge if the prosecutor wants the detention to be extended. If not, arrested suspects are released before three days and 15 have passed. Extension of police custody by a further three days, in addition to the initial 3 days and 15 hours, is possible, but rare. If this does happen, any such decision must be made by the prosecutor in person. Normally, if it is thought that further detention is necessary the prosecutor will, instead of authorising further detention in police custody, immediately request a remand in custody. This must be determined by the investigating judge, who may authorise a remand in custody for two weeks (*bewaring*). Extending police custody by three days, and requesting detention on remand after this period, means that the suspect must be brought before the investigating judge twice within a relative short period,

---

10   Art. 54 CCP.
11   Such offences include aggravated theft, public violence, most drugs offences, participation in a criminal organisation and, of course, manslaughter and the like.
12   Art. 61 CCP.
13   Art. 57 CCP; P.W. van der Kruijs, 'Kanttekeningen bij de inverzekeringstelling,' *Advocatenblad*, 1995, p. 940-946.
14   This period of three days and 15 hours derives from case law of the European Commission of Human Rights (4 November 1991, No. 18090/91 and 30 March 1992, No.19139/91) and is regarded as 'promptly' in the sense of art. 5, § 3 ECHR.

firstly to determine the lawfulness of police custody and secondly for the request for the remand in custody to be determined. For this reason, in practice extension of the police custody by three days (in addition to the 3 days and 15 hours) is only ordered when the prosecutor has reason to believe that the investigating judge would not grant a request for detention on remand and the prosecutor wants to keep the suspect for a longer period for interrogation at the police station.

2.2.3. Detention on remand

The Code of Criminal Procedure provides for two successive forms of detention on remand by order of a judge after police custody (*inverzekeringstelling*). The first is remand in custody (*bewaring*), which can be ordered by the investigating judge for a maximum period of 14 days.[15] The second is *gevangenhouding* (pre-trial detention by court order), which can be ordered by the court sitting in camera (*raadkamer*) for a maximum period of 90 days.[16] Within this period (in total 110 days and 15 hours) the case must be brought before the trial court for the first hearing. However, the court can suspend the trial for a limited or unlimited period, depending on the reason for adjournment. During this period the detention on remand stays in force until 60 days after the verdict.[17] Apart from this, detention on remand can be ordered by the trial court, where the suspect is not in custody (*gevangenneming*), for the period of the trial.[18] The period of detention on remand must not exceed the sentence that is likely to be imposed.

As mentioned above, accused persons may be held on remand (*voorlopige hechtenis*) by order of the judge if they are suspected of an offence that is punishable with a penalty of at least four years' imprisonment. A further ground for detention is that the suspect does not reside in the Netherlands and is suspected of an offence that can be punished by imprisonment.[19]

A general prerequisite for detention on remand, that is, detention authorised by a judge (normally after 3 days and 15 hours), is the existence of serious suspicion based on facts relating to the suspect. This is a higher threshold than the reasonable suspicion required for arrest and police custody: additional evidence is needed that the suspect probably committed the offence. In addition, at least one of the following five grounds must be satisfied:[20] (i) a risk that the suspect might flee, (ii) a danger that the suspect might commit another offence punishable by a penalty of at least six years' imprisonment, (iii) that the offence has seriously shocked society and the offence is punishable by a penalty of at least twelve years' imprisonment, (iv) a risk that the suspect might prevent or obstruct the investigation of the case, or (v) a

---

[15]   Art. 63 and 64 CCP.
[16]   Art. 65 CCP.
[17]   Art. 66 § 2.
[18]   Art. 65 CCP.
[19]   Art. 67 CCP.
[20]   Art. 67a CCP.

danger that the suspect may commit a listed offence (which includes some minor offences that are seen as a threat to public order, such as systematic shoplifting).

2.3. Interrogation of the suspect

During the entire investigative stage, and even after the trial has started, the suspect can be interrogated by the police. During arrest and police custody, interrogation of the suspect is the principal aim. Apart from fact-finding interrogations, there are interrogations or hearings that have a more supervisory character. For instance, before the prosecutor can request the investigating judge to authorise custody on remand (inbewaringstelling) they are obliged to personally interrogate the suspect. The aim of this interview is not principally to discover the truth, which is the function of the police, but supervision of the police, checking the information the prosecutor has received from the police, and giving the suspect an opportunity to make comments or observations. These interrogations enable the prosecutor to form their own assessment of the case and of the suspect, and enable them to decide whether they will release the suspect or request custody on remand. If the prosecutor decides to do the latter, the investigating judge will interrogate the suspect. This interrogation, by the investigating judge, has mixed objectives. The record of this interrogation normally plays an important role in the subsequent proceedings, because it is the first interview by a judge where the suspect is assisted by their counsel. This interview is intended to act as a check on the police and the prosecutor's decisions regarding the deprivation of the suspect's liberty and to scrutinize whether the alleged offences satisfy the conditions for police custody. In cases where the prosecutor requests an extension of detention on remand beyond 12 days, the suspect will be heard by the court sitting in camera, but this interview is normally very short as the court relies on the earlier interview by the investigating judge.

During the entire period of detention on remand the police may continue to investigate by all legal means, including by interrogating the suspect, even when the trial has already commenced. The police may even interview the suspect after conviction where there is to be an appeal. In the rare cases of preliminary judicial investigation, the investigating judge may delegate the interrogation of the suspect or witnesses to the police, although the police are permitted to interrogate without such delegation. The difference between being interviewed during preliminary judicial investigation and being interviewed by the police as part of their own investigation is that the accused, in principle, has the right to be assisted by counsel in the preliminary judicial investigation or when it concerns an interview delegated by the investigating judge to the police. This is not the case in an interview by the police conducted on their own initiative.

The suspect may be interrogated for as long, and as often, as is required in the opinion of the interrogating officer, provided that it is in accordance with article 29 CCP (which prohibits improper pressure and includes the right to silence). The general prohibition on improper pressure is not described precisely in any regulation. Within the limits of article 29 CCP the police are free to interrogate a suspect as long as they think is useful in order to persuade the person to talk. There are no written regulations in respect of rest, sleep or other conditions of detention and interrogation. Although the first 15 hours of arrest is divided into six hours for interrogation plus nine hours for night time rest, in practice nothing prevents the police from continuing with interrogation after midnight, and that is what regularly happens. Coffee and cigarettes are often offered when the police believe it to be helpful for creating a 'good atmosphere' during the interrogation, or, in minor cases, simply because it is customary. Although the interrogating officer must refrain from anything that leads to an involuntary confession by the suspect, it is difficult to ensure that this is complied with in practice. The Supreme Court has, however, held it to be a breach of article 29 CCP for the police to tell the suspect that they would only be released after a confession.[21] A similar judgment followed where the police used a method of interrogation, developed by a police psychologist, which consisted of the suspect being interrogated for lengthy periods in a room with photographs of the dead victim together with photographs of the suspect's family on the wall.[22]

The recording of police interviews is largely unregulated. The CCP provides that an interview should be recorded, but does not determine how this should be done. Audio-taping and videotaping of interviews are not standard practice and are only used in exceptional cases, for instance, when children are interviewed. Written records are not made verbatim, and questions and answers are not recorded literally. Most interview records read as if they were a spontaneous narrative by the suspect, but in practice they are a summary, which is written after the event.

2.4. Coercive investigative methods

The CCP enables prosecutors and assistant prosecutors to use many coercive powers in order to gather and secure evidence. In addition to the CCP, far-reaching coercive powers can be found in special statutes, for example the Opium Act (*Opiumwet*) from 1928,[23] and the Firearms Act (*Wet wapens en munitie*) from 1997,[24] which provide the police with greater powers for the investigation of possession and use of drugs and illegal arms than the powers contained within the CCP.

2.4.1. Measures against arrested persons

Photographs and fingerprints can be taken from a person who is under arrest, and in practice are routinely taken. Other investigative methods can also be used, such

---

[21]   HR 22 January 1980, *NJ* 1980, 203.
[22]   HR 13 May 1997, *NJ* 1998, 152.
[23]   *Wet van 12 mei 1928, tot vaststelling van bepalingen betreffende het opium en andere verdoovende middelen*, 1 October 1928, most recently amended *Stb.* 2004, 643. It has been amended on many occasions in order to reinforce police powers.
[24]   *Wet wapens en munitie*, 5 July 1997, most recently amended *Stb.* 2004, 290.

as participation in a 'line-up' and scent tests using trained dogs.[25] During custody and detention on remand, the suspect's contacts with the outside world can be restricted in the interests of the investigation (*bevel beperkingen*) by order of the prosecutor, or the investigating judge in the case of an official preliminary investigation. These restrictions can last until the complete file has to be disclosed to the defence (see 3.8 *infra*). This means that the suspect is not permitted to have verbal or written contact with third parties, or to read newspapers etc.[26] During this period the suspect can only have contact with their lawyer, who is not permitted to thwart the prosecutor's order by passing on messages. There is widespread discussion of, and extensive disciplinary case law on, what the lawyer is permitted to do in order to defend their client whilst these restrictions are in force. In general, defence counsel are not supposed to have contact with the counsel of co-defendants, or with the family and friends of their client, in relation to the case. This makes effective defence work difficult, especially where the defence lawyer wishes to gather evidence which may be favourable to the client's case.

2.4.2. Search and seizure

The ability and power of the police to enter premises (*betreden*) has always been connected to another legal power, such as the power to seize evidence or to arrest a person. In general, the requirements for entering a dwelling without the consent of the inhabitant are more restricted than the requirements for entering other premises.[27] A warrant is needed to enter a private home without the consent and/or knowledge of the inhabitant, according to the General Act of Entering Premises (*Algemene Wet op het binnentreden*).[28] This Act describes specific powers of civil servants and the conditions that have to be fulfilled before a warrant can be issued to enter premises or a dwelling. The person who enters the premises or dwelling is only permitted to look around, and is not allowed to search, for instance, by opening cupboards. However, there is no legal remedy where a dwelling or other premises have been unlawfully entered. Whether or not evidence obtained from an unlawful entry will be admissible as evidence depends on the circumstances of the case, but generally it will be admitted.

Search is a coercive measure that goes beyond entering premises, and must be distinguished from mere entry.[29] The appropriate authority for authorising search of premises is, in general, the prosecutor, but the search of a private dwelling or the office of a person with professional privilege must be authorised by the investigating judge. The suspect has the right to be assisted by a lawyer during the search,[30] but the authorities are not obliged to wait for the lawyer to be present.

25 Art. 61a CCP.
26 Art. 62 CCP.
27 Art. 55 CCP in case of arrest and art. 96 CCP in case of seizure.
28 *Algemene wet op het binnentreden*, 22 June 1994, most recently amended *Stb.* 1999, 194 and 207.
29 Art. 55a, 96b, 96c, 97, 98 and 110 CCP.
30 Art. 99a CCP.

Although the lawyer has no formal competence or power during the search, they can safeguard the suspect's rights by checking the legality of police conduct.

During a search, objects can be seized if they could contribute to clarifying the case, or if there is a possibility that they will be confiscated or withdrawn from circulation by a court order at a later date. The CPP contains detailed rules on who is authorised to seize goods and in what circumstances.[31] A search may include the inspection of computers at the scene of the search or at remote locations.[32] Documents containing legally privileged data may not be seized. Suspects can complain to the court about the seizure of an object.[33] Evidence obtained from an unlawful search or seizure may be admitted, but it depends upon the circumstances.

2.4.3. DNA, body-searches and mental examinations

DNA samples can be taken on the authority of an investigating judge[34] or public prosecutor (but not an assistant prosecutor) in cases where there is serious suspicion[35] that the person has committed an offence for which pre-trial detention is allowed.[36] This pre-condition also applies to a number of other coercive methods. There is no legal remedy in respect of such an order, but the suspect has the right to have the results checked by an independent expert. The public prosecutor[37] and the investigating judge[38] can order a search or an intimate body search. An intimate body search can including x-rays, and must be performed by a physician. Police officers are allowed to perform a security-search of suspects. A judge may order that the suspect be placed in a psychiatric institution in order to examine their mental faculties.

2.5. *Proactive and secret investigation methods*

The CPP provides for several secret investigative methods. These methods can be used both against persons suspected of a crime and those who are not themselves suspects, provided they serve the purpose of the investigation and there is a suspicion that an offence has been committed or is being planned. In most cases the general condition is that the investigation concerns a 'serious offence,' being an offence for which pre-trial detention is allowed (see above 2.2 *supra*).

---

[31]   Art. 94-119a CCP.
[32]   Art. 125j CCP.
[33]   Art. 552a CCP.
[34]   Art. 195a-e CCP.
[35]   As mentioned in 2.2 *supra* 'serious suspicion' is a higher threshold than the reasonable suspicion required for arrest and police custody: Additional evidence that the suspect probably committed the offence is required.
[36]   Art. 151a-c CCP.
[37]   Art. 56 CCP.
[38]   Art. 195 CCP.

The prosecutor can order the following investigative measures without prior authorisation of the investigating judge:

- covert surveillance of a person, whether or not a suspect, and in respect of any indictable offence. In the case of serious offences[39] this may include the secret entering of a private place/space, as long as it is not someone's home.[40] For the purpose of observation, technical devices may be used (e.g. transmitters, cameras) to secure traces or for surveying the place or the presence of any goods. However, the recording of private conversations is not permitted as a method of observation;

- infiltration by a police officer in respect of serious offences;[41]

- pseudo-purchase or pseudo-services by police officers in respect of serious offences;[42]

- covert and systematic collection of information by a police officer, whether or not it relates to a serious offence;[43]

- identification of telecommunication user information and number identification from telecom-organisations,[44] the supplying of personal information by financial institutions[45] and, in respect of serious offences, the supplying of data content of past financial transactions.[46]

In the case of serious offences the prosecutor can order, with the prior authorisation of the investigating judge:

- surveillance and recording of live private conversations (not necessarily the suspect's) using hidden listening devices;[47]

- tapping and recording of telecommunications equipment, telephone, fax and e-mail (not necessarily the suspect's);[48]

- banks to supply future financial data of a suspect.[49]

Moreover the investigating judge has the power, but only in the context of a preliminary judicial investigation, to order access to computerised data held by third persons or institutions.[50] In practice, the requirement for prior judicial authorisation has little impact. The judge's decision is based on police reports and

---

[39]   Mainly criminal acts that are punishable by more than four years of imprisonment, art. 67 CCP.
[40]   Art. 126g, 126k CCP.
[41]   Art. 126h CCP.
[42]   Art. 126i CCP.
[43]   Art. 126j CCP.
[44]   Art. 126na and 126 nb CCP.
[45]   Art. 125nc CCP.
[46]   Art. 126nd CCP.
[47]   Art. 126l CCP.
[48]   Art. 126m CCP.
[49]   Art. 126ne CCP.
[50]   Art. 125i CCP.

the only condition for authorisation is the interests of the investigation. Consequently, warrants are rarely refused.

2.6. Organised crime and terrorism

2.6.1. Organised crime

There are no special procedures relating to the investigation of organised crime, but the secret investigative methods outlined above may, in general, be applied not only in case of suspicion of an offence having been committed, but also proactively, i.e. in order to investigate a conspiracy to organise a crime.

2.6.2. Terrorism

In August 2004, terrorist activities were, for the first time, penalized in substantive law.[51] Apart from specific terrorist acts, the penalties for a number of common offences were increased if they are committed with a 'terrorist intention.'[52] Terrorist intention is defined as the intention to seriously frighten the population or a part of the population, to unlawfully force a government or organisation to take certain action or prevent them from taking action, or to disrupt the political, institutional, economic or social structure of a country or an international organisation. In the same legislation conspiracy, until then scarcely criminalized and almost never prosecuted, was criminalized on a significant scale, no doubt with the primary purpose of enabling proactive investigation and the use of intelligence in criminal proceedings.

Several bills have entered into force on 1 February 2007[53] which alter criminal procedural rules in cases of suspected terrorism. These special provisions include:

- extension of detention on remand before the commencement of the trial to up to two years in addition to the terms of 3-6 days remand in police custody (*inverzekeringstelling*), 14 days remand in custody (*bewaring*) and 90 days detention on remand by court order (*gevangenhouding*), without the defence having the right of access to the (complete) file;
- only 'reasonable suspicion, as opposed to 'serious suspicion,'[54] is required for the period of 14 days remand in custody (bewaring);
- the secret investigative methods outlined above can be used from the beginning of the preliminary investigative stage because they can be applied where there is an indication of terrorism and not only where there is 'a suspicion of the commission of an offence';

[51]   See, for a critical review, E. Prakken, 'Naar een cyclopisch (straf)recht,' *Nederlands Juristenblad* 2004, 2338-2344.
[52]   Art. 83a CCP.
[53]   Law of 20 November 2006, *Stb.* 2006, 580; *Stb.* 2006, 730; *Stb.* 2006, 731.
[54]   For the definition of 'serious suspicion' see 2.2 *supra*.

- intelligence can be used as evidence in a trial without the defence having a proper opportunity to challenge the evidence. Also the court has no proper opportunity to test its reliability.

3. Rights of the defendant

3.1. Information about suspects' rights

There is no legal obligation to inform a suspect of their rights apart from their right to silence (see 3.2 *infra*). A suspect has no general right to have someone informed of their arrest and detention, except for notification of a lawyer if the suspect has one. In practice some leaflets in different languages are available in most police stations for those detained. These leaflets give information about the length of detention at police stations, medical provisions, and the assignment of a lawyer from the moment the police custody has been ordered, etc. After police custody is authorised it is the responsibility of the then assigned lawyer (*piketadvocaat*) to inform the suspect of their legal position.

3.2. The Right to silence and caution

At the beginning of any interrogation a suspect has to be cautioned about their right to silence. The record of any interrogation undertaken in the absence of a caution is, in principle, inadmissible as evidence, although this omission can be circumvented by a new interrogation in which the suspect is cautioned. If this happens, most suspects do not understand the relevance of the new interview, and wonder why they are asked the same questions again. If they have already confessed in the previous interview conducted without a caution, they often think there is no point in keeping silent. Nevertheless, some politicians and lawyers have suggested that the caution should be abolished, because of its 'unnatural' character.[55] In their view there is no logic in interrogating someone in order to let them tell the truth and at the same time caution them that they may keep silent. However, there are few abolitionists and their opinion has not been enthusiastically embraced.

3.3. The Right to an interpreter

Detained suspects who do not have sufficient understanding of the Dutch language have the right to be assisted by an interpreter during interrogation and during hearings, paid for by the government. For indigent suspects who have a right to legal aid, the costs of interpreters necessary for their communication with their defence counsel are reimbursed. The suspect must be informed of the charge in a language that they understand. According to Dutch case law, the suspect who does

---

[55] One of the authors was Schipper, President of the Court of Appeal of Amsterdam. He expressed his opinion in his annual speech in 2002 as Chairman of the Dutch Lawyers Association; N.A.M. Schipper, 'Ervaringen in de strafpraktijk,' *NJB* 2002, 1295.

not understand the language also has, to a certain extent, the right to written translation of documents. This right can, however, be substituted by the presence of an interpreter during interrogation, or during the reading out of the documents at the (court) hearing where an interpreter is present.[56] According to Ministry of Justice guidelines[57] there is a right to have a translation of the following documents:

- a written translation of the essence of judicial notifications, on request;
- a complete translation of statements made by the suspect.

There is no obligation to provide a written translation of other documents, although the suspect and counsel can have the assistance of an interpreter when going through the file.

3.4. The Right to bail or release under conditions

Although the Code of Criminal Procedure acknowledges bail,[58] in practice bail in the form of the suspect making a financial payment to secure release is not a common outcome. Detention on remand is more frequently suspended on conditions, when personal circumstances so permit, and it is not to the detriment of the investigation. The general conditions are that the suspect must not flee, must not commit a criminal offence, and must appear before the police or the court when so requested. Other conditions may also be imposed such as treatment in a detoxification centre and the obligation not to go to a specified area.

3.5. The Right to be informed about the charge and existing evidence

A suspect who has been arrested must be orally informed of the reasons for their arrest and, in the case of police custody, the written order (including the grounds of arrest) must be given to the suspect. The written order only contains the article(s) of the criminal code or other statute the suspect is alleged to have contravened. There is no obligation in this phase to give information as to the existing evidence, although the police will give the suspect some information if they believe that it may persuade the suspect to confess. If the prosecutor requests custody on remand (*inbewaringstelling*) for two weeks she is obliged to provide the investigating judge and the defence, before the hearing, with sufficient information to justify the 'serious suspicion' that is necessary for the order to be granted. This information is frequently provided very shortly before the hearing.

---

[56]   HR 16 December 1997, *NJ* 1998, 352.
[57]   *Richtlijn tolkenbijstand opspsoringsonderzoek strafzaken* 11 June 1996 *Stcrt.* 168.
[58]   Art. 80 CCP.

3.6. Legal assistance

According to article 28 CCP the suspect has the right to be assisted by one or more lawyers of their own choice. Therefore a suspect has the right, from the time that they first arrive at the police station, to request a lawyer if they have one. In practice, since most suspects do not have a lawyer, this seldom occurs. It is not compulsory to have the assistance of a defence counsel, even in the most serious cases. Defendant(s) have the right to waive their right to counsel and defend themselves. When the suspect is taken into police custody (*inverzekeringstelling*), after an initial period of interrogation (of a maximum of 6 (or 15) hours), a defence lawyer is assigned to them for the period of the *inverzekeringstelling*.[59] Lawyers available for this service appear on a special register (*piket*). If the suspect has a certain preference, their choice will in most cases be respected if the chosen counsel is on the register and is willing to accept the case. If the suspect stays in detention on remand after the *inverzekeringstelling* the same lawyer will normally be assigned for the subsequent proceedings.[60] This assistance is free – lawyers are paid by the government – even when a suspect in not indigent. The suspect does have the right to replace an assigned lawyer by a lawyer of their own choice, although in that case the suspect is personally responsible for paying the lawyer.

The lawyer assigned for the period of *inverzekeringstelling* normally visits the person to whom they are assigned as soon as possible, and informs them of their rights and outlines what might happen in the following days. The lawyer is not normally provided with the existing evidence but may sometimes be given, at the police station, a copy of the record of the suspect's statement to the police. The most important tasks of the lawyer are to prepare their client for interrogation by the investigating judge if there is an expectation of custody on remand (*inbewaring-stelling*), and to discuss the defence strategy with the client. At some police stations the visits of defence counsel are restricted to half an hour, which is normally too short for effective preparation.

Although police interrogation is of crucial importance, since records of police interrogation can be used as evidence at trial, the suspect has no statutory right to have a lawyer present during police interrogation. In practice, whether defence counsel is permitted to be present depends on the interrogating officer. Lawyers are often admitted in cases of suspected tax fraud and other financial cases, but not in other cases. Suspects sometimes use their right to silence as a tactic to enforce the presence of their lawyer, but this is rare and only suspects who have previous experience will be in fact be able to choose this strategy. In 80 per cent of cases suspects give extensive statements to the police during the first 15 hours at the police station and before their lawyer arrives. Although the rights of the defence may well be irretrievably prejudiced by statements made by the suspect to the police, there is no right to consult a lawyer before interrogation. In this respect

---

[59]   Art. 40 CCP.
[60]   Art. 41 CCP.

Dutch practice appears to be in breach of the *Murray* decision of the ECtHR,[61] which suggests that a right to prior consultation derives from article 6 § 3, c of the Convention. Amongst academic lawyers and defence counsel, and even at the Ministry of Justice, a kind of consensus is developing that a right to prior consultation be established, but the police and prosecutors are not in favour.

Defence lawyers have very limited formal powers to perform their own investigation on behalf of the suspect. In the rare cases where there is a judicial preliminary investigation the defence can ask the investigating judge to carry out investigations on their behalf. Apart from that, during the pre-trial phase the only formal possibility for the defence is the so-called *mini-instructie*:[62] The suspect or their lawyer can ask the investigating judge for an investigation on a certain point, for instance the interrogation of a witness. The investigating judge has, however, a wide discretion to deny such requests on the grounds that the interest of the investigation may be impaired.

3.7. *Legal aid*

If the suspect is not deprived of their liberty and is unable to pay for counsel, they may request the assignment of a counsel. The suspect's choice of counsel will be respected. The suspect's financial position determines their level of contribution towards the cost of the counsel. There is no statutory regulation that can require a convicted person to be ordered to pay the costs of the proceedings after conviction. There is a provision, however, that the costs of legal aid can be recovered against the property of the suspect by order of the Minister of Justice (art. 49 CCP), although this provision has, to our knowledge, never been applied in practice.

Remuneration for an assigned defence counsel is not very high and is, in principle, based on a lump sum. In most cases, remuneration hardly covers office costs. To give an example, legal assistance in a relatively complex case where the suspect is in custody remuneration is € 1,090 if the legal assistance takes less than 24 hours of work and (but only with the consent of the Legal Aid Board (*Raad voor Rechts-bijstand*) € 90 for each additional hour. The relatively poor remuneration certainly has its consequences for the quality of legal services in criminal cases. Legal aid cases are mostly conducted by young lawyers in order to obtain experience, even though they are not necessarily interested in criminal cases, and by lawyers in small practices that need the remuneration to survive. However, the quality of assistance provided by lawyers specialised in criminal cases, mostly members of the Dutch Criminal Bar Association (*Nederlandse Vereniging van Strafrechtadvocaten*),[63] is satisfactory.

---

[61] ECtHR 8 Februay 1996, *Murray* v. *UK*, Reports 1996-I; ECtHR 6 June 2000, *Averill* v. *UK*, No. 36408/97.

[62] Art. 36a-36e CCP.

[63] See <www.nvsa.nl>.

3.8. The Right to disclosure

The suspect and their lawyer have the right of access to the file during the preliminary investigation from the moment the prosecutor becomes involved in the case which means, in practice, after the period of police custody of (a maximum of) 3 days and 15 hours, when the control exerted by the police has come to an end. However, if in the opinion of the prosecutor disclosure is detrimental to the interest of the investigation, certain documents can be withheld until the preliminary judicial investigation has been completed or until the suspect is served the summons for trial. Only records of statements made by the suspect or those that have been made in the suspect's presence cannot be withheld.[64] The decision to withhold documents must be notified to the defence, who may appeal to the court on the grounds that there are no adequate reasons for withholding the documents.[65] Since it is for the prosecutor to decide what should be in the file, they have a wide discretionary power to decide what information is disclosed during preliminary investigations. In practice, only a part of the file is disclosed to the defence during the investigative period. There are frequent disputes between defence lawyers and prosecutors concerning the disclosure of evidence that would lead to a discharge of the suspect or disclosure of investigative measures used by the police. The Supreme Court,[66] following the decision of the ECtHR in the *Edwards* case,[67] has decided that everything that is 'relevant' for the trial judge to reach a decision should be added to the file. This means that it can be relevant to disclose the investigative methods used, because if the police or prosecution have acted in violation of statutory provisions the prosecution can be stayed or evidence can be excluded. The final decision as to what should be added to the file lies with the trial judge who can order the prosecutor to disclose what the judge thinks is appropriate to reach a judgment.

Another difficulty is that there is no statutory definition of what should be considered as a 'document' in the sense of article 30 CCP. This can lead to equivocal decisions. For instance, a photo album used by the police to identify a suspect during the investigation is not a document, as long as it is not added to the file or as long as the court has not ordered it to be added to the file. In certain circumstances, however, if a special defence is put forward relating to the composition of the photo album, the (trial) court can order that it has to be disclosed, not because it is a document in the sense of article 30 CCP, but because it is needed to bring forward a certain defence. The court can then order that the photo album is only disclosed to the counsel, and not to the defendant, in order to protect the investigation and the privacy of the persons in the photo album.[68]

---

64   Art. 30 a.f. CCP and Art. 126aa a.f. CCP.
65   Art. 32 CCP.
66   HR 7 May 1996, *NJ* 1996, 687.
67   ECtHR 16 December 1992, *Edwards* v. *UK*, A 247-B.
68   HR 7 May 1996, *NJ* 1996, 687.

Decisions like these can put the defence in a difficult situation because counsel is not able to discuss the disclosed material with the client. This can be detrimental to the defence and can undermine the trust between counsel and client. Generally the disclosure of material only to counsel and not to the suspect is inconsistent with the principle underlying Dutch criminal procedure that the right to disclosure is a right of the defendant from which the right of counsel derives. It is also at odds with the principle that the trial court should not have more information than the defendant.

3.9. *Special protection of juveniles and other vulnerable persons*

3.9.1. Juveniles

Persons who have not yet reached the age of twelve cannot be prosecuted. Special rules apply to the prosecution and trial of persons who have not reached the age of eighteen on the date when the prosecution commences.[69] Compared to ordinary criminal proceedings the main differences are that juveniles are tried in camera, parents and guardians have a formal position, and child welfare offices are involved in the decision-making. However, during the preliminary investigation the rules on police custody and detention on remand, as well as other coercive measures, are the same as those that apply to adults, except for the places where and the way in which the detention on remand is executed. Juveniles should be kept apart from adults and various forms of bail are possible.

3.9.2. Mentally disturbed persons

For suspects with mental health issues, there are different rules in force for the prosecution and trial.[70]

3.10. *Different rights in the case of suspected organised crime and terrorism*

3.10.1. Organised crime

Some of the secret methods of investigation are more readily available in respect of those suspected of organised crime (see 2.5 *supra*).

3.10.2. Terrorism

In the past the procedural rights of terrorism suspects have been the same as those of other suspects, but as explained in 2.6 *supra* proposed legislation that is currently before Parliament will, if enacted, mean that it will be possible to postpone, for a

---

[69] Art. 486 a.f. CCP.
[70] Art. 509a a.f. CCP.

maximum period of two years and three and a half months, the right of the suspect to be informed about the precise nature of the charge and the right to full disclosure.

4. The impact of the investigative stage on the trial

4.1. The use of pre-trial statements of the accused or by witnesses as evidence at trial

As noted earlier, there is a heavy emphasis in the Netherlands on the pre-trial stage of the criminal process. The character of the trial is that of a verification of the evidence gathered by the police, and sometimes by the investigating judge, during the pre-trial period. As a consequence, the file produced during the investigative stage plays a major role at trial. The emphasis on the pre-trial stage has been facilitated by case law of the Supreme Court dating from 1926.[71] Despite the CCP, which came into force the same year and which was intended to make criminal proceedings more adversarial, the Supreme Court decided that hearsay evidence could be accepted at trial. This decision has had a tremendous impact in practice, not only because the written statement of a witness made to the police may be used as evidence, but also because the official record of a police officer containing information given by witnesses is accepted as if it were the statement of that witness. The same is true of the records made by the investigating judge during the preliminary judicial investigation. The trial judge normally only reads out the documents, or parts of it, at the trial and confronts the suspect with the results of the police investigation and of the investigation by the investigating judge, if any. The trial is restricted to discussing the value of the data collected in the pre-trial investigation. Therefore the trial itself does not take very long, especially where the suspect has confessed. Murder cases can be dealt with in one afternoon. In most cases, witnesses are not called to testify, even when the defence have not been able to put questions to them during pre-trial proceedings. Defence lawyers, supported by case law of the ECtHR, have succeeded in calling more witnesses to testify in court, but the powers of the defence to call and question witnesses is interpreted very strictly by the Supreme Court. When witnesses are called after the trial has begun, the court can refuse to hear them if it is perceived as being unnecessary. The ECtHR has condemned this practice on a number of occasions.[72] The justifications for excluding witnesses from the courtroom are expediency and financial economy. Justice has to be, and indeed is, efficient in the Netherlands! Criminal investigation in routine offences is completed within a few days and the average case takes a few months. The time provided in the CCP to investigate a case if a penalty of more than half a year imprisonment is expected is a little more than three months, although this period can be extended. Complicated cases with several counts in the

---

71   HR 20 December 1926, *NJ* 1927, 85.
72   Recently ECtHR 10 December 2005, *Bocos-Questa* v. *Netherlands*, No. 5489/00.

indictment, numerous defendants and no confessions will normally be dealt with within a year from the first arrest.

In principle, where suspects remain silent before and/or during the trial, their silence cannot be used as evidence against them. However, if the suspect remains silent when the evidence against them calls for an explanation, this can – following the case-law of the Supreme Court[73] – play a role in the weighing of the other evidence against them, both at trial and during the preliminary investigation (for instance, when a decision is taken concerning pre-trial detention). If the suspect lies, this can be used as evidence against them if there is evidence in the file that supports the assumption that the suspect is lying.[74] Suspects cannot effectively withdraw statements, such as those made to the police during the first interrogation. An accused who has given a self-incriminating statement to the police but has later withdrawn it, can be convicted on the basis of their first statement if, in the opinion of the judge, this is the more credible statement.

Dutch 'efficiency' has recently been overshadowed by two miscarriages of justice in which innocent people were convicted as a result of one-sided police work and lack of serious scrutiny in court.[75] In both cases the suspects were convicted after having (falsely) confessed to the police and withdrawn their confession afterwards. In the second case, *Schiedammer Parkmoordzaak*, the Board of Procurator-General ordered an investigation into the mistakes that had been made.[76] It appeared that the confession made during the first police interrogations, despite subsequent withdrawal by the suspect, caused so called 'tunnel vision': exculpatory evidence was ignored by the investigating authorities, and exculpatory DNA evidence was disclosed to neither the defence nor the trial judge. Various recommendations were made to the Minister of Justice to improve adversarial argument during criminal investigations and at trial.[77] It was proposed, for example, that interviews should be video-taped in serious cases, but there was no recommendation that defence counsel should have a right to be present during police interrogations. It was only because a majority in Parliament on 12 April 2006 insisted on it, that the Minister of Justice had to agree to an experiment permitting the presence of defence lawyers in a few selected districts in order to be able to evaluate the effects. The Minister had lobbied hard against such an experiment, on the grounds that it would be to costly and hinder police investigation. It is not yet known when these experiments will commence.

---

[73] HR 3 June 1997, *NJ* 1997, 584.
[74] HR 29 June 1971, *NJ* 1971, 417 and many others.
[75] HR 26 June 2001, *NJ* 2001, 564, *Puttense moordzaak*; HR 25 January 2005, *LJN* AS1872, *Schiedamse Parkmoord*.
[76] F. Posthumus, *Evaluatie onderzoek in de Schiedammer Parkmoord 13 september 2005, Bijlage TK 29800 VI, No. 168.*
[77] *Rapport Openbaar Ministerie, Versterking opsporing en vervolging, 4 november 2005, Bijlage TK 30300 VI, No. 32.*

4.2. The exclusion of illegally or unfairly obtained evidence

Evidence that is illegally or unfairly obtained in the pre-trial stage can lead to: i) the prosecution being stayed for abuse of process, ii) exclusion of evidence, or iii) a reduction of the penalty.[78] Case law tends to be lenient in applying these sanctions. Only in very exceptional cases will the prosecution be stayed, namely if the police or prosecutor have deliberately and seriously violated defence rights.[79] It is very difficult to prove that rule breaking by the police or prosecution when gathering evidence has been done deliberately in order to violate defence rights. So when the prosecution admits the mistakes, but denies that these were made deliberately to prejudice defence rights, the courts tend to believe this. Exclusion of evidence will only occur if the right to a fair trial has been violated, for instance if a statement has been given under pressure. Even an illegal search and seizure without a warrant does not lead to the exclusion of evidence where the warrant would have been granted if properly applied for. In most cases the accused will receive some reduction of their penalty. Sometimes an accused person has to be content with the establishment by the court that their rights were violated, without any compensation.

5. The role of the defence lawyer

5.1. Perception of the role of the defence lawyer

The CCP does not contain express norms prescribing the way in which criminal defence should be conducted. The Code contains a system of rights and powers, which may be exercised by the suspect and their counsel as they see fit. A characteristic of the system is that suspects have the right to defend themselves and that the power to do so resides, first and foremost, with the suspect. Counsel's powers are derived from these. Another characteristic is that in the pre-trial investigation phase virtually all rights can be restricted in the interest of the investigation. The CPP allocates no responsibility to defence counsel in exercising rights and powers derived from those of their clients. The starting point is that the suspect is *dominus litis*. At all times, the suspect is entitled to independently exercise their rights. Suspects have the right not to incriminate themselves, which means that a defence counsel is not obliged, in their capacity as defender of their client's interests, to take into account the interest of the investigation or prosecution, or the interest of an efficient justice system.

Apart from the powers derived from those afforded to the suspect, the CPP also grants separate rights and powers to counsel in their capacity as defender: access to their (detained) client, and attorney-client privilege. Unlike in the case of derived powers, the attorney bears their own responsibility in exercising these

---

[78]   Art. 591a Sv; M.C.D., Embregts, *Uitsluitsel over bewijsuitsluiting* (diss.), Deventer, Kluwer, 2003.

[79]   HR 30 March 2004, *NJ* 2004, 376.

powers and they must not abuse them. The right of access implies a right to confidential communication. It is generally accepted that supervision and regulation of contacts between counsel and their client must not make these contacts impossible, nor affect their confidential nature. In the past twenty years, under prison law, the possibilities of visiting the suspect and having access by telephone have been increasingly restricted in practice, and has been made subordinate to the internal organisation of the penal institution.

Professional privilege means that everything that comes to the knowledge of an attorney within the context of legal assistance must remain confidential although, of course, the client may authorise disclosure. Professional privilege, and the related duty of confidentiality, is not considered to be only in the interest of the individual client. It is also seen as a public interest that citizens may freely address an attorney, without having to fear disclosure of what they entrusted to them or of what was learned as a result of rendering legal assistance. Public interest requires that the attorney has a separate responsibility in exercising this privilege. Clients cannot relieve the attorney of this responsibility.

Recent law relating to the application of special investigative powers and the European provisions on combating money laundering increasingly render the guarantees of professional privilege and confidentiality subordinate to the interest of uncovering the truth. Since the Special Investigative Methods Act came into force on 1 February 2000,[80] investigative methods such as surveillance, interception of telephone conversations, direct eavesdropping or the use of informers and under-cover agents, can be deployed against lawyers even if they are not suspected of being involved in a crime themselves. Thus, confidential information may come to the knowledge of the judicial authorities without the lawyer being aware. Although the public prosecutor must immediately destroy information which is covered by lawyer-client privilege, in practice this obligation is not normally complied with.[81] The most striking fact is that it is the public prosecutor who is dealing with the investigation who, after becoming acquainted with the confidential communications that are intercepted and recorded, makes this decision.[82]

5.2. *Statutory regulations and limitations*

It was explained in 2.4 *supra* that isolation of the detained suspect from the outside world influences defence strategies. In addition, contact between the suspect and

---

[80] Act of 27 May 1999, *Stb.* 1999, 245.

[81] See for a discussion of these issues T. Spronken, 'De privileges van de raadsman,' in T. Praken and T. Spronken (eds), *Handboek verdediging*, Deventer, Kluwer, 2003, ch. 2, § 4.2.17. and ECtHR 25 November 2004, *Aalmoes e.o. v. Netherlands*, No. 16269/02; the complaint of 113 lawyers, stating that the powers of investigation under the CCP, as amended on 1 February 2000, and the regulations for implementing article 126aa of the CCP are in violation of their rights under article 8 of the Convention, was declared inadmissible.

[82] See the formal instruction on the *Destruction of intercepted conversations with persons enjoying the privilege of non disclosure* issued by the Board of Procurators General on 12 March 2002, attached to the decision of the ECtHR of 25 November 2004.

their lawyer can be restricted by the prosecutor or investigating judge[83] where there are facts substantiating a suspicion that contact between them will lead to the suspect being given information which, in the interest of the investigation, should not be conveyed to them, or that contact between them will be used to obstruct the investigation.[84] This means that some information about the investigation may be kept secret from the defendant even if their lawyer knows of it, such as the results of a line up confrontation when the defendant is denying their presence at the scene of the crime. In practice, these measures, which can only be applied for a maximum of six days, are rarely applied, but they still have an impact on strategies adopted by defence lawyers during the preliminary investigation. There is also disagreement on their implications in terms of what lawyers can properly do on behalf of their clients. Can a lawyer, for example, have contact with a potential witness who could confirm an alibi? Can a lawyer talk to journalists who want to publish a story about the case? In general, lawyers are reluctant to perform investigations in the interest of the defence because they expose themselves to the accusation of interfering with the police investigation. During the period that contact between the suspect and lawyer is restricted, another lawyer must be appointed to assist the suspect.[85] To our knowledge, the measure of restricting contact between a suspect and their lawyer has only been applied recently in cases in which a lawyer represented more than one suspect in the same case. In practice, this does not often happen because of the possibility of conflicting interests, in which case the lawyer would have to withdraw from every client they are assisting in the same case.

5.3. Professional standards and restrictions

Article 46 of the Attorneys Act (*Advocatenwet*) regulates the substance of the legal assistance attorneys render to their clients. Defence counsels' primary function is to render legal advice and assistance to their clients. Core assumptions in this respect are the principle of *ex-parte* defence,[86] safeguarding client/attorney confidentiality, quality of service and supporting due process. As to the regulation of the role of the criminal defence counsel, the conclusion can be drawn from professional disciplinary law that the principle of the suspect being the *dominus litis* in relation to their counsel remains ill-defined. Disciplinary law is subservient to the search for the truth in criminal proceedings. Counsel must refrain from actions that could reasonably be regarded as adversely affecting the lawful uncovering of the truth by the judicial authorities. This rule applies even more so where the client has been

---

[83] In cases where there is a formal preliminary investigation by the investigating judge, they are the only authority who can authorise the order to restrict contact between the lawyer and their detained client. If there is no formal preliminary investigation, this can be authorised by the prosecutor.

[84] Art. 50 § 2 CCP.

[85] Art. 50a CCP.

[86] Meaning that the role of the defence lawyer is to act in their client's best interests, even where this might have a detrimental impact on the interests of others including the interests of the prosecuting authorities.

taken into police custody or into preliminary judicial detention. If the public prosecutor or the investigating judge imposes statutory restrictions on the suspect, counsel must refrain from conduct that goes against the purpose envisaged by the imposition of such restrictions. In this type of situation, the determining factor for the judge in disciplinary cases is not the interest of the suspect and their counsel, but the interests of preserving the Bar's privileges when defending criminal cases and the trust placed in it.

As to counsel's role at trial, their use of procedural mechanisms, and their use of the media, the basic assumption in disciplinary law is freedom of defence: the lawyer is afforded great freedom in defending the client in the way they see fit. Disciplinary boards are slow in assuming that the limit of permissibility has been exceeded.

Whilst the main preoccupation of the disciplinary organs is what the defence counsel should not do, there is little concern with what counsel should do to assist clients as effectively as possible. However, there are some mechanisms that serve to improve legal services to suspects and accused persons. First, there is a mandatory course for counsel enlisted to assist suspects at police stations (*piketadvocaat*). Moreover every advocate is obliged to attend a number of courses each year in their field, and there are several courses in criminal law and criminal procedure that are attended by those lawyers who have (part of) their practice in criminal defence. Second, there is an association of criminal defence lawyers (*Nederlands Vereniging voor Strafrechtadvocaten*) that only admits lawyers for membership after they have followed an extensive specialist course in criminal defence. This association also organises courses and conferences for its members on current subjects of criminal (procedural) law.

6. Concluding remarks

The investigative stage of Dutch criminal procedure is to a large extent an inquisitorial phenomenon in which the suspect is an object of investigation. The rights of the suspect are, in principle, subordinate to the interests of the investigation, the latter being a synonym for the desire to bring a case quickly and efficiently to an end. In the process of uncovering the truth in the investigative stage, defence counsel figures only marginally. In many cases, counsel's actions are reduced to checking the lawfulness of the coercive measures imposed and (morally) supporting their client at times when they are not being examined or questioned.

Although legal assistance through counsel is easily available, it lacks the means to be effective. Access to the file during the investigative stage is difficult, and puts the defence at a disadvantage in securing exculpatory evidence. Confidential communication with clients is problematic when secret investigative methods are used. The main problem is, however, that counsel are kept out of the most essential parts of the investigative stage, i.e. the interrogation of the suspect and of witnesses by the police, whilst the impact of the investigative stage is tremendous. Mistakes and omissions made in the police station can hardly be repaired at trial. This has been demonstrated in recent miscarriages of justice.

Proposals to improve the quality of the investigation, in order to prevent mistakes, are directed at supervision of police work by superiors in the prosecution service rather than by improving the position of suspects by admitting counsel to assist during police interrogation and increasing the possibility of adversarial argument in the investigative stage.

7. Bibliography

General

J. Boksem, *Vademecum strafzaken*, Deventer, Kluwer, 2003.

Caselaw of the ECtHR can be found at the European Court of Human Rights HUDOC Portal: <http://cmiskp.echr.coe.int>, in Series A and after 1 January 1996 in Reports of Judgments and Decisions, both published by Carl Heymans Verlag KG, Köln, Germany.

C.P.M. Cleiren & J.F. Nijboer, *Tekst & Commentaar Strafvordering*, Deventer, Kluwer, 2005.

G.J.M. Corstens, *Het Nederlands Strafprocesrecht*, Deventer, Kluwer, 2005.

G.J.M. Corstens a.o. (ed.), *Handboek Strafzaken*, Deventer, Gouda Quint (loose-leaf).

A.L. Melai a.o. (ed.), *Het Wetboek van Strafvordering*, Deventer, Kluwer (loose-leaf).

Defence

M.C.D. Embregts, *Uitsluitsel over bewijsuitsluiting (diss.)*, Deventer, Kluwer, 2003.

T. Prakken & T. Spronken (eds), *Handboek verdediging*, Deventer, Kluwer, 2003.

T. Spronken, *Een onderzoek naar de normering van het optreden van advocaten in strafzaken (diss.)*, Deventer, Gouda Quint, 2001.

T. Spronken, *A place of greater safety. Reflections on a European Charter for Defence Lawyers*, inaugural lecture University Maastricht 10 October 2003.

Periodicals

Delikt en Delinkwent, Deventer, Kluwer.

Nederlandse Jurisprudentie Strafzaken, Deventer, Kluwer.

Nieuwsbrief Strafrecht, Den Haag, Sdu Uitgevers.

English literature on Dutch criminal procedural law

A.H.J. Swart, 'Chapter 10 – The Netherlands,' in C. van den Wijngaert a.o., *Criminal procedure systems in the European Community*, London, Butterworths, 1993.

P.J.P. Tak, *The Dutch criminal justice system (WODC – onderzoek en beleid)*, Meppel, Bju, 2003.

P.J.P. Tak (ed.), *Tasks and Powers of the Prosecution Services in the EU Member States*, Nijmegen, Wolf Legal Publishers, 2004.

Piotr Kruszyński

THE INVESTIGATIVE STAGE OF THE CRIMINAL PROCESS IN POLAND

1.   Introduction

Following the decline of the communist regime in 1989, the years between 1989 and 1995 saw the social and political reality in Poland change. After 1995 the Code of Criminal Procedure of 19 April 1969 underwent a process of partial reform. The amendments, which included removal of the Public Prosecutor's power to authorise the preliminary detention of a suspect, were made to humanise and democratise the criminal process. Instead of the prosecutor fulfilling this function the court was awarded exclusive power to decide upon arrest. In addition the reforms further restricted the grounds on which the Public Prosecutor could apply for preliminary detention and materially narrowed the admissibility of technical challenges open to the accused in the Court of Appeal. A series of amendments to the Code of Criminal Procedure replaced the central role of the prosecutor with an expanded role for the court, governed by the constitution. The reforms[1] did not change the fundamental structure of the criminal process except that the responsibility and power of the Prosecutor was decreased whilst the responsibility of the Judiciary in the decision-making process was increased. The Courts, and criminal process in general, began to use e-mail and other technological aids to facilitate greater efficiency.

The Polish criminal process is composed of two fundamental stages. The first, investigation, stage is conducted by the Public Prosecutor or other appropriate prosecution authority, e.g., the police under the supervision of the Public Prosecutor. This stage of proceedings aims to:

---

[1]   On 6 June 1997, the Polish Parliament passed a new Code of Criminal Procedure, which took effect on 1 September 1998. The amendments of 20 July 2000, at the behest of the Supreme Cout, restricted the ability of the parties to use the extraordinary means of appeal and to file a 'last resort' appeal. The most important amendments to the Code of Criminal Procedure were implemented on 10 January 2003, which affected nearly one third of the Code. This was an essential part of Poland's accession to the European Union. The Polish Criminal Code was 'adjusted' on the 18 March 2004 and 16 April 2004 in order that it complied with the laws of the European Union.

- determine whether a prohibited act was committed and whether this act constitutes an offence, and to detect the perpetrator;
- establish the nature and circumstances of the case;
- determine the extent of injuries to other persons; and
- gather, safeguard and record evidence for the court.

The second stage of criminal proceedings takes place before the court, and begins with an indictment brought by the prosecutor. The proceedings before the court of first instance are composed of several stages: the preliminary control of the act of accusation; preparation for the trial; and the trial itself. The judgement of the court of first instance may be appealed by any of the parties. The appellate proceedings are second instance proceedings that finally complete the process. There are two further additional, extraordinary, means of appeal in the form of cassation and the reopening of proceedings, which can only be exercised after a final (and valid) court decision. In addition to the above, the Code of Criminal Procedure also provides for specific proceedings for misdemeanours.

In Poland, judicial powers rest in the hands of courts and tribunals. The Constitutional Tribunal is the sole authority authorised to express an opinion on the Constitution. The scope of its tasks covers, *inter alia*:

- the expression of an opinion on the compliance of all laws and international treaties with the Constitution;
- the consideration of constitutional complaints made by citizens;
- answering the courts' legal questions which pertain to the compliance of a law with the Constitution;
- the settlement of pending court cases which are contingent upon answering such a question.

Furthermore, a decision of the Constitutional Tribunal constitutes grounds for re-opening criminal proceedings if, as a result of the decision, the validity of the pre-existing legal provision was successfully challenged or amended.

The European Convention on Human Rights (ECHR) of 4 November 1950 was ratified by Poland on 2 October 1992. As of 1 January 1993, it became possible to file individual complaints with the European Court of Human Rights (ECtHR). Decisions of the ECtHR are fully observed, and they often drive forward the amendment of domestic regulations.[2]

---

[2] Pursuant to article 540 § 3 of the Code of Criminal Procedure, a decision of the ECtHR can lead to the re-opening of criminal proceedings.

2. Police Powers in the Investigative Stage

2.1. *The relations between police, prosecutors and defence*[3]

In Polish criminal procedure there is no investigating judge. Specific decisions and/or investigative measures taken at the investigative stage of the process are reserved for the court to decide. For instance, it is for the court to decide on a request by the victim to have the process discontinued, to decide whether a witness should be interviewed, or to decide on preliminary detention.

The police are subordinate to the Public Prosecutor. The Public Prosecutor is the authority that conducts investigative proceedings and, in this respect, has a right to give the police binding orders, e.g., to conduct a search, to detain a person, or to bring them before the court. If the police conduct investigations they do so under the supervision of the Public Prosecutor who has a right to make decisions and to give orders or instructions as well as to change and repeal decisions made by the police. If the police do not wish to perform an action required by the Public Prosecutor, the immediate superior of the police officer who is questioning the decision of the Prosecutor may institute an official process to inform the Public Prosecutor. The actual relationship between the police and the Public Prosecutor depends upon levels of police training, technical equipment used, and the number of cases and orders dealt with.

In practice, there are contacts between defence lawyers and the prosecution authorities, and there are no restrictions in this respect. The defence lawyer can always ask for information about the stage that the investigation has reached, or on what kind of activities will be performed in the presence of their client. However, whilst proceedings are pending there is no duty on the prosecutor to respond. Furthermore, the defence only has limited access to the case file because the prosecution authorities can always refuse access, although the defence may complain about such a refusal. As a rule, defence lawyers contact the Public Prosecutor who is conducting or supervising the proceedings, because it is the prosecutor who decides on the course of the investigation.

2.2. *Arrest and detention*[4]

The police are vested with the power to arrest and detain a suspected person provided that: it can be reasonably assumed that such a person has committed an offence; there are concerns that the suspect will hide or remove evidence of an

3   P. Kruszyński (ed.), *Postępowanie karne w XXI wieku*, Warsaw, Dom Wydawniczy ABC, 2002, p. 97-123.
4   T. Grzegorczyk, *Kodeks postępowania karnego. Komentarz*, Cracow, Wydawnictwo prawnicze PWN, 2005, p. 642-687; S. Waltoś, *Proces karny. Zarys systemu*, Warsaw, Wydawnictwo Prawnicze Lexis Nexis, 2003, p. 410-433; R. Zdybel, 'Zatrzymanie procesowe w świetle rozwiązań kodeksu postępowania karnego oraz praktyki organów ścigania,' *Przegląd Sądowy*, 2003, No. 9, p. 75-107; J. Zagórski, 'Zatrzymanie przez policję oraz umieszczenie w policyjnych izbach zatrzymań,' *Państwo i Prawo*, 2004, No. 9, p. 84-97.

offence; or the police are uncertain about the suspect's identity. A fundamental pre-condition for detention is 'a reasonable suspicion' that a particular person has committed an offence. Such a suspicion requires that there is a deductive, logical connection between the available data and the suspected person. The suspected person can only be detained whilst there is due cause to do so, and as soon as the reasons for detention cease to exist the suspected person should be released without delay. The suspected person can make a written complaint about their detention to the court within seven days, and the court must consider any such complaint.

If the arrested person is not brought before the court, they must be released within 48 hours. Within this period the Public Prosecutor must decide whether they will request preliminary detention and, if so, formulate a written charge. When the detainee is brought before the court, detention may be extended by another 24 hours, within which period the court has to reach a decision on preliminary detention. The maximum period of detention (including the court detention) may, therefore, not exceed 72 hours. At this stage of detention, the police are supervised by the Public Prosecutor who will be informed, by the police or by the court, if the detainee legally challenges the detention process.

2.3. 'Suspected person' versus 'suspect'

To understand the status of the detained person at the initial stage it is important to know that before they are officially charged, the detained person does not have the status of 'suspect' but the status of 'a suspected person.' As long as a person is not officially charged, certain secret methods of investigation may be used, such as observation, 'pseudo-purchase,' or interception of communications. In addition, certain investigative measures explicitly stipulated in the Code of Criminal Procedure, may be used such as arrest and detention of the 'suspected person' for a maximum of 48 hours, inspection, photographing, and the taking of fingerprints, hair, blood and intimate samples. It is also possible for a lie detector to be used, but only with the consent of the suspected person. Preliminary detention, police supervision or confiscation of a person's passport is only possible after a person has been officially charged. Because the suspected person does not have the status of a suspect until they are charged, the police do not have to inform them of their rights. Only once a person has been charged do they have to be informed of their right to silence. The police are not permitted to interview a suspected person but, in practice at this preliminary stage, the suspected person may be 'heard,' i.e., they may make a voluntary statement to the police. If the suspected person was interviewed as a witness and they are subsequently charged, their statement may not be used at trial because of the so-called evidentiary ban.

2.4. Police interview[5]

Once a suspected person is officially charged, either orally or in writing, they are considered to be a suspect in the criminal process. A suspect can be interviewed if there is sufficient evidential data to justify the suspicion that they committed the criminal act. Prior to the interview, a suspect must be informed of their rights: to make a statement; to refuse to make a statement or to refuse to answer particular questions; to request that specific inquiries or investigations are undertaken; to be assisted by a defence lawyer; to have access to the evidential material at the end of the proceedings; to request an interview in the presence of an appointed defence lawyer. A suspect can be obliged to submit to a particular examination or test specified in the Code; to appear upon the request of the authority that is conducting the proceedings; and to provide a correspondence address. This information must be served upon the suspect in writing and confirmed by the suspect's signature.

The interview of the suspect constitutes a procedural activity. It is officially recorded, and offers the suspect the opportunity to refute the charges brought against them. The interview of the suspect begins with a statement regarding the charge, and subsequently the person conducting the interview will ask questions to supplement, clarify or verify the contents of the statement. The suspect is obliged to take part in the interview, but may refuse to offer any explanation, in which case the interview will be terminated. The interview is, in principle, an oral process, and an official record is prepared. The suspect and their defence lawyer may, however, request that the suspect give an explanation in writing, although the interviewer may refuse such a request. If the interviewer does consent, they may take steps to prevent any communication between the suspect and other persons who may be involved whilst the written explanation is prepared. Written explanations made and signed by the suspect, with the date on which they are made, are attached to the official record. The written explanation builds on and relates to the contents of the oral interview. For instance, a person suspected of defrauding a company may submit a written breakdown of financial information, but the interviewer may then request an oral explanation of the written information provided.

Interviews are not subject to maximum time limits, and they can be interrupted at any time, for example, to enable the person being interviewed to rest. In the course of the investigative process the suspect may be interviewed on several occasions depending on the requirements of the investigation. Both the police and the Public Prosecutor can conduct interviews of suspects. In practice, it depends upon who is conducting the investigation. However, in view of the supervisory role of the Public Prosecutor, they may always interview a suspect even if the police have already done so.

---

[5]   K.J. Pawelec, *Wyjaśnienia podejrzanego, zeznania świadka i instytucja świadka koronnego. Komentarz*, Warsaw, C.H. Beck, 2003, p. 21-51; P. Kruszyński (ed.), *Wykład prawa karnego procesowego*, Białystok, 2004, p. 193-210; M. Zbrojewska, 'Przedstawienie zarzutów w polskim procesie karnym – uwagi ogólne,' *Przegląd Policyjny*, 1998, No. 3-4, p. 122-132.

2.5. Preliminary detention; duration and bail

In addition to the maximum period of detention of 72 hours (referred to in section 2.2), the Polish Code of Criminal Procedure also provides for preliminary detention. It is for the court to order whether a person should be subjected to preliminary detention and the duration of such detention. The maximum period of preliminary detention is three months, although this may be extended. The general ground for preliminary detention to be ordered is that there is evidence that the accused is very likely to have committed the alleged offence. The specific grounds are as follows:

- there is a reasonable fear that the accused will escape or hide, particularly if it is impossible to establish their identity or they have no permanent place of residence;
- there is a reasonable fear that the accused will attempt to falsify evidence, make false statements or impede the criminal prosecution in any other unlawful manner;
- the accused is charged with having committed an offence which is punishable by at least eight years' imprisonment, or the court of first instance has sentenced the accused to at least three years' imprisonment;
- there is reasonable fear that the accused, having been charged with a felony or intentional offence, may commit a further offence endangering life, health or public security, particularly if there has been a threat to commit such an offence.

A person in preliminary detention may have access to the investigative file only with the consent of the person who is conducting the investigation, although refusal of access can lead to a complaint by the detainee. Before preliminary detention is authorised, the court must interview the suspect. A defence lawyer may attend such an interview, although it is not obligatory for the lawyer to be notified unless the suspect specifically requests that the defence lawyer be informed and provided that the presence of the defence lawyer will not impede the investigative process. The defence lawyer may also take part when an application is being made to extend the period of preliminary detention and may address the court on the extension of the period of detention. A failure to inform the defence lawyer of the preliminary hearing does not invalidate the decision.

Preliminary detention is ordered relatively frequently, although not as often as was the case under the previous Polish political system when the decision on preliminary detention rested with the Public Prosecutor. The maximum period that a person may be detained before a court makes a decision at first instance as to guilt is two years. In practice, it is generally only in complex cases involving corruption, economic and organised crime that such a period of detention is likely. Both the nature of the offence and the likely sentence outcome have a bearing on the decision to order preliminary detention. If it is anticipated that either a sentence of less than one year or a suspended sentence will be the outcome, preliminary detention is unlikely to be ordered. However, these considerations are not applicable where the accused absconds or fails to disclose their true identity to the court. In the absence of these factors, preliminary detention is not ordered when imprisonment of the accused would cause a serious danger to their life or health or, in exceptional cases, where detention would have severe consequences for the accused or their close family.

2.6. Coercive methods of investigation[6]

A search may only be carried out in order to detect or detain a suspect, or to seize items that are relevant to the criminal prosecution. A search may be made of premises (lodgings and other premises), other places (means of transportation, open spaces), or of the suspected person, their clothing and their possessions. In order for a search to be lawfully conducted there must be reasonable grounds to suspect that either the suspect or the aforementioned items may be found at the place to be searched.

During the investigative process the accused may be required to undergo:

- external inspection of their body and other examinations that are not regarded as a 'transgression of the bodily integrity,' e.g., fingerprints, photographs (and such data may be shown to others for the purposes of recognition);
- psychological and psychiatric tests combined with certain examinations of the body (other than surgical examination). Such actions must be necessary for the investigation and must be undertaken by a suitable person (an authorised healthcare employee who observes the medical rules) and cannot threaten the health of the accused. If the need is established, the accused may be obliged to undergo a blood test, an examination of hair and/or to submit to the taking of intimate body samples;
- a smear test of mucous membrane (from their cheeks) which is taken by a police officer, if this is essential and there are no concerns that it might threaten the health of either the accused or other persons.

Furthermore, in order to reduce the range of suspects or determine the evidentiary value of the traces detected, a person who is not considered a suspect may be required to provide fingerprints or a handwriting sample, or to permit a smear test of mucous membrane from their cheeks, or a sample of hair or saliva to be taken, or to permit a photograph or a recording of their voice to be taken. In addition, a lie-detector test may be conducted, but only with the person's consent.

The foregoing investigative methods are conducted, first and foremost, by the authority which is carrying out the investigative proceedings. The defence may also attempt to instigate such investigative methods. The parties to the proceedings are

---

[6]   J. Wójcikiewicz (ed.), *Ekspertyza sądowa*, Cracow, Zakamycze, 2002, p.79-139, 207-252, 289-372; J. Bratoszewski, L. Gardocki, Z. Gostyński, S. Przyjemski, R. Stefański, S. Zabłocki, *Kodeks postępowania karnego. Komentarz*, Warsaw, Dom Wydawniczy ABC, 2003, vol. I, p. 526-532, 878-880, 973-1015; T. Grzegorczyk, J. Tylman, *Polskie postępowanie karne*, Warsaw, Wydawnictwo Prawnicze Lexis Nexis, 2005, p. 495-507; A. Lach, *Dowody elektroniczne w procesie karnym*, Toruń, Dom Organizatora, 2004, p. 69-151; P. Świerk, 'Badanie poligraficzne po nowelizacji kodeksu postępowania karnego,' *Prokuratura i Prawo*, 2003, No. 9, p. 49-58.

informed of the outcome of such methods. If the court admits expert evidence (e.g. on toxicology or genetics) the suspect and their defence lawyer, as well as the injured party and their legal representative, must be served with a statement relating to the admissibility of the evidence and they can take part in the interview of the experts and read their opinion (if filed in writing). Familiarity with the statement allows the parties the opportunity to be informed of the issues raised by the expert, to call another expert witness, extend the scope of questions addressed to the expert, or challenge the views of the expert witness.

2.7. Secret methods of investigation[7]

Regulations concerning secret methods of investigation are included in the Code of Criminal Procedure and the Police Act of the 6th April 1990 and encompass the control and transcription of telephone calls, the control of correspondence, 'pseudo purchase,' secret surveillance and the activity of secret agents. The provisions of the Code of Criminal Procedure stipulate the procedural controls which regulate the transcription of telephone calls and the use of other technical means to monitor the content of conversations (other than telephone calls) or other communications, and e-mail. These methods of surveillance are only permitted in order to detect and procure evidence relating to pending proceedings or to prevent offences from being committed. In practice, telephone tapping is used only in respect of the most serious crimes. However, it is difficult to specify how often such methods are used because any information relating to them is kept secret. The control and transcription of telephone calls (or other communications) may only be ordered by a court, upon the request of the Public Prosecutor. In urgent cases, they may be ordered by the Public Prosecutor, but they are then required to seek validation of the decision from a court within three days. Where a Prosecutor makes a request the application is heard in the absence of the other parties to the case, and the court must make a decision within five days. Information obtained as a result of the monitoring of telephone conversations or other communications if only admissible if there is either a reasonable concern that an offence is being committed or it relates to an existing serious offence.[8]

Authorisation for these investigative methods may be granted for a maximum of three months, although this may be extended for a further three months. If the person who is subject to one of these investigative methods is aware of it, they may

---

[7]   K. Dudka, *Kontrola korespondencji i podsłuch w polskim procesie karnym,* Lublin, Wydawnictwo Uniwersytetu Marii. Curie-Skłodowskiej, 1998, p. 5 *et seq.*; T. Hanausek, *Ustawa o Policji. Komentarz,* Cracow, Zakamycze, 1996, p. 10 *et seq.*; K. Eichstaedt, 'Zarządzenie przez sąd kontroli operacyjnej w ujęciu procesowym,' *Prokuratura i Prawo,* 2003, No. 9, p. 28-48; G. Musialik–Dudzińska, 'Podsłuch pozaprocesowy (operacyjny) na gruncie znowelizowanej ustawy z dnia 6 kwietnia 1990r. o Policji,' *Przegląd Sądowy,* 2004, No. 4, p. 49-65.

[8]   For example, murder, exposure to a common danger or causing a disaster, human trafficking, kidnapping, ransom, hijacking an aircraft or boat, robbery, manufacturing, processing, trading or smuggling of drugs, participation in a criminal organisation, corruption and bribery.

appeal against the legality of the decision to authorise it. However, the Code permits the continued use of the investigative method pending the appeal. A person who is subjected to interception of their communications is normally informed of it only after it has been completed. They are then given a written notice identifying the authority that applied for authorisation, the number of the telephone that was tapped, and the duration of the interception. This is justified by the fact that earlier disclosure of this information would prevent the collection of the evidence. The court or the Public Prosecutor has a right to reproduce the recording and, in urgent cases, the police may do so as well, but only with the consent of the court or the Public Prosecutor. Access to the control register is exclusively controlled by the court or, at the investigative stage, by the Public Prosecutor.

In addition to the 'trial tap' (i.e. one applied in the course of pending criminal proceedings) there is also the so-called 'pre-trial tap,' which takes place prior to the commencement of an official investigation into a criminal offence. The 'pre-trial tap' is regulated by the Police Act which permits tapping:

- within the framework of investigative activities undertaken to prevent or detect crime, or to establish the perpetrators, but also to procure and consolidate *corpus delicti*;
- within the framework of the so-called 'operating control,' which encompasses control of correspondence and letters as well as the application of technical methods that make it possible to obtain information, evidence (and its secret transcription), and in particular the content of telephone calls and other information transferred via telecommunications networks.

The Commander-in-Chief of the Polish National Police may, with the written consent of the General Public Prosecutor (or regional commanders with the consent of the Regional Public Prosecutor), apply to the regional court for consent to operate a tap. In urgent cases, where evidence may be lost or removed, it is possible for the Commander-in-Chief or the regional commander, with the consent of the respective Public Prosecutor, to order correspondence and electronic communications to be monitored for a defined period of time. However, the validity of the order must be endorsed by the relevant regional court within five days. If the court refuses its consent, the activity must be suspended and a court order will be issued so that all the materials that have been obtained or recorded are destroyed in such a way as will prevent the reconstruction of personal data.

If, on the other hand, consent is obtained and the interception confirms the commission of an offence, the information obtained is given to the Public Prosecutor so that criminal proceedings can be initiated. The information obtained will constitute either material or documentary evidence, depending on the type of correspondence. In addition, if necessary, the persons who performed the interception may be interviewed in their capacity as witnesses. It is difficult to assess how the regulation of pre-trial tapping works in practice, and whether material recorded without consent of the court is actually destroyed, because there is no access to this type of information. Similarly, there is no access to information regarding how often pre-trial tapping is used.

The use of pseudo-purchase methods requires the consent of the relevant Public Prosecutor who is informed, on an ongoing basis, of the results of such activity. Any secret acquisition, sale or seizure of objects may be ordered for a period of up to three months, which may be extended for a further three months.

The Police Act also defines 'secret surveillance,' which is a process which occurs prior to the initiation of criminal proceedings in respect of certain offences. When it is considered necessary to determine the identity of persons who are suspected of participation, or of undertaking preparatory acts, in relation to such offences, a decision to utilise 'secret supervision' is taken by the Commander-in-Chief of the Polish National Police or the regional commander, respectively, who must immediately notify the relevant Public Prosecutor.

The police 'secret agent' is a person who, while they conceal their own identity and relationship with the police, contacts a criminal group to detect the offence and its perpetrators. The police 'secret agent' may be either a police officer or a third party. The secret agent may use documents in order to conceal their true identity.

2.8. *Terrorism and organized crime*[9]

There are no special methods of inquiry that are used to combat terrorism in the Polish legal system. The Act of 24 May 2002 established two agencies, the Internal Security Agency (*Agencja Bezpieczeństwa Wewnętrznego* — ABW) and the Foreign Intelligence Agency (*Agencja Wywiadu* — AW). Whereas the AW is concerned with external security, the work undertaken by the ABW encompasses state internal security and constitutional order. Both are concerned with terrorism, but their responsibilities extend well beyond this. The methods employed by the two agencies include 'pseudo purchase,' secret observation of premises, monitoring of correspondence and transcription and technological interception of other information transferred via telecommunications networks.

The tasks of the ABW encompass, *inter alia*:

- recognising, preventing and combating any threats to the internal safety of the state and its constitutional order, and in particular its sovereignty `and international position, independence and territorial integrity, as well the state defence system;
- recognising, preventing, detecting and prosecuting in respect of crimes of espionage, terrorism, breach of state secrets and other crimes that may jeopardise the safety of the state;
- obtaining, analysing, processing and transferring to the relevant authorities any information that may be material to safeguarding the internal safety of the state and its constitutional order;
- taking other actions stipulated in separate acts of law and international treaties.

The tasks of the AW encompass, *inter alia*:

---

9   T. Grzegorczyk, J. Tylman, *Polskie postępowanie karne*, Warsaw, Wydawnictwo Prawnicze Lexis Nexis, 2005, p. 250-252.

- obtaining, analysing, processing and transferring to the relevant authorities, any information that may be material to safeguarding the safety and international position of the state as well as its economic and defensive potential;
- detecting and counteracting any external dangers that may threaten the safety, defensive systems, independence and territorial integrity of the state;
- detecting international terrorism, extremism and international organised crime;
- detecting international trade in weapons, munitions and explosives, drugs, technologies and services which may threaten the safety of the state, as well as detecting international trade in weapons of mass destruction and any threats related to the proliferation of such arms and their carriers;
- detecting and analysing any regional threats resulting from tension, conflicts and international crises that may have a bearing on the safety of the state, and taking actions to eliminate such threats;
- ELINT, Electronic Intelligence;
- taking other actions stipulated in separate acts of law and international treaties.

Any information gathered by ABW and AW can be used in the criminal proceedings.

The Act of the 25th June 1997 modified the existing Polish legal system with regard to Crown witnesses. The Act of the 16th November 2000 made further provisions that address financial issues ranging from property valuation to the financing of terrorism.[10] Under the Act on State Witnesses a participant in certain specified forms of 'organised crime' can be given the status of a state witness provided that they fulfil certain requirements. The requirements are that the witness provides to the prosecution authority, and subsequently to the court, full information concerning any aspects of the activities of the organised crime group and of the participants. A person who has been the organiser of such acts, has committed homicide or has acted as an instigator, cannot be a Crown witness. The status of a Crown witness is designated by the court and if such a witness fulfils all the conditions stipulated by law, they are not penalised for the offence which they have committed and disclosed.

The November 2000 Act imposes an exceptionally wide range of obligations on those participating in economic transactions that exceeds € 15,000. Such transactions must be registered, in addition to any other transactions irrespective of their value. If there is a reasonable belief that such actions amount to 'money laundering' the General Inspector for Financial Control is informed, or if there is information regarding the financing of terrorism, the Public Prosecutor is notified. By virtue of the Act it is possible to suspend a transaction and block a bank account and require institutions to make available any information on financial transactions conducted by named persons. Additionally, the Act affected members of the Bar by amending the lawyer's professional obligation of confidentiality so that a lawyer

---

[10] K. Cesarz, 'Dowód z zeznań świadka koronnego na tle prawa do sądu (wybrane zagadnienia),' *Przegląd Sądowy*, 2004, No. 4, p. 65-75.

can be required to divulge otherwise confidential information regarding transactions covered by the Act.

There are no provisions in the Polish legal system that restrict the right to defend a person accused of terrorist offences.

3. The Rights of the defendant

3.1. Information concerning suspects' rights[11]

An arrested and detained suspect[12] must be verbally informed of their rights without delay by the authority that detains them (i.e., the police). Reasons for the detention must be given and the suspected person must be made aware of their right:

- to contact a lawyer;
- to request that their close friends/family/closest person (including the person designated by the detainee), employer, school or college are informed of the detention;
- to appeal to the court against the detention.

An official record of the detention is drawn up, which must indicate that the detained person has been informed of these rights. It is possible to file a complaint about the detention with the court, which immediately hears the complaint. There is no statistical data on how often complaints about detention are filed.

Following charge,[13] and before the first (official) case interview begins, the suspected person is designated as a suspect and must be informed in writing of:

- the right to make, or to refuse to make, a statement;
- the right to request that the investigator undertakes specific acts or enquiries;
- the right to select a specific defence lawyer and to have the assistance of a defence lawyer; and
- the right to familiarise themselves with the 'materials of the proceedings.'

3.2. Presumption of innocence

The presumption of innocence is guaranteed by the Constitution of the Republic of Poland and by the Code of Criminal Procedure. This means that the accused must

---

11   Z. Gostyński, 'Obowiązek informowania uczestników postępowania o ich obowiązkach i uprawnieniach jako przejaw zasady uczciwego (rzetelnego) procesu,' in J. Czapska (et al.), *Zasady procesu karnego wobec wyzwań współczesności. Księga ku czci prof. dr hab. Stanisława Waltosia*, Warsaw, Wydawnictwo prawnicze PWN, 2000, p. 362-371; R.A. Stefański, *Kodeks postępowania karnego z orzecznictwem i piśmiennictwem (za lata 1998-2003)*, Toruń, Dom Organizatora, 2004, p. 244-247.

12   See § 2.3 for the distinction between a 'suspected person' and a 'suspect.'

13   Sometimes the suspect can be charged orally. If preliminary detention is applied, however, this has to be done in a written decision.

be treated as innocent until a valid verdict of guilt has been passed. Disclosure to the news media of any material relating to the personal details of suspects, or the circumstances of the case, where there is an ongoing investigation or pending court proceedings, is forbidden unless the person(s) affected by the investigation or proceedings consent. Only if there is a wider public interest in the case can the Public Prosecutor or the court disclose the personal data or an image of the suspect. Making prejudicial statements, or offering opinions on the likely outcome, to the media before the judgement is issued is not permitted.

3.3. The right to silence and caution[14]

The suspect is under no obligation to prove their innocence nor do they have to provide any evidence to that effect. The principle of the presumption of innocence is given effect by the stipulation that the suspect has the right to provide explanations, or to refuse to provide explanations, in response to questions posed. The suspect is instructed about such rights at least twice; first, prior to the first official interview in the investigative proceedings when the suspect is notified of this right in writing, and second, when the court verbally restates the caution at trial after the indictment is read out. The notice requirements are obligatory, and any failure to give them will provide grounds for appeal against the judgement.

The fact that the accused gives a false explanation, or exercises their right to silence, may not affect the penalty imposed by a judge. The court may conclude that it did not believe the explanations given by the accused, but it may not draw any negative inference or impose a more severe penalty as a result of the accused exercising their right to silence.

3.4. The right to an interpreter[15]

The accused has a right to an interpreter or translator if they do not have a sufficient understanding of Polish, the cost of which is borne by the State Treasury. The interpreter or translator should participate in each activity in which the accused partakes, including consultations between the accused and their lawyer. The accused has the right to translated copies of the charge(s), any amendments to the charge(s), the indictment, and the final judgement.

[14] P. Kruszyński, *Zasada domniemania niewinności w polskim procesie i karnym*, Warsaw, Wydawnictwo Uniwersytetu Warszawskiego, 1983, p. 5 *et seq.*; Ł. Woźniak, 'Zasada domniemania niewinności – zagadnienia podstawowe,' in S. Waltosia, *Zasady procesu karnego wobec wyzwań współczesności*, Warsaw, Wydawnictwo prawnicze PWN, 2000, p. 354-362.

[15] K. Marszał, S. Stachowiak, K. Zgryzek, *Proces karny*, Katowice, Volumen, 2003, p. 211-213; C. Nowak, 'Prawo do korzystania z pomocy tłumacza w europejskim i polskim prawie karnym,' *Prokuratura i Prawo*, 1998, No. 10, p. 89-101.

3.5.   Legal assistance[16]

The right of a person to defend themselves is guaranteed by the Constitution of the Republic of Poland and the Code of Criminal Procedure, and it may be done either 'personally' by the defendant or by a defence lawyer. The right to appoint a defence lawyer is also vested in 'a representative in litigation' (e.g. parents) or a guardian of the defendant. If the suspect is imprisoned any such person may appoint a defence lawyer, and the defendant must be immediately informed of this.

The defendant only has a choice of lawyer if they instruct a lawyer privately. In certain circumstances the accused must have a defence lawyer irrespective of their wishes, and any objections are deemed irrelevant. The accused must have a defence lawyer for the entire criminal proceedings if they are juvenile, deaf, dumb, or blind, if there are relevant mental health issues, or when the Court finds that there are circumstances impeding the defence.

Furthermore, the accused must have a defence lawyer, but only in respect of the court proceedings, when the proceedings are pending before the regional court sitting as a court of first instance and the accused is charged with a felony, or is in prison.

3.6.   Legal aid

In cases in which it is mandatory to have a defence lawyer, and the accused has not instructed a lawyer, the president of the court having jurisdiction in the case will appoint a public defence lawyer. A suspect can also request that a defence lawyer be appointed if they can prove — by submitting documents confirming that they are in receipt of an allowance or a tax certificate confirming their income — that they are unable to pay the defence costs without prejudice to themselves or their family. There is no appeal against a refusal by the president to appoint a defence lawyer on the grounds of indigence.

Where a lawyer is privately instructed, their fee is to be agreed with the client, although the Minister of Justice has established minimum rates of payment. Where a public defence lawyer is appointed, the costs of unpaid legal assistance are borne by the State Treasury irrespective of the decision of the court.

The professional status of public defence lawyers is the same as those who are privately instructed. Any lawyer may act as a public defence lawyer and there is no separate group of lawyers who render only public legal assistance.

---

[16]   Z Czeszejko-Sochacki, Z. Krzemiński, *Adwokat z urzędu w postępowaniu sądowym*, Warsaw, Wydawnictwo Prawnicze, 1975, p. 15 *et seq.*

3.7. Legal assistance before and during police interview[17]

The interview of the suspect after charge is intended to provide, among other things, an opportunity for the suspect to exercise their defence rights. In this way, the suspect is given the opportunity to adopt a particular stance regarding the charge. If, however, the suspect decides that, for any reason, it would be premature to make a statement regarding the charge to the interviewer, such a refusal is in accordance with their rights confirmed in writing before the first interview begins.

During the interview a defence lawyer may be present if the suspect so requests. In practice, a request for a lawyer to advise at this stage is made, most frequently, by suspects who are able to pay privately. In other cases, it is unusual for a lawyer to attend the interview. There are no procedural consequences if a lawyer is not present, and there is no obligation for a lawyer to be in attendance. If a lawyer is in attendance they may actively participate in the interview, e.g. by advising the client whether to answer a question, by requesting a break in the interview for a private consultation with the client, or by requesting that the client be asked questions regarding specific facts. The right of the defence lawyer to be present during the interview is guaranteed notwithstanding the nature of the case, the status of the interviewer or the type of proceedings. Furthermore, the suspect has an unlimited right to contact the defence lawyer, including prior to the interview. However, if the suspect is in preliminary detention, they only have the right to communicate with their lawyer in private 14 days after preliminary detention commenced. Even though this contravenes European Court of Human Rights (ECtHR) jurisprudence, it constitutes Polish law and it cannot be appealed. Defence lawyers seldom agree to such a restriction and will often wait until the 14 day period has expired, advising their client to refuse to provide an explanation in the meantime. As a result, the restriction is extremely rarely imposed.

Defence lawyers are not forbidden to conduct their own investigations of the circumstances of the alleged offence. However, it is generally agreed, including by defence lawyers themselves, that investigation of the alleged offence is exclusively the preserve of the prosecution authorities.

3.8. The right to information as to the charge and evidence[18]

After charged the suspect is notified of the hearing date in order that they can familiarise themselves with the materials obtained in the investigation. The suspect may request verbal information of the basis of the charge, and that a justification for the charge be provided in writing, and in this case written information must be served on the suspect and their lawyer within 14 days. The written justification

---

[17] P. Kruszyński, *Stanowisko prawne obrońcy w procesie karnym*, Białystok, Dridt Wydaw. Filii UW, 1991, p. 10 *et seq.*

[18] K.T. Boratyńska, A. Górski, A. Sakowicz, A. Ważny, *Kodeks postępowania karnego. Komentarz*, Warsaw, C.H. Beck, 2005, p. 567-569, 575-578.

should, in particular, indicate what facts and evidence were accepted as the basis for the charge.

Once the investigative proceedings have been completed, and the suspect or their lawyer has requested disclosure of the investigative material, the body that is conducting the investigation[19] must inform the suspect and their lawyer of the final date for familiarising themselves with the case files, and of their right to review the case files within the relevant time limit. The lawyer and the suspect can request excerpts or copies of the documentation, but this is subject to the consent of the body that conducts the investigation. The defence lawyer has a right to participate in the familiarisation process, but failure by the suspect or their lawyer to participate does not prevent the proceedings from continuing.

After the suspect familiarises themselves with the case materials they have three days to request that the investigation be 'supplemented.' If such a motion is filed, the authorities cannot prevent the suspect and/or their defence lawyer from participating in the activities which they have requested. However, if the suspect is in prison this can cause serious difficulties. If the authorities decide that there is no need to 'supplement' the investigation, and the investigation is formally closed, the decision is notified to the suspect and to their lawyer.

3.9. Access to and the content of the case file[20]

It is for the prosecution authority to determine the content of the investigative case file. They are bound by the principle of objectivity so they must gather, take into account and transcribe any evidence, both favourable and unfavourable to the suspect. At the same time, the defence lawyer may submit to the prosecution authorities any evidence which is favourable to the client, e.g. bank or telephone account statements, legal opinions, resolutions of the management board of the company at issue, or any other documents, and may request that they be enclosed with the case files.

During the investigative stage the suspect and the defence lawyer have a right of access to the case files with consent of the authority that is conducting the proceedings, and any refusal of this right may be the subject of a complaint to the prosecutor. Generally, refusal is justified by reference to the interests of the investigations. However, after an investigation is closed the defence has an unlimited right to review the case files without restriction. The case file can be composed of official records, abbreviated official records and transcriptions of recorded activities.

The official record is a traditional form of consolidating procedural activities. Any explanations, evidence, statements, motions and allegations are included in the official record as precisely as possible. The persons who have participated in, or

---

[19]   The Public Prosecutor in more complicated cases, and the police in other cases. The legal provision refers to the body that conducts the proceedings, without specifying precisely who has to inform the suspect.

[20]   J. Grajewski, L.K. Paprzycki, M. Płachta, *Kodeks postępowania karnego. Komentarz*, Cracow, Zakamycze, 2003, vol. I, p. 371-394.

who are the subject of, the investigation reflected in the contents of the official record have a right to request that anything which concerns their rights and interests is included accurately in the official record. An abbreviated official record is permitted in respect of:

- audio or video recorded material;
- material that is recorded in shorthand.

In these cases the record may be limited to the most important elements of the material.

Transcripts of any audio or video recordings are attached to the official record. Any image and/or sound transcription of the recorded activity may be ordered with respect to each procedural activity, provided that the persons who participate in it are advised of this fact prior to the start of the recording process. Each party has a right to receive (at their own cost), one copy of the sound or image transcription. However, the party may not obtain such a transcription in the case of investigative proceedings or where the trial is held in camera, e.g. proceedings involving state secrets.

3.10. Special protection of juveniles and other vulnerable persons[21]

If the accused is a juvenile or suffers from some sort of incapacity, their statutory representative or custodian may undertake acts on their behalf, file appeals or motions, and appoint a defence lawyer. As noted earlier, if the accused is a juvenile, is deaf, dumb or blind, or there are justified doubts as to their mental health during the course of the entire proceedings, they must have a defence lawyer. However, if in the course of the proceedings a psychiatrist determines that there are no issues relating to the mental health of the accused, both at the time of the alleged offence and at the time of the proceedings, the further participation of the defence lawyer in the proceedings is not obligatory, and the president of the court may withdraw the appointment of the defence lawyer.

---

[21]   M. Korcyl-Wolska, 'Zasady uczciwego procesu w postępowaniu w sprawach nieletnich w Polsce na tle standardów europejskich,' in S. Waltosia, *Zasady procesu karnego wobec wyzwań współczesności*, Warsaw, Wydawnictwo prawnicze PWN, 2000, p. 371-380.

4. The impact of the investigative stage on the course of the trial

4.1. The boundaries of the indictment and the principle of immediacy[22]

The framing of the indictment by the prosecutor determines the boundaries of the criminal proceedings. The court cannot try a person who is not named in the indictment nor, unless the accused consents, can it issue a judgement in respect of an act that is not covered by the indictment. However, the court is not bound by the legal interpretation of the act as stated in the indictment and it may modify it provided that the parties are informed. Thus the court may determine that a more serious offence, with a more severe sanction, has been committed than that reflected in the indictment (e.g. robbery rather than theft). Should this occur, the accused may request an adjournment in order to prepare their defence.

The evidence obtained at the investigative stage has full evidentiary value in the court proceedings and it may constitute the basis of the verdict provided it is disclosed in the course of the trial. The principle is that the court should only rely on the evidence that has been presented during the trial and should directly examine the sources and means of evidence. However the Code of Criminal Procedure allows exceptions to the general principle and, in particular, the court may allow the official record of the statement of a witness to read aloud. This is permitted in the following circumstances:

- if the witness refuses to give evidence;
- if the witness's testimony at trial differs from that in the statement;
- if the witness states that they no longer remembers certain facts;
- if the witness is not in the country or it is impossible to serve a summons on them;
- if as a result of unforeseen circumstances the witness cannot testify;
- if the Chair of the court decides, on an application by the Prosecutor, not to summon the witness; or
- if the witness has died.

If the accused refuses to offer an explanation to the court, of gives a different explanation than that previously provided, or makes representations that they no longer remember certain facts, any previous statement made by them may be read to the court. It is important to differentiate between statements which are made in the context of the investigative proceedings, which are admissible, and those which are inadmissible, for example, statements made by the accused when they were interviewed as a witness. Such statements are inadmissible even if the accused consents to them being made available to the court.

---

[22]   T. Nowak, *Zasada bezpośredniości w polskim procesie karnym*, Poznań, Uniwersytet im. Adama Mickiewicza w. Poznaniu, 1971, p. 20 *et seq.*; B. Kurzępa, *Podstęp w toku czynności karnoprocesowych i operacyjnych*, Toruń, Dom Organizatora, 2003, p. 13 *et seq.*; B. Zając, *Przyznanie się oskarżonego do winy*, Cracow, Zakamycze, 1995, p. 13 *et seq.*; M. Błoński, 'Odczytywanie zeznań świadka, Studia Prawno,' *Ekonomiczne*, 2001, No. 63, p. 91-113.

The statements of an anonymous witness may be read out in the trial, but in this case this part of the trial is held in camera. An anonymous witness is one where neither the accused nor their lawyer is permitted to know their identity. In such cases the accused and their defence lawyer must familiarise themselves with the official record of the witness' depositions. At court an anonymous witness may be examined in a separate room, using devices that distort their voice, in order to prevent the identity of the witness from being ascertained.

It is permissible for private documents which relate to the proceedings to be adduced at trial even if the original purpose of the documents (in particular, statements, publications, letters and memoranda) did not relate to the proceedings.

If the accused pleads guilty, or offers an explanation that is consistent with their guilt, the court may sentence them without considering the evidence, or following only partial consideration of it.

4.2.   Exclusion of evidence[23]

Evidence that has been obtained contrary to the principle of fair trial, for example, evidence obtained by deceit, may be included in the evidential material presented to the court. The so-called 'fruits of the poisoned tree' doctrine does not apply in the Polish legal system. However, evidence that has been obtained unlawfully cannot be included in the evidential material or used in the criminal process. Evidence is obtained illegally if the 'evidentiary bans' applicable to trials are breached, such as the interviews of members of the clergy with regard to the contents of confessions, interviews in which violence, illegal threats or hypnosis is used, or interviews of a defence lawyer regarding any facts learned while providing legal advice or preparing a case.

5.   The role of the defence lawyer

5.1.   Perceptions of the role of a defence lawyer[24]

There has been little change in the perceived role of the defence lawyer in criminal proceedings in Poland since the decline of communism, either in theory or in practice. Their fundamental role continues to be to defend the accused and to achieve the most favourable outcome from their perspective. However, the model of criminal proceedings has materially changed, particularly at the investigative stage

---

[23]   Z. Kwiatkowski, *Zakazy dowodowe w procesie karnym*, Cracow, Zakamycze, 2005, p. 21 *et seq.*
[24]   P. Kruszyński, *Stanowisko prawne obrońcy w procesie karnym*, Białystok, 1991, p. 55 *et seq.*; T. Grzegorczyk, 'Obrona z urzędu w nowym kodeksie postępowania karnego,' in S. Waltosia, *Zasady procesu karnego wobec wyzwań współczesności*, Warsaw, Wydawnictwo prawnicze PWN, 2000, p. 311-324; P. Hofmański (ed.), *Kodeks postępowania karnego. Komentarz*, Warsaw, C.H. Beck, 1999, p. 386-406; S. Stachowiak, 'Uprawnienia obrońcy w postępowaniu przygotowawczym w nowym kodeksie postępowania karnego,' *Prokuratura i Prawo*, 1998, No. 10, p. 7-18.

of the process. Many provisions which, under communism, made it difficult or impossible for the lawyer to defend the accused, and to agree upon the defence strategy, have been eliminated. For instance, under the communist regime there was a provision stipulating that when the accused was in preliminary detention the Public Prosecutor could, when consenting to contact between the accused and their lawyer (until an indictment was filed with the court), stipulate that they be present during any consultation. The case file could only be reviewed by the defence with the consent of the investigating authority (with no right of appeal against refusal), and either the Public Prosecutor or the court could obtain access to privileged information held by the lawyer. Since the Code of Criminal Procedure of 1997 has been in force, many of these provisions have disappeared although some of them remain in a more limited form, such as the power to supervise contact between the detained suspect and their lawyer during the first 14 days of detention, and the requirement that the Public Prosecutor must consent to the accused having access to the case file during the investigative stage.

The Bar was regulated by the Act of the 26th May1982, but although this is still in force it has been amended on many occasions to adjust the law to the needs of the current political and social conditions. The governing bodies of the Bar are independent and have the right of self-regulation However, restrictions have recently been imposed in relation to their powers to control the admission of lawyers to train to become an 'attorney at law.'

In accordance with their fundamental role, defence lawyers may undertake activities only for the benefit of their client, and are prohibited from acting to their detriment. Similarly defence lawyers are prohibited from defending more than one accused person if there is a conflict of interest. Given the above, the defence lawyer must act independently in determining the defence strategy; they must act in such a way that their participation in the proceedings does not prevent the accused from acting independently and *vice versa*. However, the defence lawyer may take actions which are contrary their client's will provided that they are to the client's benefit. Such situation may lead to a conflict between the defence lawyer and the accused. The by-laws of the Bar assume that a relationship between the client and lawyer is based on trust. Therefore, a lawyer is obliged to waive the power of attorney if it is established that the client has lost confidence in their lawyer. On the other hand, if the accused has doubts regarding the defence strategy adopted the lawyer may, at any time, revoke the power of attorney, and if the lawyer is a publicly appointed lawyer, the accused may ask the court to appoint another lawyer.

In furthering the interests of the accused, it is permissible for the lawyer to deliberately prolong the duration of the trial. However, the lawyer may not falsify evidence, be involved in the production of false (witness) statements, remove material evidence, induce other persons to do so, or use evidence that, to the best of her knowledge, is false. Such conduct may amount to an offence. There is nothing to prevent the defence lawyer from advising the accused to refuse to offer any explanations, to plead guilty, to change any given explanations, or to agree the content of such explanations with the accused. If the client admits to their lawyer that they have committed an offence, the lawyer cannot disclose this to the court without the client's agreement. In such a situation, the defence lawyer is obliged to maintain that their client is not guilty.

5.2. Statutory regulations and restrictions

The Act of 26th May 1982 established that an attorney at law is obliged to keep secret any information they become aware of as a result of the provision of legal assistance. The obligation to keep professional secrets is unlimited in time. However, the provisions of the Act of 16 November 2000 on Counteracting the Introduction of Property Values Originating from Illegal or Undisclosed Sources to Financial Transactions and on Counteracting the Financing of Terrorism, removed the pre-existing blanket professional obligation of confidentiality. Subject to that, the lawyer's privilege, which is guaranteed by the provisions of the Code of Criminal Procedure, assumes that it is not permissible to interview a defence lawyer as to the facts of which they become aware whilst providing legal advice or during litigation. Likewise, the investigating authorities must not seize any of the defence lawyer's correspondence or documents that relate to their function as a defence lawyer. In practice, the duty of confidentiality, and professional privilege, is respected. The Code of Criminal Procedure does, in theory, permit the lawyer who is not the defence lawyer to be 'released' from the obligation of secrecy on the order of the court, but in practice this seldom occurs.

In performing their professional obligations the attorney at law has the same legal protection as the judge and the Public Prosecutor; they enjoy the freedom/liberty to speak and write as they see fit within the boundaries specified by the Bar and by legal regulations. Any abuse of the aforesaid freedom/liberties that constitutes an insult to or libel of a party, their attorney or defence lawyer, judicial trustee, witness, expert or the interpreter/translator, is covered by legal immunity and cannot be prosecuted, and can only pursued as a professional disciplinary matter. Similarly, if a defence lawyer breaches orders, or employs coercive means, the authority that has conduct of the proceedings may notify the Bar Council who may take disciplinary action against the lawyer.

Professional disciplinary proceedings are governed by the Act of the 26th May 1982 — the Law on the Bar — and the Decree of the Minister of Justice of the 23rd July 1998 on disciplinary proceedings relating to lawyers and trainee lawyers. The following disciplinary penalties are available: admonition; reprimand; fine; suspension from practice for a period from three months to five years; or expulsion from the Bar.

5.3. *Professional standards and restrictions*[25]

Lawyers are expected to maintain a high standard of professional work, and are obliged to undergo continuing professional development. They must defend the interests of their clients zealously and fairly, whilst being respectful and polite to the court and other authorities. When acting for a client, they must keep abreast of the developments in the case and inform the client about any progress and its outcome. The lawyer must avoid circumstances which would result in them being dependent on the client, and in particular they must not borrow money from the client account.

Only a person who conforms to the requirements of the Law on the Bar is permitted to act a defence lawyer. A defence lawyer must be an attorney at law although in exceptional cases the function of defence lawyer may be performed by a trainee lawyer who, after 6 months, may be a 'substitute' for the lawyer before district courts, and after 18 months can be a 'substitute' before other courts (other than the Supreme Court).

An attorney at law must satisfy the following requirements:

- they must be of good, untarnished, character which must be referenced by former employers, their patron/sponsor as regards their aptitude for performing such professional actions, and they must not have a criminal record or be subject to any disciplinary proceedings;
- they must fully exercise their public rights and have 'full capacity' to enter into legal transactions;
- they must have graduated in law in Poland and have obtained an M.A. or a foreign qualification that is recognised in Poland;
- they must have completed the legal training for an attorney at law in Poland and passed the final examination, although professors and associate professors in law, persons who have passed the judicial examinations, Public Prosecutor, legal counsel, and Notaries Public, are exempt from this requirement.

The Act of the 5th of July 2002 regulates the provision of legal assistance by foreign lawyers. A European Union lawyer is entitled to render cross-border services using the professional title obtained in their country of origin and expressed in the official language of their country of origin. Within the framework of provision of cross-border jurisdiction, a European Union lawyer may perform any activities that an attorney at law or legal counsel has a right to do. When rendering a cross-border service that involves the representation of the client before courts and other public authorities, they are subject to the same professional conditions that are applicable to a Polish attorney at law or legal counsel (except for conditions pertaining to place of residence and entry on the list of attorneys at law and legal counsel), and they are

---

25   Z. Krzemiński, *Etyka adwokacka. Teksty, orzecznictwo, komentarz*, Cracow, Dom Wydawniczy ABC, 2003, p. 22 *et seq.*; Z Czeszejko–Sochacki, Z. Krzemiński, *Odpowiedzialność dyscyplinarna adwokatów*, Warsaw, Wydawnictwo Prawnicze, 1971, p. 18 *et seq.*; S. Rymar, 'Dokąd ma zmierzać adwokatura polska,' *Palestra*, 2004, No. 1-2, p. 9-17.

obliged to observe the same professional rules in addition to complying with the professional rules applicable in their own country. When a non-Polish lawyer supplies a cross-border legal service in a case where Polish law requires that the accused be legally represented, the non-Polish lawyer is required to cooperate with the appointed Polish lawyer.

A European Union lawyer or a citizen of a European Union member state who has the requisite professional qualifications may be entered in the list of attorneys at law or legal counsel if:

- they are of good, untarnished, character;
- they fully exercise their public rights and has full capacity to enter into legal transactions;
- they have a command of written and spoken Polish; and
- they pass a skills test.

An entry may be refused only if the person concerned does not satisfy the requirements stipulated in the Act.

6. Bibliography

M. Błoński, 'Odczytywanie zeznań świadka,' *Studia Prawno – Ekonomiczne*, 2001, No. 63, p. 91-113.

K.T. Boratyńska, A. Górski, A. Sakowicz, A. Ważny, *Kodeks postępowania karnego. Komentarz*, Warsaw, C.H. Beck, 2005.

J. Bratoszewski, L. Gardocki, Z. Gostyński, S. Przyjemski, R. Stefański, S. Zabłocki, *Kodeks postępowania karnego. Komentarz*, Warsaw, Dom Wydawniczy ABC, 2003.

K. Cesarz, 'Dowód z zeznań świadka koronnego na tle prawa do sądu (wybrane zagadnienia),' *Przegląd Sądowy*, 2004, No. 4, p. 65-75.

Z Czeszejko–Sochacki, Z. Krzemiński, *Odpowiedzialność dyscyplinarna adwokatów*, Warsaw, Wydawnictwo Prawnicze, 1971.

Z Czeszejko-Sochacki, Z. Krzemiński, *Adwokat z urzędu w postępowaniu sądowym*, Warsaw, Wydawnictwo Prawnicze, 1975.

K. Dudka, *Kontrola korespondencji i podsłuch w polskim procesie karnym*, Lublin, Wydawnictwo Uniwersytetu Marii. Curie-Skłodowskiej, 1998.

K. Eichstaedt, 'Zarządzenie przez sąd kontroli operacyjnej w ujęciu procesowym,' *Prokuratura i Prawo*, 2003, No. 9, p. 28-48.

Z. Gostyński, 'obowiązek informowania uczestników postępowania o ich obowiązkach i uprawnieniach jako przejaw zasady uczciwego (rzetelnego) procesu,' in J. Czapska (*et al.*), *Zasady procesu karnego wobec wyzwań współczesności. Księga ku czci prof. dr hab. Stanisława Waltosia*, Warsaw, Wydawnictwo prawnicze PWN, 2000, p. 362-371.

J. Grajewski, L.K. Paprzycki, M. Płachta, *Kodeks postępowania karnego. Komentarz*, Cracow, Zakamycze, 2003.

T. Grzegorczyk, 'Obrona z urzędu w nowym kodeksie postępowania karnego,' in S. Waltosia, *Zasady procesu karnego wobec wyzwań współczesności*, Warsaw, Wydawnictwo prawnicze PWN, 2000, p. 311-324.

T. Grzegorczyk, *Kodeks postępowania karnego. Komentarz*, Cracow, Zakamycze, 2005.

T. Grzegorczyk, J. Tylman, *Polskie postępowanie karne*, Warsaw, Wydawnictwo Prawnicze Lexis Nexis, 2005.

T. Hanausek, *Ustawa o Policji. Komentarz*, Cracow, Zakamycze, 1996.

P. Hofmański (ed.), *Kodeks postępowania karnego. Komentarz*, Warsaw, C.H. Beck, 1999.

M. Korcyl–Wolska, 'Zasady uczciwego procesu w postępowaniu w sprawach nieletnich w Polsce na tle standardów europejskich,' in S. Waltosia, *Zasady procesu karnego wobec wyzwań współczesności*, Warsaw, Wydawnictwo prawnicze PWN, 2000, p. 371-380.

P. Kruszyński, *Zasada domniemania niewinności w polskim procesie i karnym*, Warsaw, Wydawnictwo Uniwersytetu Warszawskiego, 1983.

P. Kruszyński, *Stanowisko prawne obrońcy w procesie karnym*, Białystok, Dridt Wydaw. Filii UW, 1991.

P. Kruszyński (ed.), *Postępowanie karne w XXI wieku*, Warsaw, Dom Wydawniczy ABC, 2002.

P. Kruszyński (ed.), *Wykład prawa karnego procesowego*, Białystok, Temida 2, 2004.

Z. Krzemiński, *Etyka adwokacka. Teksty, orzecznictwo, komentarz*, Cracow, Zakamycze, 2003.

B. Kurzępa, *Podstęp w toku czynności karnoprocesowych i operacyjnych*, Toruń, Dom Organizatora, 2003.

Z. Kwiatkowski, *Zakazy dowodowe w procesie karnym*, Cracow, Zakamycze, 2005.

A. Lach, *Dowody elektroniczne w procesie karnym*, Toruń, Dom Organizatora, 2004.

K. Marszał, S. Stachowiak, K. Zgryzek, *Proces karny*, Katowice, Volumen, 2003.

G. Musialik–Dudzińska, 'Podsłuch pozaprocesowy (operacyjny) na gruncie znowelizowanej ustawy z dnia 6 kwietnia 1990r. o Policji,' *Przegląd Sądowy*, 2004, No. 4, p. 49-65.

C. Nowak, 'Prawo do korzystania z pomocy tłumacza w europejskim i polskim prawie karnym,' *Prokuratura i Prawo*, 1998, No. 10, p. 89-101.

T. Nowak, *Zasad bezpośredniości w polskim procesie karnym*, Poznań, Uniwersytet im. Adama Mickiewicza w. Poznaniu, 1971.

K.J. Pawelec, *Wyjaśnienia podejrzanego, zeznania świadka i instytucja świadka koronnego. Komentarz*, Warsaw, C.H. Beck, 2003.

S. Rymar, 'Dokąd ma zmierzać adwokatura polska,' *Palestra*, 2004, No. 1-2, p. 9-17.

S. Stachowiak, 'Uprawnienia obrońcy w postępowaniu przygotowawczym w nowym kodeksie postępowania karnego,' *Prokuratura i Prawo*, 1998, No. 10, p. 7-18.

R.A. Stefański, *Kodeks postępowania karnego z orzecznictwem i piśmiennictwem (za lata 1998-2003)*, Toruń, Dom Organizatora, 2004.

P. Świerk, 'Badanie poligraficzne po nowelizacji kodeksu postępowania karnego,' *Prokuratura i Prawo*, 2003, No. 9, p. 49-58.

S. Waltoś, *Proces karny. Zarys systemu*, Warsaw, Wydawnictwo Prawnicze Lexis Nexis, 2003.

J. Wójcikiewicz (ed.), *Ekspertyza sądowa*, Cracow, Zakamycze, 2002.

Ł. Woźniak, 'Zasada domniemania niewinności – zagadnienia podstawowe,' in S. Waltosia, *Zasady procesu karnego wobec wyzwań współczesności*, Warsaw, Wydawnictwo prawnicze PWN, 2000, p. 354-362.

J. Zagórski, 'Zatrzymanie przez policję oraz umieszczenie w policyjnych izbach zatrzymań,' *Państwo i Prawo*, 2004, No. 9, p. 84-97.

B. Zając, *Przyznanie się oskarżonego do winy*, Cracow, Zakamycze, 1995.

M. Zbrojewska, 'Przedstawienie zarzutów w polskim procesie karnym – uwagi ogólne,' *Przegląd Policyjny*, 1998, No. 3-4, p. 122-132.

R. Zdybel, 'Zatrzymanie procesowe w świetle rozwiązań kodeksu postępowania karnego oraz praktyki organów ścigania,' *Przegląd Sądowy*, 2003, No. 9, p. 75-107.

Ed Cape
Jacqueline Hodgson
Ties Prakken
Taru Spronken

CASE STUDY

1. Introductory information

This case study has been designed to explore the ways in which suspects are dealt with at the investigative stage of the criminal process in different EU countries in order to develop mutual understanding of the investigative process from the perspective of those who are suspected of crime. In particular it is designed to elicit information about how different EU countries approach the regulation of the investigative stage of the criminal process, and how such regulation works in practice. It concentrates on those rights that were recognised in the EU Commission Green Paper *Procedural Safeguards for Suspects and Defendants in Criminal Proceedings throughout the European Union* and the subsequent draft Council Framework Decision on the same subject.

The draft Council Framework Decision proposes, in the first stage, minimum standards in respect of:

- access to legal advice, both before trial and at trial;
- access to free interpretation and translation;
- ensuring that persons who are not capable of understanding or following the proceedings receive appropriate attention;
- the right to communicate, *inter alia*, with consular authorities in the case of foreign suspects, and
- notifying suspected persons of their rights (by giving them a written 'Letter of Rights').

In addition, the Green Paper recognised the importance of:

- rights to bail;
- fairness in the handling of evidence.

The authors were asked to describe how the issues raised by the case study would be dealt with in practice in their jurisdiction. They were asked to pay particular regard to the rights and standards referred to above, but also identify any other issues, and include any other information relevant to the way in which such a case would be dealt with in their jurisdiction.

2. Case Study

In May 2005 an international football match was held in your capital city between your country's (Country A) leading football team and a team from another European Union country (Country B). At the football match there was a violent incident in one part of the stadium involving a large number of people. Sid, a citizen of Country B, has been under suspicion of being part of an international group of people organising football violence, and he has been kept under police surveillance for some months. Jean, who is 16 years old and a citizen of your country, became involved in the violence and was arrested for assaulting another person. Georges, also a citizen of your country, took no part in the violence but was in the part of the stadium where fighting broke out. Georges is a diabetic. Sid, Jean and Georges are all arrested.

The following issues arise:

- Neither Jean nor Georges have been arrested before, and both want to know what their rights are whilst they are detained (for example, whether someone can be informed of their arrest and detention, whether they can see a doctor, their 'right to silence,' etc.), how long they can be detained, at what stage a decision must be made about whether to commence criminal proceedings against them, and whether there will be any judicial involvement in any of these decisions. Both say that they do not know why they have been arrested. Georges is very concerned that his wife should be contacted because she is expecting a baby in the near future, and she is expecting him to arrive home later that day. Sid has been convicted in Country B of a number of offences related to football violence, most recently in 2003 when he served a short prison sentence. He also wants to know what his rights are.
- Sid does not speak the language of your country and is having difficulty communicating with the police. What provisions exist for him to have access to an interpreter?
- The police tell Sid, Jean and Georges that they are to be interviewed in connection with the suspected offences. All three would like to speak to a lawyer before they are interviewed. Georges has used a lawyer before in connection with his business. Sid has used a lawyer before in his own country, but does not know any lawyer in your country. He has a job in his own country as a lorry driver. Jean has never used a lawyer before. He is still at school.
- Sid, Jean and Georges would like a lawyer to be present whilst they are being interviewed in connection with the suspected offences.
- The police tell Sid that they have been keeping him under surveillance, and Sid would like to know what evidence the police have that implicates him in the suspected crime. Georges is aware that the police have searched his company premises and he wants to know what rights they have to do this.
- Sid is aware that that in some EU countries interviews of people suspected of crime must be tape-recorded, and he wants to know whether this will be the

case when he is interviewed. If not, he wants to know how it will be documented.

- Interviews of all three suspects are subsequently conducted. During the interviews Sid answers questions put to him, and some of his answers indicate that he may be implicated with others in organising football violence. Georges refuses to answer any of the questions that are put to him because, he says, he was not doing anything wrong and the police should not have arrested him. Jean was confused, and answered some police questions and not others. Assuming that criminal proceedings are commenced against all of them what use, if any, could be made of their responses in interview at their trial?

- All three suspects are told that formal criminal proceedings are to be commenced against them. Georges is concerned about his pregnant wife and would like to be able to return home whilst he is waiting for his trial. Sid says that he wants to return to his own country as otherwise he will lose his job. Jean just wants to go home. On what grounds might any of them be refused bail?

Jan Fermon
Frank Verbruggen
Stef De Decker

CASE STUDY: BELGIUM

1. Rights whilst detained

1.1. The arrest

Initially, Georges, Sid and Jean will be placed under administrative arrest, which is a typical form of deprivation of liberty used for incidents during mass events. A person under administrative arrest can be held in police custody for up to a maximum of 12 hours. As the facts in the case study go beyond a mere disturbance of the peace and qualify as criminal offences, the administrative arrest of Georges and Sid will almost certainly be converted into a judicial arrest. After such conversion, the maximum duration of the arrest without the involvement of an independent judge is 24 hours, starting from the original deprivation of liberty. An investigating judge has to issue an arrest warrant, legally sanctioning the deprivation of liberty, within 24 hours.

As Jean is a minor (less than 18 years old), the Pre-trial Detention Act 1990 does not apply to him. The legal position of minors is determined by the Child Protection Act 1965.[1] Such cases are dealt with according to completely different procedures before a Juvenile Court. In exceptional cases involving minor offenders older than 16, the Juvenile Court can decide to remit the case to be dealt with under the normal criminal justice system. Under the influence of Strasbourg case law, minors can no longer be detained in a prison.[2] From 2002 onwards, they are remanded to secure accommodation by virtue of a Juvenile Court order.

1.2. Prisoners' rights

Until now, there has been no Act of Parliament governing the position of detained persons. To a large extent, their rights are determined by a complex tangle of secondary legislation, circular letters and internal documents. Detained persons

---

[1] Loi relative à la protection de la jeunesse – Wet betreffende de jeugdbescherming, published in the Moniteur belge, 15 April 1965.

[2] ECtHR 29 February 1988, Bouamar v. Belgium, A 129.

have almost no guaranteed rights, as penitentiary authorities have extensive discretionary powers. A brand-new Act on the legal position of detained persons provides for a comprehensive legal regime and will bring more legal certainty, but it has not yet come into effect.[3] A limited number of its articles are currently under scrutiny by the Constitutional Court as the Flemish government believes it encroaches on its competence in the field of social assistance to prisoners.

A person in pre-trial detention cannot make any telephone calls within five days of the arrest warrant being served on them, unless there is written permission from the investigating judge.[4] Consequently, Georges needs the investigating judge's consent to be able to contact his wife. When the five-day period is over, telephone calls to close relatives are allowed in principle. Foreigners like Sid can contact their embassy or consulate in Belgium. If Sid wishes to contact other persons, he can only do so with the prison governor's permission. All telephone calls are made at the prisoner's own expenses. A practical problem that arises, however, is that telephone cards must be ordered by detainees and in many prisons these cards are delivered to them only once a week. A detainee can only order a telephone card if on entry to the prison they have enough cash in their possession to buy a card. Because of these administrative limitations, it sometimes takes up to a week or even more before a detained person can effectively communicate with their family.

Prisoners who are ill will receive medical treatment from the prison physician, or they can call in a physician of their choice but at their own expenses.[5] Minor medical symptoms are often not taken seriously by the prison authorities.

The investigating judge is required to bring charges as soon as they are convinced that serious indications of guilt exist. In the present case, Georges and Sid are detained under an arrest warrant. Because only an investigating judge has the authority to issue an arrest warrant, the public prosecution service would have had to file an investigation request. Persons targeted *nominatim* in this request have the same rights (access to case file, additional inquiries, etc.) as someone who is formally charged.[6] Even though there is no legal obligation on the investigating judge to inform Georges and Sid of their rights, this information must not be unnecessarily withheld.[7] Consequently, Georges and Sid are able to exercise these rights even though they may not have been formally charged.

Although, in principle, pre-trial detention must not be used as a form of immediate punishment or to put pressure on a suspect,[8] this is often the case when foreigners are involved. In practice, pre-trial detention is looked upon as a

---

3   *Loi de principes concernant l'administration des établissements pénitentiaires ainsi que le statut juridique des détenus – Basiswet betreffende het gevangeniswezen en de rechtspositie van de gedetineerden*, published in the Moniteur belge, 1 February 2005.

4   Art. 35*bis* of the General regulations for the Penitentiary Institutions 1965.

5   Art. 96 of the General regulations for the Penitentiary Institutions 1965.

6   Art. 61*bis* Code of Criminal Procedure (CCP).

7   R. Verstraeten, *Handboek strafvordering (Companion to criminal procedure)*, Antwerp, Maklu, 2005, p. 377.

8   Art. 16 § 1, al. 2 of the Pre-trial detention Act 1990.

'punishment in advance.' Since the period of pre-trial detention is deducted from the prison sentence imposed by the trial judges, they may take it into account by imposing a prison sentence of the same as the period of pre-trial detention.

2.　Access to an interpreter

Article 31 of the Languages Act 1935 gives every person who is questioned in the course of an investigation – by the police, by a public prosecutor or by an investigating judge – the right to use the language of their choice for all their oral statements.[9] If the questioners do not understand the language of the suspect's choice, they have to call in a sworn interpreter.

Less common languages sometimes necessitate the use of two interpreters. The number of sworn interpreters in Belgium who speak Lithuanian, for example, and who are on stand-by around the clock is very limited. This is even more so in smaller, rural districts. In these cases one interpreter will translate the suspect's answers from Lithuanian into German (for example) and a second interpreter will translate this translation into Dutch or French. Needless to say, this course of action does not improve the quality of the final translation.

The costs of the interpreter(s) are met by the State. However, the costs of an interpreter for lawyer-client communication is not borne by the State unless the detained person is eligible for legal aid, Although in that case the number of hours of interpretation that the State pay for is strictly limited.

Sid will be able to communicate with the police, albeit with the use of one or two interpreters. Communication with his lawyer could prove considerably more difficult. Even though Sid, as an arrested person, is presumed to be indigent, he only benefits from a limited number of 'free' hours with an interpreter. If Sid's lawyer does not speak Sid's language, the period of interpretation that will be paid for will be totally insufficient to prepare the defence properly.

3.　Access to a lawyer prior to (police) interviews

In Belgium, it is not possible for a person who is in pre-trial detention to speak to a lawyer before they are interviewed by the investigating judge.[10] People erroneously seeking to invoke their 'Miranda rights' are reminded they are not in America. It is only after the first interview with the investigating judge that a detained person is allowed to have contact with their lawyer. During the interview, the investigating judge must inform the suspect that they have the right to choose a lawyer. If the suspect does not choose a lawyer or their lawyer of choice is unavailable, the investigating judge must notify the Dean of the local Bar association.[11] The local Bar association then appoints a legal aid counsel. In the present case, Georges is free to

---

[9]　*Loi concernant l'emploi des langues en matière judiciaire – Wet van 15 juni 1935 op het gebruik der talen in gerechtszaken*, published in the Moniteur belge 22 June 1935.

[10]　Art. 20 of the Pre-trial detention Act 1990.

[11]　Art. 16 § 4 of the Pre-trial detention Act 1990.

choose the lawyer he already knows. If they are indigent, a legal aid counsel will probably be assigned to Sid and Jean.

4. Presence of a lawyer during interviews

Lawyers are not allowed to be present whilst their clients are being interviewed. The Belgian Supreme Court has ruled that article 6.3c ECHR and article 14.3b ICCPR do not apply to interviews at the investigative stage.[12] Furthermore, the case law of the ECHR does not seem to require a lawyer to be present during interviews.[13]

In principle, the absence of a lawyer has less far reaching consequences than in other countries, as the Code of Criminal Proceedings (CCP) does not provide a legal basis for drawing inferences from the defendant's failure or refusal to answer police questions.[14] In practice, however, a defendant's silence could have negative consequences. A silent defendant is likely to be held longer in pre-trial detention, law enforcement officers are less motivated to look for evidence *à décharge*, and the trial judge's deep-down conviction will be (un)consciously influenced by this kind of attitude.

There is an exception for minors who are a victim of, or witness to, certain indecency offences or other serious offences.[15] As noted earlier, if the offender is a minor a completely different legal framework applies: the Child Protection Act 1965. Although there is no explicit legal provision that entitles lawyers to be present during interviews byJjuvenile Court judges, in practice Juvenile Courts allow lawyers to assist underage offenders during interviews.[16]

5. Secret and non-contradictory character of the investigation

5.1. Access to the case file

Because Georges and Sid are assumed to be detained under an arrest warrant, the investigation itself is transformed into a judicial inquiry, under the direction of an

---

[12] Cass. 14 December 1999, *Arr. Cass.* 1999, No. 678, <www.cass.be>.

[13] ECHR 16 October 2001, No. 39846/98 (Brennan), <www.echr.coe.int>.

[14] F. Goossens, 'Het E.V.R.M.: een argument pro aanwezigheid van de advocaat bij het politioneel verdachtenverhoor?,' (The European Human Rights Convention: an argument for the presence of a lawyers during police interviews), *Ad Rem*, 3 2005, p. 38-49.

[15] They have the right to be assisted by an adult of their choice, unless the public prosecutor or the investigating judge decides otherwise (art. 91*bis* of the Code of Criminal Procedure). It is possible that the person of his choice is a lawyer, but this will rarely be the case, as the exception does not apply to suspects, but is limited to witnesses or victims.

[16] Most Bar associations have more or less specialised lawyers, who are on stand-by around the clock.

investigating judge.[17] Although article 57 § 1 CCP explicitly states that the judicial inquiry is secret, there are two significant exceptions to this rule.

First, a person in pre-trial detention and their counsel have access to the case file each month (two days before every confirmation hearing).[18] However, there is no obligation to include all documents in the case file. In the interest of the inquiry, the reports concerning current 'covert' investigations such as interception of telecommunications or an infiltration operation will only be added to the case file afterwards.

Second, as soon as a person – who has not been or is no longer in pre-trial detention – has been charged, or targeted *nominatim* in an investigation request by the public prosecution service or by the victim, the charged person can request the investigating judge to grant them access to the case file. The investigating judge can deny access to the whole file, or limit access to parts of the file, if it is necessary in the interest of the inquiry or if it would present a danger to or violate the privacy of certain persons.[19] It is possible to lodge an appeal against the investigating judge's decision.

In practice, however, it is considerably more difficult to get access to the case file than it would appear. More often than not, defendants are denied access by means of the invariable 'word processor' formula - 'in the interest of the inquiry.' When a defendant challenges an investigating judge's decision, the decision is unlikely to be tested by many counter-arguments since the defendant has not had access to the file. It is almost impossible to have a real (contradictory) debate about the (un)fairness of the investigating judge's reasons.

5.2. Additional inquiries

Sid can request the investigating judge to make additional inquiries *à décharge*. The investigating judge can reject Sid's request if they deem the additional inquiries unnecessary for the purposes of discovering the truth or if they think the inquiries would have an adverse effect on the investigation.[20]

5.3. Search warrants

There are three exceptions to the rule that the police can only search private premises with a search warrant. The first applies where the police catch an offender 'in the act'. Needless to say, the police tend to give a very broad interpretation to the notion 'caught in the act.' The second exception applies where the police have the occupant's consent.[21] In practice, the police will often exert some pressure on the

---

[17]   It is also possible that the public prosecution service does not request the investigating judge to issue an arrest warrant. In this case, the public prosecutor will conduct a preliminary investigation, during which the suspects have less rights.

[18]   Art. 22 of the Pre-trial Detention Act 1990.

[19]   Art. 61*ter* of the Code of Criminal Procedure.

[20]   Art. 61*quinquies* of the Code of Criminal Procedure.

[21]   Art. 1, 3° and 1*bis* of the Search Warrant Act 1969.

occupants to give their consent, or do not fully inform them that they have the right to refuse. Finally, if the police hear a call for help coming from private premises, they can search these premises without a warrant.

If a search warrant is required, the investigating judge must describe the object of the search and the alleged offence on which the warrant is based. A ECtHR decision found against Belgium because a search warrant was not sufficiently justified. Until this decision, the Belgian Supreme Court had condoned the widespread practice of vaguely formulated warrants. According to the Supreme Court, it was sufficient that the police officers in charge of the search knew the offence on which the warrant was based and the kind of investigations and seizures that could be 'useful.' The ECtHR decided that the scope of a search warrant cannot be unlimited or too broadly described since that would constitute a disproportionate interference with the privacy of the concerned.[22]

Although, in the present case, it seems unlikely that the search of Georges' company premises could lead to information in connection with the alleged football violence, whether a search is necessary to discover the truth is completely at the discretion of the investigating judge.[23] However, the fact that only an investigating judge, who still remains an impartial and independent judge, can issue a search warrant should be sufficient to guarantee the fundamental right to respect for one's private life and home.

6.   Documentation of the interview

Police interviews are not normally tape-recorded. The police will summarily record their questions and the suspect's answers in the *procès-verbal* of the interview. The suspect, however, is able to counter these practices. Under article 47bis CCP, a suspect must be informed that they can request that all questions asked and all answers given be written down in the precise wording that has been used. Since 2002 it has been possible to tape-record or even video-record interviews, but only if the public prosecutor or the investigating judge give orders for this to be done.[24]

7.   Assessment of evidence

In Belgium, there are no rules directing the judge about how they must assess the evidence. A trial judge is only bound by their 'deep-down conviction' (*l'intime conviction*), and can freely assess the weight of the admissible evidence put before them.[25]

---

[22]   ECHR 9 December 2004, No. 41872/98 (Van Rossem), <www.echr.coe.int>.

[23]   Art. 56 § 1 al. 5 of the Code of Criminal Procedure.

[24]   See D. Van Daele, 'Het afnemen van verklaringen met behulp van audiovisuele media: een commentaar bij de Wet van 2 augustus 2002,' (*Police Interviews by means of audio-visual aids: a commentary on the Statute of 2 August 2002*), T. Strafr., 2003, p. 46-61.

[25]   C. Van den Wyngaert, 'Belgium,' in C. Van den Wyngaert (ed.), *Criminal procedure systems in the European Community*, London, Butterworths, 1993, p. 22.

In the present case, the judge will have to decide of the weight to be given to Sid's answers . If there is no other evidence incriminating Georges, the presumption of innocence combined with the right to silence will oblige the judge to acquit. In Belgium, it is not legally possible to draw inferences from a refusal to answer police questions. However, a failure to answer without good cause is bound to have some effect on the judge's *intime conviction*. The same principles apply to Jean. The answers he gave will be assessed by the judge, and whilst the questions he failed to answer are covered by the right to silence this may have an impact on the judge's *intime conviction*.

8.   Release on bail

A release on the payment of a financial security is usually granted for financial offences, and for minor offences committed by foreigners, to ensure that they do not abscond. In the present case, it is likely that Sid, as a non-resident whose involvement in the fighting seems minimal, would be released on the payment of a security once the inquiries are deemed complete.

The fact that Georges' wife is pregnant or that Sid will possibly lose his job, does not guarantee that they will be released. Whereas the pregnancy and the possible dismissal will, of course, be factors in the decision, the Investigative Chamber of the Court will base its judgement solely on the – broadly formulated – legal conditions for pre-trial detention. The Supreme Court is not very demanding as far as the reasons for such decisions are concerned, as it is content when the Investigative Chamber of the Court adopts – and minimally adapts – the reasons for the original arrest warrant.[26] In its essence, the decision to release a suspect or not is a highly subjective one, and therefore varies from one judge to another.

---

[26]   R. Verstraeten, *supra* note 7, p. 527-529.

Ed Cape
Jacqueline Hodgson

CASE STUDY: ENGLAND AND WALES

1. Arrest

Jean, Georges and Sid have all been arrested on suspicion of having committed one or more criminal offences. They must be informed of the fact of their arrest[1] and the grounds for the arrest[2] as soon as is practicable, although a detailed explanation does not have to be given at this stage; it would be sufficient, for example, for Jean to be told that he had been arrested on suspicion of assault, without specifying the precise form of assault. If the police fail to inform them of the fact of and grounds for arrest, the arrest is unlawful, but it will be become lawful as soon as this information is given. An unlawful arrest does not have any automatic adverse consequence for the police or prosecution, although evidence obtained from a suspect whilst they are unlawfully detained may be excluded at the trial stage.

Jean is arrested for assault.[3] Georges is likely to have been arrested for affray or violent disorder.[4] Sid is likely to have been arrested for conspiracy to commit assault (or similar) or for an offence specifically related to football violence.[5]

2. Detention – rights and procedure

Having been arrested, the men must be taken to a designated police station as soon as practicable,[6] and normally must not be questioned by the police before arrival at

---

[1]   Police and Criminal Evidence Act (PACE) 1984 s28(1).
[2]   PACE 1984 s28(3).
[3]   There are a number of forms of assault, ranging from common assault at the lower end to inflicting grievous bodily harm (or wounding) with intent at the higher end.
[4]   The maximum penalty for violent disorder is 5 years' imprisonment, and for affray 3 years' imprisonment.
[5]   There are both common law and statutory forms of conspiracy. If, for example, he was convicted of common law conspiracy to commit grievous bodily harm with intent, the maximum penalty is life imprisonment.
[6]   PACE 1984 s30(1). Under recent legislation it is possible for the police, having arrested a person, to grant them bail straight away, with a requirement that they attend the police station at a later date, but this is unlikely in this case.

the police station.[7] Research has shown that the police do engage in informal questioning – typically in the police car – but generally the courts will exclude evidence of a confession obtained in these circumstances. If a suspect does make a comment outside of a formal interview, the police are obliged to put it in writing as soon as possible and must normally ask the suspect to sign the record as being correct.

When they arrive at the police station the men will be brought before the custody officer (CO),[8] who must decide whether there is sufficient evidence to charge them with a criminal offence. If there is not sufficient evidence to charge, the CO may authorise the detention of the suspects if this is necessary to secure or preserve evidence or to obtain evidence by questioning the men.[9] If there is sufficient evidence the law says that normally a decision as to charge must be made without undue delay.[10] In practice, COs routinely authorise detention whether or not there is sufficient evidence to charge (because to refuse would undermine the decision of the arresting officer) and this has, in effect, been approved by the courts. Therefore, Jean, Georges and Sid are all likely to have their detention authorised by the CO.

Once the decision to detain them has been made, the CO will take down their details and inform the suspects of their rights (i.e. the right to have someone informed of their arrest and detention; the right to free legal advice in person or on the telephone;[11] and their right to consult the Codes of Practice), and must give them a written notice setting out these rights, together with notice of the caution.[12] This notice of rights should be available in the principal European languages and so Sid should be given a notice in his own language. The CO must ask each suspect whether they want someone informed of their arrest (Georges may have his wife informed, unless there is a risk that she will, for example, interfere with evidence[13]), whether they want legal advice, and also determine whether the suspects need medical attention, whether they require an appropriate adult, and whether they need an interpreter. The CO must note down the reasons for arrest and will inform the suspects of the grounds for their detention – but will not provide any details on the evidence which the police hold against them. The CO is responsible for the treatment of the suspects and the proper conduct of their detention – they will take

---

7   PACE Code of Practice C § 11.1. The PACE Codes of Practice are strictly not a form of legislation, but are issued with the approval of Parliament. Police officers are expected to comply with them, and failure to do so may be relevant to an application to exclude evidence obtained in breach of a code provision.

8   A custody officer is a police officer of at least the rank of sergeant who is not involved with the investigation, although recent legislation permits civilians to be appointed as custody officers.

9   PACE 1984 s37.

10   The CO can release the suspect on bail pending a charge decision by a prosecutor. PACE 1984 s37(7).

11   Code of Practice C § 3.

12   Code of Practice C § 3. The caution sets out the consequences of remaining 'silent.' See further below.

13   PACE 1984 s56.

no part in the case investigation and will not question Georges, Sid or Jean about the offence.

The normal maximum period that a suspect can be detained by the police without being charged with a criminal offence is 24 hours from the time of arrival at the police station.[14] Where a person is detained in respect of an indictable offence (an offence which may be tried either in the Crown Court or in the lower ranking magistrates' court), which all three probably are, the period of detention without charge may be extended up to a total of 36 hours on the authority of a superintendent (a senior police officer), and up to a total of 96 hours on the authority of a magistrates' court.[15] The 'evidence' will be taken to be the word of the police as to the reason for their initial arrest, and there is no further scrutiny of the evidence at this stage. In practice, it is unlikely that Jean or Georges would be detained without charge for more than 24 hours, but Sid may be, particularly if the police are trying to obtain surveillance evidence from abroad. Whilst they are detained at a police station, detention must be reviewed after six hours, and then every nine hours, by a police inspector (a middle-ranking officer) not involved with the investigation who must take the suspect to the CO for a decision to be made about releasing them if they are satisfied that the conditions for detention no longer apply.[16] In practice, although reviews are normally carried out at the appropriate times, they rarely result in the inspector deciding that detention should be brought to an end, although the inspector may apply informal pressure to the investigating officer to expedite the investigation.

2.1. Jean – under 17s

Since Jean is under 17 years old, the CO must contact his parents (or other person responsible for his welfare), and must also contact an appropriate adult. Normally, a juvenile's parents will act as the appropriate adult, but if they are not available or are unwilling to become involved, the appropriate adult may be a local authority social worker or some other responsible adult.[17] Normally, a person under 17 years cannot be interviewed by the police other than in the presence of an appropriate adult.[18] The police rarely fail to comply with the requirement to contact an appropriate adult; if they fail to do so it is likely, if the case goes to trial, that a judge would exclude evidence obtained from the juvenile (such as a confession), although exclusion is not automatic.

2.2. Sid – foreign citizens

Since Sid is not a British citizen, he must be told that he has a right to communicate at any time with the relevant consular officials, and for them to be informed of his

---

14 PACE 1984 s41.
15 PACE 1984 ss42-44.
16 PACE 1984 s40.
17 Code of Practice C § 3.
18 Code of Practice C § 11.15.

location and the grounds for his detention. If Sid asks for them to be informed, this must be done as soon as practicable, and this right cannot be denied in any circumstances.[19] As Sid does not speak sufficiently good English, the CO must call in an interpreter as soon as practicable[20] and arrange for an interpreter to be present in any police interview. If the police do not comply with this requirement, any evidence obtained from Sid may be excluded at trial, although exclusion is not automatic. The interpreter will be chosen, and paid, by the police. The Law Society has advised solicitors to obtain a separate interpreter for their consultation with the client, but although this can be paid for under the legal aid scheme, defence lawyers frequently rely on the interpreter contacted by the police. Interpreters are not covered by professional privilege, and there is no obligation of confidentiality. This means that an interpreter could tell the police what the suspect has told them even if the suspect had asked them not to, and the prosecution could require the interpreter to give evidence of what the suspect had told them, although in practice this rarely happens.

3.   Legal advice

All three suspects are entitled to consult with a solicitor, in private, at any time during their detention at the police station.[21] This is provided free under the legal aid scheme although the lawyer (or, strictly, their firm) must be under contract to the Legal Services Commission.[22] Legal advice is an absolute right, although access to a lawyer may be delayed for up to 36 hours on the authority of a police superintendent (a senior officer) where the person is detained in respect of an indictable offence. Authorisation for delay may only be given if certain exceptional conditions are satisfied, such as a belief that the lawyer will interfere with evidence or witnesses in the case.[23] If delay in access to legal advice is authorized, the suspect could be interviewed without a lawyer present, but inferences at trial could not be drawn if, as a result, he decided to remain silent in the interview.[24] In practice, delay in allowing access to a lawyer under these provisions is relatively rare, although there is evidence that the police sometimes use informal measures to discourage suspects from seeking or securing legal advice.[25]

---

[19]   Code of Practice C § 7.

[20]   Code of Practice C § 3.12.

[21]   PACE 1984 s58.

[22]   Most legally aided criminal defence work is conducted by one of the 2,700 law firms in private practice who are under contract to the Legal Services Commission (LSC). There is also a Public Defender Service (PDS), in which lawyers are directly employed by the LSC, but at present it has offices in only 8 locations.

[23]   PACE 1984 s58(8)-(12).

[24]   If, on the other hand, an interview is improperly conducted in the absence of legal advice, evidence of what was said in the interview may be excluded at trial, although the court decisions on this issue are not always consistent.

[25]   If the lawyer does not arrive after several hours and no duty lawyer can be secured, the police are likely to interview the suspect rather than delay the investigation. However, since

→

Georges has used a lawyer before in connection with his business and he may request this lawyer to attend the police station, although this will be paid for under legal aid only if the firm is under contract to the Legal Services Commission. Although Jean has not used a lawyer before, if he knows of a lawyer he may request that lawyer, but the same issues regarding legal aid apply. If he does not know of a lawyer, the CO must tell him that he can obtain the services of a duty solicitor. If he asks for the duty solicitor, the CO must make contact with the duty solicitor service. The fact that Jean is a juvenile does not affect his right to request a lawyer. Sid does not have a right to consult his own lawyer (although he could ask for the lawyer to be informed under the right to have someone informed of his arrest, as explained above), and since he does not know a lawyer in England and Wales it is most likely that he would obtain legal advice through the duty solicitor scheme. Sid may ask the UK lawyer to contact his lawyer at home in order to obtain other relevant information. The UK lawyer is obliged to follow his client's instructions (unless this is otherwise unlawful).

If Jean, Georges or Sid ask for legal advice, the CO must act without delay to secure its provision,[26] and they cannot normally be interviewed until they have spoken to a solicitor.[27] The solicitor may provide legal advice on the telephone and/or in person. Whether the advice is by telephone,[28] or in person, the communication should be confidential. The legal aid contract (which covers both 'own' and duty solicitors) sets out the circumstances in which legal advice should be provided in person, and the lawyer should attend the police station to provide legal advice in person in the case of Jean (since he is a juvenile) and Sid and Georges (because of the seriousness of the suspected offence). All three accused are entitled to have their lawyer present whilst they are being interviewed by the police. Many specialist criminal defence firms employ non-solicitors known as accredited representatives (because they have to pass a number of tests of knowledge and skills to become accredited) to provide police station legal advice.

An ongoing problem is that neither the suspect nor their solicitor have a right to be given information by the police (other than the fact of, and grounds for, arrest), although the lawyer does have a right to see the custody record that must be opened by the CO when they authorise detention, and in which all important information and decisions regarding the suspect must be entered.[29] Normally the police do give the suspect and/or their lawyer some information, but they often keep some information back in order, for example, to confront the suspect with it in interview. Therefore, the police do not have to tell Sid (or his lawyer) what

---

most firms of solicitors have out of hours duty rota, and all police stations are covered by a duty solicitor scheme, it is unlikely that legal advice could not be secured.

[26]   PACE 1984 s58(4) and Code of Practice C § 6.5.

[27]   Code of Practice C § 6.6 and Annex B.

[28]   Less than one fifth of suspects receiving legal advice are advised only on the telephone. See T. Bucke and D. Brown, *In police custody: police powers and suspects' rights under the revised PACE codes of practice. Research Study No. 174,* London, Home Office, 1997.

[29]   Although the custody record does not contain any of the evidence.

information they have resulting from the surveillance, and this is often the kind of information that the police do not disclose in advance of an interview.[30]

4.   Search of premises

With regard to Georges, the police have a number of different powers to enter and search premises. It is possible that the police will have used their powers under PACE 1984 s18, which they can use without judicial authorisation, but they could only do this if they have arrested him for an indictable offence (which they almost certainly have). Section 18 empowers the police to enter and search any premises occupied or controlled by the arrested person if they have reasonable grounds to suspect that there is on the premises evidence relating to the offence for which they have been arrested, or to some other indictable offence which is connected with or similar to that offence. A s18 search must normally be authorised by a police inspector (a middle ranking officer). However, even if Georges had been arrested for an indictable offence, it is difficult to see what evidence they would be looking for. Therefore, on the facts, the search of Georges business premises is likely to be unlawful. However, past court decisions indicate that any evidence obtained from an unlawful search is, nevertheless, likely to be admitted in evidence.

5.   Interview

In England and Wales interviews with suspects conducted at police stations in respect of indictable offences must normally be tape-recorded on audio-tape.[31] In practice, the police tape-record almost all interviews, and will record the interviews conducted with Sid. If he is charged with a criminal offence, he is entitled to a copy of the tape. The police will normally prepare a summary of the interview based on the tape-recording, and this may be adduced in evidence at a trial. Frequently, where the defendant pleads not guilty, the tape is fully transcribed, and this can be adduced in evidence provided that the interviewing officer establishes that it is a true record of the interview (which is not normally a problem). If the police fail, without good reason, to record an interview that should be recorded, a court may exclude evidence of what was said in the interview. The former practice, where the

---

[30]   Note that most forms of covert surveillance, and the interception of communications, are governed by the Regulation of Investigatory Powers Act 2000, which provides for a number of different authorisation procedures depending on the form of surveillance. The product of surveillance may never be disclosed to the accused if it is covered by public interest immunity. Further, if the surveillance consists of interception of communications that was conducted in England and Wales, there is a complete ban on its use at trial. However, if it was obtained outside of England and Wales, case law suggests that it could be used in evidence.

[31]   PACE Code of Practice E.

police conducted an interview and then prepared a statement which they asked the suspect to sign has, in practice, been discontinued.[32]

5.1. Confessions/Silence

Sid's answers indicate that he may be implicated with others in organising football violence. For the purposes of determining admissibility at trial, this amounts to a confession, and a confession made by a defendant is normally admissible in evidence at trial.[33] If, at trial, Sid asserted that his comments had been obtained by oppression or by something said or done which, in the circumstances, was likely to render his comments unreliable, then evidence of his comments would only be admissible if the prosecution could prove beyond reasonable doubt that they were not so obtained.[34] The prosecution would seek to rely on the tape recorded interviews and the custody record to demonstrate that the suspect had been treated properly. The defence may seek to rely on evidence from his solicitor if, for example, there is evidence of injury or the suspect told the lawyer of threats made at the time. This is unlikely, however, as lawyers are reluctant to testify in court, as this destroys the lawyer/client privilege and might harm the interests of the client in other respects, e.g. through the disclosure of incriminating information. The court also has a discretion to exclude prosecution evidence if, having regard to all the circumstances, admission of the evidence would have such an adverse effect on the fairness of the proceedings that it ought not be admitted.[35] This could happen, for example, if Sid's English was very poor, and the police interviewed him without an interpreter present. It is also worth noting that under recent legislation, the prosecution may be able adduce evidence of Sid's previous convictions as evidence of his propensity to commit such offences and/or as evidence as to his credibility as a witness.[36]

Georges refused to answer any police questions. At trial, in determining guilt or innocence, a court may draw adverse inferences where a defendant relies on facts in their defence which they did not tell the police about on being questioned under caution, if the court is satisfied that it would be reasonable to expect them to have mentioned those facts.[37] The Court of Appeal has decided that a court may draw inferences where they are satisfied that the suspect remained 'silent' because they had no innocent answer to give to the police, or none that would stand up to scrutiny. For example, if Georges gives evidence at trial that he was accompanied by two friends at the relevant time and that he was simply trying to find his way out of the stadium, it would be open to the prosecution to argue that, in the absence

---

[32] It is worth noting that despite initial hostility to tape-recording by some police officers, it is now uncontroversial, and almost certainly most police officers would not like to go back to having to compose a written record or statement.

[33] PACE 1884 ss76 and 82.

[34] PACE 1984 s76(2).

[35] PACE 1984 s78.

[36] Criminal Justice Act 2003 Part 11, ch. 1.

[37] Criminal Justice and Public Order Act 1984 s34.

of an adequate explanation why this was not raised during police interview, his evidence should be disbelieved. A court cannot convict on adverse inferences alone, but inferences from 'silence' could be added to other evidence so that a conviction could follow if the court is then satisfied beyond reasonable doubt of the defendant's guilt.

It is very difficult to indicate whether the court would draw adverse inferences from Georges' refusal to answer questions; the case law on the 'silence' provisions makes prediction almost impossible. If Georges was advised by his solicitor to keep silent this would not, in itself, prevent inferences from being drawn. Nor would Georges' belief that he should not have been arrested necessarily prevent a court from drawing adverse inferences. On the brief facts given, it is quite likely that a court would conclude that it would be reasonable to expect Georges to have told the police about his defence (e.g. that he did not take part in any violence, was not involved in any planning of violence, etc.), and therefore conclude that the defence he puts forward at his trial is not true. However, much would depend upon what other evidence was adduced as to his guilt, whether he had legal advice, and how convincing his evidence was as to why he did not answer police questions.

It is likely that Jean's interview will be admissible in evidence, and the prosecution would almost certainly draw the court's attention to the fact that he had answered some questions and not others, especially if the questions that he did not answer were difficult questions for a guilty person to answer without incriminating themselves. The weight that the court places on this inconsistency would depend on a number of factors such as its assessment of his maturity, whether he had legal advice, etc. It is important to note that even though he answered some questions, if he relies on facts at trial which he did not tell the police about in the interview, adverse inferences could be drawn. For example, if he told the police in interview that he did not hit the victim, but did not answer a question about whether he saw anyone hit the victim, but at trial gives evidence that he did see someone hit the victim, the court may draw the inference that (because he did not tell the police this in the interview) he is not now telling the truth when he says that he saw someone hitting the victim.

6. Bail/Continued detention

When a person is charged with a criminal offence, the CO must release them (normally on bail) pending their first court appearance unless satisfied that one or more of a number of conditions applies, e.g. there are reasonable grounds for doubting the defendant's identity, or for believing that detention is necessary to prevent them committing an offence.[38] If the defendant is not released, the first court appearance will be the same day that they are charged, or the following day. If a defendant is released on bail the CO can impose bail conditions, e.g. a condition that they reside at a particular address. A defendant who has been bailed by the police will normally have to appear in court within two days. The court will then

---

[38]   PACE 1984 s38.

make its own decision about bail, although a defendant granted bail by the police will normally also be granted bail by the court.

In the case of Jean, even if he is charged with a serious assault, it is highly likely that he will be released on bail.[39] Strictly, his age is not a relevant factor, although in practice juveniles are more likely to be granted bail than adults. If he is charged with a serious offence it is likely that the CO will impose conditions, e.g. that he reside with his parents, and does not go to any football match. If Jean is not granted bail he must be transferred to local authority accommodation pending his court appearance unless certain conditions apply (which are unlikely to be relevant in this case).[40] Unless he is jointly charged with an adult, he will appear in a youth court.

Georges will almost certainly be granted bail if he is charged with affray, and his release is likely to be unconditional (except that the fact that he is on bail will mean that his is under an obligation to attend court on the due date, and will commit an offence if, without reasonable cause, he fails to do so).

Of the three defendants, Sid is at greatest risk of being detained in custody, particularly because he has previous convictions involving football violence and is a foreign citizen. The CO is likely to refuse bail, in particular, because there are reasonable grounds for believing that he will fail to appear in court and/or interfere with the administration of justice or the investigation (particularly if he is charged with a conspiracy offence).[41] The police do have the power to grant bail subject to a security, e.g. that he hand over his passport, money, or something of value, or subject to a surety (in effect, a promise by another person that they will forfeit a certain sum of money if he failed to attend court), and/or subject to conditions, e.g. that he reside at a fixed address and does not leave the country. However, it is most likely that the CO will deny Sid bail. When Sid appears in court, the court would make its own decision about bail.

---

[39]   Since this is Jean's first offence, the police could impose a reprimand or final warning rather than prosecute him, although this would depend upon the seriousness of the assault, and would only be possible if he admitted the offence.

[40]   PACE s38(6).

[41]   PACE s38(1)(a)(ii).

Thomas Weigend
Franz Salditt

CASE STUDY: GERMANY

1. Arrest and pre-trial custody

Georges can be detained by the police until the end of the day following his arrest if he is suspected of having committed a criminal offence and if there exist grounds for keeping him in custody before trial, i.e., a risk that he might flee from justice or that he may destroy or tamper with evidence (§§ 127 § 2, 112 Code of Criminal Procedure – CCP). The police can interrogate Georges, but they must inform him of the offence of which he is suspected of and must warn him of his right to remain silent (§§ 163a § 4, 136 § 1 CCP). Warnings can be given orally, and there is no prescribed 'Letter of Rights' that the police use. Since 'un-warned' statements cannot be used against the suspect's will, the police will however take care to prepare a written record of the fact that the suspect has been informed of his rights. The police must make sure that Georges suffers no physical harm while in their custody and they must call a doctor for him if necessary.

Before the end of the following day, the police must release Georges or present him to a judge, who will then decide whether there exist sufficient grounds for keeping him in pre-trial custody. The judge will again inform Georges of the grounds of suspicion against him as well as of his right to remain silent, and the judge will give Georges an opportunity to raise issues in his favour (§ 115 § 3 CCP). If Georges has hired counsel, his lawyer has a right to be present at the judicial interrogation, and his lawyer can argue in favour of the client and can question any witnesses that may appear (§ 168c § 1 CCP). The court need not and will not, however, appoint counsel for Georges at this stage. Given the stringent requirements for pre-trial custody, it is highly unlikely that the judge will order custody in Georges' case. If the judge nevertheless does so, they will at the same time inform Georges' wife or give Georges an opportunity to talk with her (§ 114b CCP). The decision whether to file formal charges against Georges will be decided much later by the public prosecutor.

The same rules apply to Jean. In view of his youth, the judge must take special care in determining whether there exist alternatives to pre-trial custody, for example, detaining him in a secure home for juveniles (§ 72 § 1 *Jugendgerichtsgesetz* – Juvenile Court Act).

Sid has the same rights as Georges, but it is more likely that the judge will order pre-trial custody because Sid, as a foreign citizen presumably with strong ties to his own country, may be more likely to leave Germany and thus be unavailable for trial. If the violence committed by Sid both in the earlier and the present incidents was serious and a prison sentence of more than one year is likely to be imposed, the judge may also consider imposing pre-trial custody in order to prevent Sid from committing additional offences of the same kind (§ 112a CCP). It is further possible for the judge to order Sid to be kept in custody for up to one week with a view to holding an accelerated trial within that time period – accelerated trials can be held when the offence is not very serious, and the evidence is clear (§§ 127b, 417 CCP). Technically, a confession by the suspect is not a pre-requisite for an accelerated trial, but it is not likely that the case will be processed in this fashion if the defendant seriously contests the charges. The maximum penalty that can be imposed in accelerated proceedings is one year's imprisonment (§ 419 § 1 CCP), hence assault charges could well be eligible for this route. Accelerated trials are not used very often (about 4 per cent of all trials), but in the case of a foreign defendant this avenue of dealing with the case quickly may well be an option favoured by the prosecution. In Sid's case, the consulate of his country will be informed of his arrest if Sid, after being informed of his rights under the Vienna Convention on Consular Rights, so requests.

2. Right to an interpreter

Sid has a right to an interpreter for his interrogation by the police and by the judge (cf. § 187 *Gerichtsverfassungsgesetz* – Court Organisation Act). He can also use an interpreter to converse with his lawyer. The state will pay for the interpreter's fees even if Sid is eventually convicted.

3. Access to a lawyer

Suspects have a right to consult a lawyer of their choice prior to being interrogated by the police. Georges can make a telephone call to his lawyer, and when the lawyer arrives he must be permitted to speak with Georges. Sid will not be allowed to call his lawyer abroad. According to the jurisprudence of the courts, the police must offer him some help in finding a lawyer when he indicates that he wants to speak with one. They may point out that there is an existing local lawyer hotline, or they may give him a list of local lawyers.[1] The same applies to Jean. If Sid or Jean are unsuccessful in locating a lawyer after having been given a fair chance to do so, the police may proceed to interrogate them. The defendants still have the right to remain silent, however, and they can defer making any statement until they have spoken with a lawyer.

---

[1] See 42 *Entscheidungen des Bundesgerichtshofes in Strafsachen* 15; see also 47 *Entscheidungen des Bundesgerichtshofes in Strafsachen* 233.

According to the majority view,[2] the law does not accord a suspect the right to have their lawyer present during a police interview (it is different with interrogations by prosecutors or judges, see §§ 163a § 3, 168c § 1 CCP). A suspect can, however, refuse to make any statement to the police unless the police permit their lawyer to attend the interview. The police will not inform the suspect about that option but are likely to accept the lawyer's presence if the suspect insists. Only 'experienced' suspects are likely to make use of that option.

4.   Access to the prosecution file

Sid's lawyer can file a request to inspect the prosecution file (§ 147 CCP). The file, which is in fact a record of the police investigation, should include the results of police wiretapping conducted in connection with the prosecution of Sid's crime[3] (assuming that Sid has been living in Germany and was under surveillance there; the situation may be different if surveillance has been conducted in another country). The prosecutor can prevent inspection of the file if the relevant information might be used to obstruct the purpose of the investigation, for example, by allowing Sid to put pressure on witnesses named on the police tape (§ 147 § 2 CCP). In that case, Sid's lawyer would have to wait until the investigation has been declared closed (usually, shortly before a formal accusation is filed by the prosecutor); at that time, Sid's lawyer has an absolute right to inspect the file.

5.   Search of premises

The police can search Georges' premises if Georges is suspected of having committed a criminal offence and if they can reasonably expect to find evidence on the premises (§ 102 CCP). Any search is subject to the principle of proportionality, i.e., the search must be necessary for the discovery of evidence of crime, and the intrusion into the citizen's privacy must not be out of proportion to the importance of the crime and the evidence. The police would thus not be permitted, for example, to search Georges' home in order to find his entrance ticket when he did not dispute the fact that he attended the match. The police will ordinarily need a judicial search warrant (§ 105 § 1 CCP). Only if there is 'danger in delay,' that is, if there is a risk that the evidence in question would be destroyed or hidden during the time necessary to make an application to a judge, can police or prosecutors conduct a search on their own account. The Federal Constitutional Court has, in recent years, strictly limited the concept of 'danger in delay' requiring, inter alia, the police to keep a precise record of the time of their acquisition of relevant information on the

---

2   Cf. L. Meyer-Goßner, *Strafprozessordnung*, Munich, C.h. Beck, 47th ed., 2004, § 163 note 16 with further references.

3   The information may not be included in the prosecution file, however, if surveillance was conducted by the police as a measure of crime *prevention*. In that case Sid would have to apply for inspection under the relevant state police law. The possibility of using wiretaps in the context of crime prevention has, however, been severely curtailed by a judgement of the Federal Constitutional Court of 27 July 2005.

location of relevant objects and of their attempts to contact a judge before conducting a warrant-less search. Regardless of whether the search has produced evidence, Georges can subsequently obtain a judicial decision on the legality of the search. If the search is found to have been illegal, this does not necessarily mean, however, that evidence found and seized will not be admissible as evidence. Theoretically, police officers acting illegally without a judicial warrant may be criminally liable for trespass, but prosecutions of that kind do not occur in practice.

6.   Police interview

Tape-recording of police or other interrogations before trial is not required under German law. A specific provision permitting videotaping of statements (§ 58a CCP) is applicable only to witnesses, but not to suspects.[4] It is, however, not illegal to record an interrogation even without the explicit consent of the suspect if the recording is done openly. Normally, police officers and prosecutors do not make tape or video recordings of interrogations. The police officer will write down, in their own words, what the suspect has declared, and this protocol will then be read to (or by) the suspect, who can make additions or changes and will then sign the protocol. The police protocol will be entered into the official prosecution file.

The protocol of Sid's police interrogation is not admissible as documentary evidence at trial (cf. § 254 CCP, permitting the use only of protocols of judicial interrogations). If Sid decides to make a statement at the trial the presiding judge can, however, confront him with the police protocol to point out discrepancies between his prior testimony and his present statement. Regardless of whether Sid makes a statement at the trial, the police officer who conducted the interview can be called to testify as a hearsay witness – hearsay testimony being generally admissible – and the police officer can use the protocol to refresh their memory before giving testimony. The judge can also read parts of the protocol to the police officer to refresh their memory. According to the majority view, the contents of the protocol can then be used as evidence even if the officer declares that they cannot remember the details of the interview.[5] If Sid's police statement is thus properly introduced as evidence at the trial, the judgement can be based on it even if at trial Sid 'retracts' his prior statement or declares it to be false. There is no need for further corroborative evidence for conviction.

7.   Right to silence

The fact that Georges did not make any statement to the police must, in accordance with the principle *nemo tenetur seipsum accusare*, be treated as neutral; his silence

---

4   Cf. Meyer-Goßner, *supra* note 2, § 58a note 2, § 163 note 42. It is illegal and arguably even criminal (under § 201 § 1 No. 1 Penal Code), however, to *secretly* tape-record the words of the suspect without special judicial authorization (§§ 100c § 1 No. 2, 100d § 1 CCP).

5   See 3 *Entscheidungen des Bundesgerichtshofes in Strafsachen* 199 (201); for further references, see Meyer-Goßner, *supra* note 2, § 253 note 1.

must not be used as an indication of his guilt. The fact that Georges gave a reason for remaining silent does not alter that result.[6] If Georges makes an exculpatory statement at the trial, the fact that he did not make that statement when questioned by the police must not be used by the court as a reason for not believing Georges's trial statement; otherwise Georges would indirectly be forced to present exculpatory evidence at the earliest time possible, which would compromise his right to remain silent.[7]

Jean's answers can be introduced at the trial in the same way as Sid's. The fact that he selectively answered the questions put to him can, according to the courts, be used in evaluating the credibility of his statements if his responses indicate evasiveness rather than mere inadvertence.[8] His response would, for example, be regarded as evasive if he made self-exonerating statements but repeatedly refused to reply to questions that might lead to self-incriminatory statements.

8.   Pre-trial custody-bail

The fact that formal proceedings are brought against the suspects does not necessarily imply that they will be held in custody before trial. Pre-trial custody requires a high degree of suspicion and can be ordered only if the suspect presents a danger of flight or of tampering with evidence (§ 112 CCP). This is unlikely in the cases of the three suspects, with the possible exception of Sid. However, assuming that reasons for ordering pre-trial custody exist for Georges, Jean and Sid, the question arises whether execution of the custody order can be suspended. The judge must suspend execution whenever less stringent measures are available which make it likely that the suspect will appear for trial (§ 116 CCP). Such measures include requirements to report to the court or to the police at certain intervals, restrictions on leaving one's place of residence, and financial bail. If the reason for ordering pre-trial custody is the expectation that the suspect might tamper with evidence, the suspect can instead be ordered not to contact certain persons. For Georges, as well as Jean, reporting requirements and/or restrictions on changing their place of residence without judicial permission may well be sufficient safeguards since they live with their families within the jurisdiction of the court. Sid is unlikely to be permitted to return to his country in light of the difficulty of enforcing his appearance at the trial once he is abroad.[9] Depending on the seriousness of the charges against him, financial bail may still be an option, but the

---

[6]   The fact that Georges should not have been arrested might be an independent ground for rendering inadmissible any statement he makes to the police.

[7]   See 20 *Entscheidungen des Bundesgerichtshofes in Strafsachen* 281.

[8]   See 20 *Entscheidungen des Bundesgerichtshofes in Strafsachen* 298; BGH *Neue Juristische Wochenschrift* 2002, 2260.

[9]   The fact that the European Arrest Warrant makes extradition within the EU easier may change courts' policy in the future, but at present courts would still be wary of letting a foreign suspect leave Germany, especially since the German statute on the European Arrest Warrant has been declared unconstitutional.

more likely course is the holding of an accelerated trial within a few days (§ 417 CCP).

Zinovia Dellidou

CASE STUDY: GREECE

1. Arrest

Sid, Jean and Georges were all arrested during a violent incident occurring in an international football match. Sid is a supporter of the visiting team and national of country B while Jean and Georges are both supporters of the home team and are Greek citizens.

As they were all arrested while the alleged acts were being committed (or soon afterwards and, in any case, within no more than 48 hours from their commission), they were arrested for flagrant offences (art. 242 CPP).[1] That means that the police have a right and obligation to arrest them (art. 275 CPP)[2] without the need for an arrest warrant issued by the judicial authorities. An arrest warrant is required where a suspect is not caught in the act (or within 48 hours).[3]

Arrest is likely to have occurred for a number of offences. At this stage, the police will not clearly formulate the nature of the offence but must state in general terms the grounds for arresting them. All three men (Jean, who is sixteen years old is considered a juvenile)[4] are likely to have been arrested for some form of assault or incitement to violence (psychological encouragement) or for destroying public property and/or violent disorder. Most of these offences are likely to be classified as misdemeanours. However, Sid is also likely to have been arrested for a felony, i.e. being a member of a criminal organisation aimed at causing, for example, grievous bodily harm.[5]

---

[1]   Code of Penal Procedure, thereafter referred to as CPP.

[2]   A.X. Papadamakis, *Penal Procedure: Theory-Practice-Jurisprudence*, Athens-Thessalonica, Sakkoulas Publications, 2006, p. 290. See also art. 6.1 of the Greek Constitution which provides that: 'No one is arrested or imprisoned without a reasoned judicial warrant which must be served at the moment of arrest or detention pending trial, except when caught while committing the act.'

[3]   See art. 276.1 CPP.

[4]   According to art. 121 of the Greek Penal Code (thereafter PC), those between the age of eight and eighteen years are considered as juveniles.

[5]   See art. 187 PC.

2.   Detention at the police station – rights and procedure

Following their arrest by the police, the three suspects will be taken to the police station where an arrest report certifying the commission of an illegal act[6] will be compiled by the officer in charge at the police station.[7] This report will also include the details of the person arrested as well as the time of arrest.

The testimonies of the arresting officers will be taken down in writing and they will have to sign the relevant report. These testimonies will form part of the file transferred to the Attorney General (AG), who will make the decision whether to charge the defendants. Following arrest, a body search will take place to recover items that may establish the commission of the offence.[8] A report of items found on the persons arrested will also be compiled, and these items will be seized and held by the police. Those items related to the alleged crime will be then transferred to the AG (art. 280 CPP) along with the defendant and the reports compiled.[9]

If it is clear that any of the people arrested are in need of medical care they will be immediately taken to a hospital by the police. If the need for medical assistance becomes obvious after their arrival at the police station, the officer in charge will ensure medical care is afforded to those who need it (art. 60 § 3e).

As part of the pre-trial police procedure, the suspects/defendants will also be fingerprinted, and their details will be cross-referenced to investigate whether they have committed other offences. They will be allowed to make a telephone call and contact the people they wish to inform of their detention at the police station. Georges may therefore contact his pregnant wife if he wishes.

In larger police departments, where there are a large number of detainees, a specific custody officer is appointed (according to art. 67 of Presidential Decree 141/1991). As Jean is a juvenile, an effort will be made to keep him in a detention area separate from adults, although that will often depend on the size and conditions existing at the relevant police station.

3.   Police interviews

According to article 243.2 CPP an *ex officio* summary investigation can be carried out by the police in the case of flagrant offences. This examination will be directed at confirming the commission of the illegal act, ensuring that crucial evidence is not lost by the delay. Only police officers above a certain rank can conduct an *ex officio* investigation, and are considered as general investigating officers,[10] and the Attorney General must be informed as soon as possible.

---

6   B.I. Kapralos, *Criminal Litigation*, Athens-Komotini, Ant. N. Sakkoulas Publishers, 1983, p. 91.
7   Art. 60 of Presidential Decree No. 141/1991 FEK 58A/30 April 1991.
8   *Ibidem*, art. 119.c.
9   See B.I. Kapralos, *supra* note 6, p. 91.
10   See art. 33.1 CPP. Following the creation of a police academy in 1996, which introduced a change in the system of entering the police service, all graduates of that academy are now automatically considered as investigating officers and can carry out an *ex officio* summary
                                                                                                              →

Even though no charges have been formally laid, persons arrested for flagrant offences who are subject to an *ex officio* summary investigation have all the rights allowed to 'defendants' (art. 96-104 CPP).[11] This means that they can contact a lawyer and obtain legal advice. They also have a right to silence, that is, a right not to answer any questions.

If the police carry out an *ex officio* investigation they must compile reports of all acts they perform. They must inform all suspects of their rights before examining them (including the right to a lawyer and to remain silent) in a language they understand. Sid will be therefore be given a leaflet containing information on all his rights in his own language, or another language that he can understand. In addition, all his rights are printed on the form on which his statement will be recorded. Following his interview he will be asked to sign the report compiled by the police. If he refuses to sign it, the officer responsible will make a note of it on the report (art. 151 CPP).

The police must inform the suspects of the reason for their arrest, and of any evidence they may have against them, before they commence their examination (see art. 105, 104 and 101 CPP). In the case of Sid, if an interpreter is needed, the investigating officer must appoint one (see art. 233 CPP). The police have a list, compiled by the judicial council of the misdemeanours court, of interpreters and will invite one of them to attend the interview. The interpreter will be paid from government funds.

Interviews are not tape-recorded, but detailed written records of all that occurs must be kept. According to article 148-153 CPP all interviews must be documented as a statement. At the beginning of the interview, the suspects will be read their rights and then asked what they know regarding the offences of which they are accused. If their answers result from the questions posed then the questions must also be clearly recorded. The officer must also clearly indicate whether the suspect answered some or all of the questions posed to them. Apart from the officer examining the suspect, the interview must take place in the presence of a second investigating officer who will also sign the report.

Under Greek law defendants have a right to silence and no adverse consequences can result from their refusal to answer questions (art. 273.2 CPP). It should, therefore, make no difference whether they refuse to answer some or all of the questions asked by the police. The explanation Georges gave for not answering the questions posed (that he was not doing anything wrong and the police should not have arrested him) should also be clearly recorded in the report compiled.

Where the police carry out an *ex officio* summary investigation, anything the men say can be included in the file that is put before the investigating judge and/or the trial court.[12] This will not, however, be the case if the police did not respect the

investigation. See Z. Papaioannou, *The Law applicable to the Police: the functional competence of police officers in the Greek Police Force*, Athens-Thessalonica, Sakkoulas Publications, 2006, p. 5.

[11]   A.X. Papadamakis, *supra* note 2, p. 285.

[12]   The trial court will normally have had access to the pre-trial dossier before the commencement of the proceedings. However, one of the fundamental principles of the oral procedure, that of 'immediacy,' requires the trial court to give preference to the defendant's

→

suspects' rights. For example, if they did not inform them of their right to silence or to legal advice, or if the confession was obtained by oppression, their testimonies cannot be taken into account because they are considered invalid (art. 171.1.d CPP). The general rule is that absolute nullities at the pre-trial stage must be proposed[13] before the decision is irrevocably made to take the case to trial.[14] Otherwise they are treated as having been 'cured.' The courts have, however, ruled that where a confession was obtained by oppression at the pre-trial stage the defendant can raise the matter during the oral hearing. In these circumstances, if the trial court then takes the confession into account an absolute nullity will occur affecting the oral hearing which can then be proposed *ex officio* even before the Supreme Court.[15]

4.   Access to legal advice at the police station

All three suspects have the right to speak to a lawyer before they are interviewed by the police and are entitled to have a lawyer present during the interview (see art. 100, 104, 105 CPP). Communication between the lawyer and the suspect may not be interrupted in any way (art. 100.4 CPP).

Although the law does not clearly guarantee the right for a lawyer to be appointed *ex officio*, nor the right to legal aid at the police station,[16] it has been suggested that this right must apply in the case of alleged felonies or serious misdemeanours if the defendant does not have the means to pay for the lawyer himself or herself.[17] However, since the financial limits set by Law 3226/2004 (the legal aid legislation) are rather low it is unlikely that any of the suspects will have a lawyer appointed *ex officio* at this stage. Sid will, however, be appointed a lawyer *ex officio* during his examination before the investigating judge irrespective of his means. At that stage, Sid will have to accept the lawyer appointed, from a list, and will not have the right to choose his own legal counsel.

Therefore, if the suspects want to consult a lawyer during the *ex officio* investigation by the police they will probably have to pay for the lawyers' services themselves. Georges can ask the police to allow him to contact the lawyer he knows through his business. If Jean and Sid do not know of a lawyer, they can ask the police to arrange for them to contact one. Sid may talk to the lawyer he knows in his own country, but will most probably have to pay the cost of their services himself.

---

oral testimony given during the course of the trial hearing. The court can only read the relevant parts of the defendant's pre-trial testimony when the content of his/her oral testimony greatly differs from what s/he said pre-trial (art. 366.2 CPP).

[13]   *Ex officio*, by the party concerned (i.e. the defendant) or the Attorney General (see art. 173 CPP).

[14]   Art. 173 CPP. Note that relevant invalidities cannot be proposed *ex officio* and must be proposed either by the Attorney General or the party concerned (art. 173.1 CPP).

[15]   A.X. Papadamakis, *supra* note 2, p. 213.

[16]   See Law 3226/2004 FEK 24A/4 February 2004.

[17]   On the basis of art. 6.3.c of the European Convention on Human Rights. See, *inter alia*, N.K. Androulakis, *Fundamental concepts of the criminal trial*, Athens-Komotini, Ant. N. Sakkoulas Publishers, 1994, p. 272.

5. Search of premises

A search of premises is possible during an *ex officio* summary investigation of a misdemeanour or felony (although it is not possible during a preliminary inquiry) if it can be reasonably presumed that it will help or facilitate the confirmation of the commission of the offence by, for example, discovering evidence in relation to the suspected crime.[18] To be valid, this type of investigative act must satisfy the principles of proportionality and necessity.

Company premises may be searched under the same conditions as someone's home.[19] Georges has the right to be present during the search (art. 256 CPP), which must be carried out in the presence of two investigating officers, one of whom must be a judicial officer.[20] If the search is carried out in the absence of a judicial officer it will be treated as a nullity.[21] If the search was conducted during the night, a judicial officer (i.e. the Attorney General, the investigating judge, or a justice of the peace) should be in charge of it and is responsible for compiling the relevant report.[22] Once the search has been conducted, a report must be given to Georges if he requests it.

However, in Georges' case it is doubtful whether a search of premises would help discover anything relevant to the nature of the misdemeanours he is likely to be charged with. If the requirements of proportionality and necessity are not seen to be satisfied the search could be considered an invalid act. In that case, any items recovered would not be permitted to be used as evidence in court.

6. Procedure before the Attorney General

All three suspects must be brought before the Attorney General as soon as practicable and, in any case, no later than 24 hours from the time of arrest (art. 279 CPP). If the arrest occurred in the evening, it is likely that the defendants will be transferred the following morning. The Attorney General will briefly examine the documents produced by the police, hear what the defendants have to say, make a decision on the nature of offences allegedly committed, and decide whether to charge the defendants. They will then either commit them for trial on the same day or on a specific date or, if the charge relates to a felony or a misdemeanour with

---

[18] A search is also permitted where there are reasonable grounds to believe that it would facilitate or ensure: a) the discovery or arrest of the perpetrator; or b) the confirmation/revelation or restoration of the damage caused, e.g. by revealing stolen items and other proceeds of crime (art. 253 CPP).

[19] The definition of home/residence includes the place where someone exercises their professional activities (similarly to the definition given in the Constitution). See N.K. Androulakis, *supra* note 17, p. 247.

[20] Although art. 255.2 CPP provides that if no judicial officer is present the town mayor can replace them, art. 9.1 of the Constitution requires that a judicial officer must always be present.

[21] See Judicial Council of Misdemeanours Court of Herakleion 261/2005 in *PoinDik*, 2006, p. 42-45.

[22] Art. 254 CPP.

regard to which restrictive conditions can be ordered, bring the defendants before the Investigating Judge.

7. Procedure before the Investigating Judge

Those charged with a felony or a misdemeanour with regard to which restrictive conditions may be imposed must be taken before an investigating judge to be examined. This will take place as soon as possible following their appearance before the Attorney General. In this case, this is most likely to occur in the case with Sid. If Sid requests a lawyer, one will be appointed *ex officio* and they will be paid out of government funds irrespective of Sid's financial situation.[23] Before his appearance before the investigating judge, Sid has the right to communicate with his lawyer in person and in private. This right is guaranteed by article 100.4 CPP which stresses that: 'Under no circumstances can the defendant's communication with his counsel be denied.' Before the investigating judge, Sid may ask for and is likely to be granted a 48 hour delay in order to prepare his defence. During this period it is likely that he will be detained, this being a decision for the investigating judge. Sid and his lawyer may, at this point, ask to see all information contained in the investigation file and are entitled to make copies at their expense.[24]

Once the examination begins, the investigating judge will have to tell Sid the exact nature of the offence he is charged with and provide him with information on the evidence available. Sid can refuse to answer all or some of the questions put to him. If he does, the investigating judge will clearly mention his refusal in the report he compiles. Sid may also decide to testify in writing, in which case he will submit his written testimony to the investigating judge. The judge may then ask him any questions he considers necessary to elucidate the content of his pleading. These questions and the answers given will be clearly mentioned in the report compiled, which will have to be signed by Sid.

Once the examination is complete, the investigating judge will take the file to the Attorney General and they will jointly decide whether Sid should be detained until trial. If there is disagreement between the Attorney General and the investigating judge, the judicial council will make the final decision.

8. Procedure before the court

Jean and Georges, who are likely to be charged with a misdemeanour, are likely to be taken to court on the day they are charged by the Attorney General or, at the latest, the following day (art. 418.1 CPP). This decision will be made by the Attorney General who also has the option to decide to follow the ordinary procedure setting

---

[23]   See art. 100.3 CPP in conjunction with art. 6.2 and 7.2.a of Law 3226/2004 FEK 24A/4 February 2004.

[24]   N.K. Androulakis, *supra* note 17, p. 274 and 276.

a specific trial date outside those limits. If the trial takes place on the following day, they will continue to be detained until trial (art. 419 CPP).[25]

At trial, the court is likely to grant them a three day adjournment to enable them to prepare their defence. If they do not have a lawyer, the court will at this stage appoint a lawyer from a list especially compiled for that purpose. This lawyer will be paid out of government funds under the legal aid scheme, irrespective of their means.[26] The court may decide to extend their detention for another three days until trial (art. 423.3 CPP).

Jean, who is sixteen years old, is considered a juvenile. Juveniles are generally tried by juvenile courts (one-member and three-member juvenile court and three member juvenile Court of Appeal). However, these juvenile courts do not have the power to try flagrant offences under the accelerated procedure.

Since the offences allegedly committed by Jean and Georges are likely to be misdemeanours and are related, they are likely to be jointly charged. In this case, Jean will be tried under the summary procedure in the same court that tries Georges (art. 128-131 CPP). If possible, a judge of the juvenile court should be included in the composition of the court trying them (art. 130.3 CPP).

9. The use of surveillance methods

In Greece, secret investigative methods are only permitted in relation to the investigation of certain offences (those specified in art. 187 and 187A of the Penal Code, and a number of special penal laws). Article 187.1 of the Penal Code, for example, refers to the offence of being a member of a criminal organisation aimed at, inter alia, causing grievous bodily harm. However, such methods are only permitted if a) there are serious indications that one of these criminal acts has been committed, and b) the uncovering of the criminal organisation is otherwise impossible or extremely difficult (art. 253A.2 CPP).[27]

Authorisation for the use of such methods must be obtained from the judicial council, on an application by the Attorney General. If the matter is considered to be of extreme urgency, it is possible for the decision to be made by the Attorney General or the investigating judge. In that case, they must bring the matter before the relevant judicial council within a period of three days (art. 253A.3 CPP). If these provisions have not been complied with, all evidence obtained will be considered to have been unlawfully obtained. Its use may cause the proceedings to be annulled.

As noted before, Sid will be entitled to see the contents of the investigation file and make copies at his expense when he appears to testify before the investigating

---

[25] This detention period cannot last more than 24 hours from the moment the defendants were first brought before the AG. This period can only be exceeded on the express authority of the investigating judge (art. 419 CPP).

[26] See art. 423.1 CPP in conjunction with art. 6.2 of Law 3226/2004 FEK 24A/4 February 2004.

[27] If surveillance was by means of telephone tapping then law 2225/1994 also applies. If surveillance occurred by the use of camera then Law 2713/1999 is applicable.

judge. He will, therefore, be able to discover what evidence has been obtained as a result of surveillance.

10. Bail/Continued detention

As noted above, Georges and Jean are likely to be tried by the court on the day they are charged by the Attorney General,[28] or the following day, by means of the accelerated procedure. As Sid is likely to have been charged with a felony, if there are serious indications of guilt he may be released subject to restrictive conditions or be temporarily detained.

Restrictive conditions (such as the payment of a security, the obligation to appear before the authorities at regular intervals or a prohibition on leaving the country)[29] can be ordered if there are serious indications of guilt.[30] Temporary detention may be ordered in these circumstances if the defendant has no known address in the country, has made plans to facilitate his departure, or there are reasonable grounds to believe (based on past behaviour or the particular nature of the acts committed) that he may commit further offences.[31]

In Sid's case, temporary detention could therefore be ordered instead of his release on restrictive conditions. This will be decided by the investigating judge in agreement with the Attorney General.

---

[28]   As noted before, the defendants must be brought before the Attorney General at the latest within 24 hours from the time of arrest.
[29]   Art. 282.2 CPP.
[30]   Art. 282.1 CPP.
[31]   Art. 282.3 CPP.

Giulio Illuminati
Michele Caianiello

CASE STUDY: ITALY

1. Charges

Sid, Jean and Georges have been indicted for an offence contrary to article 588 of Italian Penal Code (*rissa* – fight). This article prohibits fighting and sets out the fine level (up to € 309) for those involved. In addition, article 588 § 2 of the Italian Penal Code specifies that penalties of between 3 months and 5 years' imprisonment can be imposed for taking part in a fight where someone has been injured or killed.

Sid has also been charged under article 416 of the Italian Penal Code (*associazione per delinquere* – criminal association), in connection with the above-mentioned article 588. Article 416 of the Italian Penal Code sets out the range of punishment from one to five years' imprisonment for anyone who is guilty of being a member of a criminal association. According to the Italian Penal Code, a criminal association exists, and its members are punishable, when three or more persons join together in order to commit a variety of crimes. Under article 6 of the Italian Penal Code, Italy has jurisdiction with regard to international criminal associations provided that part of the conduct occurred in Italian territory.

2. The separation of the criminal proceedings involving Jean

The criminal proceeding against Jean will be separated from those against Sid and Georges, in view of the fact that Jean is a juvenile.

3. The assignment of counsel and the rights of the arrested person

As soon as possible after the arrest, the prosecutor appoints a counsel *ex officio* for Sid and Jean, while Georges is allowed to instruct the lawyer he usually uses in connection with his business. The police immediately inform each of the three lawyers and the family of Georges and Jean of their arrest. Sid's family is not notified of his arrest. Even though article 387 of the Code of Criminal Procedure states that, if the arrested person asks for it, the police must immediately inform their family, the police observe the rule only if the arrested person is Italian. If the arrested person is an alien, the rule is rarely observed. Case law has established that non-compliance with this particular provision does not necessarily invalidate the action of arrest.

Georges, Jean and Sid are served with written notification of their rights.

Sid will be given an interpreter, but not before the arrest validation hearing. This means that although the interpreter is present at the hearing, they are unlikely to have attended the interviews, nor been present at the consultations between Sid and his lawyer. It is possible, although it is often not the case in Italy, that the lawyer is able to speak in English with Sid, or is able to find some informal solution, such as a private interpreter.

It is highly unlikely that the three arrested suspects will have been questioned by the police before the arrest validation hearing. A form of questioning could have taken place, but most probably only in an informal way, without the presence of the lawyer and without any record of the questions posed and the answers given. In practice, Sid, Jean and Georges are likely to have been interrogated for the first time by the judge at the arrest validation hearing, in the presence of their lawyers. Before the interrogation, the judge will have given the three arrested persons the caution as provided by law.

4. Validation of the arrest

Sid, Jean and Georges are arrested by the police since they were caught in *flagrante delicto*. The police informs the prosecutor of the arrest within 24 hours. In order to validate the arrest the prosecutor requests, within 48 hours of the arrest, that a judge validates the arrest by setting the date for the hearing (for the arrest validation). Within 48 hours of the prosecutor's request, the judge must make a decision regarding the legality of the arrest.

4.1. The main issues dealt with at the arrest validation hearing

The first issue the judge has to deal with at the arrest validation hearing is to ascertain whether the police acted legally in depriving an individual of their personal freedom. This requires that the police actually caught the arrested person in *flagrante delicto*, that is, in the act of committing a crime for which the arrest is permitted by law, and that the judge was requested by the prosecutor to order the detention of Sid, Georges and Jean pending the investigation phase.

4.2. The role of defence counsel at the arrest validation hearing

At the first contact with their clients, the lawyers appointed will attempt to collect sufficient information to enable them to start preparing their case. In accordance with normal practice, the first contact between the three arrested persons and their lawyers will have taken place a few hours before the validation hearing. Given that the main act of the validation hearing is the questioning of the arrested persons, the most important issue which counsel and their clients will discuss will be what strategy to adopt at the hearing. In particular, they must decide (a) whether to answer questions or remain silent before the judge; and (b) whether to involve other persons. An important consideration is that if the suspect makes a statement implicating other persons they will become a witness in relation to those facts.

An important element to bear in mind is that, even though legally co-operation should not affect the decision, in practice co-operation increases the chances of the suspect being released. Choosing to remain silent may in practice result in detention pending the investigation and, in the worst cases, even during the trial. As a general rule, the judge cannot infer the defendant's guilt from their silence. Whilst this provision is usually strictly observed in the judgment at trial, it is often infringed in the earlier phases of the criminal process, especially in connection with the decision on limitation of the defendant's freedom pending the proceedings. In other words, even though it is forbidden by article 274a of the Code, in practice judges often place the defendant in custody pending the proceeding where they remain silent during interrogations, or where they deny responsibility. Of course, in the written justification of the decision, it is not explicitly asserted that the defendant has had their freedom limited because of the fact that they did not confess their guilt; however, every time the restriction of liberty issued by the judge is justified on the basis of the 'lack of awareness by the defendant of their conduct,' or something similar, it is reasonable to conclude that such words imply that the suspect did not confess.

The concern of the defence lawyer at the arrest validation hearing is not so much to challenge the validity of the police work, as to secure the release from custody of the arrested person. This means that the strategy of the lawyer before the judge at the arrest validation hearing is not to focus primarily on the past (that is, on the police conduct), but on the future (that is, the duty to liberate the suspect or to nake a decision other than preventive detention). In other words, the main goal of the counsel is to persuade the judge that there is no basis to detain the suspect during the investigation phase.

5. The likely outcome of the arrest validation hearing

5.1. Arrest validation

On the facts of the present case study, two of the three arrests appear to be legal, that is, the arrests of Jean and Sid. Only Georges' arrest appears to be groundless and unlawful. The judge, thus, confirms the police work and validates the arrests of Sid and Jean.

It may be assumed that Georges' arrest will not be validated by the judge. However, in practice, the outcome of the decision regarding Georges is quite uncertain. Judges are normally inclined to uphold the conduct of the police, and they refuse to confirm the police actions only when it is clearly illegal. In this case, the elements on which the police operated seem to justify, at a first sight, the arrest of Georges, who was caught in the part of the stadium where the fighting broke out. The police might have reasonably perceived that Georges was involved in the fighting. Moreover, for the reasons stated before, it may be assumed that his lawyer will focus more on the judge's duty to set Georges free than on the validity of Georges' arrest. That is to say, the lawyer will challenge the arrest performed by the police, but only as an element of a strategy that is directed at persuading the judge to release Georges.

5.2. Detention pending the proceeding

At the end of the arrest validation hearing, the judge orders the detention of Sid during the investigation phase. He was caught in the act of committing a crime, he is involved with a criminal association and, last but not least, he has a previous criminal record. He is also an alien, and as a result of this factor alone, it may be assumed that the judge is keen to consider proven the need to prevent the escape of the suspect. It is possible that even in the written justification of the detention order, Sid's nationality is mentioned as an element relevant to the decision of the judge.

The judge will probably not order the detention of Jean. He is a juvenile, and the law allows the detention of juvenile suspects pending proceeding only for crimes punishable with imprisonment of nine years or more. Moreover, he has no previous criminal record, which is interpreted as evidence that he is unlikely to commit other crimes. However, taking into account the fact that that during the interrogation the answers given by Jean were not satisfactory and in some way contradictory, the judge will put in place measures that partially limits Jean's freedom, the so called 'prescription' (prescrizione).

Georges will probably be released. The main reason is that there is a lack of evidence regarding his criminal liability. Secondly, he has no previous record. Thirdly, Georges' health is barely compatible with the detention. For these reasons, the judge rejects the prosecutor's request to order Georges' detention pending the investigation. On the same basis, the judge probably refuses to order measures that, even slightly, limit Georges' freedom, such as prohibiting him from leaving the municipal district. Finally, the judge's decision will in some way be probably influenced by the fact that Georges' wife is pregnant. In this sense, detention will probably be considered by the judge as too severe, regarding the possible consequences for Georges' family.

The prosecutor decides not to validate the search of Georges' company premises since the search did not appear to be connected with the case alleged against him.

6. Indictment and trial

6.1. Sid

After the validation of the arrest, Sid is presented directly before the judge for trial. Because of the answers given by Sid during his interrogation, and in anticipation of his likely conviction at trial, Sid's counsel will suggest that Sid should opt for an alternative means of resolving the case without trial. With the consent of the prosecutor, it may be assumed that it is possible for the defendant to opt for the application of punishment at the request of the parties, proposing in this case to the judge, together with the prosecutor, a penalty amounting to about two years' imprisonment.

After the conviction, Sid can ask the judge for an alternative means of serving the sentence; release from jail subject to monitoring by the social services. The fact that Sid is an alien does not affect his right to serve his sentence outside the jail.

6.2. *Jean*

Jean will not be brought directly to trial. Even though the law permits cases involving juveniles to go directly to trial, the prosecutor and the judge must comply with specific provisions that require them, at the beginning of the proceeding, to gather information regarding the life and the social and economic conditions of the suspect and their family. For this purpose the prosecutor may seek the help of the social services at the place where the juvenile and their family live. Moreover, in juvenile cases the prosecutor must, as soon as possible, inform the social services, and the parents of the arrested person, and take steps to supply the suspect with adequate psychological help. The observation of these provisions usually takes time and does not, in practice, allow the prosecutor to shorten the pre-trial phase and go directly to trial. For these reasons, Jean's case is treated in the usual way, and following the validation of the arrest hearing the preliminary investigations will continue for some months. At the end of the investigations, the prosecutor files an indictment against Jean. The judge then fixes the date for the preliminary hearing. During the period of the investigations, Jean is assigned to the social services operating in his area and they are asked to monitor his behavior. At the beginning of the preliminary hearing, the social services produce a report regarding the behavior of Jean during that period, with a prognosis as to the prospects for his re-integration. Assuming that the report recommends that there is a high probability of his re-integration, the judge decides to acquit Jean and to close the case with a judgment of 'judicial pardon' (*perdono giudiziale*). The judicial pardon is a peculiar form of acquittal – the juvenile accused is recognized as being guilty, but the law provides for an acquittal based on the social re-integration of the accused.

6.3. *Georges*

The investigation regarding Georges is conducted in the ordinary way. Indeed, many doubts as to his criminal liability emerge following the arrest validation stage. The prosecutor, thus, carries out some other inquiries, with the aim of ascertaining more clearly the conduct of the suspect. At the end of the investigation phase, the prosecutor asks the judge to discontinue the case because of the lack of evidence gathered against Georges. If, hypothetically, the prosecutor has decided to file an indictment against Georges, it may be presumed that Georges' counsel will have suggested that Georges challenges the prosecution case at trial. At trial, the accused is guaranteed the ability to challenge the evidence presented by the prosecutor, including by cross-examination of the witnesses. Therefore, Georges will have, at trial, the best chance of securing an acquittal.

Ties Prakken
Taru Spronken

CASE STUDY: THE NETHERLANDS

1. Arrest

Arrest is permitted for any offence where the suspect is caught in the act, or where there are reasonable grounds for suspecting that the suspect has committed an act that will result in them being detained on remand. The latter is the case where the penalty exceeds four years imprisonment or where the offence is enumerated in article 67 CCP. Jean is arrested for assaulting another person, punishable as 'ill treatment' (*mishandeling*),[1] for which there is a maximum penalty of two years imprisonment.[2] However, ill-treatment is included in the list of offences for which the law allows detention on remand and therefore arrest is permitted, in order to discover the truth. The same applies to Georges, whose arrest is probably based on suspicion of having participated in public collective violence (*openlijke geweldpleging*),[3] by belonging to the group that initiated the violence. This offence is punishable with a maximum of four years' imprisonment. Presumably Jean and Georges were caught in the act. This provides, in itself, a ground for arrest regardless ofwhether detention on remand would be allowed. The position is different for Sid, who has been arrested on suspicion of membership of a criminal organisation (*deelneming aan een criminele organisatie*).[4] He had already been under surveillance for a number of months, and it is questionable whether he was caught doing anything at the football stadium. Therefore, he can only be arrested when a warrant has been issued by an (assistant) prosecutor. The police can, however, arrest Sid without waiting for the warrant if they fear he would otherwise disappear, on the condition that he is taken before an (assistant) prosecutor immediately following his arrest. The other requirements for arrest, assuming that there is a reasonable suspicion of participation in a criminal organisation (an offence which carries a maximum sentence of six years' imprisonment) are satisfied.

---

[1]   Art. 300 Criminal Code (*Wetboek van Strafrecht*).
[2]   There are a number of forms of ill treatment, ranging from simple ill treatment, ill treatment with intent, to ill treatment causing grievous bodily harm with intent, or 'terroristic' intent.
[3]   Article 141 Criminal Code.
[4]   Article 140 Criminal Code.

Having been arrested the three suspects must be taken to a police station as soon as practicable in order to be brought before a prosecutor or assistant prosecutor for interrogation. In practice a suspect is always taken before an assistant prosecutor, since in every police station there are several police officers who are also assistant prosecutors. Therefore, it is police officers who liaise between the police officers conducting the investigation and the public prosecutor.

Jean, Georges and Sid must be informed orally of the facts of and grounds for arrest by the assistant prosecutor as soon as they arrive at the police station. This is not required by the CCP, but derives from the direct applicability of ECHR article 5, § 2.[5] The men can be kept at the police station for interrogation and identification for a maximum period of six hours from the moment they arrive at the police station without any further formal requirements except that there must be a reasonable suspicion that they committed an offence.[6] However, any period between midnight and 9:00 am is effectively ignored, so that the maximum period may be extended to 15 hours. After this period the (assistant) prosecutor may order police custody for a period of three days if this is in the interest of the investigation, to secure or preserve evidence or to obtain evidence by questioning the men.

A person who has been unlawfully arrested may be released by an investigating judge, before which the suspect has to be brought within a period of three days and 15 hours after arrest.[7] The investigating judge tests the lawfulness of the police custody and can order immediate release if: a) there is no reasonable suspicion that the suspect committed the offence, b) the offence does not allow detention on remand or time limits are not complied with, c) the arrest and detention is not necessary in the interest of the investigation, or d) the arrest and detention is in breach of due process. If there are no facts or circumstances on which the police can base reasonable suspicion, Georges and Jean could apply to the investigating judge for release immediately, even before the three days and 15 hours has expired. The same applies to Sid if the results of the police surveillance do not justify reasonable suspicion. In practice, however, they would only be able to make an effective application if they had a lawyer to assist them immediately after arrest. The police are not under a duty to inform the suspects that this is possible, and even if they do know their rights, without the assistance of a lawyer it would be very difficult for them to apply for immediate release themselves. They would not be in the position to write to or telephone the investigating judge, nor would they have access to the information the police have against them at this stage of interrogation.

Georges, the only one who has used a lawyer in the Netherlands before, has the right to contact the lawyer immediately after his arrival at the police station.[8] However, even if the lawyer is able to attend the police station straightaway, the

---

5   Art. 5, § 2 ECHR provides: 'Everyone who is arrested shall be informed promptly, in a language which he understands, of the reasons for his arrest and of any charge against him'.
6   If a suspect refuses to identify themselves and does not carry any ID papers, police custody can be extended for six hours for the purpose of identification (art. 61 § 2 CCP).
7   Art. 59a CCP.
8   Art. 28 CCP.

police can prevent them from speaking to Georges before questioning takes place.[9] Therefore, the lawyer would have to wait until Georges has been interrogated before being able to gain access to him. If Georges tells his lawyer he took no part in the violence at all, his lawyer could contact the prosecutor in order to argue for his release. If the prosecutor cannot be reached or does not want to release Georges, the lawyer could try to arrange a hearing with the investigating judge. Normally, however, the lawyer will not succeed in doing anything effective at this initial stage because of lack of information as to the factual basis of the arrest and because it will be very difficult to secure an immediate hearing before the investigating judge (although in theory this should be possible). Frequently, lawyers do not undertake any action in the period during which the suspect is questioned at the police station, but wait until they are provided with information in the file, which in practice is shortly before the suspect is brought before the investigating judge. Jean and Sid cannot consult a lawyer during the period of police questioning if they do not know one or cannot afford one. This applies to Jean even though he is a juvenile. Juveniles can be questioned by the police without a lawyer or parent being present.

2.   Detention – rights and procedure

2.1.   Police interview

The assistant prosecutor can determine that the men should be released immediately if there is no reasonable suspicion that they have committed an offence, but in practice this rarely happens. Normally the assistant prosecutor will order that the men should be kept in custody in order that the police can interrogate them. If Georges mentions to the assistant prosecutor that he is diabetic and needs medicine, this will be taken care of, and he will be seen by a doctor and receive his medicine.

The police interview will normally take place within the period a suspect can be held for questioning (i.e. 15 hours where night-time is included), although it is possible, especially when a lot of people are arrested (which is often the case when football violence is involved), that Georges, Jean and Sid will not be interviewed at all within this period. If the police have enough evidence upon which to base reasonable suspicion the assistant prosecutor can, in the case of a suspected offence that allows detention on remand (see below), order that the men be detained in police custody (*inverzekeringstelling*) for a maximum period of three days in the interests of the investigation, in order to provide the police with more time for questioning and other investigations. It will be the police, rather than a prosecutor or judge, who will interview the men during the period of police custody. Georges and Jean may be confronted with other suspects, witnesses or victims who are able provide the police with evidence on their participation in the violence. The witnesses will also make statements to the police, although the police have no

---

[9]   HR 23 May 1995, DD 1995, No. 95.325 and P.W. van der Kuijs, 'Kanttekeningen bij de inverzekeringstelling,' *Advocatenblad 1995*, No. 20.

powers to force them to do so. In practice, statements of witnesses or victims are recorded by the police in the same way as statements of suspects are (see below). Sid can be confronted during questioning with the material gained from the police surveillance previously conducted.

Before the police interview starts, the interrogating officer must caution the men and inform them that they have the right to remain silent. There is no statutory requirement that they have to be informed of any other right, such as legal advice, nor that they must be given written information on their legal position. At some police stations there are leaflets that inform detainees of their rights. There is no right to have counsel present during the police interview or to have access to legal advice before the police interview.

2.2. *Caution and evidential value of police records*

The wording of the caution is normally included in the format of the document on which the interview is recorded. It reads: 'The suspect has been told that he has the right to remain silent.' Its inclusion on the document makes it difficult for a defendant to prove that the caution was not given. The caution is often mentioned casually, immediately followed by advice that it is much better to co-operate with the police, and suspects often do not remember having been cautioned. The interviews of the men will not be tape-recorded or recorded verbatim in writing. The police will prepare their own résumé of the answers they are given and the men will be asked to sign the record. If they refuse to sign, this is also recorded. It will, however, have no consequences for the evidential value of the police record: it can be used as evidence in any event. As noted earlier, the same procedure is used in respect of witnesses and victims. Usually their statements are not recorded,[10] but the record of what they say can be used as evidence in court. In Dutch criminal procedure hearsay evidence is admissible, as are records drawn up by the police or the investigating judge. Even if the defendant's statements in court differs from those made to the police and/or the investigating judge, the trial judge is free to decide which statement they regard as being the most convincing and to use that as evidence. Therefore, Sid, Georges and Jean may be confronted with their statements being used as evidence against them at their trial, even if they have refused to sign the record. This is why suspects who are familiar with the proceedings at the police station or who are able to obtain legal advice before they are arrested tend, or are advised by their lawyer, to remain silent until they are given access to the file (i.e. when they are brought before the investigating judge who considers the legality of their arrest). Many suspects, however, are not capable of following this strategy under questioning because they have had no right to access a lawyer during interrogation and, without being able to consult with their lawyer during questioning, are convinced by the police that it is better to co-operate. On the other hand, if they choose to remain silent, this can have repercussions for the length of

---

10   In exceptional cases, for instance in case of sexual abuse of children, the questioning of the children is recorded.

their pre-trial detention because the prosecutor may argue that it is in the interest of the investigation that they remain detained because it is necessary to discover the truth by means other than the statement of the suspect. When the evidence gathered by the police is strong, lawyers tend to advise their clients to admit the offence, which increases the chances of being released before trial. As noted above, well-founded legal advice can only be given after disclosure of the evidence in the file.

2.3. Interpreter

Sid, who is not a Dutch citizen, has a right to have an interpreter present during his interview by the police if he does not understand or speak the language. It is the police who decide whether an interpreter is necessary. If Sid is of the opinion that he is not able to communicate properly with the police, and the police are of a different opinion, he could use his right to silence in order to press the police to call an interpreter. The problem in practice, however, is that before the initial police interview Sid has no access to a lawyer who could advise him on this subject. There is often disagreement on the issue of whether an interpreter was necessary during a police interview. However, such disputes have to be conducted retrospectively, for instance, when the suspect is taken before the investigating judge who has to test the legality of the police custody, because the defence lawyer is rarely present during the interview. If it can be established that an interpreter was necessary, the trial judge can exclude the police record from the evidence if the interview was conducted without the assistance of an interpreter. The situation is different with regard to communication between Sid and his defence counsel. It will be for Sid's counsel to decide whether an interpreter is needed, and the lawyer may obtain one for free under the legal aid scheme when visiting their client in the police station.

2.4. Police custody and legal advice

Once police custody is ordered after the initial six (or 15) hours, Georges, Jean and Sid are entitled to consult with a lawyer who will be assigned to them during the period of police custody. This is provided free, without reference to the suspect's financial resources, by lawyers who have enlisted under the legal aid scheme (the so-called *piket service*). The police are not obliged to tell the men of their right to legal advice when police custody is ordered. They will only learn of this right when the lawyer arrives at the police station to visit them. If Georges has asked to consult his own lawyer, that lawyer can be assigned as long as they are enlisted for the *piket service*. Otherwise Georges would have to pay for his lawyer himself. He can also ask the *piket* lawyer to contact his own lawyer. In that case the *piket* lawyer and Georges' lawyer will have to make arrangements on the division of the payment for their services.

The police must immediately inform the *piket* service lawyer when custody is confirmed. Usually the order confirming police custody (*bevel inverzekeringstelling*) is sent to the lawyer on duty (or chosen lawyer) by fax. The lawyer is thus informed of the personal particulars of the suspect, and of the offence the suspect is charged with, which are mentioned in the order. Only one or two lawyers are on duty during the day in any district, which can include several police stations, and it is often the case that they are unable to visit all suspects in police custody on the day custody is confirmed. Therefore, it is possible that Georges, Jean and Sid will see a lawyer for the first time after two days of detention at the police station. Lawyers normally call the police station to make an appointment before they attend to visit their clients. Often they can only make visits during office hours, even though the police station is open for 24 hours a day and the police continue to conduct interrogations during the night. Access may also be delayed until the end of any police interrogation.

If there is more than one suspect in a case, the police will contact a lawyer for each suspect, but it is also possible that all three men in the present case will be visited by one lawyer, who will have to decide whether there are any conflicts of interest. If this is the case it is left to the lawyer to arrange legal assistance by other lawyers, and they will normally pick the next lawyer on duty on the list. The next listed lawyer will do the same if they are unable to deal with all the suspects in police custody in the district for which they are on duty.

2.5. *Detention on remand*

During the period of interrogation and police custody which, as noted, can last for three days and 15 hours, the police will try to gather as much as evidence as possible and clarify the facts. At the end of this period the prosecutor must decide either to release the suspect or request detention on remand. This is a crucial phase for the three men. In order to continue preliminary detention there must be a 'serious suspicion,' which is a heavier requirement than the reasonable suspicion required for the arrest and police custody: there must be evidence that the suspect probably committed the offence, and additional grounds are required if the investigation has been completed.[11] The likely period of detention for each of the three men in the case study is set out below.

2.5.1. Georges

If there is no proof that Georges actually participated in the violence, even by encouraging others or by creating an atmosphere of anonymity to protect others from being arrested, the prosecutor probably will decide to release him after the period of questioning of six (or 15) hours, even if Georges remains silent during questioning. Because he has remained silent, the prosecutor will need other

---

[11]   Art. 67a CCP mentions (i) a risk that the suspect might flee, (ii) the danger that the suspect might commit another offence punishable by a penalty of at least six years' imprisonment, (iii) if the offence has seriously shocked society and the offence is punishable by a penalty of at least twelve years' imprisonment, (iv) a risk that the suspect might prevent or obstruct the investigation into his case, and (v) in case of danger of recidivism of a listed number of offences, especially some minor offences that are seen as a threat to public order like systematic shoplifting etc.

evidence that Georges committed the suspected offence. If this kind of evidence is available (for instance, material from surveillance cameras in the stadium), and further investigation is needed, the prosecutor will request custody on remand for 14 days. If this is the case, Georges and his lawyer will be provided with the information in the file that will also be made available to the investigating judge who adjudicates at the hearing to decide on the lawfulness of the arrest and the associated custodial remand request. The fact that Georges refused to answer any questions has no implications for the trial in the sense that this could be held against him, but in practice it will make it more likely that the investigating judge will order custody on remand, provided that there are grounds on which to base a serious suspicion. For this, additional evidence that Georges probably committed the offence he is suspected of would be required. If there is no additional evidence the investigating judge will probably release Georges.

Even if there is additional evidence, Georges will have a good chance of being released by the investigating judge if they are not convinced that further detention is in the interest of the investigation. The fact that Georges has never been arrested before, his wife is expecting a baby in the near future, and that he has a company of his own he has to run, will be taken into account. Whether he will be released is, however, also dependent on the seriousness of the violence that has occurred and his alleged part in it. The investigating judge can decide to order custody on remand and suspend it on the conditions that Georges makes himself available for questioning or for witness confrontation. If, however, the investigating judge fears that Georges will obstruct the investigation by, for instance, influencing witnesses that still have to be interviewed by the police, it will be unlikely that the judge will suspend the remand in custody. If Georges remains silent the need for further investigation will be more easily accepted, provided that there is not enough evidence for a conviction. If, despite Georges' silence, there is enough evidence on which to found a conviction, and the investigation is regarded as completed, Georges will probably be released pending trial. Thus, if there is additional evidence that Georges was involved in the violence, whether the investigating judge orders his detention or release will depend on the impression the investigating judge forms of Georges during the hearing, the seriousness of the violence that has occurred, and whether there is a need for further investigation.

If the investigating judge orders a remand in custody for 14 days, and does not suspend the execution, Georges must be heard by the court if the prosecutor requests extension of the detention. The court can order detention on remand for a maximum period of 90 days. The court can also decide to suspend the detention on remand on certain conditions. In the case of Georges it is not likely that the court would order detention on remand after custody on remand because it is unlikely that Georges will receive a lengthy prison sentence (unless it can be proven that he actually caused grave bodily harm to somebody).

Georges' company premises were searched. Search is permitted in cases where the suspect has been caught in the act of any offence, and otherwise if there is a suspicion of an offence for which pre-trial detention is allowed. It is normally the (deputy) prosecutor who carries out the search. If the search is conducted in a home, consent of the resident or a warrant from the investigating judge is required. In that case it is the investigating judge who carries out the search, although if it is not possible to wait for the arrival of the (investigating) judge the prosecutor may start searching. Search of the premises of persons other than a suspect are permitted if evidence is 'reasonably suspected' to be found there. Therefore, the search of the premises of Georges' company is in principle permitted if the police could reasonably expect to find something relevant to the offence of which he is suspected. Given the offence of which he is suspected, it is unlikely that the police would find relevant evidence in his office. This could mean that the search is unlawful. This, however, would have no consequence if no evidence found. If, however, criminal proceedings end in Georges being acquitted, he could seek compensation if the search has caused damage to his company.

2.5.2. Jean

As Jean is under 18 years the rules concerning juveniles are applicable, which means that the juvenile court magistrate has the responsibility to test the police custody and to decide on further pre-trial detention. Jean's parents must be informed of his arrest as soon as possible and they have the right to confidential contact (visit, telephone and letters) under the same conditions as a lawyer during the first six (or 15) hours of police interrogation.[12] Jean does not have the right to have counsel or his parents present during police interview, or to consult with them before the interview. In practice neither Jean nor his parents will be informed of their right to confidential communication because the police have no duty to do so.

Pre-trial detention is allowed under the same circumstances as for adults, but detention may be ordered in the form of confinement to the suspect's home, and suspension of the detention under more or less pedagogically inspired conditions is often applied. The Child Protection Board must be informed as soon as police custody is ordered,[13] and it plays an important role from the beginning until the end of proceedings in advising the juvenile judge.

As a juvenile Jean is not supposed to be detained for a long time for an offence like this. The prosecutor can request the juvenile magistrate to order custody on remand for pedagogical reasons, but it is also possible, given that Jean has never been arrested before, that the prosecutor will send him home. Jean has the right to remain silent, and is free to answer some police questions and not others. This has no implications for trial. In this respect Jean is in the same position as Georges. The procedure for juveniles is, however, also considered to have pedagogic goals and some juvenile judges are not pleased when a juvenile chooses to remain silent or when a lawyer advises a young client to say nothing. Silence can therefore have impact on sentence. The juvenile judge can order custody on remand to be suspended under certain conditions. One of these conditions could be that Jean fulfils some pedagogically inspired tasks that may be taken into account when

---

12   Art. 490 CCP and art. 42 *Beginselenwet justitiële jeugdinrichtingen.*
13   Art. 491 CCP.

sentence is later imposed. Jean can expect a restraining order in respect of attending football matches.

2.5.3. Sid

Sid's arrest is based on police surveillance and whether there are sufficient grounds to order custody on remand will depend on the content of the surveillance material and his statements to the police. Since secret surveillance is subject to certain formalities, such as warrants and time limits, Sid has a legitimate interest in questioning its legality. He will not be able to do this during his interview with the police, because no counsel is present and the police will only tell him what they believe is in their interests in order to obtain as much information from him as possible. When he is taken before an investigating judge (within three days and 15 hours), the prosecutor will be obliged to add the results of the surveillance to the case file records. The complete results, however, are disclosed 'as soon as the interest of discovering the truth permits' and only if they are, in the prosecutor's opinion, relevant to the case. If the prosecutor determines that the surveillance records are not relevant they are only obliged to disclose in general terms the secret methods that have been used. The defence may ask for certain specified records to be put in the file, but the difficulty for the defence is that they normally will not know, without having seen them, which records are relevant. Sid's ability to scrutinise or question the lawfulness of the surveillance is, therefore, weak. In cases where the secret surveillance has taken place in the suspect's own country, the Dutch judiciary are very unlikely to be willing to review the lawfulness of such actions.

If the police are not willing to tell Sid what they know, or to reveal the source of their knowledge, he could keep silent until he can discuss the file with his counsel. However, from the case study it appears that he answered all questions and that some of his answers indicate that he was indeed implicated with others in organised football violence. These statements can be used as evidence in court, even if Sid later changes his statements or decides to remain silent in court. The court is free to use as evidence the statement they believe to be the most trustworthy.

As a foreigner, Sid's chances of being released after police custody are more problematic provided that the prosecutor can establish a 'serious suspicion.' If so, detention can be ordered on the ground that he might flee. It is possible to suspend a detention order on the payment of a sum of money, but this is rarely applied. Sid would, at least, have to convince the investigating judge that he has a fixed address in his own country and that he has a job to lose – circumstances that make it unlikely that he will abscond. If Sid does not manage to convince the court to release him, he will probably remain detained until the court hearing, that is, for a maximum period of 110 days and 15 hours. He can expect that the sentence he will receive, should he be convicted, will be of the approximate length of the pre-trial detention period. It is likely that Sid will have a sentence condition imposed that will prevent him from ever attending a football match in the Netherlands.

Piotr Kruszyński

CASE STUDY: POLAND

1.   First stage: rights during arrest and custody

Georges

Once arrested Georges must be immediately informed of the reasons for his detention, which will probably be that he has participated in a fight. He should then be orally informed by a policeman of his rights to request a lawyer, to have someone informed of his detention, and to appeal to the court in order that the grounds for, legitimacy and accuracy of the detention be examined.

Georges will subsequently be given the opportunity to make a statement to the police, rather than being interviewed by them. As long as he is not formally charged, he has the status of a suspected person. As a consequence, in this phase of police detention he is not informed of the basic rights and obligations assigned to a suspect, such as the right to silence. Georges can voluntarily make a statement with regard to the alleged offence. He has a right to contact his lawyer directly and may request them to be present. The police will compile an official record of the detention, and include any statements made by Georges, and a copy thereof will be given to him.

Georges may, himself or through his lawyer, make a written complaint about his detention to the court within seven days. At this stage, his lawyer may assist Georges in establishing that his explanations are true, for example, by calling witnesses or evidence from CCTV. If the court believes his explanation that he did not take part in any act of violence it will order that he be immediately released.

If Georges' medical condition threatens his life or health, or if he requests medical assistance, this will be provided by the closest healthcare centre. The police will arrange for him to be taken there and, depending on his condition, he may be transported by a patrol car in handcuffs, or without them, or in an ambulance under supervision of the police. After the medical assistance is provided the physician will certify whether he is fit to be detained.

With regard to the police investigation during the first period of police detention Georges, may:

- be subjected to external inspection of his body and other examinations that do not interfere with his bodily integrity, and may have his fingerprints and photograph taken, and be presented to other persons for recognition purposes;
- have blood, hair or other body samples taken by an authorised healthcare employee, provided that they are necessary and do not threaten his health;
- have a sample taken from inside his mouth by a police officer, provided it is necessary and does not threaten his health.

These procedures can be carried out irrespective of whether Georges consents, and whether or not he has been formally interviewed.

Georges may be detained by the police for up to 48 hours without a formal charge. If, however, the prosecutor requests the court to order preliminary detention within this period and, therefore, he is officially charged, he may be detained for a further 24 hours during which period the court must decide on preliminary detention. Thus Georges may be detained for up to 72 hours before the court makes a decision on his detention.

Immediately following Georges' arrest, the police will begin to gather evidence in respect of the suspected offence, and will notify the Public Prosecutor. If there are grounds for applying for preliminary detention of Georges, the prosecutor will formulate a written charge and make an application to the court for preliminary detention, in accordance with the following procedure: Georges is formally charged; he is then informed of the basic rights and obligations of a suspect; an interview is then conducted; and finally a motion for preliminary detention and referral of Georges to the court will be submitted by the prosecutor. This procedure must be carried out within 48 hours of his initial arrest. George may be formally charged only if the evidence (e.g. depositions of witnesses, any traces and evidence found in the place where the act was committed) sufficiently justifies a suspicion that Georges has committed a criminal offence. The charge must identify the suspect (i.e. Georges), and precisely determine the alleged offence (i.e. participation in a fight) and its legal definition (article 158 § 1 of the Criminal Code).

The information given to George as to his rights must be in writing, in a standard form. The rights at this stage differ from those immediately following arrest, and consist of the right to:

- give an explanation;
- refuse to give an explanation;
- refuse to answers questions;
- request that investigative acts or inquiries be conducted;
-   legal advice;
- examine the evidence on completion of the investigation;
- request the presence of the defence lawyer in interviews.

However, Georges is not entitled to a publicly funded lawyer at this stage. In practice, it is possible for him to obtain legal assistance if he knows a lawyer and can pay for his legal assistance, and if the lawyer is not available they may contact the Bar Council who may nominate another lawyer. If Georges does instruct a lawyer, they may attend the interview but it is not obligatory to inform the lawyer of the time of the hearing unless George expressly requests this.

In Georges' case it is unlikely that he will be subjected to temporary detention in view of the fact that he suffers from diabetes and his wife is pregnant. If Georges is released, there are no time limits within which the case must be dealt with, although given the nature of the case it is likely to be tried within a relatively short period.

Sid

Sid is likely to be dealt with in a similar way to Georges. If he is charged with participation in fighting it will be unnecessary for the prosecutor to prove Sid's precise role, for example, how many blows he delivered, whether he delivered them at all, or whether his role was limited to encouraging the fight. Sid's prior record in relation to football violence has no bearing on the offence with which he will be charged, although it will be taken into account by the court in sentencing him.

The fact that Sid does not speak Polish means that it is likely that he will be assigned a public defence lawyer by the court. If Sid wishes to instruct a lawyer from his own country, the lawyer appointed by the court will act until Sid's lawyer arrives.[1] Sid will be informed of his rights in the same way as Georges. The court is likely to order preliminary detention since he has no permanent place of residence in Poland

Jean

Jean is 16 years old, and since he is a juvenile the proceedings against him will be conducted pursuant to the Act on the Proceedings in Juvenile Cases of 26 October 1982. Jean will be charged with participation in a fight. He may be detained by the police, but he must be placed in a juvenile detention facility. He must be immediately informed by the police of the reasons for his detention, his right to appeal (which would be heard by a family judge) and of his other rights such as his right to assistance of a lawyer. However, the Act requires that his case be conducted, from the beginning until the end, by a family judge, and the police will perform any activities ordered by the judge as well as those that the police are explicitly authorised to carry out under the aforementioned Act.

The police must immediately inform Jean's parents or legal custodians of his detention, and they must be given the same information as is required to be given to Jean, i.e., the reasons for detention, that he has a right to legal advice, and his right to appeal to a court. The police prepare an official record of Jean's detention and must, within 24 hours after detention commences, notify the relevant family court. The court may decide to place him in a hostel for juveniles or temporarily place him in a juvenile educational institution, a juvenile socio-therapy centre or a healthcare centre or unit for up to 48 hours. Jean may be interviewed by the police and a family

---

[1]   According to the Act of 2 July 2002 on the Provision of Legal Assistance by Foreign Lawyers in the Republic of Poland, a foreign lawyer has to be on the list of European Union lawyers who intend to render legal assistance, see § 3 below.

judge. In this phase of the investigation Jean is not entitled to legal assistance *ex officio*, although he or his parents of custodian may appoint a defence lawyer if they are able to pay. However, if Jean is placed in a hostel for juveniles the appointment of a defence lawyer is mandatory, and if he or his parents have not appointed one, the family judge will appoint a public defence lawyer.

The police may interview Jean, provided that the interview takes place in the presence of his parents or legal custodians, or the defence lawyer; although if it is impossible to ensure their presence the court must call a teacher, a representative of a district family assistance centre or a representative of a social organisation to attend the interview. In practice, if parents, legal custodians or the defence lawyer are not available the police will contact an appropriate person from a list kept by them. An interview cannot take place in the absence of such an adult.

Jean must be released and transferred to his parents or legal custodians without delay:

- if the reason for his detention no longer applies;
- if the family court instructs the police to do so;
- if the family court is not notified of the detention within 24 hours from commencement of the detention;
- if Jean is placed in a hostel for juveniles etc., on the expiry of 72 hours commencing from the time he was first detained.

The decision whether to commence proceedings against Jean is taken by the family judge. He may be detained pending trial if the circumstances of the case make this necessary and there is reasonable concern that he would flee, interfere with evidence, or if it is impossible to establish Jean's identity. Detention may be by the police for a maximum of 72 hours, and thereafter must be in a hostel for juveniles. The maximum period of detention pending trial is three months, although this may be extended at three monthly intervals up to a total maximum of one year.

2. Right to an interpreter

Since Sid does not speak Polish he has a right to an interpreter paid for by the state, who must attend whenever Sid is involved in the proceedings. In addition, the formal charge, any amendment of the charge, the indictment, and any decision that may be appealed, must be translated. However, if Sid consents, only the judgement completing the proceedings need be translated provided that it is not subject to appeal.

3. Right to speak to a lawyer before the first interview

All three detainees have a right to contact their lawyer and talk to them before they are interviewed, although the detaining authority may insist on being present. At this stage the lawyer has no power to insist on a private consultation with their client. Depending on the arrangements made between the lawyer and the client, the lawyer will provide advice by telephone or attend the police station in person. The lawyer has a right to be present during the interview of the client irrespective of who the interviewer is.

In this case Georges has exercised his right and he will use the lawyer of his choice. Sid, who has a lawyer in his country of origin, may obtain the advice of that lawyer on the telephone provided that, by virtue of the Act of 2 July 2002 on the Provision of Legal Assistance by Foreign Lawyers in the Republic of Poland, the lawyer is on the list of European Union lawyers who intend to render legal assistance (such list being maintained by the regional Bar councils). In practice it will be impossible for Sid to appoint a foreign defence lawyer, who is not so listed, at short notice. If Sid's lawyer is not listed he may obtain advice from a Polish public lawyer if the court orders that, due to the circumstances which make the defence more difficult, such a lawyer should be appointed. In practice, in a situation like Sid's, a public defence lawyer is always appointed. Jean and his parents or legal custodian may appoint a defence lawyer of their choice. If Jean does not have such defence lawyer, he will be assigned a public defence lawyer, but only if the family judge has decided to place Jean in a hostel for juveniles.

4. Presence lawyer during police interview

If Sid, Jean and Georges request that they be interviewed in presence of their lawyer, then the lawyer must be permitted to attend. The right to interview in the presence of a defence lawyer is observed in practice, although generally the right is only exercised by educated persons of means, who are aware of their rights and the consequences that may flow from the interview. In practice, defence lawyers generally agree the interview date with the interviewing authority. If, for any reason, the defence lawyer is unable to attend they must inform the interviewing authority.

5. Access to the file

When the investigation is completed, Sid will be notified of the date on which he may familiarise with the investigation materials and of his right to oral and written notification of the justification for the charge(s). The written justification is served both upon Sid and his appointed lawyer within 14 days. The justification must, in particular, set out the facts and the evidence which were adopted as the grounds for the charge(s). Sid has a right of access to the case files after he is charged and with the consent of the authority that conducts the proceedings. Sid has no right to information about the evidence before he is charged.

6. Search at Georges' premises

The prosecution authorities have a right to search premises to look for material that may constitute evidence in the case or which may be seized in the criminal proceedings. To that end, they may search his office premises and other places provided there are reasonable grounds to assume that the aforementioned material can be found there. Given the offence that Georges is suspected of committing, i.e., participation in a fight, there are no grounds for searching Georges' company premise unless, for example, he used a knife, gun or any other dangerous weapon which he is suspected of hiding at the premises. When conducting the search, the prosecution authorities will have to present the authority for the search and ask the person to release the objects on a voluntary basis. If the objects are not released voluntarily or there are doubts as regards the release of all objects, the prosecution authorities will proceed with the actual search.

7.   Recording of the interview

Interviews are not normally tape-recorded, although this is possible. Any explanations of the suspect are drawn up in the official record as precisely as possible, but Sid may request that anything which concerns his rights or interests be included thoroughly in such official record. Sid has a right to request that sections of his statements included in the official record be read out to him and he also has a right to modify his statement. Sid signs the official record, but before he does so, he should read it (in this particular case it will the interpreter who will read it aloud since Sid does not speak Polish), confirm that he has done so, and sign the record. Should Sid refuse to sign the official record, this refusal and the reasons for it (if known) must be included in the record. The interpreter will also have to sign the official record. Sid has a right to raise objections as to the content of the official record, and such objections must be included in the record together with a statement by the person who performs the relevant action. If the interview is tape-recorded Sid must be given notice of this before it commences. Any recording may be confined to the most important statements made by Sid. The recording, and the transcript of it, should be attached to the official record. Similarly, if the interview is recorded by shorthand notes the record may be limited to Sid's most important statements. In such case, the stenographer will translate their shorthand notes into regular writing, and the shorthand notes and their translation will be attached to the official record.

8.   Use of police interviews at trial

If at trial the accused refuses to provide an explanation, or provides a different explanation than that previously provided, or states that they no longer remember certain facts, the official record of any previous explanation or statement may be read at trial and used as evidence. The official record is read aloud only to the extent that the accused does not give evidence, or gives different evidence, although if the accused refuses to give any explanation the whole record will be read. After the official record is read out, the judge will ask the accused to give a view on its contents and explain any discrepancies. Given that at the investigative stage Sid provided an explanation during the interview, it will be possible for the official record of that explanation to be read at trial if he then refuses to give evidence, or gives a different version of events, or states that he no longer remembers.

9. Release on bail and commencement of criminal proceedings

Preliminary detention cannot be ordered if it is sufficient to apply another preventive measure such as civil bail or a ban on leaving the country. However, the court will not accept civil bail unless it is a sufficient measure, that is, it will secure the correct course of the proceedings.

In the case of Georges, the fact that his wife is pregnant is a material circumstance that may cause the court not to order preliminary detention because his imprisonment would involve severe consequences for his closest family. If it does order preliminary detention it may order that this be changed if, by a specified date, a security is deposited. Alternatively, it may refuse to order preliminary detention in which case the Public Prosecutor may apply another preventive measure such as civil bail. If it does order preliminary detention, Georges may be detained for up to three months. If, during that time, the investigative proceedings are not completed, the detention may be extended for up to a further nine months (i.e. 12 months in aggregate). The period of 12 months may be extended by the court of appeal, but the total period of detention before the issue of the first judgement by a court of first instance may as a rule not exceed two years.

Sid is in a similar position to Georges, although if preliminary detention is not imposed, an order preventing him from leaving the country and/or requiring him to surrender his passport or other travel document, could be made. Since Sid is a foreigner, the Minister of Justice, acting *ex officio* or on the initiative of the court or the Public Prosecutor, may request Sid's home country or country in which he is a permanent resident to take over the criminal prosecution. If the prosecution is taken over in this way, the proceedings are deemed to have been discontinued. This means that the proceedings could be re-commenced if the proceedings are discontinued abroad.

As noted earlier, Jean may be placed in a hostel for juveniles, which is the equivalent of preliminary detention. At the end of the proceedings the family judge may transfer Jean to his parents or legal custodians, but may also apply one of the temporary measures: surveillance by a youth organisation, social organisation, his employers, judicial trustee, or by a trustworthy person; placement in a juvenile educational institution, a juvenile socio-therapy centre, or in an educational centre; or medical and educational measures. Placement in an appropriate place may be ordered if surveillance does not fulfil the protective purposes and is insufficient, in particular, in view of the adverse environment in which the juvenile lives.

TIMELINE ARREST AND PRE-TRIAL DETENTION BELGIUM

Time	Event
00.00	**Administrative arrest** – autonomous police power where person has e.g. disturbed public order. A trusted person may be informed of the detention. Police may question person. No caution re the right to silence. Suspect has right to copy of interview report. No access to a lawyer at this stage
	Judicial arrest can be made by the police where the person is caught red-handed. The prosecutor must be informed as soon as possible. If not caught red-handed, the prosecutor or investigating judge decide on the judicial arrest. They can only order judicial arrest when serious indications exist that the person is involved in a criminal offence. The police may question the person. Suspect has the right to a copy of the interview report. No access to a lawyer at this stage
12.00	Those under **administrative arrest** must be released, unless the prosecutor decides to convert the administrative arrest into a judicial arrest
24.00	If not released on a decision of the prosecutor before the end of that period, those under **judicial arrest** must be interrogated (without a caution) by an investigating judge within 24 hours. This is not tape recorded, but written down. Suspect has right to copy of interview report. The judge must inform the suspect of the charges against her and of the possibility that an arrest warrant will be issued. This judge must then either issue an arrest warrant (where the person is suspected of an offence for which the penalty might be one year of imprisonment or more, where it is considered as an absolute need for public safety and e.g. risk of flight, interference with evidence or witnesses) or release the suspect. The suspect may have access to a lawyer once this interview has taken place.
6 days	Detention confirmed by the Investigative Chamber of Court (or the indictment section of the Appeal Court) that sits in camera. Must then be renewed every month, or every three months for serious offences. (Defence has access to file 2 days before each confirmation hearing). The defence may make representations at the detention hearing. No limit on detention period.
Note:	No right to a defence lawyer; no caution; no right of suspect to inform another of her detention in judicial arrest; no right to be told of the charges for which initially arrested until interviewed by judge.

TIMELINE ARREST AND PRE-TRIAL DETENTION ENGLAND AND WALES

Time	Event
	Arrest – An arrested person must normally be taken to a police station as soon as practicable after arrest.
00.00 hours	**Arrival and detention at a police station** – detention decision made by the custody officer. Suspect entitled to legal advice including during police interrogation (unless delayed by police for up to 36 hours *or 48 hours*), to have someone informed of their arrest (unless delayed by police for up to 36 hours *or 48 hours*), to an appropriate adult if a juvenile or mentally vulnerable, to written notice of their rights.
06.00 hours	**First review of detention must be conducted** – *except in terrorism cases, where reviews must be conducted as soon as practicable after arrest, and then at 12 hour intervals*
15.00 hours	**Second review of detention must be conducted** – if detention continues beyond this time, reviews of detention must be conducted every nine hours.
24.00 hours	**The decision to charge must be made or the suspect released** – unless further detention without charge is authorised. If charged, the custody officer decides whether to grant bail pending the first court hearing. If bail denied, the suspect must be produced in court as soon as practicable (normally within 24 hours, although it may be longer if it is a weekend or a public holiday). If bail granted, the suspect is normally required to appear in court within 24 hours (although it may be longer if the court is not sitting within that time limit). See Note 2.
36.00 hours	**The decision to charge must be made or the suspect released** (where detention beyond 24 hours was authorised) – unless a magistrates' court authorises further detention, which can be for up to a further 36 hours. **Legal advice must be allowed** (where access to legal advice was delayed).
48.00 hours	*The decision to charge must be made or the suspect released – unless a judge authorises further detention.* *Legal advice must be allowed (where access to legal advice was delayed).*
72.00 hours	**The decision to charge must be made or the suspect released** (where detention beyond 36 hours was authorised) – unless a magistrates' court authorises further detention, which can be for up to a further 36 hours.
96.00 hours	**The decision to charge must be made or the suspect released** (where detention beyond 72 hours was authorised).
7 days	*The decision to charge must be made or the suspect released (where detention beyond 48 hours was authorised) – unless a judge authorises*

	further detention.
28 days	**The decision to charge must be made or the suspect released** (*where detention beyond 7 days was authorised*).
70 - 182 days	If remand in custody once prosecuted, trial must be within 70 days (magistrates' court) or 182 days (Crown Court).
Entries in italics refer to terrorism cases. See Note 3 for definition.	
Note 1	In non-terrorist cases (see Note 3), detention time limits run from arrival at the police station, and timing of reviews of detention run from the time detention was authorised (normally shortly after arrival at the police station). *In terrorist cases, time runs from the time of arrest.*
Note 2	There are no specific time limits within which trial must take place, although there are maximum periods for which a person can be kept in custody pending their trial, although the time limits are not absolute and may be extended by a judge.
Note 3	If a person is arrested on suspicion of a specific offence, the normal rules regarding reviews, maximum period of detention and delaying access to legal advice apply even if the offence relates to terrorism. However, instead of arresting a person on suspicion of a particular terrorist offence, the police may arrest a person on suspicion of being a terrorist without specifying a precise offence (Terrorism Act 2000 s41(1)), and in this case the special rules apply (i.e. those in italics). References to arrest under the terrorism legislation, or arrest or detention in terrorism cases are references to this legislation.

TIMELINE ARREST AND PRE-TRIAL DETENTION GERMANY

Time	Event
00.00	Provisional arrest **of suspect.**
	If police or prosecutor wish to interrogate the suspect: Tell suspect of nature of offence suspected of, right to consult with a lawyer prior to interrogation (though no right to have her present during police interrogation), right to silence, right to make written statement, right to suggest evidence be taken on her behalf and the availability of victim/offender reconciliation services.
47.59	Suspect must be brought before a **judge** or **released.**
	Judge interrogates the suspect. She informs the suspect of circumstances incriminating the suspect and of her right to remain silent. Suspect must be given an opportunity to raise facts in her favour and to refute the suspicion and the grounds for keeping her in custody (if the suspect has not been previously interrogated, the information rights mentioned above also apply).
	If not released, judge must **inform relative or friend** of suspect of her detention.
48.00	Detention (pre-trial custody) beyond 48hours must be authorised by a **judge**
6 mths no max limit	If the judge orders pre-trial detention, first instance judgment must be rendered within 6 months. Court of Appeals can extend pre-trial detention for exigent reasons, with no absolute time limit.
	Note: In 'organised crime' cases, the police enjoy greater powers but no extended detention time limits concerning police custody. If someone is suspected of being a member of a terrorist gang, written communication between the suspect and her lawyer can be monitored. If there is (additional) suspicion that the terrorist gang presently threatens the life, health or freedom of a person, and it is deemed necessary to interrupt any contact between the suspect in custody and other persons, the court can so order. The court then appoints counsel for the suspect; only appointed counsel has access to the suspect.

TIMELINE ARREST AND PRE-TRIAL DETENTION GREECE

Time	Event
00.00 hours	**Arrest.** If arrest for flagrant offence, police conduct *ex officio* summary investigation, including interview of suspect. Suspect entitled to be told of reason for arrest and detention, to contact a person of their choice (and consular officials if relevant), and to have legal advice.
	Arrest by arrest warrant (it can be issued by the investigating judge only with regard to offences carrying a minimum sentence of 3 months imprisonment).
	Summons. Defendant notified at least 24 hours in advance to appear before the investigating judge to give their testimony at the end of an ordinary investigation (art. 271.2 CPP).
	Summons. Suspect or defendant given at least 48 hours' notice to appear before investigating officers (normally a judge at the petty offences court) to give explanations during a preliminary inquiry (where no charges have yet been brought), or their testimony at the end of a summary investigation (where criminal proceedings have already commenced) (art. 245.1 CPP).
24.00 hours	**Flagrant offences:** Arrested person must be produced before Attorney General (AG) who may charge them or release them without charge. If charged with a misdemeanour, they must be taken to court immediately or within the next 24 hours. If charged with a felony or misdemeanour with regard to which restrictive conditions may be imposed, the AG must produce the defendant before the investigating judge as soon as possible.
	Other offences: The person arrested on an arrest warrant must be brought before the investigating judge (if arrest occurred outside the area of the investigating judge, the arrested person must be brought before them as soon as possible). A defendant summoned to appear before the investigating judge during the course of an ordinary investigation in order to testify appears. They may ask for a 48-hour delay (which may be extended) to prepare their defence. If they do not appear, the investigating judge may order them to appear before them by force or may issue

	an arrest warrant.
48.00 hours	**Flagrant offences**: If person is arrested for a flagrant misdemeanour, trial must take place or AG must produce them before the investigating judge who decides, within 24 hours at the latest, on the suspect's temporary detention. The person has a right, on request, to a 3-day delay to allow preparation of their defence (art. 423.1 CPP). The court will decide on whether the defendant must be detained pending trial. If a defendant charged with a felony or misdemeanour where restrictive conditions may be imposed, the investigating judge carries out investigative acts during the course of the ordinary investigation. **Other offences:** A suspect or defendant who has been summoned to give explanations or testimony (during the preliminary inquiry or summary investigation) appears before the authorities. They can ask for a 48-hour delay (which may be extended) to prepare their defence. If they do not appear, this stage of the investigation may be closed. The suspect or defendant cannot be brought before the authorities by force nor can an arrest warrant be issued.
72.00 hours	**Other offences**: A defendant, summoned to give their testimony before the investigating judge and who asked and was granted a 48-hour delay, appears before them to give their testimony.
96.00 hours	Flagrant offences: The investigating judge must issue a warrant of temporary detention or release the suspect (at the latest 3 days after the suspect was first brought before them), although this can be extended by a further 2 days on request of the arrested person or in case of *force majeure* certified by a decision of the judicial council. **Other offences:** Where a defendant is brought before the investigating judge on an arrest warrant and has given their testimony, the investigating judge must decide on whether they will be released or detained until trial. A suspect or defendant (summoned to give explanations during the preliminary inquiry or their testimony during the summary investigation), who asked and was given the 48-hour delay, appears before the authorities.
5 days	**Where arrest occurred outside the area of the issuing authority**: The investigating judge must issue a warrant of temporary detention or release the suspect (at the latest 3 days after he was first brought

	before them), although this can be extended by a further 2 days on request of the arrested person or in case of *force majeure* certified by a decision of the judicial council.
1 – 1,5 year	Maximum period of detention is 1 year for felonies (exceptionally 18 months) and 6 months for misdemeanours (exceptionally 9 months), reviewed after 6 and 3 months respectively).
Note 1:	The 3-day time limit (with a possible 2-day extension) operates in the case of a defendant brought before the investigating judge both for a flagrant offence and under an arrest warrant.
Note 2	: If the arrest (either for a flagrant offence or on an arrest warrant) occurred outside the seat of the investigating authorities, then the suspect/defendant must be brought before them as soon as possible, normally within 48 hours.
Note 3:	Temporary detention can only be ordered in relation to felonies and the misdemeanour of reckless manslaughter of more than two persons.
Note 4:	The maximum time-limits for the summary investigation and the preliminary inquiry are six (6) months and four (4) months respectively. In exceptional circumstances they can be extended for a further period of four (4) months following authorisation by the Attorney General of the Court of Appeal.

TIMELINE ARREST AND PRE-TRIAL DETENTION ITALY

Time	Event
00.00 hours	Arrest by the police of someone caught in the act or summons of suspect by the police.
24.00 hours	The police have to inform the prosecutor of the arrest. The police is not allowed to interrogate an arrested suspect. The interrogation will be done by the prosecutor, who has the obligation to inform the suspect's defence counsel in due time in order to enable the counsel to be present at the interrogation. If the suspect does not yet have a counsel, the prosecutor has to assign one and to inform him/her at the same time of the scheduled interrogation. The suspect has the right to legal advice before being questioned, but the interview with the counsel can be delayed by the prosecutor. The questioning of detained persons will be videotaped or audio recorded and a verbatim record will be made up. As it happens in every interrogation by the prosecutor, during the questioning the suspect has the right to be informed of the (provisional) charge. A letter of rights has to be handed out to the suspect from the moment he/she has the right to be assisted by counsel. The suspect has to be cautioned about his right to silence before every interrogation.
48.00 hours	The prosecutor has to request the judge for the hearing of validation (legality check) of the arrest.
96.00 hours	If the validation hearing does not take place or the judge does not deliver his/her decision the suspect has to be released. At the hearing the suspect has the right to be heard. The judge may authorise further detention on remand; if not the arrested person will be released. The decision on detention can be taken on written information. Appeal and cassation are open to the detained person. There is no right to bail, but the judge may (and often does) convert detention into house arrest or other restrictive measures. In cases involving mafia crimes detention on remand is the rule; in other most serious cases – as terrorism – detention is in practice always maintained.
5 days after the detention order by the judge	The detained person has to be heard by the judge, unless the interrogation has already been done at the validation hearing.
3 months – 1 year	The time limits of the pre-trial detention range from three

	months to one year, depending on the seriousness of the offence. Within this time the confirmation of the indictment at the preliminary hearing (not the trial itself) must take place, otherwise the detainee has to be released. (Further time limits are provided for in connection with every stage of the proceedings). There is no automatic periodical judicial review of the detention, but the detained person may ask at any time for a review.

TIMELINE ARREST AND PRE-TRIAL DETENTION THE NETHERLANDS

Time	Event
	Stop (*staandehouden*) – A person against whom a reasonable suspicion has arisen of having committed a criminal offence may be stopped by a police officer and requested to provide personal data. Anybody can stop a person caught in the act of committing an offence in order that they can be arrested by the police.
	Arrest (*aanhouden*) – Where a person is not caught in the act, arrest may be ordered by a public prosecutor or assistant public prosecutor, but only in case of a criminal offence for which the law allows detention on remand. (see note 1) An arrested person must normally be taken to a police station as soon as practicable after arrest.
06.00-15.00 hours	**Interrogation (*ophouden voor verhoor*)**– An arrested person may be held for questioning at a police station for a maximum period of six hours, not including the time between midnight and 9:00 am, in other words, for a maximum period of 15 hours. In cases where an arrested person refuses to identify themselves, this period can be extended by 6 hours if the police has not been able to identify the person. Suspects have the right to legal assistance, but the defence lawyer is not allowed to attend the police interviews or to speak to the suspect before their first interview. Suspects are informed of the criminal act of which they are suspected, but there is no official charge (see note 2).
Max. 6 days+15 hours after arrest *3 days to 6 days (plus 6 to 15 hours interrogation).*	**Police custody (*inverzekeringstelling*)** – Both the public prosecutor and the assistant public prosecutor can order that a person who is suspected of a criminal offence for which the law allows detention on remand, be held in police custody for an additional 3 days, which can be extended by a further 3 days, if the interests of the investigation so requires. Suspect will be assigned a defence counsel for the period of police custody if they have not already chosen a lawyer. Lawyers have no right to attend police interviews. Restrictions in contact with the outside world can be imposed. (see note 3)
Within 3 days and 15 hours after arrest	**Lawfulness of detention tested by investigating judge** – The suspect has to be brought before the investigating judge, who tests the lawfulness of the detention. Suspects may ask to be brought before the investigating judge before the expiry of this period of they wish to challenge the lawfulness of their

	detention.
Max. 20 days+15 hours after arrest *14 days (plus up to 6 days police custody and 6 – 15 hours interrogation)*	**Remand in custody (*bewaring*)** – remand in custody can be ordered by the investigating judge for a maximum period of 14 days after the period of police custody has expired where the suspected offence is one that detention on remand is permitted (see note 1), and there is serious suspicion based on facts relating to the suspect. In addition, at least one of the following five grounds must be satisfied: (i) a risk that the suspect might flee, (ii) a danger that the suspect might commit another offence punishable by a penalty of at least six years' imprisonment, (iii) that the offence has seriously shocked society and the offence is punishable by a penalty of at least twelve years' imprisonment, (iv) a risk that the suspect might prevent or obstruct the investigation of the case, or (v) a danger that the suspect may commit a listed (minor) offence. A remand in custody (as well as detention on remand by court order) can be suspended on conditions. The suspect has a right to be heard (note 3)
Max. 110 days+ 15 hours after arrest *90 days (plus any period in interrogation, police custody and remand in custody)*	**Detention on remand by court order (*gevangenhouding*)** – Subsequently to remand in custody, detention on remand can be ordered by the court sitting in camera for a maximum period of 90 days on the same grounds as remand in custody. The suspect has a right to be heard (note 3)
Until 60 days after sentence court in first instance	**Charge and first court hearing** – Within the period of detention on remand by court order (max 110 days + 15 hours after arrest), the suspect has to be summoned and to be brought before the trial court for the first hearing. However, the court can suspend the trial for a limited or unlimited period, depending on the reason for adjournment. During this period the detention on remand stays in force until 60 days after the verdict.
Note 1	Detention on remand is allowed if a person is suspected of an offence punishable with a penalty of at least four years' imprisonment or certain specified crimes, or if the suspect has no place of residence in the Netherlands and is suspected of an offence that can be punished by imprisonment.
Note 2	In the Netherlands there is no provision pointing out at what moment a person should be formally charged during the pre-trial investigation. Although persons, as soon as arrested, must be informed what offence they are suspected of and the prosecutor must indicate the alleged offences in the requests for preliminary detention, suspects will not learn the official

	charge until they are summoned, which will be shortly before trial commences. It is thus possible, that suspect will have to stand trial for other offences than the offences that were the reason for prelimary detention. It is – in case of preliminary detention – at the end of the period of 110 days and 15 hours that the prosecutor has to decide what eventually the charge will be, dependant on the evidence gathered in the pre-trial stage.
Note 3	During custody and detention on remand, the suspect's contacts with the outside world can be restricted in the interest of the investigation *(bevel beperkingen)* by order of the prosecutor, or the investigating judge in case of an official preliminary investigation. These restrictions can last until the complete file has to be disclosed to the defence. During this period the suspect can only have contact with their lawyer, who is not permitted to thwart the order by passing on communications. The suspect can request the court to lift the restrictions at any time, stating that they are not necessary (anymore) in the interest of the investigation.
Note 4	Concerning terrorism several bills have recenty passed Parliament,[1] *inter alia* with regard to pre-trial detention in case of terrorist offences: – To extend detention on remand before the commencement of the trial up to 2 years in addition to the terms of 3-6 days remand in police custody *(inverzekeringstelling)*, 14 days remand in custody *(bewaring)*and 90 days detention on remand by court order *(gevangenhouding)*, without the defence having the right of access to the (complete) file; – 'Serious suspicion' is not required for the period of 14 days *bewaring* (remand in custody), only a reasonable suspicion.

---

[1]   Laws of 20 November 2006, *Stb.* 2006, 580; *Stb.* 2006, 731; *Stb.* 2006, 730, entered into force on 1 February 2007.

TIMELINE ARREST AND PRE-TRIAL DETENTION POLAND

Time	Event
0.00-48 hours	**Arrest** – The police may arrest a 'suspected person' if there is good reason to believe that they have committed an offence, and it is feared that they will go into hiding or destroy evidence or their identity cannot be established. The arrested person has the right to lodge an interlocutory appeal with the court requesting an examination of the grounds, legality and appropriateness of the arrest.
	The suspected person must not be interviewed by the police before the official charge, but may be 'heard.' The person is not regarded as a 'suspect', and thus not cautioned, until they are officially charged. Legal advice is permitted, also during 'hearing' or police interview, but public funding is not available.
	The arrested person must be released within 48 hours of arrest unless the prosecutor decides to apply for preliminary detention.
48.00-72.00 hours	**Police custody (*zatrzymanie*)** – After the application for preliminary detention has been filed with the court, a copy of the detention order must be served on the arrested person within 24 hours. Thus the arrested person can be detained for a maximum of 72 (48+24) hours before preliminary detention is ordered.
	Before the preliminary detention hearing the arrested person must be officially informed of the charge(s) against them, which means that they are then a formal 'suspect' (*podejrzany*). They must be informed of their rights, including the right to silence and the right to legal advice, although state funding is not available at this stage.
72 hours- 3 months	**Preliminary detention (*tymczasowy aresztowany*)** Before ordering preliminary detention, the court must examine the suspect. The suspect is entitled to be legally represented, and state funding is available in certain circumstances. The suspect does not have a right to have legal advice in private for the first 14 days of preliminary detention.
	The initial maximum period of preliminary detention is 3

	months.
Max. 72 hours +2 years	If, in view of the special circumstances of the case, the preparatory proceedings cannot be completed within 3 months, the court of first instance having jurisdiction may, if necessary, extend preliminary detention for a period which, in total, may not exceed twelve months. The total period of preliminary detention preceding the first sentence by the court of first instance may not exceed two years. Extension of preliminary detention beyond 12 months may only be made by the appeal court in whose circuit the proceedings are pending.